CRIME AND INEQUALITY

CRIME AND INEQUALITY

EDITED BY JOHN HAGAN
AND RUTH D. PETERSON

STANFORD UNIVERSITY PRESS
Stanford, California 1995

Stanford University Press
Stanford, California

Printed in the United States of America

CIP data appear at the end of the book

Stanford University Press publications are
distributed exclusively by Stanford University Press
within the United States, Canada, and Mexico;
they are distributed exclusively by
Cambridge University Press throughout
the rest of the world.

Contents

Contributors

EMILIE ANDERSEN ALLAN is a professor of sociology at Saint Francis College of Pennsylvania. Her research interests include the relationship between crime and the labor market, organized crime, and the distribution of crime by age, sex, and race. She is the author or coauthor of articles that have appeared in the *American Sociological Review* and other sociology journals. During 1990 she served as associate director and as one of the writers of the Pennsylvania Crime Commission's study *Organized Crime in Pennsylvania: A Decade of Change*.

WILLIAM C. BAILEY is a professor of sociology at Cleveland State University. He has published extensively on the role of capital punishment in society, crime and deterrence, and urban crime patterns, with recent papers appearing in the *American Sociological Review* and the *Journal of Research in Crime and Delinquency*.

JOHN BEATTIE is University Professor at the University of Toronto, where he has been a member of the History Department since 1961. He is the author of *The English Court in the Reign of George I* (Cambridge University Press, 1967) and *Crime and the Courts in England, 1660–1800* (Princeton University Press, 1986), for which he received the François-Xavier Garneau Medal from the Canadian Historical Association. He is currently working on criminal law and the administration of justice in London in the eighteenth and nineteenth centuries.

JOHN BRAITHWAITE is a professorial fellow in the Research School of Social Sciences, Australian National University. His recent books are *Responsive Regulation: Transcending the Deregulation Debate* (Oxford University Press, with Ian Ayres); *Not Just Deserts: A Republican Theory of Crimi-*

nal Justice (Oxford University Press, with Philip Pettit); and *Crime, Shame and Reintegration* (Cambridge University Press), for which he received the Michael J. Hindelang Award from the American Society of Criminology.

DAVID CANTOR is Senior Research Associate with Westat, Inc. He is a social statistician with interests in survey research methods and criminology. He currently is conducting research designed to test criminal opportunity theories of crime and developing methods to improve the monitoring of social problems, such as criminal offending, victimization, and drug use.

JOHN HAGAN is W. Grant Dahlstrom Distinguished Professor of Sociology and Adjunct Professor of Law at the University of North Carolina at Chapel Hill and professor of sociology and law at the University of Toronto, editor of the *Annual Review of Sociology*, and immediate past president of the American Society of Criminology. His recent books are *Crime and Disrepute* (Pine Forge Press, 1994) and *Structural Criminology* (Polity and Rutgers University Press, 1989), for which he received the Outstanding Scholarship Award from the Crime and Juvenile Delinquency Division of the Society for the Study of Social Problems, and the Distinguished Scholar Award from the Crime, Law and Deviance section of the American Sociological Association.

KAREN HEIMER is assistant professor of sociology at the University of Iowa. Her research on race and crime has appeared in the *American Sociological Review*. She is currently working with Ross L. Matsueda on the development of an interactionist theory of delinquency. Her other research focuses on structural and social psychological processes underlying the gender gap in offending.

KENNETH C. LAND is the John Franklin Crowell Professor and Chairman of Sociology at Duke University. He is a social statistician with research interests in criminology, demography, organizations, and social change. In criminology, his research interests include the development and assessment of criminal opportunity theory, the study of structural covariates of crime rates, the development of micro-models of criminal careers, and the evaluation of delinquency prevention programs.

GARY T. MARX is professor of sociology at the University of Colorado at Boulder. His award-winning books include *Protest and Prejudice* (Harper & Row, 1966) and *Undercover: Police Surveillance in America* (University of California Press, 1988), and he continues to work on issues of race and ethnicity, collective behavior, social control, and deviance.

RUTH D. PETERSON is associate professor of sociology and Associate Director of the Center for Criminal Justice at Ohio State University. She has published work on subordinate status and legal/justice decisions, structural influences on crime, and punishment and deterrence, including papers in *Social Problems*, *Journal of Quantitative Criminology*, and the *American Sociological Review*.

STEPHEN T. RUSSELL is a doctoral candidate in sociology at Duke University. He has research interests in the sociology of the life course and aging, demography, and social research methods. For his dissertation, he is conducting longitudinal analyses of life antecedents of teenage parenthood in Great Britain.

ROBERT J. SAMPSON is professor of sociology at the University of Chicago. His most recent book is *Crime in the Making* (with John Laub, Harvard University Press, 1993), which analyzes longitudinal data reconstructed from the Sheldon and Eleanor Glueck archives. His numerous articles have appeared in the *American Sociological Review*, the *American Journal of Sociology*, *Criminology*, and other journals.

MARTÍN SÁNCHEZ JANKOWSKI is associate professor of sociology and director of the Chicano/Latino Policy Project of the Institute for the Study of Social Change at the University of California at Berkeley. His most recent book, *Islands in the Street: Gangs and American Urban Society* (University of California Press, 1991), received the Robert E. Park Award of the American Sociological Association. He currently is studying the underground economy.

JOACHIM J. SAVELSBERG is assistant professor of sociology at the University of Minnesota. His books include *Constructing White-Collar Crime: Rationalities, Communications, Power* (with P. Brühl, University of Pennsylvania Press, forthcoming) and *Crime, Justice, and Revolution in Eastern Europe* (in preparation for Westview Press's "Crime and Society" series). He has published chapters and articles in several languages. His current NSF-funded research investigates the conditions and changes of knowledge production in American criminology and criminal justice sciences from 1951 to 1992. Savelsberg, a former research fellow at Johns Hopkins and Harvard universities, recently moved to the United States.

DARRELL STEFFENSMEIER is professor of sociology at the Pennsylvania State University. His research interests revolve around the sociology of law, organized crime, and the structural covariates of crime (including age, gender, and race). His recent book, *The Fence: In the Shadow of*

Two Worlds, was the recipient of the 1987 Award for Outstanding Scholarship of the Society for the Study of Social Problems. During 1990 he served as a project director, chief analyst, and writer for the Pennsylvania Crime Commission's study *Organized Crime in Pennsylvania: A Decade of Change*.

WILLIAM JULIUS WILSON is a MacArthur Prize Fellow and the Lucy Flower University Professor of Sociology and Public Policy at the University of Chicago; he is a past president of the American Sociological Association. His most recent book is *The Truly Disadvantaged: The Inner City, the Underclass and Public Policy* (University of Chicago Press, 1987), for which he received the 1988 C. Wright Mills Award from the Society for the Study of Social Problems.

PETER C. YEAGER is associate professor of sociology and adjunct associate professor of management policy at Boston University. He is coauthor with M. B. Clinard of *Corporate Crime* (Free Press, 1980) and most recently published *The Limits of Law: The Public Regulation of Private Pollution* (Cambridge University Press, 1991). He recently spent a fellowship year in Harvard University's Program in Ethics and the Professions, and continues his research and writing on managerial ethics and the legal regulation of corporate wrongdoing.

Introduction

This book examines issues of social and economic inequality, crime, and criminal justice. We begin with the realization that despite a prevailing American ideology of individual freedom and equal opportunity, we live in a society where the harsh realities include glaring social and economic inequalities of class, race, and ethnicity, as well as of age and gender. Equally glaring are the realities of crime in America, including: our uniquely high rate of violent crime among Western nations, the unevenness of the social and economic distribution of crime, the high levels of fear of crime that restrict the movements of Americans, and one of the largest per capita prison populations in the world.

Linkages between social inequality and crime have been subjects of speculation as well as some dispute since the early days of European (e.g., Bonger 1916) and American criminology (e.g., Merton 1938; Sellin 1935; Shaw and McKay 1942). This book is an outgrowth of this heritage. Some chapters examine aspects of the crime and inequality relationship that are underemphasized in the research literature. Others critically assess available studies and point to further areas of investigation. Still others offer new and challenging ways of conceptualizing and better understanding the causes and consequences of crime and inequality.

This introduction provides an overview of the meaning and scope of social and economic inequality in contemporary American society and its importance to the study of crime and criminal justice. Our purpose is to set the stage for the theoretical and empirical contributions that follow.

The Meaning and Scope of Inequality

In the social sciences, concerns about socioeconomic inequality focus on the consequences of the hierarchical differentiation of attributes. Inequality implies that social categories and groups of persons are ranked and ordered in relation to one another, and that categories of individuals are socially stratified into superordinate and subordinate groups. In the United States, this hierarchical differentiation occurs along overlapping divisions that disadvantage the young, poor, minorities, and women, who are members of subordinate groups whose social position and life chances are limited by comparison to their older, more affluent, and white male counterparts.

To illustrate, U.S. Department of Commerce figures indicate that 10.4 percent of U.S. families were living in poverty in 1989. However, the comparative figures for white and black families were 7.9 and 28.2 percent, respectively. During that same year, 19 percent of all children in the United States were impoverished, but among blacks the figure was 43.2 percent compared with 14.1 percent of white children. In 1988, the median family income of African-Americans was 57 percent that of whites ($19,329 compared with $33,915). The median 1989 income of females was 55 percent that of males ($11,763 compared with $21,376). Calculated according to Monthly Labor Review statistics (1991), in 1990, the rate of unemployment in the United States was 5.5 percent. However, the unemployment rate for youth was much higher at 15.5 percent. Importantly, too, minority youth were more likely to be unemployed than white youth (31.1 percent). Clearly then, when it comes to race, gender, and age, the United States is a land of haves (whites, males, adults) and have-nots (minorities, females, youth).

These divisions have grown especially discouraging for younger Americans entering adulthood over the past two decades. The Grant Commission publication *The Forgotten Half* (1988) reports that even during the economic expansion of the mid-1980s, the social and economic position of younger Americans declined. For example, whereas in 1968 an estimated 70 percent of noncollege youth were working two years after high school graduation, only 52 percent of such youth were similarly employed in 1988. More discouraging still, as we entered the 1990s more than one-third of young black males reported no income at all for the previous year, while this was the case for only one-sixth of young white males. Wages also steadily decreased for those who were working; this was especially true for high school dropouts and for young African-Americans and Hispanics. Although wages for young adult females remained relatively constant, they were substantially below those for young adult males. African-American and Hispanic youth, male and female, increasingly confronted major and often insurmountable obstacles to making successful transitions from adolescence to young adulthood (Bound and Freeman 1992).

These patterns of inequality are connected to criminal offending, victimization, and crime control. As we illustrate in greater detail in Chapter 1, groups that are economically deprived—particularly young, disadvantaged minority males—are also heavily involved in serious criminal offenses, especially violent street crime. Data indicate that these and surrounding citizen populations also experience high rates of street crime victimization (Fingerhut and Kleinman 1989; National Research Council 1989; U.S. Department of Justice 1991a). And, have-nots disproportionately constitute the population of persons who are in contact with, and/or under the supervision of the criminal justice system (Petersilia 1985; U.S. Department of Justice 1988, 1991b, 1991c).

The differential involvement of have-not populations in crime and criminal justice has not escaped the attention of criminologists (see, for example, Braithwaite 1979; Colvin and Pauly 1983; Greenberg 1985). Indeed, various perspectives have been advanced to account for these patterns and associations. Some emphasize that subordinate groups are subjected to more crime-producing experiences than their more advantaged counterparts. For example, the early and influential social disorganization theory of Shaw and McKay (1942) focused on differences in community-based social controls as contributors to crime among have-not populations. According to this theory, social structure (the pattern of interaction between groups) provides and sets limits on the range of methods available to solve life's problems and thereby helps determine the integration of the individual into groups and society (Sykes and Cullen 1992). Criminal behavior results from the disorganization of social structure and ensuing breakdowns of social control among family, neighborhood, voluntary associations, and other institutions and groups that traditionally encourage members to abide by societal norms and assume appropriate social roles (Beirne and Messerschmidt 1991; Shaw and McKay 1942; Sykes and Cullen 1992).

These types of arguments were pursued enthusiastically during the 1940s and 1950s, but declined in popularity during the 1960s when other perspectives gained favor (including anomie, labeling, conflict, and subcultural theories). However, in recent years social disorganization themes have regained a place of importance in the analysis of crime. These new analyses provide fresh insights into the role of changes in the economic and occupational structure of the larger society in isolating and disrupting disadvantaged communities, their families, and the institutional control of peer affiliations (as discussed in Sampson and Wilson's contribution to this volume; see also W. J. Wilson 1987; Bursik 1988; Byrne and Sampson 1986; Sampson 1987; Sampson and Groves 1989).

A second perspective holds that the greater involvement of have-nots in crimes of violence has a cultural foundation. Theorists and researchers such as Wolfgang and Ferracuti (1967), Banfield (1968), Hackney (1969), Curtis (1975), Gastil (1971), and Reed (1971) have advanced economic, racial/ethnic, and regional subcultural theories of violence. Here, differential rates of criminal violence are ironically thought to partly reflect the extent to which violence is condoned by the larger group as a legitimate means of redressing offensive behavior. Judith and Peter Blau (1982) derive an alternative structural interpretation of class-, race-, and ethnicity-linked patterns of violent crime. The Blaus see violence among subordinate minority populations as a structural consequence of relative economic deprivation. Here, the greater involvement of the poor and minorities reflects diffuse aggression that stems from socially induced frustrations experienced by have-nots in an affluent society.

Messner (1989) and others have analyzed the importance of cultural factors in comparison with structural conditions of absolute (poverty-based) and relative (general and racial income inequality-based) economic deprivation in the causation of violent crime (P. Blau and Golden 1986; P. Blau and Schwartz 1984; Golden and Messner 1987; Loftin and Hill 1974; Messner 1983a, 1983b; K. R. Williams and Flewelling 1988). Related lines of research have assessed the impact of macroeconomic conditions and labor market structures on different types of street crime and delinquency (e.g., Allan and Steffensmeier 1989; also Crutchfield 1989; Kohfeld and Sprague 1988; Land et al. 1990). This literature demonstrates that glaring social and economic inequalities in our society impose correspondingly high costs in the form of street crime.

Social disorganization, cultural transmission, and structural inequality theories all attempt to explain why different groups are more or less involved in *committing* violent crimes. Meanwhile, interactionist, labeling, and conflict theorists attach a different meaning to official crime statistics. These theorists assert that the overrepresentation of subordinate groups in official crime often reflects differential law enforcement. Disadvantaged groups are viewed as victims of prejudice and discrimination that result in more frequent arrest, prosecution, and punishment for delinquent and criminal behavior. Overrepresentation of the poor and some ethnic and racial groups may also reflect lack of access to the quality of justice available to more privileged groups. Turk (1969) provides a systematic and influential theoretical formulation that emphasizes such factors (see also Chambliss and Seidman 1971; Quinney 1970).

One result of the latter theoretical contributions is an extensive literature on the impact of social and economic inequality on juvenile and criminal justice decision making. Scholars have examined the determinants of police contact, arrest, detention, adjudication, and disposition patterns with regard to the juvenile justice system. In the adult criminal justice system, comparable and additional decision points have been investigated, encompassing arrest, charging, pretrial detention, plea bargaining, disposition, and sentencing outcomes. The findings of this literature are voluminous (e.g., Chilton and Galvin 1985; Krohn et al. 1983; Miethe and Moore 1985; D. Smith 1986; Visher 1983; for reviews see Chesney-Lind 1987; Hagan and Bumiller 1983; Kleck 1981; Zatz 1987). They are also complex: for example, class-race-gender interactions are found to influence criminal justice outcomes at different decision points and for different types of crime/delinquency (Miethe and Moore 1985; Myers and Talarico 1987; Zatz 1987). Further, there is evidence that these patterns vary across time and place (Balbus 1973; Jones 1975; Myers and Talarico 1987; Peterson and Hagan 1984; D. Smith 1986). Of special concern is continuing evidence of discrimination in the use of the death penalty (Paternoster and Kazyaka 1988). Here and elsewhere in the justice system the patterns are often more subtle and difficult to discern than in the past. An example involves state capital punishment statutes that prescribe death sentences for murders that are "unusually cruel or heinous" (Mello 1984). These statutes allow politically motivated prosecutors latitude to seek the death penalty for blacks accused of killing whites (Radelet and Pierce 1985).

Just as social and economic inequality have direct implications for criminal involvement and how well persons may fare in the criminal justice system, they have similar implications for criminal victimization. Opportunity, routine activity, and lifestyle theories emphasize that subordinate populations are inadequately equipped to defend themselves against crime (L. E. Cohen and Felson 1979; Felson 1983; Garofalo 1987; Hindelang et al. 1978). Unlike their more affluent counterparts, such groups reside and work in more dangerous communities, must rely upon higher-risk forms of public transportation, and have insufficient resources to otherwise structure safe environments and lifestyles. Recent studies of victimization have attempted to further isolate resource and lifestyle factors that contribute to the supply of possible victims (and different types of victims) and the factors that facilitate and discourage victimization (Carroll and Jackson 1983; Lasley 1989; Maume 1989; Messner and Tardiff 1985). Some of this work argues that the level of victimization is a consequence of the proportion of persons in risky locations and activities and of the presence of protective "guardians." However, these efforts have only begun to measure directly the routine activities of subordinate (and superordinate) populations that make them more (or less) subject to different levels and types of victimization at the hands of different types of offenders in different types of settings.

In brief, then, criminologists have long been interested in how and why hierarchical differentiation affects the patterning of crime and criminal justice in the United States and elsewhere. As a result, a number of perspectives have been advanced to account for the greater involvement of subordinate populations in criminal victimization, offending, and crime control. These perspectives emphasize a variety of causal mechanisms and have generated a large volume of research examining how positions of superordination and subordination influence the outcomes of criminal justice decisions, and how social and economic resources and their absence contribute to offending, victimization, and patterns of criminalization more generally.

The Present Volume

Although there is considerable evidence indicating the role of hierarchical differentiation in crime and criminal justice, the articles in this volume extend our understanding and encourage further exploration of this important issue. For example, while recent empirical work sheds much light on the relative influence of some social and economic factors on crime and crime control, some researchers have been hesitant to directly address connections between race and criminal offending and the conflicts this relationship generates in American society. The politics of race in America often have discouraged systematic scholarly attention to issues of race and crime.

With this in mind, Chapter 1, "Criminal Inequality in America," focuses on the disproportionate representation of young, male African-Americans in the official and unofficial statistics of crime. This chapter documents the role of race-linked poverty in the generation of ghetto violence and property crime and considers historical and contemporary antecedents to the growing polarization of Americans around issues of race and crime. Particular attention is given to the level of hostility that characterizes minority citizens' relations with a criminal justice system that ineffectively relies on the use of incarceration to respond to these problems.

Chapter 2, by Robert Sampson and William Julius Wilson, "Toward a Theory of Race, Crime, and Urban Inequality," is a focal point of this volume. It draws from Sampson's pathbreaking research on macrolevel relationships between race, joblessness, community structure, and crime and Wilson's influential work on ghetto poverty and his book *The Truly Disadvantaged*. The result is a powerful structural and cultural analysis. A key feature of this chapter is its argument that the link between race and crime should be addressed from a macrosociological perspective. As Sampson and Wilson note, criminology of recent decades too often has discounted the insights of aggregate neighborhood and community-level research by focusing on issues of ecological validity; in the process it has often unwittingly committed an "individualistic fallacy." This fallacy can lead to an exclusive focus on individual-level attributes, such as race, when an aggregate-level phenomenon, such as the concentration of poverty, is a salient exogenous causal agent. Sampson and Wilson develop this insight into an integrated macrolevel theory. The basic thesis is that macrosocial patterns of residential inequality give rise to the social isolation and ecological concentration of the truly disadvantaged in ghetto communities. This in turn leads to structural barriers and cultural adaptations that undermine social organization and hence the control of crime. As we note next, links forged in this essay between structural, cultural, and social-psychological processes are paralleled in a number of other chapters in this volume, and implications of the concentration-of-poverty thesis are revealed throughout the book.

A central tenet in Wilson's work more generally is the proposition that "the concept 'underclass' or 'ghetto poor' can be theoretically applied to all racial and ethnic groups . . . if the conditions specified in the theory are met" (W. J. Wilson 1991: 12). Kenneth Land and his colleagues David Cantor and Stephen Russell help to establish this point in Chapter 3, "Unemployment and Crime Rate Fluctuations in the Post–World War II United States." They draw on many studies undertaken in the United States during the past half century, which support the conclusion that there is a positive and frequently significant relationship between the unemployment rate and property crime at the macrolevel. They further establish that this relationship is more robust at the intracity level of census tracts or city blocks that provide purer measures of the kind of macrolevel deprivation emphasized in discussions of ghetto poverty; and they confirm that this positive effect is more pronounced in time-series analyses that lag unemployment to reflect the accumulation of deprivation that sparks criminal motivation at the social-psychological level. These and their own time-series analysis that runs from post–World War II to the present provide compelling evidence for the kind of concentration-of-poverty argument that is central to Sampson and Wilson's theory.

Although macrolevel quantitative analyses of crime and inequality are important to Sampson and Wilson's theory, they are by no means the only source of support for the concentration-of-poverty thesis. For example, ethnographic research is providing a renewed and invigorating source of material for understanding links between crime and ghetto poverty. This work enriches our understanding by shedding light on the dynamic processes by which inequality, crime, and criminal justice responses are interrelated. Martín Sánchez Jankowski's chapter, "Ethnography, Inequality, and Crime in the Low-Income Community," assesses the merits of this research methodology for exploring links between subordinate social and economic positions and criminal outcomes. This work presents key insights into the dynamic processes by which structural subordination is transformed into particular cultural and social-psychological adaptations vis-à-vis crime and criminal justice.

Meanwhile, too little systematic attention has been given to the social and economic subordination of youth in explaining age patterns of delinquency and crime. In their chapter, "Age-Inequality and Property Crime," Darrell Steffensmeier and Emilie Allan offer a powerful argument and supporting evidence that the peak in officially recorded property crimes that occurs during mid-adolescence, and the following sharp decline, is better explained by youth inequality than by age-linked physiological changes. They then explain how age-related processes of status attainment of the larger society are reproduced within populations of criminal offenders in both the underworld and the upperworld of crime. They also draw fascinating analogies between the social worlds of sport and crime. These analyses are linked to the earlier focus in this volume on concentrated poverty and crime in ghettoized areas. This link predicts and confirms age differences in historical connections of crime, race, and class that other theories do not anticipate.

Steffensmeier and Allan also provide broad historical insights into shifting associations between age and crime that lead one to question the biological assumptions so often made about gender and crime. The next three chapters in this volume deal explicitly with gender and crime, beginning with John Beattie's rich historical analysis, "Crime and Inequality in Eighteenth-Century London." Although this chapter concentrates on several decades at the turn of the eighteenth century, it also provides a sweeping picture of property offenses over the 400 years from the sixteenth to the twentieth century. Beattie is able to cull evidence from painstakingly recreated records of Old Bailey that trends in the incidence of property crime over this period were tied to the ability of laboring families to support themselves. Particular attention is given to the very high property crime rates in the city of London from 1690 to 1720. Nearly half of the indictments during this period were against women, indicating a level of female involvement that is, of course, extraordinary when viewed from a contemporary perspective that too often includes implicit or explicit assumptions of physiological inevitability. Beattie demonstrates that the 1690s were an especially difficult decade for the working population of London. He also concludes that a fuller picture of the high level of female participation in property crime during this period involves the interaction of three factors: the immigration to the city of many women who were freed from some of the constraints they experienced in villages and small towns; irregular employment and low wages; and an anxiety-driven and punitive response from the propertied classes of London who feared a decline in "social discipline." The property crimes of women *and* the panicked penal responses to them reflected acute inequalities of the period.

Of course, recent attention has focused on the great preponderance of crime and delinquency among males in late twentieth-century Western industrial societies. Although we know less than we should about how such significant shifts in the gender composition of crime could occur, it is becoming more clear that we must recognize the time- and place-bound nature of our work. Karen Heimer's chapter, "Gender, Race, and the Pathways to Delinquency," boldly advances a new theoretical perspective to explain contemporary differences in delinquent behavior across race and gender groupings in the United States. These include differential black male involvement in assaultive behavior and white male involvement in more common forms of delinquency. The perspective proposed is an interactionist approach that emphasizes race-, age-, and gender-connected individual-level motivations. Heimer's perspective links differences in gender role ideologies to levels of involvement in violence, and damages to self-esteem and engendered tastes for risk to school deviance, theft, drug use, and other forms of common delinquency. Although all predictions of the proposed perspective are not confirmed, statistical models are estimated, which do successfully isolate social-psychological mechanisms that translate conflict over gender and racial inequality at the structural level into individual-level differences in delinquent behavior.

William Bailey and Ruth Peterson's chapter, "Gender Inequality and Violence Against Women," calls attention to the fact that, regarding women, there is much more empirical work on the role of inequality as a producer of crime than as a producer of victimization. This chapter extends feminist arguments that gender socioeconomic inequality increases female rape victimization by analyzing variation in rates of female homicide victimization across 138 American cities. The findings suggest that the gender inequality perspective is applicable to female homicides and further specify the scope conditions of the female inequality thesis: that is, they support the expectation grounded in feminist theory that in communities with higher gender inequality, married women are at greater risk of being killed by their husbands, and that in related kinds of circumstances women are also at greater risk of being killed by acquaintances and in arguments. These female homicides are a major cost of gender inequality in America.

It sometimes is difficult to fully realize the excesses of American criminality and our societal responses to crime because we observe our situation in relative isolation; American criminology has been inadequately comparative. This is unfortunate, since research that is focused on a single place or time runs the risk of drawing erroneous conclusions. This volume seeks to avoid ethnocentric and temporocentric traps by considering other periods and settings. For example, we already have noted the importance of the surprising and revealing findings that Beattie reports about gender inequality and crime in eighteenth-century London.

Joachim Savelsberg broadens our societal as well as our temporal horizons in his chapter, "Crime, Inequality, and Justice in Eastern Europe." It is difficult to miss the significance of place and time in the former state socialist societies of eastern Europe. Here former heads of state have been charged with corruption and in at least one case executed, while several former convicts have become state presidents and thousands of others have been "rehabilitated" and released. Savelsberg forcefully argues that we must combine constructionist with structuralist theories to understand the emerging crime problems of these countries. In the face of enormous difficulties of data collection, and using a critical and balanced treatment of sources, Savelsberg provides an invaluable picture of changes in crime rates in Poland and Hungary and the former Czechoslovakia, East Germany, and Soviet Union. He shows that crime rates have risen sharply during this period of rapid sociopolitical change in eastern Europe and that these increases are not due to changes in reporting or arrest practices. In analyzing this trend, Savelsberg develops the important Mertonian insight that anomie and strain can be sources of rebellion and revolution as well as sources of counterrebellion and counterrevolution. While consistently reminding us that reactions to strain are defined, experienced, or understood as either revolt or criminal behavior, depending on the structures of dominance and the legitimacy of governments, Savelsberg makes the case that eastern Europe is an extraordinarily promising site for theoretical and empirical research on the cultural and structural dynamics of adaptation to strain and anomie.

There is an intended flow and chronology to the chapters in this book. As such, the final chapters take us into technological, environmental, and philosophical aspects of crime and inequality that likely will be as much or more a part of our future as of our present and past. The first of these contributions, "The Engineering of Social Control," by Gary Marx, is only partly a futuristic discussion. Marx reminds us how far we have already progressed toward a "maximum security society" of technological social control in which the velvet glove of science is in many sectors gaining ascendancy over the iron fist of forced repression. He outlines six social-engineering strategies and a dramatic array of examples that illustrate the already well-developed capacity to control crime (or at least the places where it occurs) technologically. The existence and potential of this technology raise fascinating questions that obviously include issues of inequality. For example, will the development and dissemination of this technology simply further displace crime from those who can afford these devices to those who cannot? Marx reminds us that we have already entered the "brave new world" of social-control technology.

Peter Yeager is concerned with the current and future use of regulatory law to control the harmful behavior of business enterprises, choosing as an illustration the use made in the United States of the federal Clean Water Act to control industrial water pollution during the 1970s and 1980s. In "Law, Crime, and Inequality" Yeager thoughtfully analyzes cultural and structural constraints that make the successful regulation of harmful business practices so difficult. These constraints include culturally based utilitarian logics that favor consideration of private sector costs of compliance over less "measurable" public interests (i.e., clean environments), as well as structural features of firms and markets that make regulation by inadequately resourced legal institutions difficult. These factors combine in ways that make enforcement agents in the environmental field prone to negotiate rather than to stringently enforce compliance with the law. Yeager is not entirely pessimistic in his analysis, however, noting some progress in the environmental field.

John Braithwaite's concluding chapter, "Inequality and Republican

Criminology," gives us grounds for further hope and motivation. The republican criminology that Braithwaite advocates is not necessarily discouraged by the failures of state enforcement efforts noted, for example, in Yeager's discussion. Rather, Braithwaite emphasizes that the symbolic victories involved in getting harmful environmental practices of business into the public spotlight and onto the public agenda are of great importance. This view follows from a premise of Braithwaite's republican criminology that community-based "reintegrative shaming" is more effective in the long run for crime control than the stigmatization of state enforcement. Braithwaite takes consolation that a number of social movements—including the feminist refuge movement, the consumer movement, the trade union movement on occupational health and safety, the environmental movement, and the anti-drunk-driving movement—are successfully changing public estimations of the harm caused by crimes that too often are ignored or neglected. The power of such movements lies in their ability to provoke deep cultural changes that through mechanisms of shame and pride can on a large scale bring harmful patterns of behavior under better control in a reintegrative fashion. Without discounting the need for the threat of stronger enforcement mechanisms, Braithwaite favors regulatory over criminal law, believing that through the actions of social movements such regulatory efforts can even prevail against powerful structures of domination. This is a stimulating essay, and likely the most thoughtful and compelling argument for social action to emerge in criminological thought in recent decades.

In brief, then, this volume sheds further light on important issues of social and economic inequality and crime and criminal justice. It addresses pressing questions about how and why hierarchical differentiation affects the patterning of crime and criminal justice. These questions have a long history in criminology, but they are not simple to answer. Issues of crime and inequality are complex. While it is beyond the scope of this volume to address all aspects of this complexity, attention is given to important questions and concerns that heretofore have been ignored or given less-than-adequate attention.

Thus the chapters of this volume (1) synthesize what is known about crime and inequality in selected areas; (2) develop and integrate theoretical perspectives on the topic; (3) document the dynamics of inequality in different criminal settings; (4) examine systematically the merits of various theoretical ideas, debates, and controversies regarding crime and inequality; (5) evaluate the merits of various methodological approaches to exploring the relationship between crime and inequality; and (6) provide new research and policy agendas for continued work in this area. Collectively, these contributions help us to understand more fully the important linkages among crime, criminal justice, and inequality, and the central place of these linkages in the social organization of the United States and other nations.

THE EDITORS

CHAPTER 1

Criminal Inequality in America

Patterns and Consequences

JOHN HAGAN

RUTH D. PETERSON

Some of our most prominent theoretical and research paradigms connect the difficult circumstances experienced by disadvantaged and subordinated groups with the occurrence of crime and delinquency (e.g., Cohen 1955; Cloward and Ohlin 1960; Colvin and Pauly 1983; Merton 1938; W. Miller 1958). For example, in developing their social disorganization theory, Shaw and McKay (1942) demonstrated that the same socioeconomically depressed areas in 21 U.S. cities continued to have high delinquency rates over several decades, despite changes in their racial and ethnic composition, indicating the persistent influence of these community conditions on crime regardless of what populations experienced them. Probably the most celebrated figure in American criminology, Edwin Sutherland, however, questioned whether poverty itself was a cause of crime (see Sutherland, Cressey, and Luckenbill 1992: 225). And, some distinguished contemporary researchers assert that there is a "Myth of Social Class and Criminality" (Tittle et al. 1978) or ask "What's Class Got to Do with It?" (Jensen and Thompson 1990). This chapter is in part a response to the latter question.

Disagreement about the place of social disadvantage and subordinate status in the study of crime may reflect a deeply rooted uncertainty in American society about issues of inequality. In a society that places a premium on equality of opportunities, though not of outcomes, evidence of inequality and its consequences may be an inevitable source of distress and dispute. Nonetheless, the underlying theme of this book is that linkages between crime and inequality occupy a central place in the social organization of American society, as well as in other nations.

In this chapter we focus on intersections of race, age, sex, and economic circumstance, noting that in America the experience of crime, especially violent crime, is highly concentrated among young, disadvantaged, minority males. We emphasize the stark dimensions of this problem and locate its roots in forms of race-linked discrimination and segregation that produce crime among minorities along with diffuse patterns of resentment and aggression. We then examine the treatment of minorities within the juvenile and criminal justice systems, noting how attitudes of discontent and distrust pervade encounters between minority citizens and justice officials. Next, we suggest how the discontent and distrust stemming from the root causes of crime and the patterning of justice may have repercussions that go beyond age-graded involvements in crime. We also consider how experiences with crime radiate throughout our society, often pitting groups against one another and polarizing class relations. These problems may not be entirely unique to American society, but they are distinctive in their intensity and are too important to ignore or dismiss.

Street Crime in America

Street crimes are the common-law crimes of murder, assault, robbery, rape, burglary, and larceny that are widely considered serious law violations (Rossi et al. 1974; Wolfgang et al. 1985) and that concern most Americans (L. Harris 1973; see also Warr and Stafford 1983). The patterns and proportions of common-law criminal involvement are of great concern for impoverished Hispanic-Americans (Horowitz 1983; Moore et al. 1978; Romero and Stelzner 1985; Sánchez Jankowski 1991), for American Indians (Hagan 1985; Hayner 1942; Jensen et al. 1977; Minnis 1963; Reasons 1972; Snipp 1992; Stewart 1964; Von Hentig 1945), and for some impoverished and otherwise disadvantaged white Americans. However, our analysis focuses on how race-linked inequalities in the United States concentrate street crime among disadvantaged black Americans, especially young African-American males. There are several reasons for this focus.

First, we have far more knowledge of the juvenile and criminal justice experiences of African-Americans. In part, this derives from the recording and reporting practices of official agencies. Juvenile and criminal justice system data have been reported separately for African-Americans for many years. In contrast, the FBI has collected systematic arrest data on Hispanic-Americans only since 1980. The study of crime among Hispanics is hampered further by confusion regarding at least four sizable groups (Mexican-Americans or Chicanos, Puerto Ricans, Cubans, and "other" Latin Americans), and by tendencies to categorize Hispanics collectively as "others," "nonwhite," and as black or white, as well as Hispanic. Related problems of cultural and tribal variation have hampered the study of crime among American Indians. This research is further complicated by the small number of American Indians relative to the larger population. It is also important to keep in mind, though, that the long-term practice of separately identifying and recording crime data on African-Americans may be a part of the isolation and segregation of blacks more generally in this society. Such processes are key aspects of the race-linked inequality in American life of which crime and criminal justice are a part.

In brief then, this chapter focuses on young black American males who disproportionately encounter systems of crime and delinquency control. We do, though, also report official data for Hispanic-Americans and American Indians and refer more generically to minority and nonwhite youth, to whom in varying degrees much of the research we consider can be generalized. These references reflect the general role of ethnic- and race-linked inequality in problems of crime and criminal justice. These patterns may simply be the most pronounced, best studied, and fully documented among African-American youth.

We also give special attention to the treatment of female adolescents and young adults. Although minority males are more often the subjects of juvenile and criminal justice processing, some minority females are especially vulnerable to system contact.

High-Risk Problems and the Legacy of Minority Discontent with American Justice

Young black males who experience educational and employment problems are at exceptionally high risk for arrest and imprisonment in America (Freeman 1991). Consider the following:

- Overall, African-Americans account for one-third of all arrests and one-half of all incarcerations in the United States.
- About one-fifth of all 16- to 34-year-old black males are under justice system supervision.
- One-half of all African-American school drop-outs, and three-quarters of drop-outs who are between 25 and 34 years old, are under justice system supervision.
- Three-quarters of all black prison inmates have less than twelve years of schooling.
- African-American prisoners between 25 and 34 years of age report preprison incomes that average $11,368, compared with $20,175 for this age group in the general population.
- Homicide is the leading cause of death among African-American youth.

These facts confirm that delinquency, crime, and contacts with the criminal justice system are massive risk factors in the lives of poorly educated and economically disadvantaged black youth and young adults. There are two possible explanations for these facts.

First, race-linked patterns of discrimination, segregation, and concentrated poverty may produce pervasive family and community disadvantages as well as educational and employment difficulties, which in turn cause much delinquent and criminal behavior among young minority males. Second, it is possible that, at the hands of the juvenile and criminal justice systems, young black males are victims of prejudice and discrimination in the form of more frequent arrest, prosecution, and punishment for delinquent and criminal behavior.

Both of these explanations describe real life, even if the latter reality is today less apparent and more subtle than it was in the past. Together these realities produce an additional important problem: a legacy of suspicion and distrust of the justice system in America. This chapter argues that this legacy of discontent is one of the most corrosive and consequential features of crime in this society.

Some of this suspicion and distrust derives from the historical experience of slavery and the criminal mistreatment of African-Americans that followed. This legacy includes race-motivated torture and lynchings by white mobs (Sellin 1935) and legally sanctioned but nonetheless discriminatory use of the death penalty by white juries (Wolfgang and Riedel 1973). It includes the development of chain-gang labor practices as a source of cheap black labor for white employers in the American South (Blassingame 1977; Myers 1991); and it includes patterns of law enforcement after Reconstruction, and extending well into this century, in which the punishment of blacks for crimes against whites legally perpetuated a caste system born in slavery (Sellin 1976).

It is also the case that the civil rights revolution of the 1950s and 1960s brought with it a "due process and equal rights revolution" that mitigated at least some sources of racial injustice, while also extending some rights of adults to children and adolescents. Some blatant sources of discrimination were removed or outlawed, and the system as a whole became the subject of more intense scrutiny. In addition, affirmative action policies brought more minorities and women into jobs in the justice system.

However, the direction of reform has not been uniform or consistent. For example, in *Furman v. Georgia* (1972) several Supreme Court justices were much influenced by social science evidence showing that, with other factors held constant, poor and black Americans were at greater risk of execution. The Supreme Court held in this case that the death penalty was "cruel and unusual punishment" as then practiced. Nonetheless, this decision left open the possibility that modified statutes that presumptively addressed these practices could be deemed constitutional. And indeed, *Gregg v. Georgia* (1976) allowed new procedures to impose the death penalty, and more recently, in *McClesky v. Kemp* (1987) the Supreme Court upheld the death penalty despite sophisticated statistical evidence indicating that the race of victims still influences the use of capital punishment. Moreover, the court effectively dismissed future consideration of social science data on patterns of discrimination in capital cases (Ellsworth 1988).

In addition, institutionalized reforms were not always uniformly or consistently beneficial to those most affected, and systemic problems of other kinds therefore also persist. For example, one of the most important reforms in juvenile justice involved a shift in almost all states to handling "status offenses" (e.g., "running away from home," truancy, curfew violation, being a "person in need of supervision," being "incorrigible," etc.) differently from "juvenile crime."

The intent of this reform was to remedy a common finding that female "status offenders" were at particular risk of being institutionalized and treated even more harshly than more serious male "delinquents" (Reese and Curtis 1991: 63), especially when their impoverished families were judged to be morally or socially problematic (Cicourel 1968). The Juvenile Justice and Delinquency Act of 1974 required that states receiving federal money for delinquency prevention begin to divert and "deinstitutionalize" their status offenders (Chesney-Lind 1987). Between 1974 and 1982, the number of girls admitted to public detention centers in the United States declined by 45 percent, as did female admissions to training schools. Yet despite changes in juvenile court dispositions, girls continued to be arrested and referred to court for less serious (status) offenses than boys (Chesney-Lind 1987). And, there is a further trend in the juvenile justice system to recategorize status offenses as juvenile crime. For example, in 1981 Congress amended the Juvenile Justice Act so that any child who had violated a "valid court order" (e.g., by running away from a court-ordered placement in a foster home) would no longer be covered by the deinstitutionalization provisions of the act.

At the adult level, young adult and minority women appear to be more severely sanctioned than their male counterparts (Spohn et al. 1981–82). In addition, several recent studies indicate that young black women specifically are at risk of being treated more severely than young white women (Datesman and Scarpitti 1977; Pawlak 1977; Visher 1983). Horowitz and

Pottieger (1991: 76) speculate that "the latter may reflect the dual impact of racism and sexism, or it may be that black female arrestees and defendants are less likely than their white counterparts to exhibit submissiveness and other traditionally defined 'feminine' demeanors."

The latter speculation hints at the distrust, suspicion, and animosity noted above that characterize many interactions of justice system personnel with minority citizens in general, and with minorities accused of offenses more specifically. These are common but underemphasized sentiments revealed in studies of juvenile and criminal justice processing of minorities, male and female. This chapter suggests that these sentiments have important sources and consequences. We note that a recent shift in system attention to issues of deterrence and incapacitation may further exacerbate the animosity and distrust that are especially dangerous to young minority members who are already at high risk of criminal offending and victimization.

Common-Law Crime, Minorities, and Concentrated Poverty

We now review in greater detail evidence of the contemporary disproportionate involvement of the minority poor in delinquent and criminal behavior. To place these problems in perspective, it should be noted that African-Americans make up about 12 percent of the U.S. population, while Hispanic-Americans constitute about 8 percent, and native Indians less than 1 percent (Flowers 1988).

In the early 1990s, African-Americans are arrested for a high proportion of serious crimes against persons: as much as 40 to 50 percent of all homicides, forcible rapes, armed robberies, and aggravated assaults. Hispanic-Americans account for about 14 percent of violent crimes against persons, while American Indians account for just over one-half of 1 percent.

This involvement is strongly age-related. For example, among 15- to 19-year-old Americans, the gun homicide rate for black males per 100,000 population is more than ten times that for whites. This rate is about 68 homicides per 100,000 population for black males in their late teens, compared with about 6 for white males in the same age group (Fingerhut and Kleinman 1989).

Black Americans are arrested for a smaller but still disproportionate share of less serious property crimes: as much as a quarter to a third of all arsons, car thefts, burglaries, and larceny-thefts (Harris 1991). Hispanic-Americans account for about 11 percent of these property crimes, and

American Indians just over 1 percent. These crimes also peak in mid- to late adolescence.

Perhaps most worrisome to many Americans, however, is that U.S. arrest rates increased markedly throughout the 1960s, 1970s, and 1980s and continue at high levels into the 1990s. One researcher has calculated that more than one-half of the increase in crime in twelve of the largest U.S. cities was linked to a rise in the proportion of African-Americans living in these cities (Chilton 1986). Street crime and victimization are increasingly concentrated in the racially segregated neighborhoods of urban settings. Much of this increase can be attributed to the concentration of poverty and joblessness in the predominantly poor and minority neighborhoods of these cities (W. J. Wilson 1987). Since crime is strongly related to age, with participation concentrated in adolescence and early adulthood, the relative increase of the proportion of African-Americans in this younger age category may further contribute to these trends.

Perhaps the most striking feature of street crime in America is its link to the concentration of poverty in urban settings. Recent epidemiological studies focusing on census tracts indicate that at higher socioeconomic levels, blacks and whites experience similarly low rates of homicide (see Lowry et al. 1988; Centerwall 1984; Munford et al. 1976). It is only in census tracts with high concentrations of poor households that blacks have much higher levels of homicide victimization.

Ethnographic studies are especially persuasive in describing the ways in which urban concentrations of poverty affect rates of crime in minority neighborhoods (see Anderson 1990; Hagedorn 1988; Lehmann 1991; Sánchez Jankowski 1991; Sullivan 1989). Journalistic descriptions of such settings also evocatively depict the danger, anger, risks, and strains of ghetto poverty and crime. For example, in *There Are No Children Here*, Alex Kotlowitz (1991) follows the early teen years of the brothers Pharoah and Lafayette Rivers who live in a Chicago housing project where the prospects for escaping poverty and crime seem remote. The younger brother poignantly confides, "I worry about dying, dying at a young age, while you're little."

It is sometimes difficult in aggregate-level studies to fully disentangle the factors that concentrate poverty and cause problems of violence to proliferate. For example, in a meta-analysis of 21 macrolevel studies, Land et al. (1990) find a cluster of factors that have a clear and pervasive causal influence (including median income, percentage of families below the poverty line, an index of income inequality, percentage of population that is black, and percentage of single-parent families), but these factors cannot be fully decomposed into more specific causal effects. In Chapter 3 of this volume, however, Land, Cantor, and Russell argue convincingly that aggregate lagged rates of unemployment have specifiable effects on property crime. This appropriately focuses attention on issues of joblessness that are central to the concentration-of-poverty argument.

The possible importance of joblessness and other factors is further illustrated in aggregate- and individual-level quantitative studies focused specifically on the causal mechanisms that link concentrated poverty and family disruption to crime among young minority citizens. Sampson (1987) examined race-specific rates of robbery and homicide in over 150 U.S. cities. He found that the scarcity of employed black men increased the prevalence of families headed by women in African-American communities, which in turn substantially increased the rates of black murder and robbery, especially among juveniles (see also Matsueda and Heimer 1987). Sampson emphasized that family disruption produces similar effects on white crime and therefore "cannot be attributed to unique cultural factors in the black community" (Sampson 1987: 377). Most likely these effects reflect macrolevel patterns of social and community control. Sampson and Wilson's essay on race and urban poverty, which follows this chapter, articulates a compelling theoretical perspective on the mechanisms by which concentrated poverty and joblessness produce person and property crime.

In his penetrating analysis "American Apartheid," Douglas Massey (1990) reveals much about the root causes of the concentration of poverty and its consequences. He demonstrates that during the 1970s racial segregation was the key factor responsible for the social transformation of many black communities and the concentration of poverty. He uses experimental simulations and regression models based on census tracts to show how a pernicious interaction between rising poverty rates and high levels of segregation created the population often identified as an "underclass." These models illustrate how racial segregation makes it possible for economic changes, including industrial restructuring, to produce rapid and dramatic concentrations of poverty that can change low-income communities from places where welfare-dependent, female-headed families are a minority, to places where these are the norm. When this occurs, patterns of formal and informal community control may be undermined, in turn producing high rates of crime and related problems.

Racial segregation and related forms of discrimination may produce violent crime in another way. Blau and Blau (1982) note that race-linked inequalities find expression in forms of "diffuse aggression" and "hostility." They point out that such pronounced and highly visible inequities imply that there are great riches within view but not within reach of many people destined to live in poverty (see also Farnworth and Leiber 1989). The result is that there is much "resentment, frustration, hopelessness, and alienation," producing a "sense of injustice, discontent, and distrust" (Blau and Blau 1982: 119). The Blaus' point is that while inequality generally promotes criminal violence, racial inequities are especially productive of such violence, because of the feelings just described. The following sections of this chapter discuss the sense of distrust, suspicion, discontent, and injustice that characterize minority contacts (those of offenders and of the general citizenry) with the American justice system. Indeed, we argue that recent changes in the system may have broadened and intensified these feelings among African-Americans.

Common-Law Crimes and Law Enforcement

In part because of a belief that bias in police arrest practices might account for some of the racial disproportionality in less violent crime, social scientists developed survey methods to record offender and victim reports of their experiences of delinquency and crime. In a pattern that partly parallels the official figures for property and person crimes reported above, adolescent self-report studies show small or no differences by race for many kinds of minor law violations, but significant and consistent differences for more serious, especially violent, offenses. This suggests that discrimination is more manifest in minor discretionary contexts of police decision making about common and less serious forms of delinquency than in contexts of more serious and violent youth crime. As Sampson (1986: 884) notes, "if we . . . focus on the most serious offenses where police discretion is limited and prior record is not a factor (e.g., robbery and homicide arrests), the effects of SES and other non-legal factors (race, delinquent friends) are diminished and hence official records reasonably . . . [can] be used as proxies for offending behavior."

In this context probably the most widely referenced self-report study of adolescents finds that:

> Black males disproportionately and consistently . . . report being involved in what could be characterized as face-to-face *violent* offenses often involving theft: "used club, knife or gun to get something; threatened to beat someone up if he didn't give you money; used physical force to get money; carried a razor, switchblade, or gun; pulled a knife; hit a teacher; beat up someone so badly they probably needed a doctor; jumped or helped jump somebody" (Hindelang et al. 1981; see also Elliott and Ageton 1980).

In research that asks prison inmates to self-report past criminal involvements, most of which date from their youth, parallel racial differences emerge (Petersilia 1985).

The patterns that emerge from self-report surveys and official data are also consistent with what victims of common-law personal crimes report regarding the race of assailants and with what such studies show about the race of the victims themselves (Hindelang 1978). These data reflect a crucial aspect of crime and race in America: not only are rates of offending and arrest high in African-American communities, but so too are rates of victimization. That is, crime is predominantly intraracial.

Annually, the U.S. Department of Justice undertakes the National Crime Survey (NCS), a nationwide residential survey of the general public about their experiences as victims of crime. According to NCS reports from the mid-1980s, African-Americans have experienced rates of rape, aggravated assault, and armed robbery that are approximately 25 percent higher than those for whites. Rates of motor vehicle theft for blacks exceed those for whites by about 70 percent, and robbery victimization is more than 150 percent higher for blacks. Other sources reveal that for much of the past half century, rates of African-American homicide deaths have ranged from six to seven times those for whites (Hawkins 1986; Ross and McClain 1990).

The point is that the experience of crime is felt heavily in the African-American community. Moreover, it is felt disproportionately by the young and the poor, the near-poor, and the middle socioeconomic segments of this community. To illustrate, NCS data indicate that rates of robbery victimization decrease monotonically from over 1,000 per 100,000 population for 1- to 15-year-olds, to one-third this rate for persons 65 or older (Gottfredson and Hindelang 1981). For many ghetto youth, victimization is a consequence of the risk of living in a highly criminal environment. For other youth, it is a consequence of direct participation in the criminal activities prevalent in this environment (Fagan et al. 1987). Sometimes victimization can lead to offending. Some crime in minority neighborhoods may be a product of retaliation, a form of what one researcher calls "self help" (Black 1983). These compensating and revenge-seeking acts are a frequent part of gang and peer group associations. In these contexts, the lines between victimization and offending are frequently unclear. The overlapping nature of these events is partly a reflection of and partly a cause of the animosity and aggression that Blau and Blau (1982) describe.

Even living in proximity to high-crime areas may be dangerous, because of substantial spillover effects. The National Research Council's (1989) report *A Common Destiny: Blacks and American Society* dispels two common misconceptions: that it is the white community that suffers disproportionately from black crime, and that poor blacks suffer the most from all types of black crime. This review of the evidence reveals that although poor blacks do suffer greatly from crime victimization, "middle-class and near-poor blacks seem to suffer significantly greater losses than poor blacks or than whites of any income level" (p. 471).

Popular sources and public opinion surveys indicate that many middle-class black Americans believe that the police and the courts fail to protect them from these growing problems of crime and at the same time mistreat them. These viewpoints are most apparent where survey items dealing with the police and courts are linked to issues of inequality, poverty, and race (see Hagan 1989: 131). In recent years, these perceptions have been reinforced by brutal police-citizen encounters in several cities, including the Rodney King beating in Los Angeles and the police killing of Malice Green in Detroit. Middle-class African-Americans, including some of America's finest athletes, have long complained of such harassment. A quarter century ago, the star center of the Boston Celtics basketball team, Bill Russell (1966), wrote in his autobiography of the harassment he had experienced in encounters with the police. More recently, the Boston Celtics' Dee Brown received an apology from suburban Boston police for "racial implications" in his forcible search by officers looking for a bank robber (*New York Times*, Nov. 4, 1991, VIII: 1). Research confirms that black Americans, especially those who have achieved positions of high status, share a pervasive perception of criminal injustice that reflects Russell's and Brown's experiences (Hagan and Albonetti 1982).

The lack of confidence in the ability of the juvenile and criminal justice system to respond effectively to crime in minority urban communities, coupled with the fact that young minority citizens are disproportionately swept into the criminal justice system, presents a major public policy problem. In the view of many, the justice system is more a symptom of America's problems with urban minority youth crime than a source of solutions to these problems. This view is reinforced by research on the policing, prosecution, and punishment of ghetto youth.

Policing Minority Communities

Mixed into the evolving picture of law enforcement in America is much evidence that the police perceive the attitudes and behaviors of minority youth as hostile and threatening. The consequences are many: increasing levels of contact between young minorities and the police, more negative police–community relations, and for the affected youth a greater likelihood of harassment, brutality, and arrest.

Contextual analyses of policing indicate that police perceive minority youth in general as hostile and threatening. Scholars offer a variety of plausible reasons. Skolnick (1966) suggests that the danger of violence in policing results in the police's treating large parts of the public as "symbolic assailants," with young minority males being especially prone to this kind of stereotyping. After studying policing in three of the largest U.S. cities, Black and Reiss (1967) reported that a majority of the police expressed "antiblack" attitudes. And Reiss and Bordua (1967) note that a common tactic in police–citizen encounters is for police to "take charge" and "freeze" situations through verbal and physical expressions of authority. These factors combine to make police–suspect encounters emotionally charged and confrontational. They are especially likely to characterize police encounters with minority youth, and to increase the risks of police brutality and indiscretion.

Empirical analyses of situational determinants of arrests indicate that legal variables such as seriousness of the offense and prior record play an important role in arrest decisions. These studies also show that suspects' demeanor and behavior may also be important in police decision making. For example, in their classic study of policing of juveniles, Piliavin and Briar (1964) suggested that beyond having a prior arrest record, adolescents who do not display respect toward officers are the ones most likely to be arrested. Additional studies confirm that a confrontational demeanor or lack of contriteness of minority youth partially accounts for their greater risk of arrest (Black 1970; Ferdinand and Luchterhand 1970; Sykes and Clark 1975).

Sykes and Clark (1975) place this finding in the context of an "asymmetrical status norm." They suggest that policing is characterized by a normative expectation requiring that officers receive more deference than they give; so, for example, a policeman or policewoman will expect to be addressed as "officer," but will address citizens in general, and youths in particular, by given names, at best. This asymmetry exists in part because the police represent the authority of the law, and probably also because officers are often older and of higher occupational status than the suspects they encounter. The asymmetry becomes more problematic when minority youth are involved.

For example, even an unprejudiced officer's expectation of general deference may be interpreted by a minority youth as indicating the officer's own ethnic group superordination. Likewise, an officer may view a minority youth's refusal to express deference as a refusal to acknowledge assumed social obligations of all citizens and the officer's symbolic status. So a simple observation of the asymmetrical status norm can convey double meanings, placing both officers and minority youth in double binds. Sykes and Clark's study shows that this kind of problem often leads to more punitive treatment of minorities.

More recently, in a study of 742 suspect encounters with police in 24 American cities, Smith and Visher (1982) report that antagonistic suspects are much more likely to be taken into custody than suspects who display deference, that black suspects are more likely to be arrested than whites, and that part of this race effect can be explained by the more hostile or antagonistic demeanor of the black suspects.

Status-linked expectations may play a role in the treatment of females as well. While it is sometimes thought that female delinquents benefit from "chivalrous coddling" by the police, recent studies suggest that "paternalistic punitiveness" may often be the more pressing problem (Krohn et al. 1983; McEachern and Bauzer 1967). Visher (1983) suggests that:

> When law enforcement officials (e.g., police, prosecutors, judges), most of whom are male, interact with female violators, the encounter is transformed into an exchange between a man and a woman. In this situation, appropriate gender behaviors and expectations may become more salient than strictly legal factors in the official sanctioning of female offenders. Indeed, if women fail to conform to traditional female roles, then the assumed bargain is broken and chivalrous treatment is not extended.

Further, Visher and others (e.g., Chesney-Lind 1987) have noted that "chivalry" is not likely to be extended to minority or young females.

In addition, field studies of street prostitution indicate that young minority women are routinely harassed by police, taken into custody because they are "known" prostitutes, and sometimes brutalized (Horowitz and Pottieger 1991; LaFave 1965). These types of experiences produce distrust and suspicion. This antagonism is a thread of consistency that carries through a range of contacts of minority citizens in general, and minority youth in particular, with the criminal justice system, ultimately adding to the risks of this endangered group.

Finally, findings regarding the ecological patterning of police work refocus our attention on the links between racial inequalities of discrimination and segregation and the concentration of poverty and crime in poor minority settings. Sometimes it is argued that densely populated ghetto settings increase anonymity and freedom from surveillance and control

(Newman 1972; Thrasher 1927). It is more likely, though, that the press of people in dense underclass areas imposes upon residents a unique kind of community organization characterized by a high level of mutual surveillance (see Jacobs 1961; Plant 1957). This restricts residents' privacy, making their activities, both legal and illegal, more frequently "public" (Stinchcombe 1963). A result is that the same act detected, reported, and recorded as illegal in a densely populated minority community may go undetected, unreported, and unrecorded in less densely populated middle- and upper-class settings. But this is only one way in which some social and geographical areas are more "offensible" than others.

The term *offensible space* has been used to refer to areas in which the police perceive a disproportionate incidence of deviant behavior and beyond this take some *initiative* in processing offenders (Hagan et al. 1978). Although most police work is "reactive," in response to citizen complaints, some is "proactive," or police-initiated, and some is a mixture of both. For example, Black (1970) notes that "citizens occasionally provide the police with intelligence about *patterned* juvenile behavior, such as complaints provided by businessmen about recurrent vandalism on their block or recurrent rowdiness on their corner. These may lead the police to increase surveillance in an attempt to 'clean up' the area" (p. 66n). Smith (1986: 316) goes further in suggesting that:

> Based on a set of internalized expectations derived from past experience, police divide the population and physical territory they must patrol into readily understandable categories. The result is a process of ecological contamination in which all persons encountered in bad neighborhoods are viewed as possessing the moral liability of the area itself.

In other words, offensible space or "ecological contamination" involves areas where prior police conceptions encourage an aggressive and stereotyped pattern of police work.

A study designed to assess the effects of police conceptions of offensible space was undertaken in a Canadian community called Westport (Hagan et al. 1978). Using a mixture of quantitative and qualitative techniques, this study showed that official areal delinquency rates can be better explained by police conceptions of offensible space and citizen complaints than by aggregated self-reported measures of delinquent behavior. That is, this study confirms that there is a contamination effect associated with offensible space that results in the overpolicing of youth and adults from stigmatized areas. However, this study also concludes that, "Once past the areally influenced stage of detection and selection, individualized decision making may become more visible, and the decisions correspondingly more legalistic, depending on the organizational constraints and decision makers involved."

A similar set of conclusions emerges from Sampson's (1986) contextual analysis of data from the Seattle Youth Study (see also Smith 1986). He finds a strong inverse effect of neighborhood socioeconomic status (SES) on police processing of juveniles that is independent of self-reported law-violative behavior. He then concludes that "the influence of SES on police contacts is contextual in nature, and stems from an ecological bias with regard to police control, as opposed to a simple individual-level bias against the poor" (p. 884). The implication is that this is a kind of community-based discrimination that is felt by individuals, even though it is not revealed in individual-level analyses. It is a process that lowers the threshold for the entry of the poor and minorities into the juvenile and criminal justice systems, and it is a part of the experience that builds resentment and distrust among these populations.

Processing Minority Defendants

Once caught up in the justice system, the risks for young minority members increase. Even prolonged contact with the system itself often is detrimental, not only in terms of justice system outcomes, but also in terms of lost employment and earnings—so much so that Malcolm Feeley (1979) argues, "The process is the punishment." This, combined with the problems already noted, makes it unsurprising that minority defendants would be relatively uncooperative during the process of prosecution, adding to the problems of suspicion, distrust, and hostility discussed above.

This pattern is apparent in research on the prosecutorial process. The pervasive concern at the prosecution stage is with charge and plea bargaining, which has been defined as "the exchange of official concessions for the act of self-conviction" (Alschuler 1979: 213). A key issue is what kinds of charges and cases get "bargained down" or dismissed instead of fully prosecuted. Research suggests that much of this process in the juvenile and criminal courts involves a stereotyping of cases according to case-specific characteristics, including racial assessments of the credibility of the victim and offender as witnesses (see Cicourel 1968; Myers and Hagan 1979; Sudnow 1965). Nonwhite victims tend to be considered less credible witnesses, while white victims, especially of nonwhite defendants, are considered highly credible (Newman 1966).

Although there is variation in results, two patterns commonly emerge in analyses of the prosecution of minorities, who are disproportionately young and male. The first is a tendency to dismiss more cases involving nonwhite defendants. The second pattern is for nonwhite defendants to receive plea bargains less often than white defendants. These patterns probably are not contradictory.

For example, in a large study in California, Michigan, and Texas, Petersilia (1983) found higher dismissal rates for African-American defendants. Petersilia speculates that this difference results from the tendency of the police to arrest minority suspects with insufficient evidence or probable cause; this speculation is supported by a finding that warrants are used more extensively in arrests of whites than nonwhites. Prosecutors may simply use dismissals to eliminate their weakest cases against minority defendants.

When attention is focused on cases not dismissed, Petersilia and other researchers find that minority defendants are less likely to plea bargain and more likely to go to trial (LaFree 1980; Mather 1979; Petersilia 1983; Uhlman 1979; Welch et al. 1985; Zatz and Lizotte 1985). This finding suggests that whites are getting better "deals" in the plea bargaining process. Several studies support this view (e.g., Welch et al. 1985; Zatz and Lizotte 1985).

Scholars speculate that this pattern results from the suspicion, distrust, and hostility minority suspects have for the prosecutorial process. We can now begin to see the mounting costs of these sentiments. On the one hand, the justice system bears the costs of procedure and delay that fully prosecuting a greater proportion of minority defendants brings. Meanwhile, these defendants are caught up in a system that is time-consuming and costly in other ways, not the least of which is an increasingly greater likelihood of imprisonment.

Punishing Minorities

Perhaps the most important contemporary development in the sentencing and punishment of offenders has been the shift from an emphasis on rehabilitation and treatment to an emphasis on just deserts, incapacitation, and deterrence. In criminology this transition has involved resurrecting theories of crime that emphasize the consequences of punishment, with an associated view toward the protection of society. The reemergence of deterrence theory and strategies of selective incapacitation are a part of this shift of attention. Associated with this shift is increased use of institutionalization and incarceration, especially of high-risk minority youth. The aggregate numbers in our state prisons, which hold 92 percent of our nation's inmates, are in themselves dramatic. In little more than a decade, commitments to prison increased nationally nearly two and one-half times, from less than 100,000 in 1974 (96,073), to over 200,000 in 1986 (232,969). Langan (1991: 1568) reports that as of December 31, 1989, state prisons nationwide held a record 610,000 inmates, 63,000 more inmates than a year earlier.

The use of institutional placements for juvenile offenders has also increased, although its growth has been less pronounced than is the case for adults. In 1975 juveniles were confined in juvenile facilities at a rate of 241 per 100,000 juveniles between age 10 and the age of majority. By 1987 the figure was 353 per 100,000 such juveniles. Over the 1975–89 period, the number of children in custody in public facilities increased by 19 percent, from nearly 47,000 in 1975 to over 56,100 in 1989.

There are many reasons why the use of imprisonment could have grown over this period, including increasing levels of reported crime and arrests, more specific increases in drug crime and arrests, and changes in the proportion of young people in the population. However, Langan's (1991) analysis indicates that changes in overall reported crime and arrest account for only 9 percent of the increase in imprisonment from 1974 to 1986, while changes in drug arrest and imprisonment explain 8 percent. Changes in the proportion of young people in the population are responsible for 20 percent of this growth. And the largest factor by far, accounting for more than half of the change, is simply a renewed preference for imprisonment.

Because crime is concentrated so heavily among youth and minorities in American society, the increased use of imprisonment falls heavily on young minority males. For example, during the 1974–86 period, the national rate of incarceration for African-Americans was more than six times as high as the rate for white Americans (Chilton and Galvin 1985). Between 1978 and 1982 alone, the percentage of adult black males in the U.S. population sent to prison increased by 23 percent (Bureau of Justice Statistics 1985: 5). In light of these patterns, it becomes relevant to inquire about the consequences of contact, especially imprisonment, with the justice system for minority youth and young adults.

To date, much of this inquiry has focused on the issue of discrimination in sentencing. Early studies of race and sentencing conducted in the 1940s and 1950s often concluded that racial discrimination occurred, but these studies often did not control for relevant legal variables (Hagan 1974). When controls for prior record and seriousness of offense were introduced in later studies, the evidence of racial discrimination often was reduced. Nonetheless, a number of recent contextual analyses indicate that ethnic- and race-based sentencing is still apparent for some types of offenders, at some decision points, and in some times and places (Hagan and Bumiller 1983; Myers and Talarico 1987; Peterson and Hagan 1984; Zatz 1987).

A number of efforts have been made in recent decades to prevent discrimination by reforming sentencing practices. Reforms have included rules and guidelines for plea bargaining, mandatory minimum sentences, statutory determinate sentencing, presumptive or prescriptive sentencing guidelines, and the establishment of sentencing councils. In light of these reforms and the findings of some research investigating their impact (e.g., Miethe and Moore 1985), the National Research Council's report *A Common Destiny* (1989: 487) notes that:

> Few criminologists would argue that the current gap between black and white levels of imprisonment is mainly due to discrimination in sentencing or in any of the other decision-making processes in the criminal justice system. The higher rate of crime among blacks explains much of the differential.

Yet these same reforms have made imprisonment more likely for young minority males in much the same way that the professionalization of police work increased risks of arrest for youth (see J. Q. Wilson 1968): that is, more young minority males are imprisoned through an evenhandedness that includes increased severity for convicted whites as well as nonwhites.

Chesney-Lind (1987) points out that this type of evenhandedness has also been extended to women such that in recent years judges have been sentencing women to prison in record numbers. She reports that, "between 1974 and 1984, for example, the number of girls and women arrested increased by 203 percent . . . and the number of women in prison jumped 258 percent (considerably steeper than the male increase of 199 percent)" (p. 114). Again, even if this involves an evenhandedness that extends to white as well as nonwhite women, the biggest effect will be felt by young minority women who encounter the system in disproportionate numbers. Black women constitute the majority of female prisoners (Chilton and Galvin 1985).

Consequences of the Criminalization of Young Minorities

Much of the support for the increased processing and punishment of offenders seems to derive from a mistaken optimism about the crime-reducing prospects of incapacitating a large number of highly active offenders. This policy for crime reduction often is referred to as selective incapacitation, a strategy that focuses on "career criminals."

A National Research Council panel undertook an evaluation of a large body of research on selective incapacitation and concluded that, despite concentration of crime among some highly active offenders, it would not be possible to reduce crime significantly without very substantial increases in prison populations. This is because the capacity to predict future careers in crime is limited, there is relatively little specialization by type of crime, most criminal careers are brief, and new offenders quickly replace those who desist. The apparent accuracy of this assessment is suggested by the fact that the record use of imprisonment in recent years has been accompanied by increasing, not decreasing, amounts of violent crime.

There are a variety of hypotheses about why repressive efforts may not be effective. One is that institutionalization results in "prisonization," a process in which new detainees take on the attitudes and values of older inmates. Although this may be true to some degree, there is also evidence that by the time disadvantaged minority youth encounter the justice system they already have the self-concepts, attitudes, and values that time in prison would foster (see Ageton and Elliott 1974; Harris 1976). This should not be surprising, if our arguments regarding the extensiveness of hostile attitudes toward the justice system among blacks have merit. This might also account for some of the weakness of deterrent and incapacitation effects associated with justice system contacts for minority youth.

Justice system experiences may have the further effect of solidifying networks of association that make unemployment and continued involvement in crime more likely. For example, ethnographic research in prisons suggests that racial associations and conflicts are imported from home communities and perpetuate gang activity within these settings (Lockwood 1980). One effect of these continuing associations may be to maintain connections with illegal markets that persist in prison and beyond (see Jacobs 1977; Moore et al. 1978). These underground markets are alternatives to conventional employment. For example, in the book provocatively titled *"Getting Paid": Youth Crime and Work in the Inner City*, Mercer Sullivan (1989) makes the point that for many ghetto youth these markets offer subculturally legitimized lines of economic opportunity.

Evidence of the more general detrimental consequences of the processing and punishment of youthful offenders, especially in terms of adult economic outcomes, continues to mount. At least since the pioneering work of Schwartz and Skolnick (1964), there is evidence that contacts with the criminal justice system have especially negative effects for the already economically disadvantaged. Schwartz and Skolnick found that working-class males with conviction records were uniquely disadvantaged in finding employment. And even if most youth who are arrested do not go to jail, the experience of arrest and conviction can have long-term, even intergenerational repercussions for criminal as well as conventional occupational careers (Hagan and Palloni 1990; Hagan 1991).

Both Freeman (1991) and Grogger (1991) report that a criminal arrest record has detrimental consequences for labor market outcomes, with negative effects on employment as much as eight years later. Some of this is likely due to the reluctance of employers who check for criminal records to employ ex-offenders. However, there are other possibilities.

Incarceration, or even prolonged processing through the criminal justice system, can date job skills and networks of contact for employment. Attitudes and interests that signal employability to prospective employers may be undermined and otherwise discouraged, while attitudes of distrust and hostility may increase. Anderson (1990) notes in his ethnographic research that while factory jobs in the manufacturing sector once allowed for a toughness of demeanor among young minority males, such attitudes are disabling in the new jobs of the service economy. Juvenile and criminal justice system contact seems to be a part of the process that perpetuates these attitudes.

A number of studies point to the problems that youth who participate in delinquency and experience criminal justice agency contact have in securing and holding jobs. In Robins's classic study in St. Louis, *Deviant Children Grown Up* (1966), adult employment problems were experienced disproportionately by former delinquents. Similar findings emerge in Sampson and Laub's (1990) reanalysis of the Gluecks' (1950) panel data on former delinquents traced into adulthood in Boston.

A recent thirteen-year panel study reports that youth from working-class families who identify with a subculture of delinquency are distinctly disadvantaged in terms of occupational outcomes when compared with middle- and upper-class youth who also were involved in this subculture (Hagan 1991). This study directly measures attitudes that impair the formation of social and cultural capital that is important in the process of occupational attainment. It also provides evidence that contact with the justice system diminishes the cultural capital of working-class youth.

These studies, from communities dispersed in time as well as location, all suggest that former delinquents experience unique difficulty in securing and holding jobs. When we add the implications of the elements of hostility, suspicion, and distrust noted above, the situation becomes bleak. Christopher Jencks (1988: 27) offers this chilling assessment of the employment prospects of many African-American youth:

> Even when young ghetto blacks manage to get a job, they are not likely to keep it long. Many quit because they take offense at the way their supervisors treat them, or get fired because their employers take offense at the way they behave. If we want to understand racism in the 1980s, we must look at conflicts of this kind.

If these comments have general currency, they likely have further salience for minority youth who come into conflict with the law. It is difficult to separate the effects of involvement in crime and delinquency from the effects of contacts with the criminal and juvenile justice system. Both may have their influence, and they may interact to produce additional problems, especially the animosity and distrust we have emphasized. Freeman (1991: 18) writes that, "either way, declining labor market opportunities for the less-educated and participation in crime seem to reinforce each other for growing fractions of less-educated young males." Little or nothing about juvenile and criminal justice system contact and experience seems to improve these prospects for young disadvantaged minorities.

Conclusions

This chapter points to fundamental and consequential inequalities that begin with broad patterns of segregation, isolation, and discrimination and that lead to concentrated problems of poverty, crime, and violence. To begin at the end of this story, limited data indicate that Hispanic-Americans are overrepresented in crimes against persons and property, while American Indians are overrepresented in property- and alcohol-related offenses. For reasons that seem only partly to involve racial discrimination in justice system processing, high levels of crime, especially violent street crime, are most fully documented among young black males in American society. As Chilton and Galvin (1985: 4) note, "given the economic situation of most black Americans, these facts are inconvenient for those who suggest that social class is unrelated to crime."

We have cited evidence developed by W. J. Wilson (1987) and others that high levels of crime among African-American youth are causally associated with the concentration of poverty and joblessness in black neighborhoods. Concentration of poverty has coincided with the entry into the crime-prone years of adolescence and early adulthood of the large postwar birth cohort, and this may partly account for the peaking of homicide and other forms of crime in the United States in the late 1970s. The aging of that birth cohort might have been expected to produce some relief from these high rates of criminal violence in following years, but after some positive signs in the early 1980s, rates have moved upward again. New applications of deterrence theory, strategies of selective incapacitation, and escalating rates of imprisonment have not altered these trends, but instead have coincided with them. Young minority males have continued to experience high levels of crime as well as punishment.

Why has crime among young blacks been so prolific and violent over the past several decades? Massey (1990) persuasively argues that patterns of ethnic and especially racial segregation created the conditions in which economic downturns and restructuring could have rapid and devasting consequences in urban minority communities. He demonstrates that residential segregation concentrated race and poverty in ways that savagely disrupted the social fabric of black American communities. This disruption has simultaneously aggravated stereotypes of ghetto settings and led to overpolicing and other kinds of discriminatory treatment that compound the difficulties of such communities. Blau and Blau (1982) suggest how race-linked inequalities generate diffuse feelings of injustice, hostility, and aggression. This hostility can be disorganizing and disruptive in ways that make crime and violence common. In Chapter 2, Sampson and Wilson systematically articulate the economic and social mechanisms through which this occurs.

Race-linked inequalities of segregation and discrimination further aggravate problems in an array of institutional settings where blacks and whites meet. Because community-level policing practices in ghetto settings display discriminatory patterns, and because nonetheless the justice system is expected to embody high standards of fairness and equal treatment, justice system interactions have become particularly difficult forums for black–white relations. We have cited a variety of kinds of evidence that the juvenile and criminal justice systems are perceived with suspicion, distrust, animosity and despair by minority citizens, who are too often stereotypically treated as suspects by the police and others. This negative atmosphere is likely intensified by the increasing use of imprisonment. A result is that many disadvantaged minority youth grow up in environments of animosity toward the justice system. It is not surprising that when such youth come into conflict with the law their attitudes both aggravate their contacts with the system and in the longer term predict poor occupational prospects.

Meanwhile, the large-scale use of arrest and imprisonment to deal with ghetto youth is incredibly costly in financial terms. Growing fear of crime and concern about the demoralization of our cities is an added cost of the street crime problem in this society (Skogan 1990; Skogan and Maxfield 1981). One response has been a substantial growth in firearm ownership for self-protection.

The number of guns in America has more than doubled over the past two decades, from less than 100 million before 1970 (Newton and Zimring 1969), to about 200 million in 1990 (Reiss and Roth 1993). Many of these guns are owned for self-protection. Smith and Uchida (1988) find that protective gun ownership increases with income, is higher among males, and is split about evenly by race. Perhaps most significantly, they find that high income and perceived risk of crime interact to stimulate the acquisition of guns as a means of self-protection against crime. This is a form of "class fortification against crime" that reflects a society increasingly polarized around issues of criminal inequality (Hagan 1992).

Although historically residential segregation in America may have functioned to give whites a feeling of separation and protection from blacks, a recent unintended consequence may be a society that is more dangerous than ever before and uniquely violent among Western nations. The irony is that policies and practices that residentially segregate and concentrate race and poverty also produce increasing problems of crime that threaten to explode beyond the boundaries in which they form. Recognizing this, white as well as black Americans increasingly arm and otherwise attempt to secure themselves within their homes and communities. Yet a recurring urban nightmare troubles the unprepared victims in a variety of urban folk tales, such as *The Bonfire of the Vanities*, *Do the Right Thing*, and *Grand Canyon*, in which unsuspecting citizens become subjects of the polarization of fear and violence that stalk our city streets. Issues of inequality and crime are no longer of interest to criminologists alone. These issues are at the heart of growing concerns about the quality of life available to citizens in this society, whether white or black, male or female, poor or affluent.

CHAPTER 2

Toward a Theory of Race, Crime, and Urban Inequality

ROBERT J. SAMPSON
WILLIAM JULIUS WILSON

Our purpose in this chapter is to address one of the central yet difficult issues facing criminology—race and violent crime. The centrality of the issue is seen on several fronts: the leading cause of death among young black males is homicide (Fingerhut and Kleinman 1990: 3292), and the lifetime risk of being murdered is as high as 1 in 21 for black males, compared with only 1 in 131 for white males (U.S. Department of Justice 1985). Although rates of violence have been higher for blacks than whites at least since the 1950s (Jencks 1991), record increases in homicide since the mid-1980s in cities such as New York, Chicago, and Philadelphia also appear racially selective (Hinds 1990; James 1991; Recktenwald and Morrison 1990). For example, while white rates remained stable, the rate of death from firearms among young black males more than doubled from 1984 to 1988 alone (Fingerhut et al. 1991). These differentials help explain recent estimates that a resident of rural Bangladesh has a greater chance of surviving to age 40 than does a black male in Harlem (McCord and Freeman 1990). Moreover, the so-called drug war and the resulting surge in prison populations in the past decade have taken their toll disproportionately on the minority community (Mauer 1990). Overall, the evidence is clear that African-Americans face dismal and worsening odds when it comes to crime in the streets and the risk of incarceration.

Despite these facts, the discussion of race and crime is mired in an unproductive mix of controversy and silence. At the same time that articles on age and gender abound, criminologists are loath to speak openly on race and crime for fear of being misunderstood or labeled racist. This situation is not unique, for until recently scholars of urban poverty also consciously avoided discussion of race and social dislocations in the inner city lest they be accused of blaming the victim (see W. J. Wilson 1987). And when the topic is broached, criminologists have reduced the race–crime debate to simplistic arguments about culture versus social structure. On the one side, structuralists argue for the primacy of "relative deprivation" to understand black crime (e.g., Blau and Blau 1982), even though the evidence on social class and crime is weak at best. On the other side, cultural theorists tend to focus on an indigenous culture of violence in black ghettos (e.g., Wolfgang and Ferracuti 1967), even though the evidence there is weak too.

Still others engage in subterfuge, denying race-related differentials in violence and focusing instead on police bias and the alleged invalidity of official crime statistics (e.g., Stark 1990). This in spite of evidence not only from death records but also from survey reports showing that blacks are disproportionately victimized by, and involved in, criminal violence (Hindelang 1976, 1978). Hence, much like the silence on race and inner-city social dislocations engendered by the vociferous attacks on the Moynihan Report in the 1960s, criminologists have, with few exceptions (e.g., Hawkins 1986; Hindelang 1978; Katz 1988), abdicated serious scholarly debate on race and crime.

In an attempt to break this stalemate we advance in this chapter a theoretical strategy that incorporates both structural and cultural arguments regarding race, crime, and inequality in American cities. In contrast to psychologically based relative deprivation theories and the subculture of violence, we view the race and crime linkage from contextual lenses that highlight the very different ecological contexts that blacks and whites reside in—regardless of individual characteristics. The basic thesis is that macrosocial patterns of residential inequality give rise to the social isolation and ecological concentration of the truly disadvantaged, which in turn leads to structural barriers and cultural adaptations that undermine social organization and hence the control of crime. This thesis is grounded in what is actually an old idea in criminology that has been overlooked in the race and crime debate—the importance of communities.

The Community Structure of Race and Crime

Unlike the dominant tradition in criminology that seeks to distinguish offenders from nonoffenders, the macrosocial or community level of explanation asks what it is about community structures and cultures that produces differential rates of crime (Bursik 1988; Byrne and Sampson 1986; Short 1985). As such, the goal of macrolevel research is not to explain individual involvement in criminal behavior but to isolate characteristics of communities, cities, or even societies that lead to high rates of criminality (Byrne and Sampson 1986; Short 1985). From this viewpoint the "ecological fallacy"—inferring individual-level relations based on aggregate data—is not at issue because the unit of explanation and analysis is the community.

The Chicago School research of Clifford Shaw and Henry McKay spearheaded the community-level approach of modern American studies of ecology and crime. In their classic work *Juvenile Delinquency and Urban Areas*, Shaw and McKay (1942) argued that three structural factors—low economic status, ethnic heterogeneity, and residential mobility—led to the disruption of local community social organization, which in turn accounted for variations in crime and delinquency rates (for more details see Kornhauser 1978).

Arguably the most significant aspect of Shaw and McKay's research, however, was their demonstration that high rates of delinquency persisted in certain areas over many years, regardless of population turnover. More than any other, this finding led them to reject individualistic explanations of delinquency and focus instead on the processes by which delinquent and criminal patterns of behavior were transmitted across generations in areas of social disorganization and weak social controls (1942, 1969: 320). This community-level orientation led them to an explicit contextual interpretation of correlations between race/ethnicity and delinquency rates. Their logic was set forth in a rejoinder to a critique in 1949 by Jonassen, who had argued that ethnicity had direct effects on delinquency. Shaw and McKay countered:

> The important fact about rates of delinquency for Negro boys is that they, too, vary by type of area. They are higher than the rates for white boys, but it cannot be said that they are higher than rates for white boys in comparable areas, since it is impossible to reproduce in white communities the circumstances under which Negro children live. Even if it were possible to parallel the low economic status and the inadequacy of institutions in the white community, it would not be possible to reproduce the effects of segregation and the barriers to upward mobility (1949: 614).

Shaw and McKay's insight almost a half century ago raises two interesting questions still relevant today. First, to what extent do black rates of crime vary by type of ecological area? Second, is it possible to reproduce in white communities the structural circumstances in which many blacks live? The first question is crucial, for it signals that blacks are not a homogeneous group any more than whites are. Indeed, it is racial stereotyping that assigns to blacks a distinct or homogeneous character, allowing simplistic comparisons of black–white group differences in crime. As Shaw and McKay recognized, the key point is that there is heterogeneity among blacks in crime rates that correspond to community context. To the extent that the causes of black crime are not unique, its rate should thus vary with specific ecological conditions in the same way that the white crime rate does. As we shall now see, recent evidence weighs in Shaw and McKay's favor.

Are the Causes of Black Crime Unique?

Disentangling the contextual basis for race and crime requires racial disaggregation of both the crime rate and the explanatory variables of theoretical interest. This approach was used in recent research that examined racially disaggregated rates of homicide and robbery by juveniles and adults in over 150 U.S. cities in 1980 (Sampson 1987). Substantively, the theory explored the effects of black male joblessness and economic deprivation on violent crime as mediated by black family disruption. The results supported the main hypothesis and showed that the scarcity of employed black males relative to black females was directly related to the prevalence of families headed by women in black communities (W. J. Wilson 1987). In turn, black family disruption was substantially related to rates of black murder and robbery, especially by juveniles (see also Messner and Sampson 1991). These effects were independent of income, region, density, city size, and welfare benefits.

The finding that family disruption had stronger effects on juvenile violence than on adult violence, in conjunction with the inconsistent findings of previous research on individual-level delinquency and broken homes, supports the idea that the effects of family structure are related to macro-level patterns of social control and guardianship, especially for youth and their peers (Sampson and Groves 1989). Moreover, the results suggest why unemployment and economic deprivation have had weak or inconsistent direct effects on violence rates in past research—joblessness and poverty appear to exert much of their influence indirectly through family disruption.

Despite a tremendous difference in mean levels of family disruption among black and white communities, the percentage of white families headed by a female also had a large positive effect on white juvenile and white adult violence. In fact, the predictors of white robbery were shown to be in large part identical in sign and magnitude to those for blacks. Therefore, the effect of black family disruption on black crime was independent of commonly cited alternative explanations (e.g., region, density, age composition) and could not be attributed to unique cultural factors within the black community given the similar effect of white family disruption on white crime.

To be clear, we are not dismissing the relevance of culture. As discussed more below, our argument is that if cultural influences exist, they vary systematically with structural features of the urban environment. How else can we make sense of the systematic variations *within* race—for example, if a uniform subculture of violence explains black crime, are we to assume that this subculture is three times as potent in, say, New York as in Chicago (where black homicide differs by a factor of three)? In San Francisco as in Baltimore (3:1 ratio)? These distinct variations exist even at the state level. For example, rates of black homicide in California are triple those in Maryland (Wilbanks 1986). Must whites then be part of the black subculture of violence in California, given that white homicide rates are also more than triple the rates for whites in Maryland? We think not. The sources of violent crime appear to be remarkably invariant across race and rooted instead in the structural differences among communities, cities, and states in economic and family organization.

The Ecological Concentration of Race and Social Dislocations

Having demonstrated the similarity of black-white variations by ecological context, we turn to the second logical question. To what extent are blacks as a group differentially exposed to criminogenic structural conditions? More than 40 years after Shaw and McKay's assessment of race and urban ecology, we still cannot say that blacks and whites share a similar environment—especially with regard to concentrated urban poverty. Consider the following. Although approximately 70 percent of all poor non-Hispanic whites lived in nonpoverty areas in the ten largest U.S. central cities (as determined by the 1970 census) in 1980, only 16 percent of poor blacks did. Moreover, whereas less than 7 percent of poor whites lived in extreme poverty or ghetto areas, 38 percent of poor blacks lived in such areas (W. J. Wilson et al. 1988: 130). In the nation's largest city, New York, 70 percent of poor blacks live in poverty neighborhoods; by contrast, 70 percent of poor whites live in nonpoverty neighborhoods (Sullivan 1989: 230). Potentially even more important, the majority of poor blacks live in communities characterized by high rates of family disruption. Poor whites, even those from "broken homes," live in areas of relative family stability (Sampson 1987; Sullivan 1989).

The combination of urban poverty and family disruption concentrated by race is particularly severe. As an example, we examined race-specific census data on the 171 largest cities in the United States as of 1980. To get some idea of concentrated social dislocations by race, we selected cities where the proportion of blacks living in poverty was equal to or less than the proportion of whites, *and* where the proportion of black families with children headed by a single parent was equal to or less than that for white families. Although we knew that the average national rate of family disruption and poverty among blacks was two to four times higher than among whites, the number of distinct ecological contexts in which blacks achieve equality to whites is striking. In not one city over 100,000 in the United States do blacks live in ecological equality with whites when it comes to these basic features of economic and family organization. Accordingly, racial differences in poverty and family disruption are so strong that the "worst" urban contexts in which whites reside are considerably better than the average context of black communities (Sampson 1987: 354).

Taken as a whole, these patterns underscore what W. J. Wilson (1987) has labeled "concentration effects," that is, the effects of living in a neighborhood that is overwhelmingly impoverished. These concentration effects, reflected in a range of outcomes from degree of labor force attachment to social deviance, are created by the constraints and opportunities that the residents of inner-city neighborhoods face in terms of access to jobs and job networks, involvement in quality schools, availability of marriageable partners, and exposure to conventional role models.

The social transformation of the inner city in recent decades has resulted in an increased concentration of the most disadvantaged segments of the urban black population—especially poor, female-headed families with children. Whereas one of every five poor blacks resided in ghetto or extreme poverty areas in 1970, by 1980 nearly two out of every five did so (W. J. Wilson et al. 1988: 131). This change has been fueled by several macrostructural forces. In particular, urban minorities have been vulnerable to structural economic changes related to the deindustrialization of central cities (e.g., the shift from goods-producing to service-producing industries; increasing polarization of the labor market into low-wage and high-wage sectors; and relocation of manufacturing out of the inner city). The exodus of middle- and upper-income black families from the inner city has also removed an important social buffer that could potentially deflect the full impact of prolonged joblessness and industrial transformation. This thesis is based on the assumption that the basic institutions of an area (churches, schools, stores, recreational facilities, etc.) are more likely to remain viable if the core of their support comes from more economically stable families in inner-city neighborhoods (W. J. Wilson 1987: 56). The social milieu of increasing stratification among blacks differs significantly from the environment that existed in inner cities in previous decades (see also Hagedorn 1988).

Black inner-city neighborhoods have also disproportionately suffered severe population and housing loss of the sort identified by Shaw and McKay (1942) as disrupting the social and institutional order. Skogan (1986: 206) has noted how urban renewal and forced migration contributed to the wholesale uprooting of many urban black communities, especially the extent to which freeway networks driven through the hearts of many cities in the 1950s destroyed viable, low-income communities. For example, in Atlanta one in six residents was dislocated by urban renewal; the great majority of those dislocated were poor blacks (Logan and Molotch 1987: 114). Nationwide, fully 20 percent of all central-city housing units occupied by blacks were lost in the period 1960–70 alone. As Logan and Molotch (1987: 114) observe, this displacement does not even include that brought about by more routine market forces (evictions, rent increases, commercial development).

Of course, no discussion of concentration effects is complete without recognizing the negative consequences of deliberate policy decisions to concentrate minorities and the poor in public housing. Opposition from organized community groups to the building of public housing in their neighborhoods, de facto federal policy to tolerate extensive segregation against blacks in urban housing markets, and the decision by local governments to neglect the rehabilitation of existing residential units (many of them single-family homes), have led to massive, segregated housing projects that have become ghettos for the minorities and disadvantaged (see also Sampson 1990). The cumulative result is that, even given the same objective socioeconomic status, blacks and whites face vastly different environments in which to live, work, and raise their children. As Bickford and Massey (1991: 1035) have argued, public housing is a federally funded, physically permanent institution for the isolation of black families by race and class and must therefore be considered an important structural constraint on ecological area of residence.

In short, the foregoing discussion suggests that macrostructural factors—both historic and contemporary—have combined to concentrate urban black poverty and family disruption in the inner city. These factors include but are not limited to racial segregation, structural economic transformation and black male joblessness, class-linked out-migration from the inner city, and housing discrimination. It is important to emphasize that when segregation and concentrated poverty represent structural constraints embodied in public policy and historical patterns of racial subjugation, notions that individual differences (or self-selection) explain community-level effects on violence are considerably weakened (see Sampson and Lauritsen 1994).

Implications

The consequences of these differential ecological distributions by race raise the substantively plausible hypothesis that correlations of race and crime may be systematically confounded with important differences in community contexts. As Testa has argued with respect to escape from poverty:

> Simple comparisons between poor whites and poor blacks would be confounded with the fact that poor whites reside in areas which are ecologically and economically very different from poor blacks. Any observed relationships involving race would reflect, to some unknown degree, the relatively superior ecological niche many poor whites occupy with respect to jobs, marriage opportunities, and exposure to conventional role models (quoted in W. J. Wilson 1987: 58–60).

Regardless of a black's individual-level family or economic situation, the average community of residence thus differs dramatically from that of a similarly situated white (Sampson 1987). For example, regardless of whether a black juvenile is raised in an intact or single-parent family, or a rich or poor home, he or she will not likely grow up in a community context similar to that of whites with regard to family structure and income. Reductionist interpretations of race and social class camouflage this key point.

In fact, a community conceptualization exposes the "individualistic fallacy"—the often-invoked assumption that individual-level causal relations necessarily generate individual-level correlations. Research conducted at the individual level rarely questions whether obtained results might be spurious and confounded with community-level processes. In the present case, it is commonplace to search for individual-level (e.g., constitutional) or group-level (e.g., social class) explanations for the link between race and violence. In our opinion these efforts have largely failed, and so we highlight contextual sources of the race–violence link among individuals. More specifically, we posit that the most important determinant of the relationship between race and crime is the differential distribution of blacks in communities characterized by (1) *structural social disorganization* and (2) *cultural social isolation*, both of which stem from the concentration of poverty, family disruption, and residential instability.

Before explicating the theoretical dimensions of social disorganization, we must also expose what may be termed the "materialist fallacy"—that economic (or materialist) causes necessarily produce economic motivations. Owing largely to Merton's (1938) famous dictum about social structure and anomie, criminologists have assumed that if economic structural factors (e.g., poverty) are causally relevant it must be through the motivation to commit acquisitive crimes. Indeed, "strain" theory was so named to capture the hypothesized pressure on members of the lower classes to commit crime in their pursuit of the American dream. But as is well known, strain or materialist theories have not fared well empirically (Kornhauser 1978). The image of the offender stealing to survive flourishes only as a straw man, knocked down most recently by Jack Katz, who argues that materialist theory is nothing more than "twentieth-century sentimentality about crime" (1988: 314). Assuming, however, that those who posit the relevance of economic structure for crime rely on motivational pressure as an explanatory concept, is itself a fallacy. The theory of social disorganization *does* see relevance in the ecological concentration of poverty, but not for the materialist reasons Katz (1988) presupposes. Rather, the conceptualization we now explicate rests on the fundamental properties of structural and cultural organization.

The Structure of Social (Dis)organization

In their original formulation Shaw and McKay held that low economic status, ethnic heterogeneity, and residential mobility led to the disruption of community social organization, which in turn accounted for variations in crime and delinquency rates (1942; 1969). As recently extended by Kornhauser (1978), Bursik (1988), and Sampson and Groves (1989), the concept of social disorganization may be seen as the inability of a community structure to realize the common values of its residents and maintain effective social controls. The *structural* dimensions of community social disorganization refer to the prevalence and interdependence of social networks in a community—both informal (e.g., the density of acquaintanceship; intergenerational kinship ties; level of anonymity) and formal (e.g., organizational participation; institutional stability)—and in the span of collective supervision that the community directs toward local problems.

This social-disorganization approach is grounded in what Kasarda and Janowitz (1974: 329) call the "systemic" model, where the local community is viewed as a complex system of friendship and kinship networks, and formal and informal associational ties are rooted in family life and ongoing socialization processes (see also Sampson 1991). From this view social organization and social *dis*organization are seen as different ends of the same continuum of systemic networks of community social control. As Bursik (1988) notes, when formulated in this way, social disorganization is clearly separable not only from the processes that may lead to it (e.g., poverty, residential mobility), but also from the degree of criminal behavior that may be a result. This conceptualization also goes beyond the traditional account of community as a strictly geographical or spatial phenomenon by focusing on the social and organizational networks of local residents (see Leighton 1988).

Evidence favoring social-disorganization theory is available with respect both to its structural antecedents and to mediating processes. In a recent paper, Sampson and Lauritsen (1994) reviewed in depth the empirical literature on individual, situational, and community-level sources of interpersonal violence (i.e., assault, homicide, robbery, and rape). This assessment revealed that community-level research conducted in the past twenty years has largely supported the original Shaw and McKay model in terms of the exogenous correlates of poverty, residential mobility, and heterogeneity. What appears to be especially salient is the *interaction* of poverty and mobility. As anticipated by Shaw and McKay (1942) and Kornhauser (1978), several studies indicate that the effect of poverty is most pronounced in neighborhoods of high residential instability (see Sampson and Lauritsen 1994).

In addition, recent research has established that crime rates are positively linked to community-level variations in urbanization (e.g., population and housing density), family disruption (e.g., percentage of single-parent households), opportunity structures for predatory crime (e.g., density of convenience stores), and rates of community change and population turnover (see also Bursik 1988; Byrne and Sampson 1986; Reiss 1986). As hypothesized by Sampson and Groves (1989), family disruption, urbanization, and the anonymity accompanying rapid population change all undercut the capacity of a community to exercise informal social control, especially of teenage peer groups in public spaces.

Land et al. (1990) have also shown the relevance of *resource deprivation*, *family dissolution*, and *urbanization* (density, population size) for explaining homicide rates across cities, metropolitan areas, and states from 1960 to 1980. In particular, their factor of resource deprivation/affluence included three income variables—median income, the percentage of families below the poverty line, and the Gini index of income inequality—in addition to the percentage of population that is black and the percentage of children not living with both parents. This coalescence of structural conditions with race supports the concept of concentration effects (W. J. Wilson 1987) and is consistent with Taylor and Covington's finding (1988) that increasing entrenchment of ghetto poverty was associated with large increases in violence. In these two studies the correlation among structural indices was not seen merely as a statistical nuisance (i.e., as multicollinearity), but as a predictable substantive outcome. Moreover, the Land et al. (1990) results support Wilson's argument that concentration effects grew more severe from 1970 to 1980 in large cities. Urban disadvantage thus appears to be increasing in ecological concentration.

It is much more difficult to study the intervening mechanisms of social disorganization directly, but at least two recent studies provide empirical support for the theory's structural dimensions. First, Taylor et al. (1984) examined variations in violent crime (e.g., mugging, assault, murder, rape) across 63 street blocks in Baltimore in 1978. Based on interviews with 687 household respondents, Taylor et al. (1984: 316) constructed block-level measures of the proportion of respondents who belonged to an organization to which coresidents also belonged, and the proportion of respondents who felt responsible for what happened in the area surrounding their home. Both of these dimensions of informal social control were significantly and negatively related to community-level variations in crime, exclusive of other ecological factors (1984: 320). These results support the social-disorganization hypothesis that levels of organizational participation and informal social control—especially of public activities by neighborhood youth—inhibit community-level rates of violence.

Second, Sampson and Groves's analysis of the British Crime Survey in 1982 and 1984 showed that the prevalence of unsupervised teenage peer groups in a community had the largest effects on rates of robbery and violence by strangers. The density of local friendship networks—measured by the proportion of residents with half or more of their friends living in the neighborhood—also had a significant negative effect on robbery rates. Further, the level of organizational participation by residents had significant inverse effects on both robbery and stranger violence (Sampson and Groves 1989: 789). These results suggest that communities characterized by sparse friendship networks, unsupervised teenage peer groups, and low organizational participation foster increased crime rates (see also Anderson 1990).

Variations in these structural dimensions of community social disorganization also transmitted in large part the effects of community socioeconomic status, residential mobility, ethnic heterogeneity, and family disruption in a theoretically consistent manner. For example, mobility had significant inverse effects on friendship networks, family disruption was the largest predictor of unsupervised peer groups, and socioeconomic status had a significant positive effect on organizational participation in 1982. When combined with the results of research on gang delinquency, which point to the salience of informal and formal community structures in controlling the formation of gangs (Short and Strodtbeck 1965; Sullivan 1989; Thrasher 1963), the empirical data suggest that the structural elements of social disorganization have relevance for explaining macrolevel variations in crime.

Further Modifications

To be sure, social-disorganization theory *as traditionally conceptualized* is hampered by a restricted view of community that fails to account for the larger political and structural forces shaping communities. As suggested earlier, many community characteristics hypothesized to underlie crime rates, such as residential instability, concentration of poor, female-headed families with children, multi-unit housing projects, and disrupted social networks, appear to stem directly from planned governmental policies at local, state, and federal levels. We thus depart from the natural market assumptions of the Chicago School ecologists by incorporating the political economy of place (Logan and Molotch 1987), along with macrostructural transformations and historical forces, into our conceptualization of community-level social organization.

Take, for example, municipal code enforcement and local governmental policies toward neighborhood deterioration. In *Making the Second Ghetto: Race and Housing in Chicago, 1940–1960*, Hirsch (1983) documents in great detail how lax enforcement of city housing codes played a major role in accelerating the deterioration of inner-city Chicago neighborhoods. More recently, Daley and Mieslin (1988) have argued that inadequate city policies on code enforcement and repair of city properties contributed to the systematic decline of New York City's housing stock, and consequently, entire neighborhoods. When considered with the practices of redlining and disinvestment by banks and "block-busting" by real estate agents (Skogan 1986), local policies toward code enforcement—that on the surface are far removed from crime—have in all likelihood contributed to crime through neighborhood deterioration, forced migration, and instability.

Decisions to withdraw city municipal services for public health and fire safety—presumably made with little if any thought to crime and violence—also appear to have been salient in the social disintegration of poor communities. As Wallace and Wallace (1990) argue based on an analysis of the "planned shrinkage" of New York City fire and health services in recent decades: "The consequences of withdrawing municipal services from poor neighborhoods, the resulting outbreaks of contagious urban decay and forced migration which shred essential social networks and cause social disintegration, have become a highly significant contributor to decline in public health among the poor" (1990: 427). The loss of social integration and networks from planned shrinkage of services may increase behavioral patterns of violence that may themselves become "convoluted with processes of urban decay likely to further disrupt social networks and cause further social disintegration" (1990: 427). This pattern of destabilizing feedback (see Skogan 1986) appears central to an understanding of the role of governmental policies in fostering the downward spiral of high crime areas. As Wacquant has recently argued, federal U.S. policy seems to favor "the institutional desertification of the urban core" (1991: 36).

Decisions by government to provide public housing paint a similar picture. Bursik (1989) has shown that the planned construction of new public housing projects in Chicago in the 1970s was associated with increased rates of population turnover, which in turn were related to increases in crime. More generally, we have already noted how the disruption of urban renewal contributed disproportionately to housing loss among poor blacks.

Boiled down to its essentials, then, our theoretical framework linking social-disorganization theory with research on urban poverty and political economy suggests that macrosocial forces (e.g., segregation, migration, housing discrimination, structural transformation of the economy) interact with local community-level factors (e.g., residential turnover, concentrated poverty, family disruption) to impede social organization. This is a distinctly sociological viewpoint, for it focuses attention on the proximate structural characteristics and mediating processes of community social organization that help explain crime, while also recognizing the larger historical, social, and political forces shaping local communities.

Social Isolation and Community Culture

Although social-disorganization theory is primarily structural in nature, it also focuses on how the ecological segregation of communities gives rise to what Kornhauser (1978: 75) terms *cultural* disorganization—the attenuation of societal cultural values. Poverty, heterogeneity, anonymity, mutual distrust, institutional instability, and other structural features of urban communities are hypothesized to impede communication and obstruct the quest for common values, thereby fostering cultural diversity with respect to nondelinquent values. For example, an important component of Shaw and McKay's theory was that disorganized communities spawned delinquent gangs with their own subcultures and norms perpetuated through cultural transmission.

Despite their relative infrequency, ethnographic studies generally support the notion that structurally disorganized communities are conducive to the emergence of cultural value systems and attitudes that seem to legitimate, or at least provide a basis of tolerance for, crime and deviance. For example, Suttles's (1968) account of the social order of a Chicago neighborhood characterized by poverty and heterogeneity supports Thrasher's (1963) emphasis on age, sex, ethnicity, and territory as markers for the ordered segmentation of slum culture. Suttles found that single-sex, age-graded primary groups of the same ethnicity and territory emerged in response to threats of conflict and community-wide disorder and mistrust. Although the community subcultures Suttles discovered were provincial, tentative, and incomplete (Kornhauser 1978: 18), they nonetheless undermined societal values against delinquency and violence. Similarly, Anderson's (1978) ethnography of a bar in Chicago's South-side black ghetto shows how primary values coexisted alongside residual values associated with deviant subcultures (e.g., hoodlums), such as "toughness," "getting big money," "going for bad," and "having fun" (1978: 129–30, 152–58). In Anderson's analysis, lower-class residents do not so much "stretch" mainstream values as "create their own particular standards of social conduct along variant lines open to them" (1978: 210). In this context the use of violence is not valued as a primary goal but is nonetheless expected and tolerated as a fact of life (1978: 134). Much like Rainwater (1970), Suttles (1968), and Horowitz (1987), Anderson suggests that in certain community contexts the wider cultural values are simply not relevant—they become "unviable."

Whether community subcultures are authentic or merely "shadow cultures" (Liebow 1967) cannot be resolved here (see also Kornhauser 1978). But that seems less important than acknowledging that community contexts seem to shape what can be termed *cognitive landscapes* or ecologically structured norms (e.g., normative ecologies) regarding appropriate standards and expectations of conduct. That is, in structurally disorganized slum communities it appears that a system of values emerges in which crime, disorder, and drug use are less than fervently condemned and hence expected as part of everyday life. These ecologically structured social perceptions and tolerances in turn appear to influence the probability of criminal outcomes and harmful deviant behavior (e.g., drug use by pregnant women). In this regard Kornhauser's attack on subcultural theories misses the point. By attempting to assess whether subcultural values are authentic in some deep, almost quasi-religious sense (1978: 1–20), she loses sight of the processes by which cognitive landscapes rooted in social ecology may influence everyday behavior. Indeed, the idea that dominant values become existentially irrelevant in certain community contexts is a powerful one, albeit one that has not had the research exploitation it deserves (cf. Katz 1988).

A renewed appreciation for the role of cultural adaptations is congruent with the notion of *social isolation*—defined as the lack of contact or of sustained interaction with individuals and institutions that represent mainstream society (W. J. Wilson 1987: 60). According to this line of reasoning, the social isolation fostered by the ecological concentration of urban poverty deprives residents not only of resources and conventional role models, but also of cultural learning from mainstream social networks that facilitate social and economic advancement in modern industrial society (W. J. Wilson 1991). Social isolation is specifically distinguished from the culture of poverty by virtue of its focus on adaptations to constraints and opportunities rather than internalization of norms.

As Ulf Hannerz noted in his seminal work *Soulside*, it is thus possible to recognize the importance of macrostructural constraints—that is, avoid the extreme notions of the culture of poverty or culture of violence, and yet see the "merits of a more subtle kind of cultural analysis" (1969: 182). One could hypothesize a difference, on the one hand, between a jobless family whose mobility is impeded by the macrostructural constraints in the economy and the larger society but nonetheless lives in an area with a relatively low rate of poverty, and on the other hand, a jobless family that lives in an inner-city ghetto neighborhood that is influenced not only by these same constraints but also by the behavior of other jobless families in the neighborhood (Hannerz 1969: 184; W. J. Wilson 1991). The latter influence is one of culture—the extent to which individuals follow their inclinations as they have been developed by learning or influence from other members of the community (Hannerz 1969).

Ghetto-specific practices such as an overt emphasis on sexuality and macho values, idleness, and public drinking are often denounced by those who reside in inner-city ghetto neighborhoods. But because such practices occur much more frequently there than in middle-class society, largely because of social organizational forces, the transmission of these modes of behavior by precept, as in role modeling, is more easily facilitated (Hannerz 1969). For example, youngsters are more likely to see violence as a way of life in inner-city ghetto neighborhoods. They are more likely to witness violent acts, to be taught to be violent by exhortation, and to have role models who do not adequately control their own violent impulses or restrain their own anger. Accordingly, given the availability of and easy access to firearms, knives, and other weapons, adolescent experiments with macho behavior often have deadly consequences (Prothrow-Stith 1991).

The concept of social isolation captures this process by implying that contact between groups of different class and/or racial backgrounds either is lacking or has become increasingly intermittent, and that the nature of this contact enhances effects of living in a highly concentrated poverty area. Unlike the concept of the culture of violence, then, social isolation does not mean that ghetto-specific practices become internalized, take on a life of their own, and therefore continue to influence behavior no matter what the contextual environment. Rather, it suggests that reducing structural inequality would not only decrease the frequency of these practices; it would also make their transmission by precept less efficient. So in this sense we advocate a renewed appreciation for the ecology of culture, but not the monolithic and hence noncontextual culture implied by the subculture of poverty and violence.

Discussion

Rejecting both the "individualistic" and "materialist" fallacies, we have attempted to delineate a theoretical strategy that incorporates both structural and cultural arguments regarding race, crime, and urban inequality in American cities. Drawing on insights from social-disorganization theory and recent research on urban poverty, we believe this strategy provides new ways of thinking about race and crime. First and foremost, our perspective views the link between race and crime through contextual lenses that highlight the very different ecological contexts in which blacks and whites reside—regardless of individual characteristics. Second, we emphasize that crime rates among blacks nonetheless vary by ecological characteristics, just as they do for whites. Taken together, these facts suggest a powerful role for community context in explaining race and crime.

Our community-level explanation also departs from conventional wisdom. Rather than attributing to acts of crime a purely economic motive springing from relative deprivation—an individual-level psychological concept—we focus on the mediating dimensions of community social organization to understand variations in crime across areas. Moreover, we acknowledge and try to specify the macrosocial forces that contribute to the social organization of local communities. Implicit in this attempt is the incorporation of the political economy of place and the role of urban inequality in generating racial differences in community structure. As Wacquant observes, American urban poverty is "preeminently a *racial poverty* . . . rooted in the *ghetto* as a historically specific social form and mechanism of racial domination" (1991: 36, emphasis in original). This intersection of race, place, and poverty goes to the heart of our theoretical concerns with societal and community organization.

Furthermore, we incorporate culture into our theory in the form of social isolation and ecological landscapes that shape perceptions and cultural patterns of learning. This culture is not seen as inevitably tied to race, but more to the varying structural contexts produced by residential and macroeconomic change, concentrated poverty, family instability, and intervening patterns of social disorganization. Perhaps controversially, then, we differ from the recent wave of structuralist research on the culture of violence (for a review see Sampson and Lauritsen 1994). In an interesting methodological sleight of hand, scholars have dismissed the relevance of culture based on the analysis of census data that provide no measures of culture whatsoever (see especially Blau and Blau 1982). We believe structural criminologists have too quickly dismissed the role of values, norms, and learning as they interact with concentrated poverty and social isolation. In our view, macrosocial patterns of residential inequality give rise to the social isolation and concentration of the truly disadvantaged, engendering cultural adaptations that undermine social organization.

Finally, our conceptualization suggests that the roots of urban violence among today's 15- to 21-year-old cohort may stem from childhood socialization that took place in the late 1970s and early 1980s. Consider that this cohort was born between 1970 and 1976 and spent its childhood in the context of a rapidly changing urban environment unlike that of any previous point in U.S. history. As documented in detail by W. J. Wilson (1987), the concentration of urban poverty and other social dislocations began increasing sharply in about 1970 and continued unabated through the decade and into the 1980s. As but one example, the proportion of black families headed by women increased by over 50 percent from 1970 to 1984 alone (W. J. Wilson 1987: 26). Large increases were also seen in the ecological concentration of ghetto poverty, racial segregation, population turnover, and joblessness. These social dislocations were, by comparison, relatively stable in earlier decades. Therefore, the logic of our theoretical model suggests that the profound changes in the urban structure of minority communities in the 1970s may hold the key to understanding recent increases in violence.

Conclusion

By recasting traditional race and poverty arguments in a contextual framework that incorporates both structural and cultural concepts, we seek to generate empirical and theoretical ideas that may guide further research. The unique value of a community-level perspective is that it leads away from a simple "kinds of people" analysis to a focus on how social characteristics of collectivities foster violence. On the basis of our theoretical framework, we conclude that community-level factors such as the *ecological concentration of ghetto poverty*, *racial segregation*, *residential mobility* and population turnover, *family disruption*, and the dimensions of local *social organization* (e.g., density of friendship/acquaintanceship, social resources, intergenerational links, control of street-corner peer groups, organizational participation) are fruitful areas of future inquiry, especially as they are affected by macrolevel public policies regarding housing, municipal services, and employment. In other words, our framework suggests the need to take a renewed look at social policies that focus on prevention. We do not need more after-the-fact (reactive) approaches that ignore the structural context of crime and the social organization of inner cities.

Unemployment and Crime Rate Fluctuations in the Post–World War II United States

Statistical Time-Series Properties and Alternative Models

KENNETH C. LAND

DAVID CANTOR

STEPHEN T. RUSSELL

The relationship between aggregate rates of unemployment and aggregate rates of crime (hereafter the U-C relationship) surely is one of the "big" issues of criminology—because of its relevance to both the construction of theories of crime and the formulation of economic and social policy. With the cumulation of attention by many social scientists in recent years, it has become apparent that this relationship is complex and multifaceted. Indeed, perhaps most frustrating of all is the fact that conclusions reached from the study of one facet of the U-C relationship may be contradicted by conclusions from another.

In this chapter, we focus on a precisely defined aspect of the general U-C relationship—namely, the temporal relationship between levels of and fluctuations in aggregate annual unemployment rates and fluctuations in annual crime rates for the United States in the post–World War II period. This topic was the focus of a thesis of joint crime motivation and crime opportunity effects put forward by Cantor and Land (1985). Recently, the Cantor-Land formulation has been critiqued by Hale and Sabbagh (1991), who also put forward an alternative formulation of temporal dependence. Other empirical analyses that may shed some light on the Cantor-Land thesis also have appeared in recent years.

Given these recent contributions to the literature, and the longer annual time series now available, we update the Cantor-Land empirical analyses and study the statistical time-series properties of the unemployment and crime rate series. Based on these properties, we evaluate the merits of the Cantor-Land model with respect to the criticisms raised by Hale and Sabbagh (1991). We conclude with a discussion of conditions under which the temporal U-C relationship will be operative and of ways in which the links between the rates of unemployment and crime can be more fully articulated and estimated.

Before presenting the details of our analyses of the temporal aggregate U-C relationship, we review briefly the published research on the general U-C relationship and describe in more detail the Hale and Sabbagh critique as well as other relevant research. This review documents the complexity of the U-C relationship and positions the present study within the general subject.

Research on the General U-C Relationship

Four major surveys of published cross-sectional and time-series studies of the relationship of unemployment and crime rates have appeared in the past two decades: Gillespie (1978)—13 studies reviewed; Long and Witte (1981)—16 studies reviewed; Freeman (1983)—18 studies reviewed; and Chiricos (1987)—63 studies reviewed.[1] By far the most comprehensive of these is the Chiricos review: he surveyed some 42 studies that use cross-sectional data (at the intracity, city, county, state/province, or nation levels) and 21 studies that use time-series data. Most of the latter were based on national-level U.S. time series, although some focus on other nations or use city- or state-level U.S. data. Most of the cross-sectional studies surveyed by Chiricos use data from 1960 or 1970, but some date back to 1950 and others are based on various years in the 1970s. Most of the time-series studies are based on annual data for the post–World War II years and end in the 1970s, but some go back as far as 1935 (U.S. data) and others as far as 1894 (England and Wales data).

Substantively, Chiricos notes that the first three of these literature reviews concluded (or were subsequently interpreted by other analysts to conclude) that the U-C relationship is positive but weak and generally insignificant. This, he argues, created a "consensus of doubt" in the mid-1980s about the existence of a consistent, definite, positive relationship between unemployment and crime rates.

Based on his analyses and comparisons of many estimated U-C relationships in these studies, Chiricos concludes, by contrast, that "evidence favors the existence of a positive frequently significant U-C relationship" and that this is especially true since 1970 for *property crimes* (1987: 203). Elsewhere, he concludes that the positive and significant U-C relationship is more likely to be found in studies based on *less-aggregated units of analysis* such as intracity studies. To explain this, he suggests that there is less aggregation bias at the lower levels of analysis; that is, "the lower and smaller units of analysis are more likely to be homogeneous, thereby reducing variation within each unit and allowing for more meaningul variation between units" (1987: 195). This focus on the identification of those *conditional or contextual circumstances* under which a definite relationship between unemployment and crime rates will be found is a major contribution of Chiricos's survey of extant U-C research.

On the basis of our assessment of the summary of the research literature provided by Chiricos (1987) and other published research, we agree that the likelihood of finding a positive statistically significant U-C relationship is higher for *property crimes*. Even among property crimes, however, there is variability—with the U-C relationship more likely to be positive for burglary and larceny than for motor vehicle theft. A major task for current theoretical efforts, therefore, is to explain the differential variation of the U-C relationship by type of crime.

Regarding the contextual effects of *levels of analysis*, we believe that the key effect of aggregation bias pertains to the *meaning* of the unemployment rate at different analytic levels. For instance, at the intracity level of analysis, the unemployment rate may be a comparatively pure (cross-sectional and/or longitudinal) indicator of the relative degree of deprivation or affluence of, say, census tracts or city blocks. Under conventional assumptions about the relationship of deprivation to criminal motivation and about the conditions under which a local community can control the criminal behavior of its inhabitants, it then follows that one should find a positive U-C relationship.

By contrast, at the city, metropolitan, or state level, the unemployment rate appears relatively orthogonal to, or independent of, other indicators of the relative deprivation/affluence level of a community (Land et al. 1990) and, accordingly, may be less likely to produce a consistent, positive U-C relationship.[2] In addition, the unemployment rate may be even less solely indicative of levels of deprivation in time-series analyses at the national level. Indeed, at the national level, it is well known that the unemployment rate is a "coincident" indicator of business cycles (see, e.g., Granger 1980: 144) with corresponding implications for variations in systemic economic and social activity. Consequences of this for the confounding of the U-C relationship in national time-series studies were developed by Cantor and Land (1985).

The Cantor-Land Thesis

That an increase in crime rates should be associated with increases in, and/or higher levels of, unemployment rates in capitalist or market-driven economies is considered obvious both in conventional wisdom and in many criminogenic theories that are motivationally focused. Cantor and Land note, for example, that strain, rational choice, and conflict theories differ in the causal mechanisms by which each relates unemployment to crime rates (1985: 319). Nonetheless, each would be consistent with the following setup. Array the members of a population along a continuum of low to high motivation to commit criminal offenses according to their levels of motivation. All other things being equal, these *criminal motivation* theories then lead to the assertion that an increase in unemployment produces a shift in the density distribution of the population along this continuum toward its higher end. Thus, the central tendency (mean, median) of the motivation density will have shifted upward. Furthermore, if it is assumed that the level of crime rates experienced by the population is an (unconditional) increasing function of the level of this central tendency, then it follows that the crime rates will increase.

Cantor and Land observed that this formulation does not assert that the upward shift in the density distribution is due solely to changes in motivational levels of the specific individuals who are unemployed. Some fraction of the density shift may be due to individuals who, while not becoming unemployed themselves, are nonetheless adversely affected by economic downturns. However, theories of criminal motivation have traditionally emphasized the primacy of an individual's becoming unemployed relative to the compositional effect of group economic hardship, even though aggregate unemployment rates have been used in empirical tests.

Noting the coincident relationship of the unemployment rate to business cycle fluctuations, Cantor and Land suggested that there may exist countervailing *criminal opportunity* effects of unemployment on crime rates. For one thing, a higher unemployment rate generally signals a slowdown in production and consumption activities for both employed and unemployed persons. Thus, the unemployment rate can be viewed as an index of *total system activity*, a lower level of which (i.e., a higher unemployment rate) corresponds to a lower rate of circulation of people and property.[3] Second, by removing some individuals from employment outside the household, a higher unemployment rate may lead to an increased concentration (in the population, on average) of sustenance and leisure activities within primary-group locations (residences, neighborhoods), where individuals and their property are at reduced risks of victimization. Both of these effects, the *system activity effect* and the *guardianship effect*, respectively, lead to the inference that, all other things being equal, a higher unemployment rate produces lower rates of concurrence of motivated offenders with ineffectively guarded, suitable property crime targets, and hence, lower property crime rates.

In the case of violent crimes, Cantor and Land suggested that the main mechanism of negative influence of levels of economic activity on violent crimes will be through the types of situations in which individuals find themselves. Specifically, if a high unemployment rate leads to a concentration of sustenance and leisure activities within such primary-group locations as homes and neighborhoods, this may lead to lower crime rates because a substantial fraction of violent crimes involve casual acquaintances or strangers.

In brief, there are two distinct and potentially counterbalancing mechanisms—crime motivation and crime opportunity—through which unemployment levels and fluctuations therein may affect crime rates in the aggregate. Most traditional explanations have emphasized the former, while crime opportunity/routine activities theory concentrates on the latter. A consequence of the simultaneous presence of both mechanisms, moreover, is that the overall relationship of unemployment and crime rates is hopelessly underidentified *if* it is maintained that both structural effects of unemployment must be *contemporaneous*. But, Cantor and Land argued, there is no reason why this must be assumed.

To break through the identification problem, they argued that the primary crime opportunity (system activity and guardianship) effects ought to be *relatively instantaneous* and primarily associated with the *level of the unemployment rate* (as a coincident indicator of business cycles). By contrast, because of the buffering effects of public unemployment benefits as well as familial and other private support, the primary criminal motivation effects are likely to be *lagged* and associated with the amount of change in the unemployment rate from one period to the next (as an indicator of the rate of change in the population of unemployed persons). That is, Cantor and Land operationalized these motivational impacts by comparing the level of unemployment in one time period with that in the previous period (i.e., by using *first-differences in the unemployment rate*). If the former is higher than the latter, and if this change in the level of employment results in a positive motivational impact on crime, then this should produce upward fluctuations in crime rates. Similarly, economic recoveries and the associated declines in the unemployment rate should produce downward perturbations in crime rates.

It should be noted that Cantor and Land (1985) postulated only *indirect* effects of unemployment rate levels and fluctuations on crime rate fluctuations. That is, their model hypothesizes that the relationship of unemployment rates to crime rates is not a direct relationship, but rather an indirect relationship through the crime opportunity and crime motivation mechanisms. One implication of this is that the models they estimated are what are termed *reduced forms* or *semireduced forms* in the literature on structural equation models (e.g., Duncan et al. 1972: 23–30). That is, the coefficients of effects of the unemployment rate and its first-differences on crime rate fluctuations in the Cantor-Land models represent composites of structural coefficients from more elaborate models (hypothetical or operational, depending on whether the requisite data are available) that contain explicit indicators of the intervening crime motivation and crime opportunity mechanisms. Another implication is that the explicit incorporation of data on such intervening mechanisms (e.g., direct measures of the opportunity for property crimes, such as an index of motor vehicles per population unit for motor vehicle theft or direct measures of variables hypothesized to affect crime motivation such as the imprisonment rates in models discussed later herein) may reduce estimates of the coefficients of the unemployment rate or its fluctuations to zero (or at least to statistical insignificance)—if the postulated intervening variables are, in fact, operative empirically.

Cantor and Land (1985) developed their model in reference to trends and fluctuations in national unemployment and crime rate data—a level of analysis for which the interpretation of the unemployment rate as a coincident indicator of business cycles certainly is appropriate. It is possible that similar models could be applied to the analysis of temporal trends in regional or local populations. Empirical applications to date have been limited to annual time series, although, as we will show, monthly series also can be used to evaluate the plausibility of the differential lag structures of the Cantor-Land thesis.

Time-Series Properties and Statistical Models

Hale and Sabbagh (1991) recently argued that the Cantor-Land model is "fundamentally flawed," "statistically misspecified," and "a priori . . . cannot be valid." Using a different approach to time-series model specification, they also claimed to find only criminal motivation (positive) effects of the unemployment rate on rates of theft, burglary, and robbery for annual data on England and Wales, 1952 to 1984.

The Hale-Sabbagh critique of the Cantor-Land thesis is based on a statistical analysis of the regression models for time-series analysis specified by Cantor-Land. These regression models take the form

$$DC_t = \alpha + \beta_1 U_t + \beta_2 DU_t + \varepsilon_t \qquad (1)$$

or

$$D^2C_t = \alpha + \beta_1 U_t = \beta_2 DU_t + \varepsilon_t \qquad (2)$$

(or similar expressions in natural logarithm transformations of the variables), where C_t represents a particular FBI Index crime rate in year t (murder or nonnegligent homicide, forcible rape, aggravated assault, robbery, burglary, larceny-theft, and motor vehicle theft); U_t is the unemployment rate in year t; D is the difference operator—that is, $DX_t = X_t - X_{t-1}$, and $D^2X_t = D(DX_t) = X_t - 2X_{t-1} + X_{t-2}$; β_1 is the parameter associated with the relatively instantaneous criminal opportunity effect of the unemployment rate; β_2 is the parameter associated with the lagged criminal motivation effect; and ε_t is a stochastic error or disturbance term. If the Cantor-Land thesis about the relative lag structures of these two effects is operative in the data, then β_1 should have a negative estimated value and β_2 should be estimated as positive.

The Hale-Sabbagh claim that the models in equations (1) and (2) are statistically misspecified is based on the logic of recent work in linear time series/econometric methodology. In this context, Engle and Granger's (1987) article on co-integration and error correction models has been particularly influential. A general guideline for model specification that emerges from the analysis of Engle and Granger is that one should not specify models that contain explanatory or regressor variables of a "higher order of integration" than the dependent or response variable, or vice versa (Maddala 1988: 217).

For instance, suppose a response-variable time series is an independently distributed normal variable with zero mean and constant variance—often called Gaussian white noise.[4] Then the series is said to be *stationary* or both stationary (constant) in its mean and its variance with autocovariances that do not depend on time. Such a series is said to be *integrated of order zero* (Maddala 1988: 217), and is denoted by I(0). Variables of a higher order of integration may then be derived in a recursive way from variables of lower orders of integration. For instance, if a time series X_t follows a *random walk model*, that is,

$$X_t = X_{t-1} + \varepsilon_t \tag{3}$$

where ε_t is I(0), then we get by substitution,

$$X_t = \sum_{j=0}^{t-1} e_{t-j} \quad \text{if} \quad X_0 = 0. \tag{4}$$

Thus, X_t is a summation of ε_j, and

$$DX_t = \varepsilon_t \tag{5}$$

which is I(0). In this case, X_t is said to be I(1)—that is, *integrated of order one*—and it can be shown that the variance of X_t increases without bound or becomes infinite as time increases. Generally, a time series X_t is said to be *integrated of order d*, denoted by I(d), if $D^d X_t$ is I(0).

According to the statistical theory developed by Engle and Granger (1987), an analyst should include only similarly I(0) variables as regressors to explain an I(0) variable. For to include regressors of another type, such as random walk variables, leads to mathematical contradictions. Specifically, there will not be real numbers that satisfy the postulated regression relationships between the response and regressor variables, because the variance of the response variable is finite while that of the regressor increases to infinity as time increases. In the terminology of Engle and Granger (1987), the variables will not be "co-integrated."

Within this time-series modeling framework, Hale and Sabbagh apply various tests for stationarity and co-integration to unemployment and crime rate time series for England and Wales. From these tests, they conclude that, in each case, the time series consisting of levels of the rates are nonstationary and those consisting of the first differences are stationary. The combination of these two properties, in fact, implies that the time series of the levels of the rates are I(1). Accordingly, the specification of an I(1) series, namely the unemployment rate, as a regressor in a model of a first-differenced, or I(0), crime rate series, as in regression models (1) and (2), is a misspecification. Based on the presumption that the annual unemployment rate series for the United States similarly is an I(1) series, this is the crux of the Hale and Sabbagh (1991) critique of the Cantor-Land thesis. As an alternative to models of the form (1) and (2), Hale and Sabbagh then propose autoregressive distributed models of the form:

$$DC_t = \alpha + \beta_1 DC_{t-1} + \beta_2 DU_t + \beta_3 DU_{t-1} + \varepsilon_t. \tag{6}$$

As indicated, their empirical results from application of models of this form to annual time-series data for England and Wales, 1952 to 1984, suggest only criminal motivation (positive) effect coefficients for the differenced unemployment rate.

In response to Hale and Sabbagh, Cantor and Land (1991) note that the proposition that the annual U.S. unemployment rate series is I(1) is untenable, except as a local approximation (i.e., for a relatively short sample period). The reason is that the annual unemployment rate is bounded, by definition, by 0.0 and 100.0, and, in practice, in the post–World War II years has varied between a lower bound of about 3.5 and an upper bound of about 10.0. This implies that the variance of the unemployment series is bounded, which is at odds with the variance of a random walk, or I(1) series, which necessarily increases linearly with time to infinity. Cantor and Land (1991) also note that the U.S. annual unemployment rate empirically fails to satisfy the I(1) model for the period 1946 to 1982, but because of space limitations did not present a complete empirical analysis. For time series updated through 1990, we next present a full analysis of this question and thereby an assessment of the Cantor-Land and Hale-Sabbagh models.

Annual Unemployment and Crime Rate Time-Series Analyses, 1946–90 Data

Analyses were conducted for the post–World War II United States for seven Index crimes—murder, forcible rape, aggravated assault, robbery, burglary, larceny-theft, and motor vehicle theft—published in the Federal Bureau of Investigation's (FBI) *Uniform Crime Reports* (UCR), Maguire and Flanagan (1990), and the revised series for the early post–World War II years published by the Office of Management and Budget (OMB) (1974). In 1958 the UCR system instituted major changes in the collection of their data that make pre- and post-1958 data incompatible. The OMB series accounts for this discontinuity in ways consistent with the original trend in the UCR (Cantor and Cohen 1980). Thus, for the years 1946 to 1959, the crime rate data for each of the seven Index crimes analyzed herein were obtained from the OMB publication. For the years 1960 to 1979, corresponding annual estimates were obtained from Maguire and Flanagan (1990), and, for the years 1980 to 1990, from the Federal Bureau of Investigation (1991).

In the case of larceny-theft, a change in the UCR definition from "larcenies of $50 and over" to "larceny-theft" was made in 1973. The latter definition has since been applied in recent volumes of the *Uniform Crime Reports* to produce a consistent series of revised estimates back to 1960. But there is a clear discontinuity at that point with prior data because the larceny-theft category includes a larger number of crimes. To adjust for this change in levels of the larceny-theft series from 1959 to 1960 and yet remain faithful to the historical patterns before 1960, we divided the average of the 1960 to 1961 larceny-theft rates by the average of the 1958 to 1959 larcenies of $50 and over rates and used this quotient as a multiplier for the latter rates for the 1946 to 1959 years.[5]

Annual average unemployment rates for the United States, 1946 to 1990, were obtained from the *Economic Report of the President* (Executive Office of the President 1991).

Models and Methods

As noted above, the central feature of the Hale and Sabbagh (1991) critique of the models specified in Cantor and Land (1985) is the presumption that the annual unemployment time series for the United States is a I(1) series (i.e., that this series is not stationary in its mean or variance), whereas the first- or second-differenced crime rate series are I(0). By contrast, the analysis strategy employed by Cantor and Land, for the years 1946 to 1982, was based on the premise that, as a coincident indicator of the business cycle, the unemployment rate series is stationary in both mean and variance, that is, I(0). This premise was not evaluated empirically, however, both because of long-standing extant research on the business cycle behavior of the unemployment rate and because of the relatively short sample period dealt with by Cantor and Land.

With an additional eight years of data now available from updating the unemployment and crime rate series through 1990—bringing the total length of the series to 45 observations—it now is possible to use modern statistical time-series models to subject these assumptions to empirical tests and thus to address the pivotal point of the Hale-Sabbagh critique.[6] Specifically, we initially employ techniques of Auto-Regressive Integrated Moving Average (ARIMA) time-series modeling (see, e.g., Box and Jenkins

1976; Brockwell and Davis 1991; Granger and Newbold 1986; McCleary and Hay 1980) to study the properties of these time series.[7] This is followed by an updated estimation of the time-series regression models (1) and (2), as specified by Cantor and Land (1985).

Results

Figure 3.1 reports the estimated autocorrelation and partial autocorrelation functions for the undifferenced annual unemployment rate series for lags zero through ten years. To ease the interpretation of the statistical significance of the numerical values, band widths corresponding to two standard errors also are given in the plots. Of major interest is the rapidity of the decline in the autocorrelation function toward zero or effectively zero values. If the decline is slow (i.e., takes many lags), then this would indicate nonstationarity of the time series. Conversely, if the decline is relatively quick, then it can be inferred that the series is stationary.

It can be seen that the autocorrelation function in Figure 3.1 decreases rapidly towards a zero value: after a two-year lag, the autocorrelations are well within the two-standard-error bound, and, after a five-year lag, they are of very small size. In brief, the estimated autocorrelation function provides no evidence of nonstationarity in the annual U.S. unemployment series. Combining information from the autocorrelation and partial autocorrelation graphs, in fact, it can be inferred that the annual unemployment series is a first-order autoregressive process or an autoregressive process of order (lag) one, denoted by AR(1). That is, while both the lag-1 and lag-2 autocorrelations are of substantial size and significance, only the lag-1 partial autocorrelation is significant. By conventional ARIMA inferential procedures, this implies that the process should be well represented as AR(1).

This inference is confirmed by the model parameter estimates and goodness-of-fit statistics reported in Table 3.1. This table reports the estimated constant term, autoregressive, and moving-average parameters for the AR(1) model as well as two models that incorporate additional parameters and within which the AR(1) model is nested: the second-order autoregressive model, AR(2), and the autoregressive, moving-average model of order one in each of the autoregressive and moving-average parts, ARMA(1,1).

The table also gives the values of two summary statistics that indicate the relative goodness-of-fit of the models: the Ljung and Box (1978) Q statistic (for lags one through six) and the Akaike Information Criterion (AIC) for each model. The Ljung-Box Q statistic is a measure of the extent to which the autocorrelation function, after model estimation, is

Autocorrelations

Lag	Covariance	Correlation	−1 9 8 7 6 5 4 3 2 1 0 1 2 3 4 5 6 7 8 9 1	Se
0	2.598499	1.00000		0
1	1.947858	0.74961		0.149071
2	1.331720	0.51252		0.217247
3	1.027880	0.39557		0.242633
4	0.979728	0.37704		0.256564
5	0.853004	0.32827		0.268595
6	0.514990	0.19819		0.277367
7	0.319199	0.12284		0.280496
8	0.085234	0.03280		0.281689
9	0.046426	0.01787		0.281774
10	−0.035440	−0.01364		0.281799

Partial autocorrelations

Lag	Correlation	−1 9 8 7 6 5 4 3 2 1 0 1 2 3 4 5 6 7 8 9 1
1	0.74961	
2	−0.11274	
3	0.12155	
4	0.14150	
5	−0.04567	
6	−0.14963	
7	0.05898	
8	−0.16690	
9	0.09084	
10	−0.06331	

Fig. 3.1. Estimated autocorrelation and partial autocorrelation functions for the U.S. unemployment rate series, 1946–90. • marks two standard errors. Data on unemployment rates are from the *Economic Report of the President* (Executive Office of the President 1991).

indicative of white noise residuals. Use of the Q statistic for model evaluation is predicated on the model-building criterion that, for a fitted model to be acceptable, its residuals should be distributed as white noise. The Q statistic is asymptotically distributed as a chi-square variate, and the adequacy of a model is rejected at level α if the computed value of Q exceeds the $1 - \alpha$th percentile of a chi-square distribution with degrees of freedom equal to the number of lags in the autocorrelation function minus the number of parameters estimated (i.e., if the p-value of the statistic is greater than $1 - \alpha$). The AIC was designed to be an approximately unbiased estimate of the Kullback-Leibler index of a fitted model relative to the true model (Brockwell and Davis 1991: 302). Informally, the AIC trades off a likelihood function measure of the goodness-of-fit of alternative models with the numbers of parameters they require to be estimated. It thus can be used to compare alternative models—with lower values of the statistic indicating better fits of the associated models.

It can be seen from Table 3.1 that the AR(1) model indeed fits the annual U.S. unemployment series well and that no additional autoregressive or moving-average parameters are statistically significant or yield a better fitting model. That is, none of the additional parameters in the AR(2) and ARMA(1,1) models have statistically significant t-ratios, thus indicating that they are not necessary to model the unemployment time series. In addition, the Ljung-Box Q statistic indicates that there is nothing in the residuals of the AR(1) model to reject the null hypothesis that they are white noise. Finally, the AR(1) model yields the smallest AIC statistic.

With respect to the question of whether the unemployment series displays nonstationary or random walk behavior, note that the estimated standard error (0.097) for the autoregressive parameter in the AR(1) model is such as to yield 95 percent confidence bounds that do not include the 1.0—which is the value that this parameter would take if the unemployment series were governed by a random walk model. Thus, we conclude that the critical empirical assertion upon which the Hale and Sabbagh (1991) critique of the Cantor and Land (1985) regression models is based is itself not empirically valid.[8]

For comparison, Figure 3.2 reports the estimated autocorrelation and partial autocorrelation functions for the first-differenced unemployment series. While the patterns in these graphs are not very strong and do not reach statistical significance because of the relatively short series on which they are based, their decaying and oscillating patterns are consistent with an

TABLE 3.1
Estimated Parameters and Goodness-of-Fit Statistics for Alternative Time-Series Models of the Annual U.S. Unemployment Rate, 1946–90

	Parameters				Goodness-of-fit statistics	
Model	μ	φ_1	φ_2	θ_1	Q(6)	AIC
AR(1)	5.47*	0.75*			4.13 (p = .53)	136.93
	(9.12)	(7.75)				
AR(2)	5.49*	0.82*	−0.10		3.44 (p = .49)	138.44
	(9.87)	(5.45)	(0.68)			
ARMA(1,1)	5.49*	0.67*		−0.18	3.16 (p = .53)	138.25
	(9.97)	(4.64)		(0.91)		

SOURCE: Data on unemployment rates are from the *Economic Report of the President* (Executive Office of the President 1991).

NOTE: Estimates are maximum-likelihood metric coefficients; μ denotes the constant term of the model, φ_1 and φ_2 are the autoregressive parameters, and θ_1 is the moving-average parameter; figures in parentheses are t-ratios; Q(6) = Ljung-Box residual statistics for lags one through six; AIC = Akaike Information Criterion.

*Significantly nonzero at $\alpha = .01$.

Autocorrelations

Lag	Covariance	Correlation	Se
0	1.265950	1.00000	0
1	−0.036869	−0.02912	0.150756
2	−0.324192	−0.25609	0.150883
3	−0.181020	−0.14299	0.160458
4	0.057338	0.04529	0.163328
5	0.137081	0.10828	0.163613
6	−0.160263	−0.12659	0.165234
7	0.032889	0.02598	0.167424
8	−0.104393	−0.08246	0.167516
9	−0.040515	−0.00320	0.168436
10	−0.112325	−0.08873	0.168437

Partial autocorrelations

Lag	Correlation
1	−0.02912
2	−0.25715
3	−0.17132
4	−0.04272
5	0.02986
6	−0.15302
7	0.04794
8	−0.14134
9	−0.04296
10	−0.16790

Fig. 3.2. Estimated autocorrelation and partial autocorrelation functions for the first-differenced U.S. unemployment rate series, 1946–90. • marks two standard errors. Data on unemployment rates are from the *Economic Report of the President* (Executive Office of the President 1991).

ARMA(2,1) model—that is, an Auto-Regressive Moving Average model with an autoregressive component of order 2 and a moving-average component of order 1. It is shown in the Appendix that this is precisely the pattern that a first-differenced series should display if it is derived from an AR(1) parent series.

What are the corresponding time-series properties of the seven Index crime rates studied by Cantor and Land (1985)? They are: first-differences of murder, rape, and motor vehicle theft exhibit AR(1) behavior; first-differences of robbery, burglary, and larceny-theft exhibit AR(2) behavior (i.e., are well represented as autoregressive processes of order [lag] 2); and second-differences of aggravated assault also have AR(2) patterns.[9]

Several implications can be drawn from these time-series properties of the U.S. unemployment and crime rate series during the post–World War II period. First, there is no evidence to support Hale and Sabbagh's

(1991) claim that the annual unemployment time series is an integrated process. Rather, this series is well represented as an AR(1) process. Therefore, the "statistical misspecifi[cations]" asserted by Hale and Sabbagh concerning the Cantor-Land time-series regression models (1) and (2) simply do not hold up. Similarly, the time-series properties assumed for the annual unemployment series in Hale (1991) are invalid. It follows that it is not necessary to replace the Cantor-Land regression models (1) and (2) with the autoregressive distributed-lag specifications (6) of Hale-Sabbagh.

Second, these properties can be used to clarify the statistical foundations of the Cantor-Land time-series regression models (1) and (2) for those property crime Index crime rate series for which Cantor and Land (1985) estimated statistically significant coefficients for both the criminal opportunity and criminal motivation mechanisms. In brief, the time-series properties of the undifferenced and first-differenced unemployment rate series imply that the regression models (1) and (2) correctly embody an AR(2) type of time-series behavior—which is what they should exhibit in order to successfully predict the AR(2) time-series behavior of the robbery, burglary, and larceny-theft crime rate series (for a detailed derivation, see the Appendix). These time-series properties also imply that an application of the Cantor-Land regression specifications to those crime rate time series that do not exhibit AR(2) behavior probably would result in statistically insignificant estimated coefficients for one of the two effects specified in the models—which was the case in the empirical estimates reported in Cantor and Land (1985).

Given this clarification of the statistical time-series basis of the Cantor-Land regression models (1) and (2), Table 3.2 displays results of a re-estimation of these models for our extended time period, 1946 to 1990, for each of the seven Index crime rate series studied herein.[10] Generally, the estimated regression coefficients are of the same orders of magnitude and levels of statistical significance as those previously reported in Cantor and Land (1985). As anticipated on the basis of the analysis of the statistical properties of these regression models in the Appendix, all seven regression models exhibit serially correlated errors, which are adjusted for by the estimation of first-order autoregressions in the errors. Taking into account both the regressions in the unemployment rate and its first-differences as well as the autocorrelated errors, the total coefficients of determination for the three crimes with a property component (robbery, burglary, and larceny-theft) indicate that about 30 to 45 percent of the time-series variance is explained—with about half to two-thirds of this due to the regression or structural part (i.e., that associated with the U and DU variables)

TABLE 3.2

Estimates of Coefficients and Summary Statistics for the Effects of Unemployment Levels and Fluctuation on Index Crime Rates, 1946–90

Dependent variable[a]	Intercept	U_t	DU_t	$\hat{\rho}$	Reg R^2	Tot R^2
Murder	0.808*	−0.136*	0.058	−.476	.137	.392
	(2.556)	(2.506)	(1.168)			
Rape	1.155	−0.070	−0.182	.388	.066	.227
	(1.289)	(0.654)	(0.242)			
Assault	10.098	−0.311	−0.310	.293	.002	.122
	(1.322)	(0.236)	(0.022)			
Robbery	33.139*	−5.137*	5.279*	.462	.288	.433
	(3.673)	(3.324)	(3.681)			
Burglary	181.292*	−29.250*	27.987*	.480	.301	.469
	(3.771)	(3.556)	(3.731)			
Larceny	247.717*	−33.994*	32.751*	.403	.151	.293
	(2.921)	(2.334)	(2.287)			
Motor vehicle theft	46.863*	−6.495*	1.584	.474	.125	.397
	(2.802)	(2.269)	(0.603)			

SOURCE: Data on unemployment rates are from the *Economic Report of the President* (Executive Office of the President 1991). Data for crime rates for 1946–59 are from Office of Management and Budget (1974); for 1960–79, from Maguire and Flanagan (1990); and for 1980–90, from Federal Bureau of Investigation (1991).

NOTE: Estimates are metric coefficients obtained by generalized least squares with an estimated autoregressive parameter; figures in parentheses are t-ratios; $\hat{\rho}$ = estimated lag-one residual autocorrelation coefficient; Reg R^2 = coefficient of determination for the structural or regression part of the model after transforming for the autocorrelation; Tot R^2 = a measure of fit using both the regression part of the model and the past values of the residuals.

[a]All dependent crime rate series except assault are transformed to stationarity by taking first-differences prior to regression; for assault, second-differences were necessary to achieve stationarity.

*Significantly nonzero at $\alpha = .01$.

of the models. By comparison, the models for the other crime rates indicate substantially less ability to account for the time-series fluctuations.

The results in Table 3.2 replicate the principal substantive findings reported in Cantor and Land (1985) quite closely. First, both the expected negative contemporaneous (crime opportunity) unemployment rate effect and the expected positive first-differenced (crime motivation) unemployment rate effect are estimated to be statistically significant only for three Index crime rates with a property component: robbery, burglary, and larceny-theft. Second, for murder and motor vehicle theft, only the negative contemporaneous effect is statistically significant. Third, for rape and assault, both the contemporaneous and the first-differenced effects are estimated as negative. Each also is far from statistically significant, so that there is no evidence of either expected effect.[11]

Discussion: Interpretation of the Temporal U-C Relationship

In brief, we have clarified the statistical time-series properties of the regression models specified in Cantor and Land (1985) and have successfully replicated, on updated time series, the empirical results reported therein. We now turn to a discussion of related studies that help to: (1) determine the applicability of the Cantor-Land thesis to age- and race-specific population groups; (2) specify intervening variables in the linkages between unemployment and crime rates; (3) assess the microlevel foundations of the Cantor-Land thesis; and (4) identify the short-term lag structures of the crime motivation and opportunity mechanisms.

Application to Disaggregated Age and Race Categories

With a focus on systemwide relationships, Cantor and Land (1985) originally formulated and tested their model on total or aggregated unemployment and Index crime rates. It is this aggregated model that has been updated and replicated here. The question remains, however, to what extent the negative crime opportunity-related and positive crime motivation-related effects exist among race- and age-specific groups. Smith, Devine, and Sheley (1990) recently addressed this question for the crimes of murder, robbery, and burglary.

Using annual time series on Index crime arrest rates by age group (ages 16 to 19, 20 to 24, 25 to 34, and 35 to 44) and race categories (white, black) in UCR arrest data, 1959 to 1987, Smith et al. (1990) found: (1) fluctuations in unemployment rates exert a greater motivational influence on robbery and burglary rates than on homicide rates (this is consistent with the findings reported herein and in surveys of research literature described above); (2) for all three crimes, the effects of both unemployment levels and changes are significant, with few exceptions, for every age group—but the negative (contemporaneous) influence of the unemployment level decreases with age and the positive influence of changes in the unemployment rate is weak for homicide; and (3) though whites and blacks alike demonstrate strongly negative coefficients with the opportunity component, whites appear to be more susceptible to the motivational influence of unemployment rate change.[12] Smith et al. (1990) also found that these effects hold even when controlling for the potential influence of other variables (the rate of consumer price inflation, spending on police and public relief welfare, and general changes in the crime opportunity/routine activity structure of the society) identified in recent research as having an impact on the unemployment-crime relationship.

Identifying Intervening Linkages in the Temporal U-C Relationship

We have interpreted the estimated negative effects of the unemployment rate on Index crime rates throughout this chapter as indicative of the crime opportunity (system activity and guardianship) mechanisms postulated by Cantor and Land (1985). Recently, however, an alternative specification of the mediating mechanism for the negative U-C linkage has been suggested by Cappell and Sykes (1991), namely, through a form of *increased imprisonment rates/general deterrence process*. Using annual data on unemployment and aggregate Index crime rates, for 1933 to 1985, and a simultaneous-equation modeling strategy, Cappell and Sykes (1991) find, first, a positive direct effect of annual changes in the unemployment rate on annual changes in the aggregate crime rate. They interpret this (as we have) as evidence for the criminal motivation effect of the unemployment rate. Second, Cappell and Sykes find a positive direct effect of annual changes in the unemployment rate on annual changes in state prison commitment rate and a negative direct contemporaneous impact of the latter on annual changes in an aggregated Index crime rate for the period 1933 to 1985.

The product of the latter two direct effects then is an indirect negative effect of changes in the unemployment rate on changes in the aggregate crime rate. Cappell and Sykes (1991) interpret this negative indirect effect as due to the aggregated effect of individual sentencing decisions that are more likely to result in imprisonment if an individual is unemployed and an incapacitation/general deterrence effect of an increased imprisonment rate on the crime rate.

The Cappell-Sykes study has three substantive limitations, however.[13] First, because the Cappell-Sykes models included only the first-differenced unemployment rate and the first-differenced unemployment rate lagged 1 period and not both the contemporaneous level and first-difference of the unemployment rate, as specified in the models of Cantor and Land (1985), it is impossible to ascertain whether the negative (crime opportunity) effect postulated by Cantor-Land would continue to be evidenced in the Cappell-Sykes models. Second, the use of an aggregated Index crime rate prohibits any determination of differential effects across various Index crimes. Both because the U-C estimates reported herein and in other studies have shown substantial variability of direction and strength of relationship to unemployment rates and fluctuations across Index crime categories, and because general deterrence is generally acknowledged to have variable effects for different crimes, it is to be expected that the relationships estimated by Cappell and Sykes would have substantial intercrime variability. Third, Cappell and Sykes's "preferred" simultaneous-equation model permits a contemporaneous impact of the prison commitment rate on the crime rate in year t, but not vice versa. While the time delay between arrest and commitment to prison is often greater than one year for many crimes, it nonetheless is the case that many persons arrested for crimes committed in year t also will be sent to prison within that same year. Thus, a simultaneous dependence specification is called for, and its absence in the Cappell-Sykes preferred model is a weakness of the specification.[14]

The Cappell-Sykes findings are not consistent with the empirical results from monthly time-series analyses discussed below. Specifically, given the pattern of positive and negative effects of monthly fluctuations in the unemployment rate on fluctuations in crime rates found by Cantor and Land (1987), one would have to argue for a response by the criminal justice system to increases in crime within approximately one to two months. While this might occur at the most immediate tier of the system (e.g., arrest rates), it is unlikely that this would be the case for conviction and imprisonment rates.

For the post–World War II United States, we attempted to replicate the Cappell-Sykes analysis of first-differences in crime rates by incorporating data on exogenous variables they found to have statistically significant effects—the lagged first-differenced crime rate and the lagged first-differenced state prisoner commitment rate into the Cantor-Land U, DU models for which we reported estimates in Table 3.2.[15] We also included the Cappell-Sykes youth population (ages 15 to 44) rate, because many studies have found a strong effect of changes in age structure on Index crime rates.[16] All rates were defined per 100,000 population, as in Cappell and Sykes (1991).

Briefly, the statistical estimates of this model reproduced the statistically significant negative-positive pattern of algebraic signs for the U, DU variables reported in Table 3.2 for the Index crimes of robbery, burglary, and larceny-theft. For the other Index crimes, the estimates also are similar to those in Table 3.2, but with somewhat stronger U or DU effects. As might be expected, the youth population rate also exhibits a strong statistically significant effect, but neither the lagged Index crime rate nor the prison commitment rate attained significance.[17] A complete detailed analysis of the U, DU model in the presence of other exogenous variables and with the possibility of simultaneous dependence of imprisonment rates taken into account will be given in another research report. The essential point here, however, is that these estimates suggest that the negative and positive effects of the unemployment rate and its first-differences—which Cantor and Land (1985) associated with the crime opportunity and crime motivation mechanisms, respectively—are not mediated by imprisonment rate/general deterrence effects.

Evidence from Studies Based on Microdata

While the Cantor-Land thesis about the differential lag structures of the crime opportunity and crime motivation mechanisms was formulated to facilitate the interpretation of the *aggregate* effects of unemployment levels and fluctuations on crime rate fluctuations, this thesis itself can, in principle, be subjected to a longitudinal, *microlevel* empirical test. However, probably because the data and analytic demands to do so are quite extensive, we are not aware of any detailed tests of the Cantor-Land model to date using microdata. Nonetheless, Schmidt and Witte (1984) estimated negative effects of the "unemployment rate of the county of release at the time of release" on arrest rates in a longitudinal, microlevel study of recidivism among samples of adult men released from prison in North Carolina (in 1969, 1971, and 1975). Working from a standard economic (consumer demand and labor supply) model, they found these coefficients "unexpectedly negative" (Schmidt and Witte 1984: 254).

Good, Pirog-Good, and Sickles (1986) similarly found a negative effect of the "general community unemployment rate" on rates of police contact in a longitudinal, microlevel study of youths (aged 13 to 18) in Philadelphia. The latter authors also found a negative effect of the youth's own *current employment* on her/his rate of police contact. Since for individuals in the labor force current employment is the obverse of current unemployment, this implies a positive effect of current unemployment on rate of police contact. Although Good et al. do not explicitly address the lag structure specified by the Cantor-Land thesis, at least the pattern of algebraic signs (positive for personal unemployment, negative for community unemployment rate) is consistent therewith.

On the basis of these and other studies, it can be concluded that the strength of the contemporaneous relationship of employment status to criminal involvement varies with age. For teenagers and young adults, being unemployed is positively associated with criminal behavior (indicated by police contacts or arrests). Furthermore, in the data of Thornberry and Christenson (1984), this relationship becomes stronger as the individuals studied age from their twenty-first to their twenty-fourth birthdays. In the case of adult ex-prisoners, Berk, Lenihan, and Rossi (1980) similarly find that the amount of time an individual is employed over the study period is negatively related to the number of times he is arrested. On the other hand, there is some evidence to suggest that most adult, habitual property offenders are "moonlighters"—that is, they are employed at the time of the commission of the offense (Holtzman 1983). In brief, it appears that, during the mature adult years when most offenses are committed by "career criminals" (Gottfredson and Hirschi 1986), the impact of being unemployed on criminal involvement is less than it is during the teenage and young adult years.

It is also noteworthy that several of the above studies find a significant negative, contemporaneous reciprocal relationship between having a criminal record and employability. This connection appears to be more stable across all age groups than the connection between employment status and criminal activity. In the context of the aggregate U-C relationship, however, the individual-level criminal record–employability relationship is less important, because the aggregate unemployment rate is more strongly determined by other aggregate economic forces than by the arrest records of individuals.

Analyses Based on Monthly Data

In brief, the Cantor-Land regression models (1) and (2) appear to be applicable to age- and race-specific population categories as well as to population aggregates. In addition, there is some evidence from studies based on microdata to support the proposition that an individual's probability of criminal involvement is affected both by his/her unemployment status and by the general level of unemployment in the surrounding community—with an algebraic pattern of signs consistent with that suggested by Cantor and Land (1985). But these studies also suggest that there may very well be a contemporaneous positive relationship between an increase in the unemployment rate in a given month and the rates of crimes of property theft (especially larceny and burglary) in that month—and hence that the lag structures for the crime motivation component of the aggregate U-C relationship specified by Cantor and Land (1985) should be modified for these property crimes.

But annual movements in aggregate unemployment rates, as demonstrated above, tend to be correlated over time as the economy contracts or expands. Age-specific unemployment rates also tend to be positively correlated across age categories, so that an increase in, say, teenage unemployment in any given month will be associated with an increase in unemployment in the same or subsequent months in other (older) age categories. Some of the latter individuals will be parents or relatives of unemployed teenagers. The unemployment of the former may increase the level of adult supervision of the latter. Some of the older unemployed also will spend more time in locations (e.g., domiciles) with relatively low rates of victimization or risk for themselves and their property. Thus, the obvious next question pertains to the implications of all of these lifestyle changes for the time pattern of the relationship between a change in unemployment and crime rates.

Because this question is intrinsically about the aggregate consequences of a population-interactional phenomenon, it cannot be answered by individual-level studies of unemployment rates and criminality. Rather, although such studies may suggest hypotheses to be investigated, these hypotheses must be studied by ascertaining the degree to which changes in the aggregate unemployment rate are related to changes in aggregate crime rates. Furthermore—in order to specify more precisely the forms of the lag structures between unemployment fluctuations and increases in criminal motivation as well as the variability of such lag structures among the Index crimes—it is helpful to examine the temporal U-C relationship with monthly unemployment and crime rate data. This is what Cantor and Land (1987) did.

Using monthly U.S. unemployment and crime rate data for the years 1969 to 1985 and bivariate seasonal ARIMA time-series model-building strategies, Cantor and Land (1987) indeed found a positive, statistically significant effect of an unemployment rate fluctuation in month $t-1$ on the rates of burglary and larceny in month t—an indicator of a virtually simultaneous increase in crime motivation. This was followed, however, by a nearly equal negative, statistically significant effect of an unemployment rate fluctuation lagged two months ($t-2$) on the rates of burglary and larceny in month t. With no other lagged unemployment rate fluctuations (up to lag-12) being statistically significant, the total effects for burglary and larceny across a full year then average out to a relatively small and not statistically significant value.

For each of the other Index crime rates studied here, Cantor and Land (1987) found only negative effects (reaching statistical significance at various lags up to twelve months)—which, of course, is consistent with the relative contemporaneity of a crime opportunity mechanism as postulated by Cantor and Land (1985). In interpreting these differences among the Index crimes, Cantor and Land (1987) noted that the contemporaneous effect of personal unemployment status on criminal involvement found in microstudies appears to occur primarily for crimes of theft and burglary and primarily for teenagers and young adults. They also noted that these individuals are least likely to be cushioned by the availability of government unemployment benefits and social aid mechanisms cited by Cantor and Land (1985).

In sum, with the exception of burglary and larceny—the Index crimes most likely to be influenced by the unemployment of adolescents, teenagers, and young adults—monthly bivariate analyses of the temporal U-C relationship suggest that the initial effects of an upturn in the unemployment rate will be negative. Indeed, for those crimes with a violent component (murder, rape, assault, robbery), the only statistically significant unemployment effects are negative.

Conclusion

We noted at the outset that the accumulation of research findings has demonstrated the complex and multifaceted nature of the general U-C relationship. The present study has focused on the temporal aspects of this relationship. Several conclusions are warranted. First, given the annual time-series properties of the unemployment and crime rates studied herein, the forms of the regression models specified by Cantor and Land (1985) are statistically acceptable. Second, with annual time series extending from 1946 through 1990, these models remain successful in identifying and estimating both the negative (crime opportunity) and positive (crime motivation) effects postulated by Cantor and Land (1985). Third, other related research demonstrates that these effects (1) are evident across age- and race-specific population categories; (2) are not mediated by imprisonment/general deterrence processes; (3) are generally consistent with evidence from microlevel studies; and (4) are consonant with studies based on monthly unemployment and crime rate time series.

In brief, the pattern of effects of unemployment levels and fluctuations postulated by Cantor and Land (1985) has substantial empirical support for some Index crime rates. Future research should document more fully the intervening mechanisms for these effects and what, if any, portions to attribute to imprisonment/deterrence and/or other mechanisms. Variation in these effects across different categories of crime also requires explanation.

APPENDIX

Time-Series Properties of Differenced Unemployment: Suppose that the undifferenced unemployment rate series is centered so that its mean is zero and that it is an AR(1) process:

$$U_t = \varphi\, U_{t-1} + \delta_t, \tag{A1}$$

where φ is the autoregressive parameter relating the value of the unemployment rate in period t to its value in the preceding period $t-1$ (recall that in Table 3.1 we estimate this parameter to be about 0.75) and δ_t is zero-mean white noise. Then:

$$\begin{aligned} DU_t &= U_t - U_{t-1} \\ &= (\varphi U_{t-1} + \delta_t) - (\varphi U_{t-2} + \delta_{t-1}) \\ &= \varphi U_{t-1} - \varphi U_{t-2} + (\delta_t - \delta_{t-1}), \end{aligned} \tag{A2}$$

which is an Auto-Regressive Moving Average process of order two in the autoregressive part and order one in the moving-average part—that is, an ARMA(2,1) process.

Time-Series Properties of the Cantor-Land Regression Models: Suppose that the undifferenced and centered unemployment rate series is AR(1) as in (A1) and that the first-differenced unemployment rate series is ARMA(2,1) as in (A2). Then, with ε denoting a zero-mean white noise process, the Cantor-Land regression model (1) for first-differences of an Index crime rate can be written (with the expected pattern of algebraic signs as indicated):

$$\begin{aligned} DC_t &= \alpha - \beta_1 U_t + \beta_2 DU_t + \varepsilon_t \\ &= \alpha - \beta_1(\varphi U_{t-1} + \delta_t) + \beta_2(\varphi U_{t-1} - \varphi U_{t-2} + \delta_t - \delta_{t-1}) + \varepsilon_t \\ &= \alpha - \beta_1\beta_2\varphi^2 U_{t-1} - \beta_2\varphi U_{t-2} + \varepsilon_t^* \end{aligned} \tag{A3}$$

where

$$\varepsilon_t^* = \varepsilon_t + 2\delta_t - \delta_{t-1}. \tag{A4}$$

If error term ε_t of the regression model is independent of the error term δ_t of the AR(1) process generating the unemployment rate series, this implies that the error term ε_t^* in (A4) is a first-order moving average process—that is, a MA(1) process. But since the coefficient of the δ_{t-1} term in (A4) is not greater than 1, this MA(1) process is invertible and therefore equivalent to an AR(∞) process (Granger and Newbold 1986: 24). In practice, for the estimation of the regression model (A3) in the applications reported in the text, the latter autoregressive representation of the error process is approximated by a p-th order autoregressive specification used in the SAS AUTOREG program. Empirically, we found $p=1$ suffices for this approximation.

To draw out the implications of (A3) and (A4) for the ability of the Cantor-Land regression models (1) and (2) to explain temporal variations in Index crime rates, assume next that the DC_t term on the left-hand side of the regression model

(A3) represents a first-differenced Index crime rate series for which we have found in the text that an AR(2) model is an appropriate representation (robbery, burglary, or larceny-theft). Then note that the regression model in lagged values of the unemployment series on the right-hand side is in the form of an autoregression in the unemployment rate of order two. Thus, the autoregression in the unemployment rate on the right-hand side of (A3) will yield an AR(2) type of behavior—which should provide an appropriate representation for the AR(2) behavior of the left-hand side. This is affirmed in the estimated regressions reported in Table 3.1 of the text.

On the other hand, for those Index crime rate series that display AR(1) time-series behavior (murder and motor vehicle theft), it probably is the case that only the first-order part of the right-hand side of (A4) will be significantly related to the dependent series—which is, of course, exactly what we find in Table 3.1 of the text. In the case of rape and assault, the results in Table 3.1 show that even the first-order parts of the unemployment rate regressions are not significantly related to the dependent series.

Ethnography, Inequality, and Crime in the Low-Income Community

MARTÍN SÁNCHEZ JANKOWSKI

Crime in the United States has often been likened to a social malignancy that threatens the health of the social body of which it is a part. Interestingly, the issue of crime has presented the same policy dilemmas that often confront medical researchers. The pressures to find intervention strategies that will either eradicate crime or put it into remission have influenced the sociological and criminological research community to develop agendas in the direction of deterrence. The problem is that we still know very little about the nature of crime and those who become involved in it. In essence, we simply do not understand the etiology of crime as a social disease, and there has not been enough research to develop the kind of understanding we need.

Two general problems have contributed to an overemphasis on deterrence and crime control in recent research. The first is pressure from the public (and as a result, political pressure) to provide greater protection from those who would prey on law-abiding citizens. The second has more to do with method—more precisely, with the difficulty of gaining close access to those who are actively involved in crime. Those individuals actively engaging in crime have not been readily available, or they have not been willing to be the subjects of research. Crime researchers have generally been forced to undertake analyses of aggregations of data collected through the use of: (1) survey instruments with closed-question formats, (2) in-depth interviews with open-ended formats, and/or (3) official records of various public agencies. These methods of data gathering have generally involved *ex post facto* research in that they have asked individuals to recreate past incidents and attitudes. Then, with the use of background data, researchers have had to account inductively for various types of crime, for individuals' motivations for becoming involved, and/or for the estimated propensity of individuals to become involved in criminal activity. These methods have been much used in the development of deterrence research and policy.

Although these methods have been sufficient for identifying, explaining, and predicting certain aggregate trends, they have been inadequate in providing an understanding of crime and of the individuals who become involved in criminal activity. By this, I simply mean that although these data can be used to explain criminal events in a limited sense, they are not especially effective in helping us understand how these events come about. The ethnographer can better provide this understanding of crime. Ethnography, if used properly, should include participant-observation as the primary method of data collection.[1] Participant-observation implies that the researcher is closely associated with the daily activities of the subjects under study and is in a position to observe the events involving these subjects as they naturally occur. If enough time is spent in the field there should be sufficient data to establish a pattern that provides an understanding of how, why, and under what conditions certain events (including criminal events) have taken place.

Ethnography can clarify a good many of the causes and ramifications of social activity. It does so by categorizing the relationships between phenomena and by identifying the processes by which certain events occur. In so doing, it establishes the foundations for causality.

In this chapter, I discuss some of the contributions of ethnographic data to understanding the dynamics that exist between conditions of inequality and acts of crime. Before proceeding, it is appropriate to identify the data sources that I draw on. First, I use data from an ethnographic gang study that I conducted from 1977 through 1988. In this study, I followed 37 gangs in Los Angeles, New York, and Boston over ten years to analyze the conditions under which they rose and thrived, declined and died.[2] Second, I use data from an ethnographic study I began in 1988 (and that is still in progress) on various elements of the illicit underground economy of four American cities.

Inequality and Crime in Low-Income Neighborhoods

The purpose of this chapter is to examine some of the relationships between crime and inequality. Most studies addressing these relationships begin by identifying crime as the event to be explained and inequality as one of the variables that contributes to its explanation. Recent research (and debate) on inequality and crime has focused primarily on two independent variables—heredity and environment. Those who include heredity as a predictor often suggest that heredity produces gene inequality among individuals, which in turn produces individuals who are more ignorant and aggressive and who have "present-oriented" traits (i.e., they live for today and do not plan for the future). These individuals perform poorly in the market, experience frustration as a consequence, and therefore have a greater propensity to engage in crime. The argument is that the foundations of criminal behavior lie in heredity's influence on the production of bad character among individuals (Wilson and Herrnstein 1985). Those who emphasize the environment argue that crime is more likely to occur in areas with great disparity in income inequality. They suggest that being poor is the most important factor influencing individuals to become involved in crime (Currie 1986).

The problem with both analyses is that the root variables of inequality and heredity (not to mention crime) are too broad; this leads to inaccurate explanations of criminal events, as well as to an inability to understand them. For example, the assumption that most people at the bottom of some specified inequality scale involve themselves in crime for similar reasons underestimates the complex nature of the condition of inequality—even for those who are in fact at the bottom of such a hierarchy. The environmental explanation fails to account for the fact that people do not share a common "inequality" experience, nor do they have similar motives for being active in crime; and the process by which they move from a motive to commit a crime to the act itself is related to the individual and the situation. Aggregate data analysis is simply an insufficient means of assessing the relationship between crime and inequality.

As mentioned, one of the primary problems in assessing the relationship between crime and inequality is with our understanding of the terms themselves. Most research treats inequality as synonymous with poverty. This is, of course, an inaccurate treatment. There are two general conditions of inequality: in one, people are, objectively, living in conditions of poverty; in the other, people are experiencing inequality relative to others. Even if we focus our attention only on the low-income community, these two conditions exist.

The category of crime involves many acts that are not necessarily similar. The two categories of criminal acts that affect people most profoundly are economic crimes and crimes of violence. Violence and economic crime may, of course, occur within the same event, but in many cases they are separate. If we are to understand the relationship between inequality and crime in the low-income community, we must address the dynamics of economic and violent crimes separately.

Inequality and Economic Crime

In a recent book on social policy, Christopher Jencks suggests that "while the poor commit more crimes than the rich, they do not commit these crimes solely because they have low incomes" (Jencks 1992). My own studies and those of others suggest that this assertion is not completely accurate. In order to assess its accuracy we must look at the motives of those from low-income areas who become involved in crime.

For people in poverty, there are three general motives for engaging in crime. First, there are those who engage in crime in order to become socioeconomically mobile (Anderson 1990). For these individuals, crime is nothing more than an economic activity that they hope will alleviate their impoverished condition. In fact, nearly all the individuals who become involved in crime for this reason believe that crime is the only activity that will give them a realistic chance of improving their economic status. Nearly all these individuals have socioeconomic values similar to those of other citizens who are not involved in crime. They want to be rich and famous, or at least comfortable, but they do not know any way of achieving this goal other than through criminal activity. Most of these individuals live in areas where there are few chances for upward socioeconomic mobility. What most observers have not fully appreciated is that these individuals do assess their situation and consider the options available to them to better their position. They make choices using some calculus that makes sense to them (William 1989). This calculus is likely to involve an assessment of personal investments, risks, and returns (Sánchez Jankowski 1991: 113–36; Sullivan 1989: 106–22). The fact is, they may not always make an accurate assessment, and an inaccurate assessment can lead to setbacks in achieving their goals and to further personal hardship. Yet they nearly always engage in some form of analysis. It is these individuals who challenge Jencks's assertion. Poverty alone does not cause them to become involved in crime, but poverty along with a desire to be upwardly mobile and a perception that few opportunities exist in the legitimate economy cause them to become involved. The comments of RR, a 21-year-old male from New York, are typical of those who are poor and want to have more:

> I ain't never been involved in any big crime or anything like that in my life. But I been thinking that I might take this job with CC [a local drug dealer]. I haven't done this [crime] before 'cause I thought there might be something I could do that was legal, but I been at it for quite awhile now and there just ain't no jobs or they won't hire you. You say that to people and they think you just be making excuses or something, but they ain't down here. Fuck 'em, I been trying and I mean, I don't want to live like this [poor] all my life. My parents lived like this, but I sure the hell ain't going to.[3]

Three weeks later he joined CC and began to sell drugs. He subsequently became an independent drug retailer and then moved into one of the larger drug syndicates in his section of the city.

Second, there is a contingent of individuals experiencing poverty who commit criminal acts in order to maintain themselves economically. For these individuals, crime is simply a means (a necessary means) of maintaining their present socioeconomic condition, no matter how depressed it may be. Most of these individuals live in low-income areas where there are few economic possibilities (W. J. Wilson 1987; 1989). Thus, many of the youth from these areas, who face the most constricted job opportunities, will engage in crime as a means of supplementing any meager allowances they may get from their families (Sullivan 1989: 124; William and Kornblum 1985). I have also found this to be true for a significant number of adults in similar economic situations. Take the comments of TT, a 37-year-old male who has been unemployed for fourteen months:

> As you know I've been involved in some break-ins recently. I ain't keen on doing them, but I ain't got no choice right now. I ain't got work and I got me a family to provide for. I really don't make that much off robberies once I share it with the other two guys, but it's enough for me to pay the rent in this shit hole and buy some food.

Ironically, although the money TT makes from burglary pays his rent, it is not enough to pay for his family's food. He uses the money to supplement the family's food-stamp allowance. It is important to realize that significant numbers of individuals engage in crime for no other reason than to supplement their individual (or family) income.[4]

Another group of people who engage in crime for the purposes of maintaining their present condition are those addicted to drugs. In low-income communities throughout the United States, growing numbers of people are addicted to drugs (especially crack cocaine). Large numbers of these people have become active in crime, particularly burglaries, prostitution, and drug sales, to support their addiction. Many researchers have known this but have failed to link drug addiction to issues of inequality and poverty. What many have assumed about why individuals in low-income areas consume drugs turns out to be only partially confirmed empirically. Many people within the low-income community do not begin to use drugs because they have given up on life. Rather, most begin using drugs as a way of trying to have fun. They report that their initial contact with drugs was within the context of a social event and they merely tried a particular drug to see what it was like and to have some fun. Addiction for most of these individuals developed over an extended period of revisiting similar social situations where drugs were present. Thus, they did not use drugs for purposes of socioeconomic escape, but for purposes associated with leisure. Further, they do not continue their use of drugs in order to escape the realities of low-income life. Rather, crime allows them to escape the harsh physical realities of addiction. Therefore, inequality, drug addiction, and crime can be linked, to a large extent, to the lack of options that face low-income people living in low-income areas. The comment of YY, a 23-year-old crack addict, is representative:

> Yeah I been robbing houses and people on the street for some time to get the money I need for my drugs. . . . I don't really know how I got this way. . . . Hell, my friends and I didn't have much money so there weren't a whole hell of a lot we could afford to do for fun, so we used to go mostly to local parties. Once we was just at this party on my block and somebody asked me if I wanted to try some crack. I thought it might be fun so I checked it out. Now I be really all messed up.

The relationship among economic inequality, drug addiction, and crime can be seen as a quasi-bridge between the motive of maintenance described above and a third motive, that of pursuing pleasure. Among those experiencing poverty are a number of individuals who engage in criminal acts to secure the economic means to buy some type of fun. For example, they may use the money from drug sales, burglaries, or running numbers to pay for a movie, a restaurant, or a concert, or to buy drugs and alcohol (Anderson 1990: 88–89; Sánchez Jankowski 1991: 133–35). Those in this category commit crime with no intention to accumulate wealth, but merely for the means to consume. Most (but by no means all) of these individuals are young people whose families are on public assistance or whose major income earner is employed in the secondary labor market. Although I observed that the vast majority of these individuals are young, many are in their late twenties and early thirties; and most fluctuate between being periodically employed in the secondary labor market and receiving public assistance. What distinguishes the people whose motive is the pursuit of pleasure from other people is that in general they are capable of providing basic food, shelter, and clothing for themselves and their families, but after doing so they have no money left for pleasure. The comments of FF, a 43-year-old woman on public assistance, are representative:

> Sure I run numbers for one of the local joints, but I really don't get too much for it. I do it for a little extra money so I can have a little fun. I mean, I can make ends meet barely with what I get from welfare, but I don't have anything left to go out for a drink or go to the movies. So this job gets that for me, that's all.

The comments of TT, an 18-year-old woman from Los Angeles, are also representative:

> I been passing dope for this here gang for about six months. I do it cause it gives me some money to play with. You know, I get money to get some weed [marijuana] or sometimes even some cocaine. I don't mean that I get that much money at this job. I really could never live on it or anything. Don't get me wrong, I been trying to get a job, but I ain't had any luck. But at least this job gives me something to have fun with.

People who are not poor, but who feel the effects of inequality, also engage in crime as a means of ameliorating their perceived relatively deprived condition. Although this motive for crime can be observed in white middle-class society in the United States, it can also be observed in the urban neighborhoods that have been called ghettos and barrios.

A sense of relative deprivation among some elements of the ethnic/racial middle class in the United States provides another example of how inequality can influence participation in economic crime. For most people, inequality is synonymous with low incomes, but it need not be. In the following examples, inequalities in housing opportunities and intrafirm mobility were principal factors in explaining why certain middle-class people became involved in crime. The perceived presence of racial and ethnic inequality was the root cause of the relative deprivation that these people felt. Thus, middle-class minorities whose group has faced long-term discrimination and who continue to observe inequality in their occupational and residential environments are more likely to feel relatively deprived than members of groups not faced with such conditions. Most will not engage in crime as a result, but some portion will. Let us take the example of housing.

Because of racial discrimination in the housing market, African-Americans and Latinos have found it difficult to move into ethnically integrated white neighborhoods; this difficulty has led to the creation of nonwhite, ethnically defined geographic districts called ghettos and barrios, which are home to people with different socioeconomic statuses.[5] Within these social-ecological niches, I have found middle-class people of color who feel relatively deprived compared to members of the white middle class outside their community; such feelings of relative deprivation have influenced some of them to become involved in crime. Drug selling and running prostitution and gambling houses were the crimes they turned to most often. Probably the most common reason these middle-class individuals became involved in crime was impatience. Most of the individuals I observed became frustrated by how long it took them to acquire material benefits in sufficient quantity and quality as compared with others in society. This frustration led them to look to crime as an alternative for speeding up the process. Some of the middle-class people I observed simply switched occupations. They went from being professionals in legal businesses to being professionals in criminal activity. Take the case of BB, a 32-year-old with a bachelor of arts degree in management, who now works for one of the local crime syndicates in New York:

> You [the researcher] knew me when I was working for [a large electronics company]. Well, I was making a pretty good salary there. I really wasn't unhappy working for them, but I was unhappy about how long it would take to get the big-time money. I was sort of looking around to see what my options were when I ran into an old friend of mine. He was working for one of the syndicates in town and asked if I would be interested in something. I was trying to be polite and so I just said maybe. Well he got back to me with this offer. It was a position in his company [the syndicate], but it involved me using nearly all of the skills I had learned in college, so I listened. I really didn't know what I was going to do. I thought about it for awhile, I knew the company I worked for would eventually promote me; but I decided to go with my friend's business because I knew I could get the good life much faster. It's funny, now I work in the neighborhood I always wanted to get out of, but I live in a much better section and I didn't have to wait!

Other middle-class individuals moonlighted in crime as a second job. These people were nearly always in a job where they were frustrated by the length of time it would take them to be promoted. They usually believed that they would be promoted, but that it would take an inordinate amount of time. Most thought that the slowness of their promotion was due mainly to prejudice. It was their impression that their employers were generally skeptical about the competence of minorities and that they would extend the time between promotions to ensure that the individual minority member was capable. The comments of EE, a 33-year-old who works for an industrial manufacturing company but also deals in drugs, are representative:

> I have worked hard here at [the firm] and I have been promoted a couple of times. But the promotions seem to take an enormous amount of time and I always get promoted after most of the other white guys. No one says anything, but I believe that they wait because they want to be sure that I can handle the responsibilities at the next step. I don't feel enormously discriminated against, but I do feel penalized because while I wait, my salary is lower and I don't get to buy some of the things that I would like to. So I have been doing some extra work selling drugs to get the things that I want. The funny thing is that I sell nearly all of my product [cocaine] to white yuppies like the ones I work with. . . . Having such different jobs is a bit crazy, but it is capable of giving you what you want.

Inequality and Violent Crime

Much of the research on the relationship between inequality and crime uses violent crime as the dependent variable. Although there may be reasons why violent crime is a poor dependent variable to test this relationship, a more significant problem is that researchers usually consider only one type of violent crime—homicide (Blau and Blau 1982: 114–29; Jencks 1992: 114–19). Using homicide may be convenient, but it has great potential to underestimate the impact of inequality on crime. The problem is that when crime is equated with homicide it confuses a result with an act. It is not against the law to have a corpse, but it is against the law to act in such a way as potentially to cause death. No doubt this is why the law criminalizes a number of actions that do not result in death, such as attempted murder and reckless endangerment. Therefore, sociologically, violence must be understood to be the functional method or technique by which actors seek to achieve their goals.

If we are to understand the relationship between violent crime and inequality, and start from the premise that violence is an instrumental act, then a number of distinctions must be made concerning its use. One must start by making a distinction between violence used in pursuit of material goals and its use in situations where material concerns are not directly present.

Economic Crime and Violence

A whole host of crimes are associated with violence. The majority of these crimes involve the attempt to secure material possessions through the use of force. In these cases, violence is merely a tactic. For people who have low incomes, inequality in its objective state directly influences the decision to commit a crime, but it does not have a direct impact on the use of violence itself. That is to say, the low-income person may carry the instruments of violence, but the decision to use them is mostly determined by the situation.[6] In situations involving economic crime, the factor that most influences whether violence is used is the condition of fear. I have found that when individuals who are engaging in a crime become fearful that they will not achieve their objective, or that they will be physically hurt, or that they will be apprehended, they have a very high propensity to use the instruments of violence.[7]

Noneconomic Crime and Violence

In a large number of incidents violence does not involve the pursuit of economic goals. For example, one can start with the low-income family. Many studies find a growing number of low-income families to be dysfunctional. Leaving aside the question of whether these families are truly dysfunctional, I have found a good deal of violence within the ones I have observed. This violence has been between husband and wife, parents and children, and siblings. Ironically, although there are laws against domestic violence, this violence is seldom considered by researchers as part of the equation that has been specified to address the relationship between inequality and crime. Yet my own research suggests that it may be one of the primary crimes related to inequality. The principal causes of family violence are frustration and identity preservation. Frequently, frustrating job conditions lead to violent confrontations at home. Job frustrations can include being passed over for a promotion, being harassed on the job, being bored on the job, or being fatigued by job duties. The frustration-generating condition only sets the stage—that is, it is only a precondition for the violent act in the home. It takes another incident or series of small incidents for violence to emerge. The case of YY, a 28-year-old male worker in a New York paper bag manufacturing company, is representative of the other individuals and situations I observed:

> Sorry you had to see this [he just physically beat up his wife]. Every day I go to this work and the line works so fast it is tiring. Then I got this fuckin' asshole that is on my ass constantly to keep working fast and watch how I'm doing this and watch how I'm doing that. All day, I get this shit and then I come home and my old lady starts with we need this and that and where's the money for it and why I didn't do this or that to get it. Then, even after you tell her that you want her to stop, she just keeps it up. So, you got to create some place for yourself that's all. . . . Yeah I should punch out the jerk that supervises me, but then I lose my job and then what am I going to do? What kind of job can I get and for how long?

Thus, faced with the frustrations of the job and the feelings of impotence associated with his inability to ameliorate the problem, he and others like him often displace the problem to the home. Home violence must be seen as a crime because there are laws making it so; and it is related to inequality because much (though not all) of it can be associated with inequality in the labor market. This relationship has been called one of the "hidden injuries of class" (Sennett and Cobb 1972). Ethnography can provide evidence of when domestic violence is and is not associated with inequality. It can also specify the conditions under which inequality is likely to produce such violence.[8]

In addition to the violence that is found in the low-income family, there are other situations in which violence can be associated with the condition of inequality. One such case is when individuals feel physically threatened. Because low-income communities have scarce resources, the competition for those that exist is intense. There are many predators in these communities, and every resident is socialized to be vigilant in watching for them. In many cases both women and men take on a posture of being able and willing to use whatever force is necessary to deter a threat.[9] If that tactic is not successful and a person does feel threatened (by a perceived predator from within or outside the community), he or she usually uses violence quickly to prevent physical harm. Because failure to act can have serious consequences, people in these communities do not leave anything to chance.

Another potentially violent situation occurs when a person's self-worth is threatened. Many people living in low-income communities struggle with issues of self-worth. This struggle develops from their attempt to negotiate the social interactions associated with their daily lives and to reconcile their present socioeconomic situation with that associated with the middle and upper class. Respect is especially important to such people. Perceived or actual challenges to these individuals' sense of self-worth nearly always lead to violent confrontation. There are two reasons for this. First, in the absence of material possessions, respect and honor are all that many of these individuals have to offer as evidence of social status within their community. They become possessions that must be defended. This is especially true of honor. Honor and respect are often used interchangeably, but they are not sociologically the same. In some cultures, especially those of the Mediterranean and Latin America, honor is one of the organizing principles for interpersonal relations (Gutierrez 1991: 176–206; Peristiany 1965; Pitt-Rivers 1968: 503–11). In these cultures, honor is something that is given to everyone at birth and not something that is achieved (in contrast to respect). A person with honor must guard against losing it because if lost, it cannot be regained easily (if at all). In addition, honor encompasses not only the person, but the person's entire family. When a family member's honor is offended, the honor of the entire family is offended. Therefore, an attack on a person's honor usually results in a violent confrontation (Horowitz 1983: 88–97). This is especially the situation for low-income people who, because they use their honor to achieve status and favors within their communities, treat it as a precious commodity that must be protected.

Respect can also be functional for people who live in low-income areas. Many low-income residents cultivate respect because it can act as a deterrent to those who might want to prey on them. This is particularly true for gang members, but it is true for others in the low-income community as well (Sánchez Jankowski 1991: 141–44). Middle-class individuals also use respect in this way, even though they also have other resources to draw on.

Finally, a number of violent crimes in low-income areas result from status inequality, which creates jealousies among people who live there. In most cases, the violence is directed against property and not other individuals, yet the victims usually feel violated and resentful. The most common example is of people who for one reason or another feel jealous and resentful of what one of their fellow residents has been able to acquire. Over a significant period of time, I have observed people who would rob or even attempt arson against a business establishment owned and run by a person of the same ethnic group. Nearly all of the persons involved were envious of the success that one of their group had achieved. The fact that the successful person was a member of their own ethnic group intensified the situation by exacerbating feelings of inadequacy in those who had not been able to start a business.

In each of the situations that I have described, violence was used to achieve some goal or objective. These crimes, whether reported or not, must be seen as functions of inequality. In cases where violence was instrumental to achieving a material goal, there was a direct relationship between income inequality and the engagement in violent crime. In others, the relationship was indirect. These cases generally involved issues of status inequality, which is directly linked to economic inequality; for these cases, economic inequality must be understood indirectly to influence violent crime.

Inequality and Crime: The Decision-Making Process

What is the process by which someone who is experiencing inequality moves to participate in crime? Drawing from my ethnographic work on gangs and my subsequent research on crime in low-income areas, I have thus far found two routes that individuals have followed in making their decisions to engage in crime.[10]

In the area of economic crime, the process begins when individuals assess the material condition in which they live. They then decide that the condition (or a perceived threat to worsen the condition) is neither desirable nor acceptable. Next, they make a commitment to pursue a strategy to alleviate this condition. Here the goal can be variable. As reported earlier, some may want only to maintain their present condition (or prevent it from worsening); others may want to experience some recreation that their condition does not afford; still others may want to escape the present condition through socioeconomic mobility. Their next step is to rationalize the commission of a criminal act.[11] They then formulate a general strategy, deciding on the resources (which can include weapons) necessary to be successful and the tactics to be employed. Finally, they commit the criminal act itself when the benefits of the specific situation (targeted opportunity) seem to outweigh the risks.

The noneconomic violent crime involves a slightly different process. Here, too, individuals first compare their own living conditions with the conditions of those who live in different socioeconomic situations. These calculations are embedded in a worldview—who lives in the community, how they live, how they behave, what the dangers are, what the cues for danger and safety are. Individuals are sensitive to the cues associated with danger (physical and psychological) and safety. This sensitivity may make it possible to avoid interactions that would leave the individual susceptible to perceived unpleasantries, status deprivation, and/or attacks on self-worth, or vulnerable to bodily harm. When an individual sees no possibility for escape or does not desire to escape, he or she usually decides very quickly what action to take. Action almost always will be based on what is known about the event/situation, the assessed competence of the adversaries compared with that of the individual, cues that signal the adversary's likely next move, and what is a sufficient and/or appropriate line of action. Within this decision-making process, three types of action can (and do) occur: (1) the individual decides on a first-strike line of action using all the force at his or her disposal; (2) the individual decides on a plan of action that simply retaliates proportionally to the actions of the adversary; or (3) the individual decides strategically to withdraw, plans a course of retaliatory action at a more advantageous time, and then executes the action. Regardless of what course of action is taken, the final stage in the thought process is to begin rationalizing the use of violence immediately after the act and then to further rationalize the moral reasoning that led to the act.

Conclusion

There has always been some debate about the relationship of inequality to crime, but the major problem has been assessing this relationship. More often than not, inferential statistics are used in much the same manner as in epidemiological studies of disease or related kinds of problems. Using aggregate statistics is simply not adequate; there may be more subtle causal processes that such methods have difficulty discerning. In addition, even when a relationship is found using aggregated data, the etiology, characteristics, and behavior associated with that relationship cannot be specifically detailed or easily understood. In order to provide such specifications, more closely focused research is needed. In sociology this research will often need to be ethnographic.

In a recent chapter on the relationship between inequality and crime, Christopher Jencks uses homicide rates for particular cities and countries. After analyzing the aggregate patterns of poverty and homicide, he says that "crime rates depend on how people respond to economic inequality rather than on the actual level of inequality" (Jencks 1992: 118). Finding no consistently strong relationship, he felt the need to modify the specified relationship to account for inconsistencies in the aggregate trends. Yet his statement is also indicative of the problems associated with this type of analysis. He may be perfectly correct in arguing that there is a relationship between crime rates and how people respond to economic inequality. However, the data in this chapter indicate that the crimes an individual is more likely to commit are in fact related to the level of inequality that the person has experienced. Whether a person experienced economic deprivation (at the level of poverty or not), or status deprivation in relation to others, had a significant influence on whether that individual would engage in crime, on the type of crime, and on the rate of participation. There are places in the world where inequality may not lead to crime, but aggregate data cannot tell us why this is so. At the same time, the data here would also tend to confirm that Jencks may be correct in suggesting that the way people respond to inequality affects the crime rate. But such a finding might lead two ways. For Jencks, the influence of culture might lead people to deal with their inequality by not participating in crime—that is, it would reduce the crime rate (Jencks 1992: 117–18). For others, the response to inequality would in certain situations be to increase their involvement in crime. This is why ethnographic work is so vital: It can clarify the content of the relationship. For example, the research presented here was able to show a relationship between inequality and crime that might well have been overlooked, and it was able to show the differentiated ways that this relationship exists. It has been shown here that the type of crime engaged in was influenced by the motives of those individuals who were attempting to deal with the inequality they experienced. More specifically, the type of crime (economic or violent) was influenced by whether the individual was trying to be socioeconomically mobile, trying to maintain the present economic position, or merely trying to have some fun.

The data also indicated that there was a relationship between inequality and violent forms of crime and that this relationship was indirect and often hidden by the seemingly more direct effects of frustration, resentment, and jealousy. The research was therefore able to specify circuitous routes taken by inequality to influence crime.

Finally, my data show a relationship between inequality and crime only in certain situations, with perhaps a relatively small number of people associated with each situation. Some researchers interested in social policy may find the absence of a more universal or general relationship unsatisfying. The relationship between crime and inequality is complicated, however, and the varied forms this relationship takes are of critical importance for understanding the social dynamics of social settings.[12]

Age-Inequality and Property Crime

The Effects of Age-linked Stratification and Status-Attainment Processes on Patterns of Criminality Across the Life Course

DARRELL STEFFENSMEIER

EMILIE ANDERSEN ALLAN

The purpose of this chapter is to explore selected issues related to age, inequality, and crime. Age is a potent mediator of inequality in both the legitimate and illegitimate opportunity structures of society. Just as the low-wage, dead-end jobs of the legitimate economy are disproportionately held by the young, so too are high-risk, low-yield crimes committed disproportionately by the young. At the opposite end of the opportunity scale, it is rare to find young people in well-rewarded positions of power and influence in business or politics; likewise, relatively few young people score big in the world of white-collar crime or in the lucrative rackets of organized crime.

In this chapter we examine how age-stratification processes of the larger society shape the age distribution of property crimes, focusing on two different patterns of age-crime distribution:

1. For low-yield, high-risk crimes the age curve peaks sharply in the mid-teens, with a very rapid drop-off in offending as youths enter their late teens and early twenties.
2. For high-yield, low-risk types of crime, the age-crime curve is much flatter, involving a preponderance of middle-aged and older offenders.

These two patterns are depicted in Figure 5.1, which depicts the age curves for three crimes: burglary, which is typical of the curves for low-yield, high-risk crimes, along with fraud and gambling, two (*Uniform Crime Reports*) offense categories that may be considered to have somewhat lower

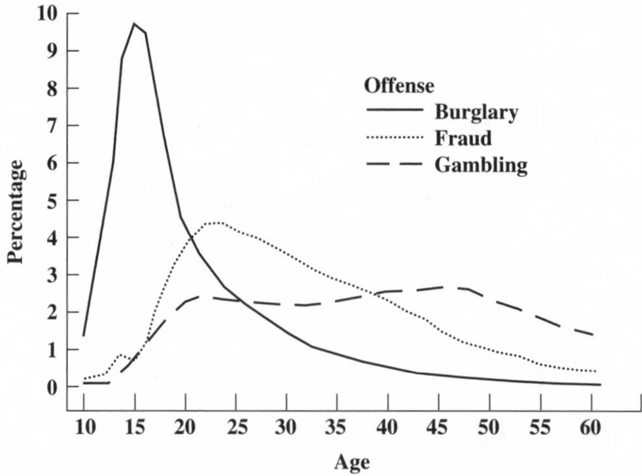

Fig. 5.1. Age curves for burglary, fraud, and gambling, 1980. The percentage of arrests has been adjusted for the population size of each group. Based on *Uniform Crime Reports* arrest data for 1980.

risks and stronger potential for higher yields. (See also Figures 5.4 and 5.5.)

We examine first the relationship between youth inequality and the high concentration of offending among adolescents for ordinary property crimes. Much more is known about the association between youth and conventional crimes than about the age distribution for lucrative crimes. The tendency of rates for conventional crimes to drop—at least gradually—with age has been recognized since at least the time of Quetelet (1831).

The widespread incidence of this inverse relationship between age and conventional crime has led some to suggest that the pattern is "invariant" (Hirschi and Gottfredson 1983), or that it can best be explained by age-linked physiological changes (Gove 1985). After exploring the latter argument briefly, we explicate the age-inequality explanation for the traditional age-crime curve, building on the work of others (e.g., Greenberg 1985; Hagan 1991; Tittle 1988) to examine (1) interrelationships among crime, age-inequality, and other dimensions of inequality such as race; and (2) variations in the age-crime curve in connection with cultural and historical variations in age-inequality.

We then turn to the links between age and involvement in lucrative property crimes—that is, to the issue of status attainment or upward mobility within the population of criminal offenders of both the underworld and the upperworld. Much less is known of such patterns, but they appear to parallel the relationship between greater maturity and status attainment in the legitimate economy.

Finally, we examine similarities in the age curves of athletes and criminals, which provide an intriguing model for understanding similarities in the interaction between age stratification and other dimensions of inequality in both legitimate and illegitimate opportunity structures.

Youth Inequality and the Concentration of "Ordinary" Property Crime Offending Among Adolescents

We begin with a consideration of the age pattern for involvement in "ordinary" property crimes such as burglary, robbery, and larceny. Such crimes typically involve younger persons, are not very profitable, have high social visibility, are risky (in terms of costs and benefits), and are sometimes physically demanding. Age-specific arrest rates for such crimes typically rise rapidly with age among preteens and peak during the mid-teens, after which age-specific rates drop sharply. Specific features of the age curve (e.g., peak age, precise shape and slope of the curve before and after the peak age) vary somewhat among different crimes in this group, and vary also over time and between males and females, blacks and whites.

Key questions about the age distribution of ordinary property crime in the contemporary United States center on the extreme skewness of the curve. Why do the age-specific rates of offending rise so sharply during the early teens and peak during the mid-teens? Why do the rates then drop with equal abruptness during the late teens and early twenties and continue to taper off with advancing age?

The "stress and storm" of adolescence have been noted since ancient times, and some increase in "delinquency" can be seen simply as a stage of growing up. The traditional sociological position has been that a certain amount of experimental misbehavior seems to be natural to youth. Sociological interpretations have also acknowledged the role of biological and psychological factors: During early adolescence young people are not only undergoing powerful hormonal changes that produce strong sensate experiences, but—unlike younger children—they possess the physical prowess required to commit the ordinary property crimes, at the same time that their stage of cognitive development limits prudence concerning the consequences of their behavior.

The inequality of youth has also had a central position in traditional sociological interpretations of the age curve of ordinary crimes. Adolescents become increasingly aware not only of the differences between what juveniles and adults are allowed to do (e.g., drink, have sex) and to have (e.g., automobiles, money), but also of the different sets of rules that adults apply to their children and to themselves. When awareness of this "double standard" and the conspicuous nature of adult freedoms is combined with youthful egocentrism, a feeling of oppression at the hands of adults is virtually inevitable, providing young people with a convenient rationale for misbehavior and rebellion.

Some decline in crime would therefore be expected as young people move into adult work roles, establish permanent relationships, and generally "settle down." Individuals become more accepting of societal norms, more comfortable in social relations, and more concerned with the meaning of life and their place in the scheme of things. Prudence increases with age and greater psychological maturity; the casual delinquencies of youth come to be seen as childish or foolish. With advancing age, declining physical skills eventually diminish the ability to carry out physically demanding crimes.

Physical Prime Explanation of the Age-Crime Curve

Some writers have argued that "nature" can explain these skewed distributions better than "nurture"—especially the precipitous drop in offending rates after the peak age. Because of the surprisingly cordial reception accorded at least one recent physiological explanation of the age-crime curve among some social scientists, we examine briefly Walter Gove's physical prime theory (1985) before proceeding with a more detailed examination of the relationship between inequality and youth crime.[1]

Focusing mainly on physically demanding crimes, Gove holds that the abrupt decline in risky physical crime with age is due largely to an equally abrupt decline in physical prime and to hormonal changes. Gove writes:

> To explain the rapidity of the decline in deviant behavior with age, we need to look at physical strength, energy, psychological drive, and the reinforcement effect of the adrenaline high. We have pointed out that these variables peak at the same time deviant behavior peaks and suggest that their rapid decline is a major contribution to the rapid decline in deviant behavior. If this argument is correct, it would tend to explain why the age-deviance relationship seems to be universal across societies and historic time (1985: 138).

Gove also asserts that the principal sociological theories of crime are unable to explain the inverse relationship between age and crime since (according to Gove) these theories predict an amplification in crime with age: "This is particularly true of labelling theory, conflict theory, and, to a

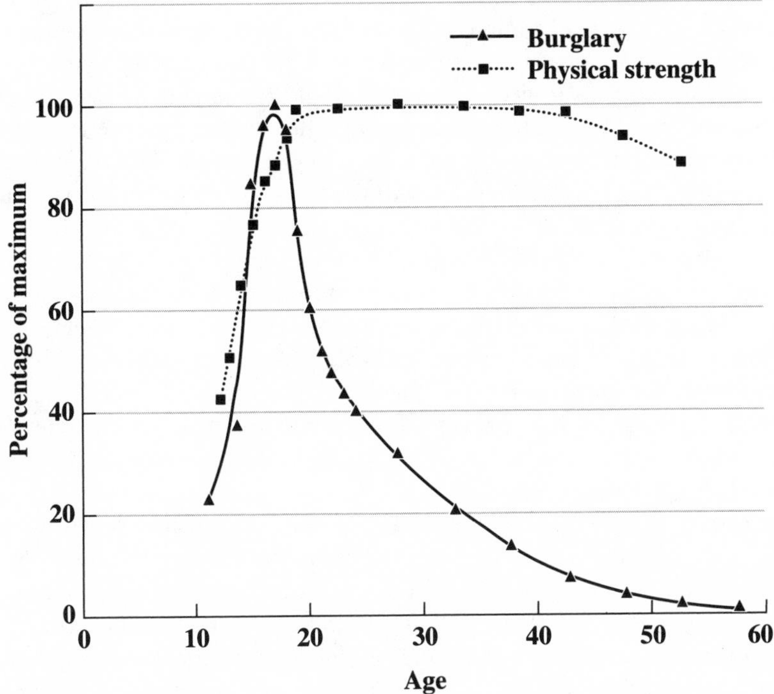

Fig. 5.2. Age curves for burglary and physical strength. Data from Montoye 1975; Tecumesh Community Health Survey; *Uniform Crime Reports* 1990.

slightly lesser extent, control theory, functional theory, and the theory of differential association" (p. 123). This argument has been challenged both by Tittle (1988) and by Steffensmeier and Allan (1990), who show the parsimony of major sociological theories in explaining both the amplification of crime with age for career criminals and the desistance from crime that is reflected in the age curves for common-law crimes.

To assess the argument that the rapid decline in the age-crime curve is matched by a corresponding decline in the age curve for physical fitness, Figure 5.2 compares the age curves for physical strength and burglary. Physical strength is regarded as a robust proxy for maximum work performance (Shock et al. 1984; Spirduso 1982), is strongly correlated with other performance criteria for the evaluation of fitness (Finch and Schneider 1985), and is singled out by Gove as a physical prime indicator. Burglary is a predatory offense requiring the kinds of physical advantage (e.g., strength, endurance) and risk-taking described by Gove. To provide a common metric, both the physical prime variable and the crime data are expressed as percentages of the maximum rate at the peak age (which is 100 percent).

Consistent with other evidence on biological aging, Figure 5.2 strongly contradicts the physical prime theory.[2] Specifically, the peak age for high-risk, physically demanding crimes such as burglary is much younger than the peak age for physical abilities; and the speed of the decline from peak age is slow or gradual for the fitness variables but very abrupt for the high-risk crimes. The research literature on biological aging (see especially Shock et al. 1984) indicates that peak functioning is typically reached between the ages of 25 and 30 for those physical variables—strength, stamina, recovery capacity, motor control, and speed of movement—plausibly assumed to affect one's ability to commit crimes. Although decline sets in shortly thereafter, it is not abrupt. Rather, the decline is gradual, almost imperceptible, until the mid-fifties or so, after which a steady decline persists through the final period of life.

Other commonly mentioned physical variables, such as testosterone levels, peak in the late teens but then remain at or near the peak level until middle age or older (Shock et al. 1984). In short, while it is reasonable to assume that biological/physiological factors such as strength and testosterone help explain the increase in delinquent behavior during early adolescence, neither can explain the abrupt decline in the age-crime curve after the peak age. Only in the sphere of age-stratified roles and statuses do changes of corresponding abruptness occur.

Age Stratification and Youth Crime

In many respects, young people constitute an oppressed minority, but a minority that eventually acquires full majority status. It is significant that juveniles today are referred to as "minors" and that the age at which juveniles legally assume adult status is commonly referred to as the "age of majority." Youth inequality as an aspect of age stratification is a phenomenon found in all societies, but the intensity of the inequality and the abruptness of the transition to adult status varies among groups, over time, and across cultures. If the concentration of offending among adolescents is in part a rebellion against perceived inequality in status, then one would expect that the age-crime curve would vary in response to variation in the nature of youth inequality and the transition to adulthood.

Where youth inequality in comparison with older groups is less marked, or where the transition to "majority" (adult) status is gradual, the age curve for ordinary property crimes should be less skewed (i.e., flatter). Where the inequality of youth (or the perceived inequality) is more pronounced or the transition to adulthood more abrupt, the curve should be more sharply skewed, with a younger peak age and steeper slopes. A review of historical, cross-cultural, and intergroup data indicates that this is indeed the case (see discussion below).

For example, Greenberg (1977) and others (Steffensmeier et al. 1989; Steffensmeier and Allan 1990) have observed that the current highly skewed age curve for index crimes reflects the intensification of youth inequality during this century through processes of industrial and postindustrial economic change that have produced a narrower and more rigidly scheduled time-span for the transition to adulthood. Modell writes: "the nineteenth-century family allowed far greater latitude, providing individuals were prepared to satisfy familial obligations. 'Timely' action to nineteenth-century families consisted of helpful response in times of trouble; in the twentieth century, timeliness connotes adherence to a schedule" (1976: 30).

That "schedule" in modern societies involves two distinct and highly stratified phases of "growing up." Phase 1 (roughly ages 12/13 to 16/17) involves loss of childhood roles but continued segregation from productive adult roles, making the transitions both ambiguous and stressful. Phase 2 (roughly ages 17 to 22) involves role acquisition rather than role loss, coupled with role transitions that mark the beginning of movement into majority status. Despite the stresses of making crucial life choices, these appear to be largely positive experiences.

Phase 1 is characterized by youth inequality and pressures to "fit in" or "find oneself." Although autonomy expands somewhat, it is still restricted and coupled with low responsibility, lack of meaningful integration into the adult world, and social expectations that young people will engage in socially disapproved behavior.

In *Growing Up Absurd*, Goodman (1960) concluded that the greatest problem facing adolescents today is their own *uselessness*. Segregated from productive activities and dependent upon adults for economic and emotional support, youth are a powerless class in modern societies. Their exclusion from the adult labor market makes it more difficult for youth to support their leisure activities and generates fears of adult unemployment. A sense of oppression and of being subject to a double standard fosters alienation and encourages the formation of adolescent subcultures oriented toward consumption and hedonistic pursuits. The latter are enhanced further by the media and other influences that have heightened the subjectively defined needs of youth (Greenberg 1977, 1985). Furthermore, young teens (roughly ages 13 to 16) in modern societies are faced with expanding opportunities and greater sources of reinforcement for offending:

money, sex, autonomy, identity claims, various forms of substance abuse, strong sensate experiences, and peers who similarly value independence, or even defiance of conventional morality.

Phase 2 is the period of transition from juvenile (minority) status to adult (majority) status in contemporary society, as the individual crosses the boundary between the family and the adult world. It is characterized by a clear-cut shift from relative dependence and powerlessness to high autonomy and enhanced status. A period of expanding responsibilities, this phase involves the taking on of most of the rights and obligations of adulthood, and meeting the social expectation that young adults "settle down." This phase is the beginning of the end of youth inequality.

Unlike minorities that are confined to subordinate status for their whole lives, most young people eventually mature out of that status, and late adolescence is the period during which youths both anticipate and begin to assume adult roles and behaviors. This is the time when young people take significant charge of their lives and make choices (often stressful ones) that will to a large extent shape the rest of the life course (e.g., work, college, military, marriage). They face the sudden transition from dependence on families for income, status, and security to enhanced status and greater responsibilities for jobs, further education, and families. What is important *structurally* is not necessarily the actual assumption of adult-like roles but, owing to the powerful effects of anticipatory socialization, the *availability* of adult roles at the societal level.

We summarize below the important changes that mark the shift toward adult (majority) status during late adolescence and early adulthood and that thus help explain the sharp decline in ordinary property crime offending that occurs at this time. The changes, which take place in at least five major spheres, are driven largely by age-stratification processes of the larger society and their ripple effects on social control, social integration, and social development:

1. greater access to legitimate sources of material goods and excitement: jobs, credit, alcohol, sex, and so forth
2. age-graded norms: externally, increased expectation of maturity and responsibility; internally, anticipation of assuming adult roles, coupled with reduced subjective acceptance of deviant roles and the threat they pose to entering adult status
3. peer associations and lifestyle: reduced orientation to same-age/same-sex peers and increased orientation toward persons of the opposite sex and/or persons who are older or more mature
4. increased legal and social costs for deviant behavior
5. patterns of illegitimate opportunities: with the assumption of adult roles,

opportunities increasing for crimes (for example, gambling, fraud, and employee theft) that are less risky, more lucrative, and/or less likely to be reflected in official statistics.

These same social factors, responsible for the sharp reduction in age-specific crime rates for the *majority* of those in their late teens and early twenties, also work to sustain a high rate of offending over a longer portion of the life cycle among labeled persons and among youths who become alienated from conventional society and remain bonded to unconventional networks (Hagan 1991; Tittle 1988). Thornberry and Christenson (1984), using the Philadelphia cohort data, documented the manner in which arrest histories suppress subsequent opportunities for work. Similarly, minority youths enter adulthood with less access to good jobs and other valued roles normally associated with adult status that facilitate desistance from delinquent behavior.

For some groups, in other words, the ordinarily integrative processes are disintegrative instead, forging a subpopulation of perpetual adolescents, as it were, or—worse still—"career criminals." As noted earlier, the power of sociological theories lies in their parsimony in explaining *both* the desistance from crime by the majority of the population during late adolescence *and* the amplification of criminal behavior and identity for the subpopulation of career offenders.

Minority Differences in the Age-Crime Curve

A youth-inequality interpretation of the age curve for ordinary crimes explains the rapid drop-off in age-specific offending rates for youths who enter majority status in late adolescence or early adulthood. But what about those youths who are less able to "mature" out of their minority status? To complete the maturation process successfully, it is crucial to have access to productive activities—such as college attendance or employment at adequate wages. In the inner cities of this nation, where the labor market for young adults is dominated by marginal jobs with low hours, low pay, high turnover, and limited benefits and opportunities for advancement, the other goals of a conventional life—marriage, family, community involvement—are more difficult to attain, and the proportion of the population still attracted to illegitimate alternatives will be greater (Allan and Steffensmeier 1989; Greenberg 1977).

For black inner-city youths, the high level of youth inequality that characterizes modern societies is compounded by the problems of living in a racist society, and they are less able to leave behind the inequality of

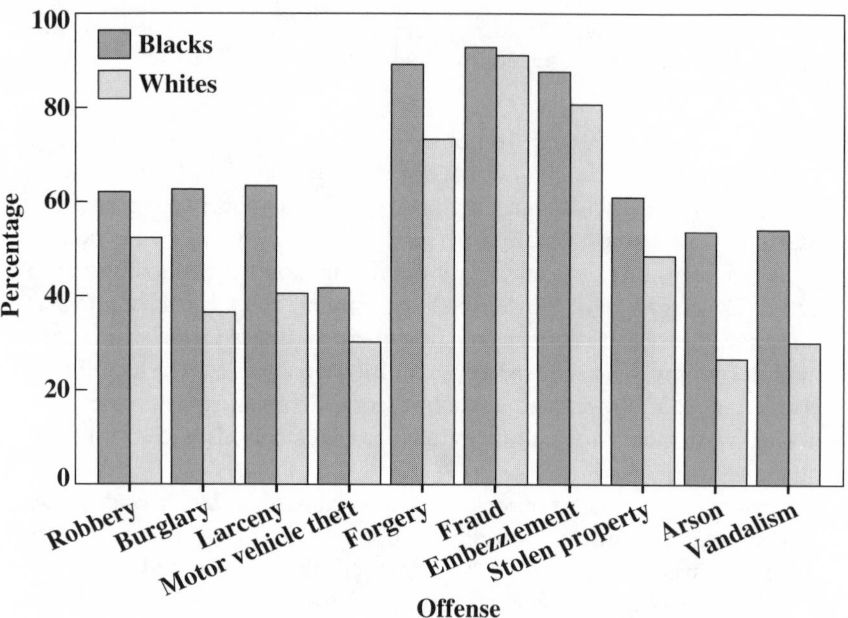

Fig. 5.3. Adult property crime arrests, 1990. Based on *Uniform Crime Reports* arrest data for 1980. This figure shows the percentage of total arrests accounted for by adults of each race, after controlling for population differences between adults (18 and older) and juveniles. In other words, for each race and arrest category, the percentages represent what the adult percentage of all arrests would be if the population were equally divided between adults and juveniles. The actual formula used is (adult arrest rate)/(adult arrest rate + juvenile arrest rate), calculated separately for each arrest category and each race.

youth status (W. J. Wilson 1987; Jaynes and Williams 1989). As they move into young adulthood they continue to experience limited access to the adult labor market. The inequality perspective predicts that levels of adult offending among blacks will therefore continue to be higher than those among whites, and that the proportion of total black crime that is committed by black adults will be greater than the proportion of total white crime that is committed by white adults.

This hypothesis is confirmed by Figure 5.3, which compares the percentage of black and white adults arrested for property crimes (controlling for differences in juvenile and adult populations).[3] Across all crime categories, the adult percentage of arrests (APA) is greater for blacks than for whites, in some cases strongly so. Significantly, the property crime categories for which the black APA is closest to the white APA are those categories for which blacks might be assumed to have less access to criminal opportunity: fraud, forgery, and embezzlement.

The inequality perspective would also predict that conditions of increased economic stress on minority populations would increase the adult percentage of arrests still further among minorities, at least in the case of economically motivated crimes. A comparison of black and white APAs for 1970, 1980, and 1990 reveals that black APAs for most property crimes increased over the two-decade period that witnessed deterioration of inner-city conditions and growth of the urban underclass (W. J. Wilson 1987). White APAs were more likely to have remained stable (or declined), as was the case with black APAs for violent crimes and many other non-economic categories. Finally, the age-stratification model would predict greater longevity in the offending careers for black offenders than for white offenders, a pattern confirmed in the cohort and "criminal careers" research (Wolfgang et al. 1987).

Finally, a caveat: contextual variations in the age-crime curve across population subgroups will tend to be fairly small, since we would expect the age-stratification processes of the larger society to powerfully affect all population subgroups within a given society. As we discuss next, the contextual effects of age stratification will be much greater when comparing age-crime distributions across cultures and historical periods.

Cross-cultural and Historical Differences in the Age-Crime Curve

The hypothesized relationship between age stratification and the steep rise and fall in the age curve for ordinary property crime is also supported by cross-cultural and historical differences in the age-crime curve. If age-inequality is indeed a major determinant of the skewed shape of that curve in contemporary society, then a flatter shape would be predicted for societies and for historical periods in which the culture provides for a smoother transition from youth to adulthood.

For example, in small preindustrial societies, the passage to adult status is relatively simple and continuous. Formal "rites of passage" at relatively early ages (compared with the modern United States) avoid much of the status ambiguity and role conflict that torment American adolescents. Youths often begin to assume responsible and economically productive roles well before they reach full physical maturity. It is not surprising, therefore, to find that such societies have significantly flatter and less skewed age-crime patterns (see Steffensmeier et al. 1989 for a review).

Much the same is true for earlier periods in the history of the United

States and other industrial nations. The traditional school calendar, with its long summer vacations, testifies to the integral economic roles of youths when agriculture was the dominant economic activity of the nation and the help of young people was crucial to the harvesting of many crops. Youth economic productivity continued through the early years of industrialization when wages were so low that working-class children were expected to leave school at an early age and help to support their families. The responsible roles assumed by many youths in earlier periods forestalled the feelings of rebellion seen among contemporary teens who are isolated from truly productive roles within their families.

The past century, however, has witnessed a radical move away from a family-based economy. The labor surplus created by industrialization freed families from dependence on the labor of their dependents. The course to adulthood came to involve more nonfamilial institutions, especially those concerned with training and occupation, coupled with greater freedom from familial obligations. The shift toward greater dependence and economic "uselessness" of contemporary youths began around the turn of the century when, in an efffort to drive wages up, unions supported reforms that limited the work of women and children. Although many youths do hold jobs today, they do not typically contribute their wages to family support, but use them to support leisure activities and other "lifestyle" consumption patterns dictated by media advertising and peer pressures. Historical data also suggest that contemporary age-crime curves are much more skewed than in the past (Greenberg 1977; Steffensmeier et al. 1989).

Age and Status Attainment in Property Crime Offending

> Vertical social mobility [status attainment] functions for criminal persons as well as for noncriminal, with criminals being "on the make" in their status framework as well as others. (Lemert 1951: 323)

Youth are largely blocked from involvement in lucrative property crimes by the same mechanisms of age-stratification that shape youth inequality in the arena of legitimate opportunity structures as well as youth motivation for involvement in high-risk, low-yield crimes. The relatively flat age-crime curves found for FBI arrest data on fraud and gambling (shown in Figure 5.1) only hint at the age distributions to be expected for *highly profitable* frauds and gambling enterprises.

It is well recognized that age contributes to status attainment within the legitimate opportunity structure through the cultivation of skill and the acquisition and accumulation of experience, educational credentials, and

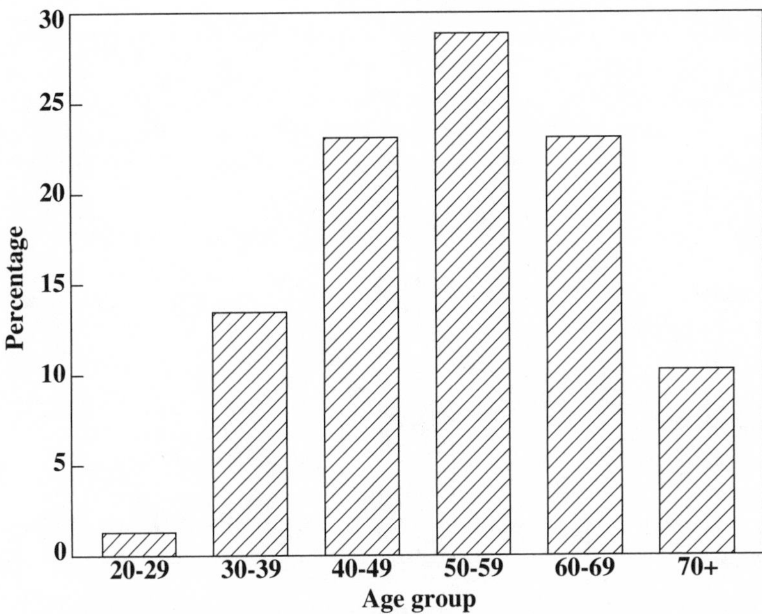

Fig. 5.4. Age distribution of Pennsylvania "racketeers," 1990. All ages are as of 1990. Data compiled from the Pennsylvania Crime Commission's *1990 Report.*

financial resources. Since at least the publication of Sutherland's *Professional Thief* (1937), criminologists have recognized that similar status-attainment processes are at work in illegitimate opportunity structures. Advancement into higher-ranking criminal occupations such as "con man" or "racketeer" depends upon age-related factors such as skill, experience, financial success, and the ability to avoid imprisonment (although a prison record can also enhance an individual's credibility in the underworld, just as educational credentials do in the business world). And, as in the business world, the right "family connections" can sometimes enable a younger criminal to skip several rungs on the ladder.

Unfortunately, relatively little is known about the age distribution of persons who commit the more lucrative crimes, but fragmentary evidence suggests that the majority are middle-aged or older. Figure 5.4 shows the age distribution of persons identified as major gambling and loansharking racketeers in the state of Pennsylvania.[4] It is apparent that the age curves for racketeering not only peak much later, but also tend not to decline with age. Most gambling and loanshark kingpins are between their mid-forties and mid-sixties, and some continue to practice their trade well into their

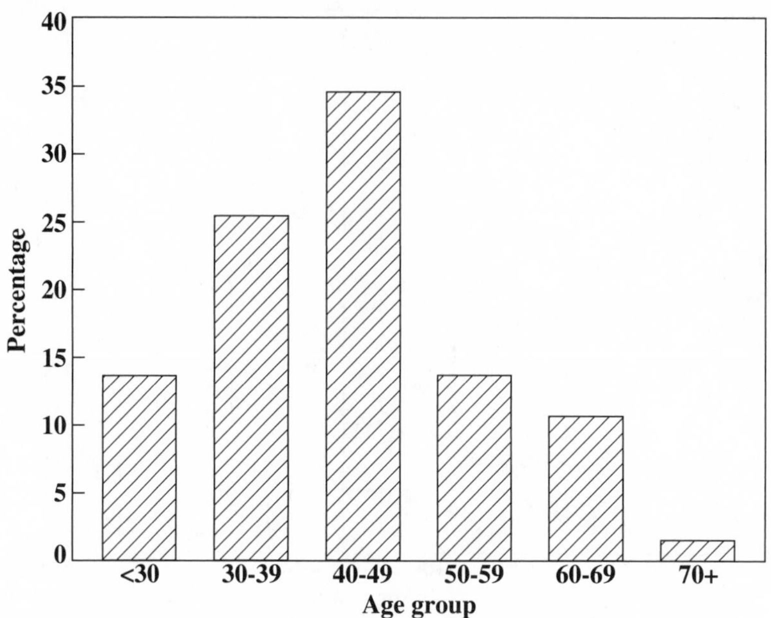

Fig. 5.5. Age distribution of "wayward capitalists." Data from the *New York Times*, 1987–90. The ages used are as of the dates these articles were published.

seventies. Evidence suggests that other lucrative rackets in the underworld are also largely populated by older persons. Fences of stolen goods, for example, are typically middle-aged or older (Walsh 1977; Steffensmeier 1986).

Still less is known of the age distribution of "respectable" or "upperworld" offenders who commit lucrative business crimes such as fraud, price fixing, bribery, and so forth. Of course, one would not expect youths to hold the types of legitimate positions that provide access to such criminal opportunities. Although data on the age distribution of such crimes are not plentiful, media reports typically include information on age of offenders in business crime cases that attract public attention. Figure 5.5 displays the age curve for persons who committed "lucrative" business crimes during the 1987 to 1990 period, using data extracted from articles on those crimes as reported in the *New York Times*. A lucrative crime is defined here as one involving gains of $25,000 or more.[5] Figure 5.5 reveals a wide age spread for persons engaged in highly profitable white-collar criminality but with a preponderance of middle-aged or older offenders. The modal age falls between ages 40 and 50.

These age figures from the survey of *New York Times* articles are consistent with other fragmentary evidence on the age distribution of lucrative forms of white-collar or corporate offending. Shapiro's investigation of securities fraud, for example, found the following age range for the "wayward capitalists" on whom age data were available: 6 percent were under 30, 30 percent were 30 to 39, 22 percent were 40 to 49, 21 percent were 50 to 59, 12 percent were 60 to 69, and 9 percent were over 70. Shapiro writes: "the majority of individual suspects are male, middle-aged, organizational leaders with considerable securities and/or industry experience—a far cry from the prototypical crime suspect" (1984:42).

These findings on lucrative kinds of white-collar criminality suggest how the age stratification of the larger society is reproduced in the world of crime. Many corporate/white-collar offenders apparently reach their peak level of criminality at about the time they reach the peak of their occupational careers. This correspondence partly reflects age-related opportunities for criminal behavior that emerge as a result of one's position within a firm that, either directly or indirectly, encourages shady business practices. But the involvement of older offenders also reflects the ongoing learning of perspectives favorable to law violation, as well as the accumulation of skills, insight, and wit, and the greater ability of older persons to inspire confidence in their victims.

The Age Curves of Athletes and Criminals: Physical Prime or Age Stratification

> In much of life, age is only a number. But in a boxing ring, age is everything. Especially when the rounds click by. (source unknown)

Our understanding of the relationship between age stratification and age patterns in crime can be illuminated further by examining the relationship between age and participation in sports. We suggest that physical prime and age-stratification variables contribute substantially to many criminal careers in much the same way that peak physical functioning and youth inequality contribute to athletic careers.

As anecdotal support for his linkage between physical prime and crime prime, Gove offers an analogy between sports and crime. At the age when some people are winning Olympic medals, others their age are busy committing assaults, robberies, and burglaries: "Both groups consist of young adults who withdraw from the field as they age" (1985: 139).

The comparison of criminality with athletics is a useful one (although we disagree with Gove's interpretation of that comparison). Adolescents who pursue sports (and/or delinquency) do so both for "fun" (including physical pleasure) and for a variety of social rewards such as status with their peers. Those who reduce their participation in sports upon leaving school (or even before), do so not because of a sudden decline in physical abilities, but because the assumption of new responsibilities (or the anticipation thereof) precludes many of the activities that used to occupy their spare time.

Many of the new adult responsibilities, moreover, provide social rewards exceeding those available from sports. Even athletically gifted young people may judge that other opportunities hold greater promise, so that those progressing into professional (or college) sports will disproportionately represent groups in society that have less access to conventional opportunities. The overrepresentation of blacks and Hispanics among professional athletes is thus not unlike their overrepresentation among those arrested for crimes. But for most "amateur" delinquents and criminals as for most "amateur" athletes, declining rates of participation have very little, if anything, to do with changes in level of physical functioning.

Ages of peak performance among professional athletes may conform closely to the ages of peak fitness cited earlier, however. Some reviews, for example, report that the ages of most champions (e.g., those in tennis, boxing, and baseball) fall between the mid-twenties and early thirties (Landers 1984; Wright 1989). Available data are not adequate to determine with any certainty whether the age distribution of crime over individual careers of professional criminals (at least those involved in physically demanding types of crime) corresponds more closely to the physical prime curves described above. However, it is reasonable to assume a closer fit than has been found for cross-sectional age-crime data.

Eventually, professional criminals—like professional athletes—reach a point in their lives when they seek less arduous careers. This is scarcely remarkable. (It is also a pattern widely recognized by criminologists.) Just as athletes eventually move on to less demanding activities and often seek opportunities in related fields such as sports broadcasting, so too a talented thief with appropriate resources and connections may seek a related career in fencing stolen property (Steffensmeier 1986). Sam Goodman, the fence studied by Steffensmeier, commented on his switch from burglary into fencing as follows: "I was tired of crawling in windows [was getting too old]. So, I had someone crawl into windows for me."

Implications

Our analysis has important implications not only for the inequality, age, and crime issue, but also for broader sociological and criminological concerns relating to patterns of criminality across the life cycle and to the effects of overall stratification processes on crime patterns.

First, much crime and delinquency can be seen as more-or-less isolated time-bound events (or brief series of events) that occur in the transition from childhood to and through adolescence, and that more or less cease during the actual transition from adolescence to adulthood. Yet we still know very little about the dynamics of termination of offending during the late teenage years and how this desistance is influenced by particular life events marking the transition from adolescence to adulthood, such as marriage, employment, college, joining the military, leaving the neighborhood, or finding new friends.

We do not yet know whether one or more of these key events is necessary to bring about termination, or, from among the many role changes that are occurring, which ones are more crucial in bringing about a crime reduction. Nor do we know whether the actual or the prospective assumption of these roles is more important. In light of the importance of anticipatory socialization, after the mid-teens, before youths actually assume the adult roles of work or college or marriage, the *expectation* of soon assuming these roles already contributes to greater prudence about committing the high-risk, exploratory delinquencies of younger teens. To illustrate, picture the 17-year-old entering his senior year in high school, who—wanting to ensure his chances of acceptance into college or the military—suddenly begins to display a semblance of planned competence that entails less "goofing off" and more "buckling down."

Theoretical and empirical work is needed both to elaborate the systems of norms that channel age-appropriate behavior and to gauge just how age norms and accompanying sanctions operate to govern behavior and interaction during the adolescence-to-adulthood transition. Little empirical work has been done in this area in the decades that have intervened since the work of Neugarten and colleagues (1965).

Both cross-sectional and longitudinal research are needed to further explicate the manner in which the adolescence-to-adulthood phase molds the characteristics and behaviors of individuals, and how this molding is affected by the changes in social expectations, the roles the individuals play, the situations they encounter, the individuals who become significant others to them, and the subjective meanings attached to all these changes.

Useful reviews of cross-sectional and prospective longitudinal surveys for capturing the onset and termination of event histories or experiences—including the collecting of information on both crime and the adolescence-to-adulthood transition—are available in Hagan and Palloni (1988) and in Blumstein et al. (1986).

Second, just as the adolescence-to-adulthood transition may lead to a sharp reduction in exploratory, outwardly directed, and antisocial forms of crime/deviance, it simultaneously may lead to increases in other kinds of crime/deviance such as suicide, substance abuse, or violence between intimates that arise because young adults face stressful life choices, more intimate and havoc-producing relationships, and social environments where heavy drinking or drug use is expected (e.g., in college or the military). The adolescence-to-adulthood phase may be crime-reducing in some ways but crime-producing in other ways, so that the broader age-crime relationship will depend on the forms of crime/deviance we are referring to.

Third, although Gove is unsuccessful in explaining the age-crime relationship, his biosocial approach does offer more promise than earlier theories of biological determinism such as those of Lombroso, Hooton, or Sheldon. Such theories sought to explain crime in terms of alleged biological *differences* between criminals and noncriminals. Social scientists have generally found such deterministic approaches not only inimical to but incompatible with sociological theory (see, e.g., Merton and Montagu 1940). Since Gove's approach is based on physiological developmental processes common to both criminals and noncriminals, it has the potential for contributing new insights to traditional social and psychological perspectives on crime (Akers 1985).

Nevertheless, sociologists wanting to include biological variables in sociological models of behavior should proceed cautiously, forewarned that the state of the art of knowledge about biological aging is far less sophisticated than many social scientists believe. The quantitative assessment of physical fitness is one of the most complex and controversial problems in applied physiology. For example, there is no general agreement on what constitutes fitness for withstanding various types of stress, or on what measurements allow valid comparisons to be made among individuals exposed to the same stress. Furthermore, much of the research makes the erroneous assumption that cross-sectional age differences, essential for examining physical functioning at different points in the life span, are always accurate indicators for longitudinal changes over the life spans of individuals.

Consequently, there is considerable uncertainty in the research literature pertaining to how fitness characteristics change with age in various populations of subjects, the time course of these changes, the effect of physical inactivity, the impact of disability and disease, and the separate impact of gender (Buskirk and Segal 1989). Sociologists and other social scientists may be surprised to find out that as much is known about social aging as is known about biological aging.

Fourth, age has always permeated the sociological imagination, and sociologists have much to contribute toward understanding the aging process and its effects on behavior and personality, including crime, alcoholism, mental illness, and other forms of deviance. Riley et al. write, "Because of their broad concern with both social structures and the lives of individuals in society, sociologists have taken the lead in integrating the divergent and often confusing biological, psychological, and sociological perspectives in the ways individuals grow older" (1988: 248).

A central theme of sociological work on aging is that the aging process varies with social structure (e.g., stratification) and social change. On the one hand, there is plasticity in the aging process within each individual life, as social processes interact with biological and psychological processes to influence the ways in which people change from childhood through adulthood to old age. On the other hand, there is collective diversity among individuals in the ways they grow older, depending on their locations in a society, their relationships with other people, their lifestyle adaptations (including how active or physically fit they are), and their development of a social self. This diversity was noted earlier when reference was made to comparisons across cultures and historical periods in the presence or absence of "adolescence" as a life stage and its bearing on the age-crime relationship, particularly with respect to age of peak criminality and the rate of decline from the peak age.

There is a need, in particular, to integrate the research on crime and age stratification for examining the effects of race and class on the proportionate criminal involvement of adults as compared with juveniles. Although their age distributions will be more similar than different (see earlier discussion), the age curve for common-law property crimes will decline more rapidly for whites and youths with middle-class backgrounds than for blacks and youths with working-class and lower-class backgrounds. The data we presented earlier showed that black arrest rates drop off less sharply than white arrest rates. Elsewhere, Hagan (1991) has presented data that suggest a parallel outcome with regard to social classes—that arrest rates of working-class youth decline less rapidly than rates of nonworking-class youth. Apparently, access to productive economic activities remains more restricted for working-class youth; also, detrimental labeling effects and identification with a delinquent subculture interfere more strongly with adult status-attainment outcomes of working-class than nonworking-class youth.

Finally, there is an obvious need for research on lucrative forms of property crime within both the underworld and the upperworld, to determine how age stratification and inequality in the larger society are reproduced in the world of crime. Unfortunately, criminologists too often treat "delinquency" as the endpoint of their research. That approach has contributed to a somewhat distorted view of crime in the field.

Conclusion

We hope our analysis will encourage researchers interested in age-related patterns of crime to broaden their vision to include notions of inequality and stratification. For example, one of the established findings in sociological criminology is that conventional crime tends to peak in adolescence and declines thereafter. But, owing to contextual variations in age-stratification processes, the parameters of the age-crime curve such as peak age and speed of decline from peak age differ across historical periods and cultures. In addition, there are differences in age curves across offenses that reflect age-related status-attainment processes of the larger society. The latter in particular remains a relatively unexplored area in criminology. There is a need here to distinguish crime opportunities relative to whether they involve lucrative or petty crime and whether they are situated mainly in the upperworld or the underworld. Differentiating crime opportunities in this fashion helps to decipher how age-stratification processes influence age differences in crime by making differentiated options available to young and older persons for solving economic problems, seeking excitement, and so forth; and by creating or providing constraints that influence the decision to adopt a particular option.

In recent years, an increasing number of criminologists seem prone to adopt a biological or physical explanation of crime, including the age-crime relationship. A half-century ago, Merton and Montagu (1940) warned that we are still almost completely in a world of the unknown as regards the relationship between criminality and physical functioning or the endocrine system, and to resort to physical explanations of criminality is to attempt to explain the known with the unknown. The situation has changed some since Montagu's assessment, but (historically) biosocial treatments of crime that are sensible and data-driven are still exceedingly difficult to locate. Social scientists contemplating the inclusion of biological variables in their models are cautioned to comb carefully the biological literature and to forbear interpretations that go beyond what biologists themselves hold. An age-stratification perspective provides a more robust explanation of many and varied features of crime across the life span.

Crime and Inequality in Eighteenth-Century London

JOHN BEATTIE

Inequality in the distribution of wealth, of status, of power, of opportunity—indeed in all aspects of life—has been the ruling condition in Western societies over most of their history. Until the possibility of equality began to be raised in the eighteenth century, it was a fundamental assumption that poverty was an inevitable condition ordained by God and that society could not be maintained without the cement that a hierarchical social order provided, without the stability and permanence that arose from rank and degree. In this view, social order depended on the natural harmony that sprang from the fixed and settled relationships of men (and, through men, women) in a hierarchy of status groups bound one to the other by obligation and deference. Indeed, such groups were long conceived as but links in a much larger scheme of order—a "great chain of being"—that bound mankind to God and the hierarchy of Heaven, as well as to the more lowly creatures of God's creation on earth (Lovejoy 1942: 59, 189–207). There was little room in such a view of society for notions of equality among men or between men and women.

It is true that by the fifteenth century in England, after the erosion of feudal obligations, few distinctions of rank and privilege were set out in law. Equality before the magistrate and protection from oppression by government were universally claimed by the eighteenth century and were widely regarded as rights and liberties that were part of the birthright of the English. But formal protections against the overweening power of government and against illegality in the courtroom did not translate into entitlements to equal treatment in other areas of life—into the recognition of the equal worth of the individual and access to the full rights of citizenship. The idea of equality was in the process of formation by the eighteenth century, but, as J. R. Pole has said in his study of egalitarian ideas in American history, it "had to struggle for existence in an almost entirely hostile world, for it was subversive of all received and almost all conceivable ideas of order" (Pole 1978: 5–6).

In the premodern world, the acceptance of fundamental inequality—of a radically unequal division of property and of inequities in the distribution of power—inevitably shaped the criminal law, the offenses that were prosecuted, and the way the law was administered. In exploring that vast area, I must draw some sharp limits around the subject of this chapter. I concentrate on English material in the early modern period, primarily the seventeenth and eighteenth centuries, when evidence about crime and the administration of the law becomes reasonably plentiful. I deal mainly with crimes against property—principally robbery, burglary, and larceny—the offenses most likely to have arisen from poverty and deprivation, and, incidentally, the offenses most commonly prosecuted before the major courts in England. And because the effects of poverty were experienced most starkly in urban areas, I deal with the patterns of prosecuted crime in London, the largest city in England and indeed the largest city in Europe by the beginning of the eighteenth century. The broad theme of the chapter is the relationship of poverty and crime in London. But I pay particular attention to the patterns of women's crime, because in the period we are dealing with women were unusually prominent among property offenders at the Old Bailey, and women were the targets of some of the principal responses of the authorities to the problem of crime in London. The prosecution of women, and their experience in the life and work of the metropolis, are among our central concerns. But we need to place those matters within the broad pattern of prosecuted crime in London in general and within the wide range of initiatives being taken by the state to combat what the authorities clearly regarded as the growing menace of property offenses in London. As a way of putting this larger subject into context, I begin with a brief discussion of the way in which patterns of prosecution for property crime have been treated in the historical literature over the past twenty years.

Historical Patterns of Prosecution

The historical study of crime in England is bedeviled by the problem of data. It was only in 1805 that the state began to collect information about the numbers of accused sent to trial for serious offenses and about the outcomes of those trials. By the second half of the nineteenth century systematic evidence was being gathered of the work of the magistrates' courts and of the by then greatly increased numbers of accused being dealt with under summary jurisdiction (Gatrell and Hadden 1972). National judicial data thus became available in the nineteenth century in increasing detail and gave rise to the practice of criminology. But the recent flowering of interest in the social history of crime before 1800 has required historians to build up the pattern of recorded offenses case by case from the court records, and for the most part county by county, the jurisdictions within which the major courts operated. The incompleteness of the surviving court records (and the labor required for such detailed work on documents that are all too frequently difficult to decipher) has placed some serious restrictions on the geographical range and the time periods of the work reported on so far. But by putting that work together with Gatrell's recent reworking and penetrating analysis of the nineteenth-century data, it is possible to discern a broad pattern of prosecutions for property offenses over the 400 years from the sixteenth to the early twentieth centuries that can be summarized briefly.[1]

Over this long period there were frequent short-term fluctuations in the level of prosecutions for property offenses, fluctuations that were occasionally very striking from year to year. But a more general and long-term pattern has also become clear. From the 1550s into the early decades of the twentieth century, two long periods of significantly increasing prosecutions for property crime can be discerned, separated by two equally long periods of stagnating or even falling rates. The first period in which prosecutions rose to exceptionally high levels ran from the last decades of the sixteenth century to the second quarter of the seventeenth, particularly in the 1590s and again in the 1620s and 1630s. This was also a period of sharply rising population and of serious economic difficulties for large numbers of the poor especially. The Elizabethan and early seventeenth-century surge in population perhaps in itself explains some of the increase in charges for property offenses in that period, but it cannot account for the sharpness of the upturn (Lawson 1986). These increasing levels of indictments came to an end in the 1630s and were followed by a very long period, stretching well into the middle decades of the next century, in which there was a leveling off both in the rate of population increase and in prosecutions for crimes against property. This long period of greater stability in prosecutions was punctuated from time to time by a number of short-term reversals and, as we will see, there was also a significant general exception in London, where prosecutions fluctuated strongly and tended if anything to increase over time. But over most of the country the trend from the mid-seventeenth to the mid-eighteenth centuries was for prosecutions for property offenses to remain relatively stable and even to decline gradually (Sharpe 1984: 57–59).

By the second half of the eighteenth century this pattern changed again as prosecutions began to increase in many parts of England. There was a strong upturn in crimes against property in the 1780s, but the sharpest increases were to come in the nineteenth century. From the end of the Napoleonic wars in 1815 into the middle decades of the century, huge increases in prosecutions raised the levels of indictable offenses in England and Wales to heights hitherto unimagined. Prosecutions rose sevenfold between 1805 and 1842. The population also increased very rapidly; indeed, the population of England and Wales increased by two and a half times between 1780 and 1850. And in this period of social and economic transformation that is at the heart of the Industrial Revolution, an increasing proportion of that population was concentrated in urban areas and in manufacturing work. Again, an increase in population goes some way toward explaining a rapid increase in prosecutions for property crime, but in fact the huge advances in offenses brought to court outpaced the population growth by a considerable margin. Over the first half of the nineteenth century the rate of property crime increased by more than four times (Gatrell 1980: 239). The number of charges grew to such an extent that many cases hitherto tried before judges and juries at quarter sessions and assizes were shifted to summary trial before a magistrate in a massive reorganization of court jurisdictions in the middle decades of the century (Gatrell and Hadden 1972: 355–58; Philips 1977: 132–36).

That surge of prosecutions peaked in the 1840s, and once again a period of rapid increase was followed by one of stability, even of decline, in the levels of indicted crime. The second half of the nineteenth century saw steadily declining levels of prosecutions in England and Wales, even though the population continued to increase strongly. Gatrell has shown that between the 1860s and the end of the nineteenth century the rate of indictable crime declined by 43 percent before rising again in the difficult economic times before the First World War and again in the two decades between the First and Second World Wars (Gatrell 1980: 281–83).

There has thus been no steady advance of recorded crimes against property in England over the past 400 years, not even since the onset of the massive transformations brought on by the Industrial Revolution and the urbanization of the nineteenth century. Rather, the pattern of prosecutions suggests that there have been periods in which the level and the rate of charges of property crime have increased significantly, and others—quite long periods—in which the rate of such offenses has stabilized or even fallen.

How such patterns might be explained has given rise to a good deal of debate. The long-term trends, especially the coincidence of periods of rising and falling levels of prosecution for property offenses with periods of changes in the standard of living of the working population, suggest that the incidence of such crime was tied to the ability of laboring families to support themselves by legitimate means. But broad trends in indictments are subject to myriad influences, and the study of shorter-term fluctuations—the changing pattern of prosecutions from year to year, for example—has seemed to a number of historians to provide a more reliable basis for such an argument. Several studies over the early modern period have shown that annual fluctuations in indictments for property offenses very often bear a relationship to changes in the standard of living of the working population. No one who has studied the court data is inclined to minimize their problems as guides to criminality, or to insist that there was a direct and invariable relationship between crime and changes in the economic circumstances of the working population. But the frequency with which short-run changes in the standard of living are reflected in the direction of change in prosecutions does suggest that property crime was in some respects a response to adversity.[2]

I pursue this argument at some length in this essay because it relates fundamentally to the theme of crime and inequality. But we must be conscious of the limitations of the data and also of the objections of those who consider judicial evidence in this period to be useful only as a guide to the activities of prosecutors, rather than of those who broke the law. There are clearly good reasons to be cautious. Until comparatively recently, the administration of the criminal law in England depended on the initiative of the victims of crime to undertake what was essentially a private prosecution. It was only toward the end of the nineteenth century that the police began to take on the burden of prosecuting even serious offenses (Hay and Snyder 1989). Before that, over most of the period we are dealing with, prosecutions depended on the willingness of victims to go to the trouble of bringing a charge and to bear the costs of a court case. And that in turn, it is clear, could have been influenced by their circumstances, by their attitudes toward particular offenses or a suspected offender, and by their view of the punishment that might follow upon conviction. More general anxieties operating in society about the level of contemporary crime could also act to encourage or impede prosecution. In addition, a decision to bring charges and initiate a prosecution might well have depended on the alternatives available—for example, how effective more private and informal means of extracting compensation, or revenge, might have been perceived to be. Such influences could have altered victims' behavior significantly over time and thus the changing level of prosecutions. The alternatives available to the magistrates who heard the charges in the first place and whose responsibility it was to send cases to trial could also have shaped the number of accused offenders appearing before the courts. And changes in the criminal law or in the administrative machinery—the development of a larger, more organized and better controlled police force in the nineteenth century, as an obvious example—might also have altered the proportion of cases being reported and brought forward for trial.[3]

In examining prosecutions for theft and related offenses in the late seventeenth and early eighteenth centuries we have reason to take account of such cautions. But I do so without abandoning the view that the patterns of changing prosecutions over time are also likely to bear some relationship to the real world of theft and robbery. The record of prosecutions in the courts was a product of numerous influences, and changes over the short term in the numbers of cases brought to trial do not reflect in any straightforward way either the changing incidence of crime or changes in prosecutorial vigor. The pattern of indictments, in this view, was the outcome of an interaction—an interaction that could easily vary over time, depending on a host of circumstances—between the number of transgressions that might have been charged and the willingness and ability of victims, the police, and the judicial authorities to bring suspects to trial. Public alarm—which amounted at times to serious panic—might well have encouraged victims to prosecute and the authorities to be more vigilant. Such anxiety was no doubt stirred when numerous reports of violent offenses appeared in the press, when the dock at the eight annual sessions at the Old Bailey, the main London court, was crowded with accused, and when large numbers of convicts were brought to a bloody end at the hanging place at Tyburn. But the relationship between alarm and prosecution, between state action and crime, is not likely to run simply one way. Crime had its own determinants, its own history, and the level and the character of offenses must have been shaped by changing local conditions and circumstances. My hope is that by bringing together a range of evidence relating to the criminal prosecution in London over a crucial 30-year period, the court record may be encouraged to yield up its fullest meaning.

Criminal Prosecutions in London, 1690–1720

The data I am concerned with arise from the cases prosecuted in the City of London, that is, the ancient city that by the eighteenth century formed only one part, though an immensely important part, of the larger metropolis of London. That metropolis had become the largest city of Europe by 1700 as the result of a striking increase in population and geographical reach over the previous century and a half. From a city of 120,000 in 1550, metropolitan London had grown to almost half a million inhabitants by the end of the seventeenth century. Within it, the population of the old City of London was about 100,000 at the end of the seventeenth century, roughly a fifth of the larger metropolis.[4]

The City was immensely important in both the capital and the country. It had long enjoyed a great deal of political influence because of its size and proximity to the royal court and the central administrative departments in Westminster, and because it was at the center of the financial world, a position that was being increasingly strengthened in the period we are dealing with (Brewer 1989; Dickson 1967). The City had also long been one of the main manufacturing centers of the country and continued to be so in the late seventeenth century. Work was shifting by then to the suburban parishes to the north and east, outside the walls of the old city, parishes that were freer of guild controls and growing rapidly in size and importance (Beier 1986: 115–40; George 1964 [1925]: chap. 4). But the City of London retained a large and diversified work force in the building trades, clothing and textiles, and a range of other enterprises. Along with the rest of the metropolis it was also a center of increasingly conspicuous consumption, a massive consumer of food, and stimulant of a national market in foodstuffs and other products (Fisher 1948: 37–50; Fisher 1954: 134–51; Wrigley 1967).

The City was wealthy and politically important. By the beginning of the eighteenth century it contained a plutocracy of vast wealth, an extensive and broadening middle class of merchants and shopkeepers, and larger numbers of more modestly prosperous masters and journeymen in skilled trades, in manufacturing, and in retail trades. But the City also included a larger unskilled working population who lived in the greatest insecurity because they depended on work that was by its nature uncertain and irregular. Many of the City's parishes were overcrowded and poor. Even in the wealthiest districts there were pockets of poverty. But in the largest wards on the outskirts of the City, which had grown particularly rapidly in the seventeenth century, a considerable proportion of their large populations lived constantly on the edge of disaster (Beier 1986; George 1964 [1925]). We will explore that more fully later as we inquire into the relationship between property crime and the social and economic landscape of the City. We will also return to the political and cultural makeup of the City when we consider responses to what seemed to many of the prosperous citizens of the capital to be the great threat of crime and disorder.

Old Bailey

Let us turn now to the record of the Old Bailey—or at least to the cases in that court that arose from the City of London, which are my main concern. The City and the urban parishes of the county of Middlesex, which formed the main components of the metropolis north of the River Thames, were separate jurisdictions in criminal matters. The City and the county had their own justices of the peace, their own courts of quarter sessions, their own clerical staffs. But because they shared a common jail—the prison of Newgate, located on the western edge of the City—they also shared the court sessions that dealt with the prisoners in that jail, and thus it was that the serious offenses arising across the whole of the metropolis north of the river, including most crimes against property, were dealt with at what was by far the busiest and most important criminal court in England, the Old Bailey.[5]

The total number of City cases over the 30 years we are dealing with is set out in Table 6.1. Two features of these figures are notable: the proportion of capital offenses and, even more striking, the number of women among the accused. Both require elucidation. But two related issues that are not disclosed in these data need to be addressed first because they help to put those matters into context. The first is the relatively high level of prosecutions in London compared to other parts of the country. The second is the absence from the data in Table 6.1 of charges for the most minor form of theft, petty larceny.

Eighteenth-century population estimates can only be inexact, but one can say roughly that over the three decades we are dealing with, the annual rate of prosecution for offenses against property from the City of London revealed in Table 6.1 was in the neighborhood of 140 per 100,000 population on average. That figure will strike a modern observer as remarkably low. But in its eighteenth-century context—and to contemporary observers—it was very high indeed. The equivalent rate in the county of Essex in the decade of the 1680s and in Sussex over the period 1690 to 1721 was in the neighborhood of 23. In Surrey, which included a large and

TABLE 6.1
Crime Against Property: City of London Cases at the Old Bailey, 1690–1720

Offenses	Total	Percent
Noncapital offenses		
Men	1,242	49.7
Women	1,256	50.3
Total	2,498	100.0
Capital offenses		
Men	993	56.5
Women	764	43.5
Total	1,757	100.0
All offenses		
Men	2,235	52.5
Women	2,020	47.5
Total	4,255	100.0

SOURCE: Sessions Files and Minute Books, Corporation of London Record Office.

growing urban area—in fact the southern suburbs of the metropolis of London along the south bank of the Thames—the rate over the late seventeenth and early eighteenth centuries was a little over 60 indictments per 100,000 population, considerably more than in the largely rural counties of Essex and Sussex, but still distinctly fewer than in the City of London (Beattie 1986: 182; Sharpe 1983: 145, 183).

There are, in addition, good reasons to think that the London rate was systematically reduced by the way that reports of property offenses were dealt with in the metropolis. Of course, in all jurisdictions prosecutions represent only a fraction of the crimes that might have been charged. But there is evidence that in London in this period the magistrates (who heard complaints and initiated criminal charges) regularly filtered out some of the most minor offenders by sending a significant number of suspects to Bridewell, the City's house of correction, instead of to trial at the sessions or the Old Bailey, perhaps because they were already feeling the pressure on the established courts of the numbers of offenders. The result was that few charges of the offense known as petty larceny—that is, thefts in which the stolen goods were valued at less than a shilling—were brought to trial in London.[6] Outside London, such offenses continued to be prosecuted at the county assizes and quarter sessions: they accounted for about 13 percent of the property crime brought to the Surrey courts over the period

1660 to 1800 and 25 percent in Sussex, for example (Beattie 1986: 147). But not at the Old Bailey, where virtually no petty larceny cases were heard. It is difficult to get an exact count of the number of accused diverted in this way from the London courts, but the records of the lord mayor (who was the City's most active magistrate during his year in office) suggest that these magisterial practices might have reduced the level of noncapital property offenses in the 1690s by at least a fifth or a quarter.[7] The rate of officially prosecuted property crime in London was thus even higher than the data in Table 6.1 reveal, and the difference between the reported crime in this urban world and the rest of the country even greater than we suggested earlier. And given the fact that women were more likely than men to be charged with minor offenses and (the lord mayor's records suggest) more likely to be sent to the house of correction instead of to trial, it is also clear that women would have been even more prominent among the defendants at the Old Bailey had these diversions not taken place.

The consequences of this take us back to the evidence reported in Table 6.1 and to the two prominent features of those data: the level of capital offenses and the strikingly high proportion of women among the defendants.

London had a reputation for being a violent and a dangerous place, and these figures perhaps suggest why. Not only were there more prosecutions in the metropolis than elsewhere, but a high proportion were for capital offenses, many of them offenses that had been made punishable by hanging because they threatened violence. Robbery and burglary had both been made capital offenses in the sixteenth century, and (along with murder) they continued to be the most feared offenses at the end of the seventeenth.[8] Highway robbery was not confined to the areas around the metropolis of London. But it was very common on the busy roads leading into the capital, particularly in the 1690s and in the first decades of the eighteenth century. Indeed, the city may have been at its most vulnerable to mounted highway robbery in this period. Targets were plentiful, and with internal trade growing and passenger traffic, particularly stagecoach services and private coach travel expanding, opportunities for highway robbery were becoming more plentiful with time. But the metropolis not only provided targets. It also provided cover. A mounted man could stop a number of coaches on a lonely stretch of road on the outskirts of the city and get back to the relative safety and anonymity of a densely populated parish before an alarm could be sounded, especially given the weakness of the policing forces. But what distinguished robbery in this urban setting was not so much the activities of single highwaymen as the attacks of street robbers, who were much more likely than highwaymen to use violence to make their escape.[9]

Street robberies appear to have been especially frequent in London in this period. Reports of violent attacks and confrontations were common, and they created an obvious sense of anxiety that spurred the national government and parliament and the authorities in the City to search for ways to defend the public. Measures were taken in the City, for example, to improve street lighting and to strengthen the night watch; and parliament extended capital punishment to forms of housebreaking that involved the threat of violence. But perhaps the most significant responses to the fear of violent crime in this period were the efforts made in parliament to encourage prosecutions by promising pardons to accomplices who turned king's evidence, and by instituting a substantial reward—in fact a sum that exceeded the annual income of a laborer—for the successful prosecution of a robber. These rewards underlay the least savory aspect of eighteenth-century criminal administration, for they came to attract people on both sides of the law (most famously Jonathan Wild), many of whom exploited the rich possibilities that "blood money" presented not only for the direct profits of "thief-catching," but also the opportunities it offered for malicious prosecutions and control over thieves. In other hands, statutory rewards also provided an underpinning for the development well before 1829 of more "professional" policing than the old parochial and ward systems of constables nightwatchmen could have managed (Howson 1970; Paley 1989: 301–40; Radzinowicz 1948; Styles 1983).

The strengthening of surveillance and the encouragements to prosecution were responses to what were perceived to be violent and frequent robberies by footpads in the streets of London and attacks by mounted men on the roads leading into the capital. And, although such offenses happened elsewhere in the countryside and small towns of England, there is no doubt that violence of this kind was associated with London, and that it was from London that the defensive measures mainly originated. But crime in London was different from that in the rest of the country in other ways too, and the particular experience of crime in the metropolis helps to explain several other features of the responses to crime in the late seventeenth and early eighteenth centuries. For crime in London was not only occasionally violent and threatening; it was also pervasive. London experienced crimes against property in a different way from the rest of the country mainly because the population of the metropolis was so much larger than that of even the largest provincial city. More people produced more offenses and more reports of offenses. But beyond that, the circumstances of life in the city gave rise to forms and rates of crime that were not experienced elsewhere, and that encouraged responses that were different from those then available to the courts—more vigorous, certainly more varied, responses. Crime in the capital was often violent, but it was also characterized by the number of minor offenses that were especially difficult to prevent—offenses such as shoplifting, theft from stalls and wagons and coaches, thefts from the docks or ships in the Thames, theft by servants and other employees, and theft from people in crowds.

Many of the property crimes included in the noncapital category in Table 6.1 were offenses of this kind, undoubtedly because of the opportunities that the city provided.[10] Shoplifting became a problem because this period saw a major transformation in retailing, an aspect of what has been characterized as a revolution in consumption. Shops began to display goods in windows and glass cases, making them more attractive and more easily available to be scrutinized and examined. By the late seventeenth century, shops that sought customers in these ways were to be found in towns and cities all over England, but they were particularly common in London, in Cheapside, and many other streets in the central wards of the City.[11] But as they attracted customers, they also attracted thieves, and at least by the 1690s a growing anger and anxiety about the extent of shoplifting was clear among the shopkeepers of London. Because some of them were among the City's leading citizens, shoplifting became a major issue. The grand jury of London complained about it, and shopkeepers successfully petitioned parliament in 1699 to give them more protection. What this meant was the protection of the gallows, because there were as yet no established noncapital punishments for felonies like larceny. Shoplifting to the value of five shillings or more was made a capital offense in 1699 and, though not many convicted offenders were actually hanged, theft from shops was among the most commonly prosecuted capital offenses in the first two decades of the eighteenth century (Beattie 1992).

The response to shoplifting in parliament was undoubtedly as massive as it was because of the effectiveness of the London lobby and because there was not as yet an agreed upon and easily available secondary punishment for felonies. Similar reasons explain why another minor property offense was made capital in 1713, in this case theft of goods from a house or warehouse to the value of forty shillings or more, an enactment aimed at servants who stole their employer's goods. Again it followed complaints about how common such offenses had become and about the weakness of the law. But there are other reasons why such essentially minor offenses as shoplifting and servants' theft were countered with such extreme violence in this period. The common involvement of women may have been one such reason, and a desire to bring them under control. At least eight out of ten of those charged with shoplifting under the new statute in its first two decades of operation were women; and while women did not form such a large proportion of those prosecuted for servants' theft, they were nonetheless very prominent among the accused. And their involvement in both offenses was linked to what was perhaps the most important underlying anxiety in parliament as well as among the shopkeepers and employers of London about these offenses: the conviction that thieving servants and shoplifters could not have been simply working on their own, but must have been linked to gangs that were in turn directed by large-scale receivers. The possible connection especially of young female domestic servants with lovers who were members of gangs to whom they would spirit away silver and other valuables or, even worse, to whom they would open the house in the night and allow them to rob and pillage their employers, was a frequently expressed anxiety in this period. There was also a more general concern about receivers—that they inspired and instigated crime. This was almost certainly greatly exaggerated, but there is no doubt that stolen goods could find a ready market in London in this period. Pawnbrokers were common, especially in the poorer parishes of the city; street markets provided ample opportunities to get rid of even tiny bundles of goods; and publicans and petty traders of all kinds, including many women, were clearly willing to eke out a precarious living by taking in goods on which they might turn a modest profit (George 1964 [1925]: 73, 285).

Receivers had long been thought to be a major cause of crime because they provided safe havens and conduits for stolen goods or even organized robberies and burglaries. It was a common saying that without receivers there would be no thieves. They were also very difficult to catch, convict, and punish. But the prominence of women among the accused is a reflection of a particular anxiety: the imagined connection between women and receivers and between women and gangs conjured up the fear not only of plunder, but of violence. The reports of domestic theft and the prosecutions of large numbers of women thus helped to encourage a sense that society was changing in some important ways, that the natural feelings of deference and obedience that underlay social order were shifting, that the old controls that underpinned the cohesion of society were being undermined. There was a widespread belief in the growing "insubordination" of servants, and in their untrustworthiness, a belief that was undoubtedly increased by the rapid turnover among domestic servants (Hecht 1981). A number of attempts were made in parliament and elsewhere to impose controls on servants by requiring their registration and establishing a system of references (Shoemaker 1992; Beattie 1992).

These anxieties were focused by the behavior of women in the city, but they flowed broadly from the comparative weakness of informal controls over the working population in general in this urban world compared to the kind of surveillance that arose quite naturally in a village or small town from neighbors, parish officials, clergymen, magistrates, and employers. And informal punishments—chastisement or the threat of exposure or of dismissal from work—also presumably worked less effectively in large urban environments than in small-scale societies where reputation was an even more important determinant of a man's or a woman's place in the community and of his or her ability to earn a living. Informal surveillance and controls were not impossible in the settled communities of the city, but they were weaker in the large suburban parishes in which the laboring poor found cramped shelter in courts and alleys.[12] For many, especially perhaps the young of both sexes who came to London to look for work and to establish a new life, the relative weaknesses of such surveillance meant a measure of freedom. Certainly there was a strong sense among critics concerned with a variety of social problems that people were being allowed to live "at their own hand," to live self-indulgently, and that this encouraged them in immoral habits—laziness, blasphemy, drinking, gambling—that would inevitably lead them to worse and worse crimes. It was to combat that detachment, that sense of freedom, and the immorality that it spawned, that active campaigns for the "reformation of manners" were conducted in London in the 1690s and the early decades of the eighteenth century seeking to bring blasphemers before the magistrates, to rid the streets of prostitutes and to suppress immorality of all kinds (Shoemaker 1992). The changes in the criminal law in this period and the efforts to stimulate prosecutions and to tighten up surveillance in the streets were similarly aimed at what were thought to be the consequences of a growing social indiscipline.

Economic Inequalities

The city provided more opportunities and targets for theft than most other parts of the country, and relative freedom for sections of the working population. But this freedom was linked to another consideration that perhaps more than any other explains the higher rate of crime in this urban world compared to the rural. That is the patterns of work in the city, and in particular the dependence of so many of the poor on sources of employment that frequently fell short of what was necessary to support even the most basic standard of life. The crucial consideration in explaining the rate of prosecutions for property crime in London in the early eighteenth century was inequality—the inequality that arose from inadequate wages and serious underemployment, from poverty and simple necessity.

The city contained a large number of men and women who were tempted to steal because of the difficulties they found themselves in. A large proportion of the working population depended on unskilled or semiskilled work that was seasonal and casual by its nature. Work in the important textile and clothing trades was closely tied to the fashions and activities of the social season; work on the river was also irregular, dependent as it was on seasonal flows of trade; and jobs in the market gardens that ringed the city, in carrying and selling fresh vegetables and fish and the hawking of other products that provided employment for so many, especially women, as well as work in the building trades and similar sources of employment, were inevitably irregular. At the best of times casual employment provided a precarious living for those who had to depend on it. Many trades were overstocked. But there was competition for all work because of the steady immigration to the city of large numbers of young men and women from all over the British Isles. It has been estimated that some 8,000 immigrants arrived in London every year in the early eighteenth century, many of them young men in their teenage and young adult years coming to serve apprenticeships, and young women seeking work as domestic servants (Beier and Finlay 1986: 9–10; Kitch 1986: 226; Wrigley 1967). Not all succeeded in finding settled places. Unemployment and underemployment were normal features of the lives of many of the working poor in the metropolis, and the circumstances that gave rise to those conditions fluctuated from season to season and from year to year (George 1964 [1925]: 156–59, 168–70, 211–13, 269–70).

Two main considerations determined how well or how badly the working population of London could sustain themselves: food prices and the level of employment, especially in a period such as this, when wages were low and it would have been difficult for the poor to put money aside for bad times. The price of basic foodstuffs was largely determined by the state of the harvests, and in a number of years over this period bad weather led to some significant shortages and very high prices, from 1694 to 1699 and in 1709 and 1710 in particular. Bad harvests also led to shortages of work, but unemployment and underemployment in London resulted more directly from interruptions in trade and fluctuations in the size of the labor market. Either high food prices or a shortage of work might be offset by

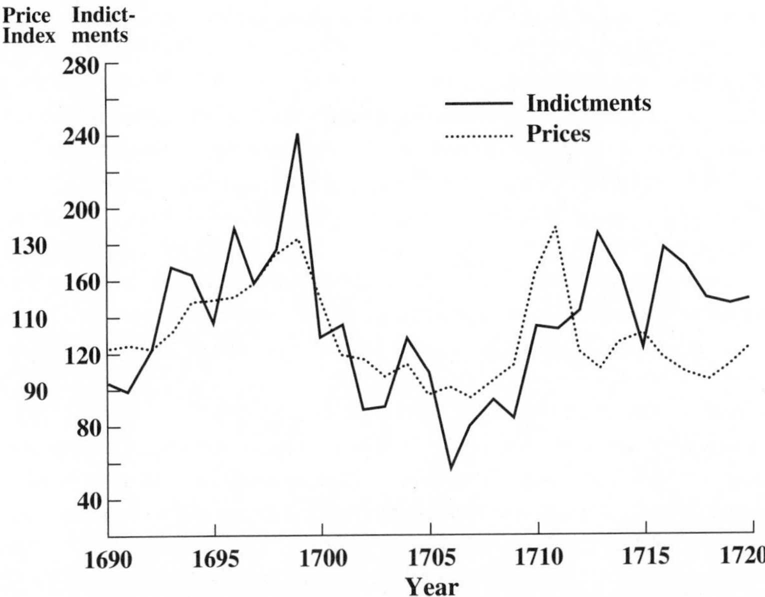

Fig. 6.1. Indictments at the Old Bailey and consumer prices, 1690–1720. Data on indictments from Sessions Files and Minute Books, Corporation of London Record Office. Data on price index from B. R. Mitchell and Phyllis Deane, *Abstract of British Historical Statistics* (Cambridge: Cambridge University Press, 1962), p. 468.

good times with respect to the other—though lack of work caused problems in all circumstances. But when both came together the results could be devastating. And at such times economic difficulties were particularly likely to be reflected in the level of prosecutions for property offenses.

It was characteristic of such prosecutions that they often fluctuated, sometimes sharply, from court session to court session and from year to year, as can be seen in Figure 6.1, which sets out the annual levels of property offenses coming before the Old Bailey from the City of London. Prosecutions over the 30 years can be divided broadly into thirds: a period of rising levels in the 1690s; a contrasting decade of lower totals; and a third period in which prosecutions were again broadly higher. There is a striking relationship between this pattern of prosecutions and one indicator of the movement in prices, the Schumpeter-Gilboy price index (A and B), which is also displayed in Figure 6.1, and which can be taken as a rough guide to changes in the cost of living over that period (Mitchell and Deane 1962: 468–69). The movement of this index confirms what other evidence strongly suggests, that the 1690s were a very difficult decade for the working population, with especially bad years in the middle of the decade and again in the poor harvest years of 1697 and 1698. There followed a number of years in which harvests were good and food plentiful. Over most of the first decade of the eighteenth century, indeed, prices fell relatively sharply, until further bad harvests in 1709 and 1710 drove prices up again before they moderated once more. The fluctuations in the level of prosecutions did not follow this pattern of food prices in detail, but the broad congruence of prosecutions and prices until the last few years of the period suggests at least some general relationship between the numbers of charges being laid and short-term changes in the standard of living of the working population.

Those conditions were influenced even more directly by another factor: the market for labor. It is impossible to get a measure of the changing availability of work for the large segment of the London population that depended on wages. But there are clear indications that the last decade of the seventeenth century was particularly difficult for large numbers of the working poor. This is suggested, for example, by a frequently expressed concern about vagrancy and the numbers of beggars in the streets of the capital, by a renewed interest in this period in the use of houses of correction as a means of disciplining the laboring population, and by the establishment of workhouses in which to put men and women to work who would otherwise press for outdoor relief under the Poor Laws (Innes 1987: 79–84). London was the center of this effort to provide employment for the able-bodied who were out of work. In 1699, the so-called Corporation of the Poor established such a workhouse (Macfarlane 1986: 254–58).

Though direct evidence of the levels of employment cannot be found, some indication of the importance of shifting work opportunities for the level of prosecution is suggested by the fluctuating pattern of indictments for property crimes in alternating periods of war and peace. For war had a direct effect on the labor market and the competition for work in London. As wars began, large numbers of young men were carried off to the army and navy, willingly or not. Their removal from the capital must have created better opportunities to find work for those left behind, especially since war also stimulated some aspects of the economy. Later, the coming of peace created a problem for all those seeking work in London. The forces were always demobilized rapidly, and in London this created massive competition in the labor market just as war-stimulated work was coming to an end. The invariable experience in the eighteenth century was that the coming of peace abroad was accompanied by violence at home, as the number of reported robberies and other property crimes rose alarmingly. The level of prosecutions generally moderated slightly as the immediate peacetime crisis passed, but peacetime levels were virtually always higher than those experienced during wars. War thus provided some relief from the conditions that normally ruled in the London labor market—underemployment and shortages of work—and some relief too from the relatively high levels of prosecutions for offenses against property that were also the norm in the capital.[13]

The movement of prosecutions in the 30 years we are dealing with confirms much of that pattern. The period saw two long and bloody wars in which Britain was heavily engaged in a European coalition against Louis XIV: the so-called War of the League of Augsburg (1689–97) and the War of Spanish Succession (1702–13). Several of the features that were to become commonplace in the succession of wars that followed over the eighteenth century were experienced in this period. The exception was the period of war in the 1690s during which prosecutions increased rather than diminished; any advantage that might have been won by the removal of young men from the labor market was offset during this war by harvest failures that kept food prices at a high level, and by trade disruptions due to blockades and naval action before a convoy system could be worked out to keep the trade routes open (Jones 1972: 319–26). Unemployment remained high in the 1690s and made for what has been called "a decade of distress for the London poor" (Macfarlane 1986: 259). As we have seen, the distress on the streets of London helped to stimulate a campaign of social and religious discipline and the establishment of a workhouse in which the unemployed who might otherwise claim relief would be set to work. The peace of 1697 only made things worse by adding demobilized troops to the London labor market, and the level of prosecutions for property crimes rose even more rapidly than it had throughout the decade. The fall in prices in 1700, though, and even more the war that began two years later, had a decisive influence on the level of prosecutions in London. Indictments fell sharply until, again, the advantages of a wartime economy were offset by a sharp upturn in food prices from 1709 to 1711 after two disastrous harvests. In 1713, prosecutions for property crime rose even more sharply as the war ended and the troops were demobilized, even though food prices had moderated by then.

The pattern of prosecutions during the war years in the 1690s are a reminder that several economic circumstances influenced the lives of the working population of London; wage levels and the price of necessities were as important as the availability of work. The best combination of circumstances for the laboring population, however—plentiful work and low prices—were most commonly provided by warfare and good harvests. In the years in which these coincided, 1702 to 1709, prosecutions for property offenses were well below the average for the period. On the other side, in peacetime the only year in which the indictment level was below average was 1701, a year in which food prices were also well below average.

These are crude measures of the standard of living of a diverse working population whose experiences differed from trade to trade. And with such small numbers of indictments, the fluctuations of prosecutions for property crime cannot provide anything more than a possible indication of the direction of change in the level of "events" that might have led to a charge being laid. Nonetheless, the conjunction of changes in the standard of living of the working population with the broad trends in the offenses brought to the Old Bailey provides some suggestions about the nature of property crime in this period. In particular, the relationship of prosecution and economic factors suggests that crime against property arose in large part from the inequalities under which a large part of the population all too frequently labored.

Women's Property Crime

These movements in prosecutions also provide some clues about what is perhaps the most striking feature of the pattern of indictments at the Old Bailey in this period: the high level of women's property crime. Women were rarely as prominent among accused felons as they were at the Old Bailey in the late seventeenth and early eighteenth centuries.[14] Studies from several centuries have found that women commonly accounted for a much smaller proportion of offenders accused of serious crimes (Hanawalt 1979: 115–25; Philips 1977: 147–51; Sharpe 1983: 95; Wiener 1975; Zedner 1991). In the rural parishes of Surrey over the period we are dealing with, about 13 percent of the accused were women; and in Sussex, 19 percent.[15] The fact that over the same period women accounted for 38 percent of those accused of property crimes in the urban parishes of Surrey, which were part of the larger metropolis of London south of the River Thames, suggests that the presence of an unusually large proportion of women before the criminal courts was an urban phenomenon.[16] Even so, that women accounted for close to 48 percent of those accused of property offenses in the City of London between 1690 and 1720 makes this period entirely unusual.[17] Some of that distribution is explained by the fact that 20 of these 30 years were years of war and a large number of young men were away in the army or navy. But even in years of peace in this period more than

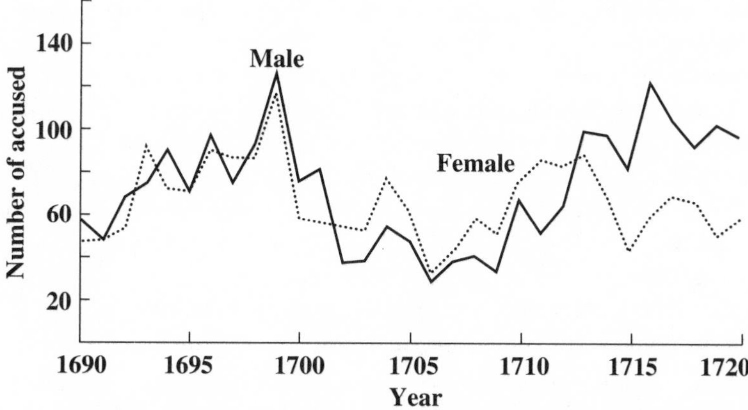

Fig. 6.2. Numbers of male and female accused at the Old Bailey, 1690–1720. Data from Sessions Files and Minute Books, Corporation of London Record Office.

40 percent of the accused at the Old Bailey were women; and if one were to add the defendants who were every year diverted to the house of correction and away from jury trial—a number that always included more women than men—that figure would be even higher.[18]

Women were more likely than men to be charged with offenses that did not involve the threat of violence and the direct confrontation with a victim. They stole more by indirection and stealth. But, while their forms of appropriation differed, the prosecution of men and women for crimes against property followed broadly similar tracks over the period, as Figure 6.2 reveals. In the 1690s as many women as men were indicted, and their numbers declined at the same time and to the same extent as men's when first the sharp fall in prices and then the war made for better times for the working population of London after 1700. Women were not quite as prominent as men at the Old Bailey in the years of peace after 1713, but over the whole period they had virtually equaled the number of men in that court, and the patterns of their prosecution had been very similar.

The decline of prosecutions of women for property offenses during the war that began in 1702 is significant in that it diminishes the possibility that the reason the general level of prosecutions commonly fell during wars was that the prosecutors and the authorities used the recruitment needs of the army and the navy as a way of diverting young men from the courts. Instead of going to the expense of bringing such men to trial, the argument has been made, prosecutors and magistrates were likely simply to have turned them over to recruiting sergeants and the press gang, thereby punishing them effectively and discouraging others from like offenses, while saving themselves a good deal of trouble. The fall in levels of prosecuted crime during wars in the eighteenth century may thus be linked more to changes in judicial administration than to changes in the labor market (Innes and Styles 1986: 393; King 1984: 64–73). There is no evidence that such diversions were taking place in the first decade of the eighteenth century. But the prosecution of women also casts doubt on this explanation of the effect of war on the pattern of accusations brought against men for property offenses. The fact that the pattern of charges against women during the war that began in 1702 virtually duplicated that of men (and could not have been because the magistrates were sending them to the army) diminishes the possibility that the diversion of men to the army and navy was the primary reason for a pattern of prosecution that was to be duplicated in every war in the eighteenth century.

Women may have been prosecuted at an unusually high level in the late seventeenth and early eighteenth centuries because of heightened anxiety about their behavior and greater willingness of victims and the authorities to bring women to court. There is some suggestion of such an anxiety in the reformation-of-manners campaigns that began soon after 1689; these groups of reformers wanted to eradicate all evidence of irreligion and immorality wherever they found it, but their principal targets were the "lewd and disorderly," primarily prostitutes (Shoemaker 1992). Perhaps more directly, the shoplifting statute of 1699 and the act that made servants' theft a capital offense in 1713 reveal a particular anxiety about women. This extension of capital punishment suggests that the propertied classes of London and members of parliament thought that women's crime had extended beyond all expectation and needed to be reined in, that women needed to be controlled. And the public anxieties about women that led to the passage of this legislation might also have encouraged victims to prosecute; a form of "moral panic" might thus account for some of the increase in the number of female defendants before the courts in those years. It is also true that an accused could be more readily identified and arrested in some of the offenses that women typically committed—shoplifting, pilfering by employees, the robbery of a client by a prostitute—than in many of the more violent offenses that men engaged in. If there was widespread determination to prosecute these offenses in order to discourage others, a number of accused women would almost certainly be readily at hand.

Such considerations surely shaped the number of charges brought to trial. But can they in themselves explain the patterns of Old Bailey cases over these 30 years? It seems to me as likely that the anxieties about women arose at least in part from women's behavior, from changes in the pool of offenses they were actually committing. And those behavioral changes seem to me to have resulted from increased difficulty in the ability of large numbers of women to earn a living. Perceptions of women's behavior were surely important, but they were almost certainly formed because women were unusually hard-pressed to make ends meet in London and because theft was one of a number of options—the poor law, charity, the support of friends and relatives, begging, and prostitution were others—when starvation threatened.

A large proportion of the women in London had come to the capital—typically in their early twenties—in search of work (Earle 1989: 331). Indeed, so many women had migrated to London (as well as to other towns) over the late seventeenth century that a significant gender imbalance seems to have developed in urban areas (Clark and Souden 1987: 23, 35). The problems that such women faced arose from their position of fundamental inequality: they were very largely confined to a limited range of occupations and their wages were significantly lower than men's. Most of the work they could seek was unskilled or semiskilled, badly paid, and sensitive to seasonal variations. That was particularly true of work in the textile and clothing trades, but it was also true of large numbers of other jobs in a variety of trades in London and in street selling and work in the market gardens, in taverns and shops, and so on. Domestic service, which attracted large numbers of young women, carried no guarantee of continuous work.[19]

The justification for low wages arose from the notion of the woman as dependent, the notion that women were expected merely to supplement the earnings of a male. The reality was that such wages (and the irregularity of work) left many women destitute, or at least close to the edge and easily tipped into serious circumstances. The wives of the large number of poor unskilled men, who themselves could only patch together a living, had to work to supply simple necessities to their families, and commonly had to work hardest during their child-raising years because extra mouths could not be fed without their labor (Earle 1989: 338). But single women, or widows with children (and demographic realities and warfare ensured that there were many widows with families to support), or wives who had been deserted by their husbands (a situation that was all too common among the very poor) were likely sooner than others to feel the threat of starvation from loss of work or a sudden increase in prices (Rogers 1991:

133–35). "A very high proportion of London women," Peter Earle has concluded, "were wholly or partly dependent on their own earnings for their living" (1989: 337).

The dislocations in the economy caused by the interruptions in trade during the war, compounded by the effects of several disastrous harvests, made the 1690s a time of hardship for all the poor of London, but particularly for women. When prices fell in the early years of the eighteenth century, and especially when the war began and took large numbers of men out of the London labor market, women were likely to have been more easily able to support themselves in the capital.[20]

The pattern of prosecutions thus suggests that women stole for the same reason that men stole in this period—largely as a means of survival, as a way of supplementing inadequate wages or of supplying the most basic wants. And the frequency with which women were brought before the courts suggests too that women found themselves in difficulties in the city much more often than in small towns and rural parishes. For single women especially, the capital offered a greater degree of independence and privacy—a certain freedom from the surveillance and controls of patriarchal and paternalistic social relationships. Inevitably, however, the urban world forced on them a greater need for self-reliance. That must have been true of single women and widows in particular, and it is therefore hardly surprising that fully 80 percent of the women before the Old Bailey on property charges were unmarried.[21] For many of these women crime may well have been a matter quite simply of survival.

The unusually high level of prosecution of women in this period may thus derive from a combination of factors: from a pattern of immigration that allowed women to enjoy relative freedom in the city from the constraints that hedged in the lives of most women—married and single—in the villages and small towns in which most of the population lived; from the severe difficulties that many such women experienced in London from time to time given the irregularity of work and the low wages they could command; and from the responses of the propertied classes of London to the efforts of women in trouble to make ends meet, responses made all the more severe by the apparent weakness of the courts and of the criminal justice system in the capital. Anxiety no doubt contributed to the sense of panic that was so often expressed about the threat of crime, which perhaps encouraged victims to complain and the authorities to take more vigorous action than they might otherwise have done. But the charges brought to the Old Bailey against women as well as men arose too from the reality of offenses being committed. The patterns of prosecution suggest that property offenses in London in this period were largely a response to the changing conditions in which a large part of the laboring poor lived and worked, and in particular to the inequalities under which they labored.

Gender, Race, and the Pathways to Delinquency

An Interactionist Explanation

KAREN HEIMER

Gender has recently become more central in research on delinquency. Old explanations that simply applied traditional theories of male offending to females have been challenged (Klein 1973; Smart 1976) and new perspectives proposed in their place (Hagan et al. 1979, 1987; Hagan et al. 1985; Messerschmidt 1986; Simpson 1991). Most contemporary analyses focus on structural factors, arguing that the gender gap in offending reflects gender differences in access to political and economic power. Broadly speaking, these explanations are rooted in the conflict tradition in criminology. The social-psychological underpinnings of these structural explanations rarely are articulated, however. When they are, they tend to be based on the assumptions of control theories. Because control and conflict theories contain contradictory assumptions about social order, human nature, and human motivation, perhaps a more fruitful way to link macro and micro processes would specify a social-psychological model based on a conflict approach.

This chapter proposes a social-psychological explanation of the processes giving rise to the gender gap in delinquency that is rooted in the conflict tradition in criminology and therefore is consistent with contemporary structural-level arguments. Based on an interactionist theory of delinquency (Heimer and Matsueda 1994; Matsueda 1992), my explanation proposes that forms of structural-level conflict, such as gender inequality, influence the meaning that actors give to themselves, situations, and behaviors such as delinquency. My argument also is informed by Greenberg's (1977) work on the relationship between age and delinquency, which critically examines power at the structural level and its implications for social-psychological pathways leading to delinquency. Specifically, I reframe the pathways that Greenberg identifies from an interactionist perspective and argue that variation across gender in these social-psychological mechanisms leads males to break the law more often than females.

The second goal of this chapter is to address an issue that has received too little attention in the literature—namely, the role of race in the process leading to gender differences in delinquency. As several authors have noted, research has not adequately addressed gender-race patterns of law violation (Lewis 1981; Hill and Crawford 1990; Chilton and Datesman 1987; Simpson 1991). Although recent work has begun to explore the structural relationships among race, gender, and offending (e.g., Messerschmidt 1986; Simpson 1991), the underlying social-psychological mechanisms have not yet been identified. I examine whether an interactionist framework can elucidate the mechanisms by which race and gender intersect to produce delinquent behavior.

The chapter proceeds in four sections: The first section briefly discusses structural explanations of the gender and race gaps in delinquency. The second section develops an interactionist explanation of the influence of gender and racial inequality on delinquency, which focuses on three key social-psychological pathways. The third section presents results from a covariance structure analysis, using data from the Monitoring the Future survey (Bachman et al. 1990b). Finally, the fourth section discusses implications for future development of an interactionist perspective on gender, race, and delinquency.

Gender, Race, and the Structural Roots of Law Violation

Gender Inequality and Law Violation

Studies relying on official, victimization, and self-report data all find that females are much less likely than males to break the law (see Hindelang 1971, 1979; Steffensmeier and Steffensmeier 1980; Steffensmeier and Cobb 1981). Furthermore, self-report data show that while males commit crime and delinquency more frequently than females, their patterns of involvement are the same; the offenses that are committed most and least are the same across gender (Hindelang 1971; Weis 1976). Yet the magnitude of the gender gap varies with offense, being most pronounced for violent offenses and least pronounced for less serious offenses, such as minor property crime, drug use, and status offenses (Hindelang 1971, 1979; Weis 1976; Steffensmeier and Cobb 1981).

Recent work on socialist feminist criminology (Messerschmidt 1986;

Simpson 1991) and power-control theory (Hagan et al. 1979, 1985, 1987; Hagan 1989) locates the source of gender differences in offending in structural inequality. Both perspectives assume that gender inequality is rooted in conflict, arguing that law reflects the interests of the powerful. Indeed, research indicates that law and the legal system do reflect the interests of powerful sectors in a capitalist, patriarchal system (e.g., Chesney-Lind 1973; Nagel and Hagan 1982; Smart 1984).

From the perspective of socialist feminist criminology, patriarchy gives rise to the gender gap in law violation by dampening the motivations of females to commit all forms of crime and delinquency (Messerschmidt 1986). In addition, the capitalist system structures imbalances in political and economic power among both genders, which are consequential for law violation (Messerschmidt 1986; Simpson 1991; see also Smart 1976). Powerful males commit white-collar crime, both petty and major; powerful females also engage in white-collar offenses but theirs are less serious and somewhat less frequent, because of restricted opportunity and patriarchal ideology (Daly 1989). Violent street crimes, in contrast, are said to be more prevalent among the economically and politically marginalized of both genders, consistent with the arguments of other critical perspectives (e.g., Quinney 1977: 52–54; Colvin and Pauly 1983). Yet marginalized females engage in less violence than do their male counterparts. According to socialist feminist criminology, this is because all males—even those who are economically and politically marginalized—are afforded power on the basis of their gender (Messerschmidt 1986: 58). One way for marginalized males to demonstrate the power that they do possess is through the display of machismo and male posturing, which can evolve into violent street crime (Greenberg 1977; Schwendinger and Siegel-Schwendinger 1985; Messerschmidt 1986; see also Miller 1958). Marginalized females, in contrast, are not afforded power on the basis of gender. The result is that when males are marginalized, they respond with more serious, often violent crime; when females are marginalized, they respond with nonviolent property crime (Smart 1976; Giordano et al. 1981; Box and Hale 1985; Messerschmidt 1986).

Power-control theory also maintains that the gender gap in law violation is spawned by inequality in power at the structural level. From this perspective, males and members of more powerful social classes are freer from societal controls and therefore are more apt to violate the law (Hagan et al. 1985, 1987). At first glance, this view appears to contradict the socialist feminist contention that street crime is more common among those who are economically and politically marginalized. Yet this discrepancy reflects a difference in focus rather than a difference in theoretical assumptions. Power-control theory attempts to explain common delinquency, such as minor theft, vandalism, and status offenses, while socialist feminist criminology focuses more on violent street delinquency, such as assault and robbery. The assumption underlying both of these perspectives is that members of all segments of society commit acts that are harmful to others, but the specific form of these acts varies with position in the power structure. Both socialist feminist criminology and power-control theory agree that persons who are afforded power engage in behaviors that are viewed by our society as less serious, such as common delinquency, while persons who are economically and politically marginalized commit offenses that are seen as more serious, such as violent street delinquency. Both perspectives also agree that patriarchal constraints serve to reduce rates of both common and violent delinquency among females.

Together, these perspectives predict the following patterns: Among males and females, violent street delinquency is more likely among those who have limited economic and political power, while common law violation is more likely among those who have greater access to power. Moreover, patriarchy serves to reduce female rates of offending more than it does male rates for both violent street offenses and common "less serious" delinquency.[1] These arguments together imply that at the social-psychological level, the motivational pathways to law violation vary somewhat according to the nature of the offense. Before addressing the question of social-psychological processing, however, I turn to discuss structural explanations of race differences in delinquency.

Racial Inequality and Law Violation

The relationship between race and delinquency is less clear-cut than the relationship between gender and delinquency. Both official and victimization data show large race differences in offending, while most self-report surveys find small race effects (cf. Gold 1966; Wolfgang et al. 1972; Hindelang 1978; Hindelang et al. 1981; Tracy et al. 1990).[2] Some researchers have argued that this discrepancy arises because official and victimization data weight serious street crimes more heavily, while self-report surveys capture common, less serious delinquency (Elliott and Ageton 1980). Consistent with this, research shows that young African-American males are involved disproportionately in street crime, especially violent and major property offenses (Wolfgang et al. 1972; Elliott and Ageton 1980; Tracy et al. 1990), but does not report higher levels of common delinquency, such as status offenses, public order violations, and drug use for African-American youths than for whites (Elliott and Ageton 1980: 95).[3]

Some researchers propose that the disproportionate involvement of African-Americans in street crime reflects the existence of an "underclass" in the most poverty-stricken areas of our inner cities (Glasgow 1981; W. J. Wilson 1986, 1987; Sampson 1987). They argue that economic inequality, segregation (W. J. Wilson 1987), and discrimination (Massey 1990) have combined to marginalize inner-city blacks, thereby creating conditions that foster high rates of under- and unemployment, welfare dependency, female-headed households, and violent street crime (Hogan and Kitagawa 1985; W. J. Wilson 1986, 1987; Sampson 1987; Lichter 1988). In short, race is consequential for violent crime and delinquency because segregation and discrimination have limited the economic and political power of African-Americans.

There is less discussion in the literature of why African-Americans are overrepresented in statistics on violent delinquency but not in self-reports of common offending.[4] Although some researchers argue that the processes that explain common delinquency also account for involvement in violent and predatory law violation (e.g., Gottfredson and Hirschi 1990), other work indicates that the mechanisms underlying race ratios of violent offending may differ from those giving rise to race ratios of less serious law violation (Blau and Blau 1982; Simpson 1991). Thus, the question of whether the effect of race on law violation varies with offense remains unresolved.

One limitation of research on race and delinquency is that most studies of racial differences in law violation are limited to males (e.g., Sampson 1987; Matsueda and Heimer 1987). Research rarely has examined the possibility that race may have different implications for law violation across gender. When research does examine offending by minority females, it points to the importance of cultural contexts and structural dislocations (e.g., Lewis 1981; Campbell 1984; E. Miller 1986; Hill and Crawford 1990). This work, however, often targets only females and, like studies that focus only on males, is unable to illuminate the ways in which gender and race combine to produce differences in law violation.

We can apply my earlier arguments based on socialist feminist criminology and power-control theory to explain gender-race patterns of offending. Specifically, crime and delinquency emerge because the restricted power afforded to African-Americans plays itself out differently across gender. Black males are more apt than white males to experience restrictions of their political and economic power. Yet they are afforded power on the basis of gender in our patriarchal society, which when displayed through male posturing can result in violence. The power of black females, in contrast, is limited on the basis of both race and gender; in other words, black females are not afforded power based on their gender and thus are less likely than their male counterparts to engage in violent law violation (Messerschmidt 1986: 58; Simpson 1991).[5] Moreover, the combined arguments of socialist feminist and power-control theories suggest that the relationship between race and delinquency will vary with the nature of the offense. We can expect that offenses that are associated with positions of greater power—such as common delinquency and white-collar crime—will occur more frequently among whites. In addition, because patriarchal structures and ideologies diminish the power of females relative to males, white males constitute the gender-race group with the most power at the structural level and hence should be the most likely to engage in common law violation.

An Interactionist Perspective on Gender, Race, and Delinquency

This structural analysis assumes that society is characterized by conflict. Yet recent social-psychological explanations of the gender gap in delinquency are rooted in control theory (Hagan et al. 1985, 1987; Hagan 1989; Gottfredson and Hirschi 1990), which assumes consensus across groups in society with regard to the law. The control view also assumes that the motivation to deviate is constant across groups and thus nonproblematic; the focus is instead on restraints from deviance. Consequently, social-control explanations of gender and delinquency tend to focus largely on gender differences in restraints and do not link conflict at the structural level with individuals' motivations to break the law at the social-psychological level.

In the remainder of this chapter, I develop an explanation that shows how structural conflict gives rise to gender and race differences in motivations to break the law. My explanation employs recent work on an interactionist theory of delinquency (Heimer and Matsueda 1994; Matsueda 1992) to reconceptualize the pathways to law violation identified by Greenberg's (1977) critical analysis of delinquency. The interactionist perspective has the virtue of providing an explanation of links among social structure, groups, individuals, and situations (Heimer and Matsueda 1994). Moreover, the perspective is internally consistent; it assumes that society is characterized by diverse groups, whose members negotiate definitions of situations and the law that sometimes conflict with those of other groups

(Matsueda 1988; Heimer and Matsueda 1994). To specify the content of motivational processes, I draw on Greenberg's work. Reframing his analysis from an interactionist perspective weaves the structural and individual level explanations into a unified sociological framework. In this section, I first specify some of the basic principles of symbolic interactionism and then interpret Greenberg's arguments from this viewpoint, showing how the pathways that he identifies may explain the consequences of gender and race for delinquency.

Laying the Foundation: A Symbolic Interactionist Theory of Delinquency

The interactionist perspective on delinquency views individuals, groups, and the broader organizational context as intertwined in an ongoing social process (Heimer and Matsueda 1994; Matsueda 1992). According to the symbolic interactionist tradition in sociology, individuals give meaning to themselves, others, and situations by considering these social "objects" from the perspectives of significant others and reference groups (see, e.g., Mead 1934; Shibutani 1961, 1986; Goffman 1959; Turner 1962; Blumer 1969; Stryker 1980). The capacity to engage in role-taking allows actors to jointly construct definitions of situations. This joint negotiation of definitions makes cooperative social action possible (Mead 1934; Shibutani 1961, 1986; Turner 1962; Stryker 1980; Hewitt 1987). Such cooperative social action in turn produces social structures such as positions and communication networks, which together constitute the broader social organization of society. Thus, social organization is ultimately a product of the meaning that individuals give to situations; yet at the same time, the structuring of positions and communication networks influences this meaning.

From an interactionist perspective then, gender and racial inequality are consequential for law violation because they restrict the positions of females and minorities and thereby constrain communication networks and power to influence others. Hence, these forms of structural inequality influence definitions of situations because they partially determine the significant others and reference groups considered in the role-taking process. Through shaping definitions of situations, gender and racial inequality contribute to the patterning of crime and delinquency.[6] Thus, consistent with the tradition of differential association in criminology, an interactionist theory of delinquency argues that there will be differences across groups in definitions of situations and the law to the extent that communication networks vary (Heimer and Matsueda 1994).

At the individual level, when youths encounter the opportunity to break the law they consider themselves and the situation from the perspectives of significant others and reference groups, and construct definitions of the situation that are either consistent or inconsistent with delinquent lines of action. When role-taking leads to defining a situation as one in which delinquency would be rewarded—through nonsocial reinforcement, positive reactions from others, or enhanced esteem in the eyes of others—youths will be likely to break the law. When role-taking leads to defining the situation as one in which delinquency would be disapproved or would damage self-image, youths will be unlikely to break the law (see Heimer and Matsueda 1994 and Matsueda 1992 for more detailed discussions).

In short, gender and racial inequality restrict the others with whom youths interact and therefore are consequential for the role-taking process that occurs when youths contemplate delinquency. The motivation to break the law will therefore vary across gender and racial groups. This conclusion does not, however, tell us the direction of the influence of gender and race on definitions of situations that provide delinquent opportunities. To begin to answer this question, I draw on Greenberg's (1977) critical analysis of delinquency, with some elaboration based on the structural arguments of socialist feminist criminology and power-control theory.

Building on the Foundation: Interaction and the Pathways to Delinquency

In his critical analysis of the relationship between age and delinquency, Greenberg (1977) argues that youths in our society have been stripped of power through their removal from productive roles in the labor force. This, combined with mandatory education, has resulted in the age segregation of daily activities, with youths in schools and adults in the work place. The conflict inherent in this situation sets the scene for the development of high rates of law violation by youths. Age segregation fosters heightened importance of the peer group and its symbols of status. The school context itself restricts independence and exposes youths to degradation ceremonies, which together challenge their self-efficacy and self-esteem. These factors then merge to form a social milieu that fosters high rates of delinquency.

Although Greenberg does not employ principles of symbolic interaction, his arguments can be augmented and reframed to be quite consistent with an interactionist perspective. First, the segregation of youths in schools restricts communication networks so that peers are the group most readily accessible when youths negotiate definitions of situations; thus, the reactions of these others are weighted heavily in youths' decisions about delinquency. This age segregation, combined with the practices and ceremonies that Greenberg identifies as characteristic of the school context, have important implications for youths' definitions of self, each other, and appropriate behavior. Consequently, youths as a group can be expected to negotiate definitions that are at times in conflict with those of adults and, indeed, the law.

Greenberg's discussion also implies that these structural and contextual factors combine to create pathways to delinquency that vary somewhat, depending on the nature and *meaning* of the offense. Specifically, his discussion implies somewhat different motivational pathways to breaking school rules, to stealing, and to violence. To the extent that gender and racial inequality influence these motivations, we can expect somewhat different patterns of behavior across gender and race groups.

In the following sections, I discuss three of Greenberg's pathways to delinquency from an interactionist perspective. I also broaden his original statements to account for differences in the influence of gender and race on delinquency by deriving implications from the structural arguments of socialist feminist criminology and power-control theory. In this way, I begin to build an explanation that links gender and racial inequality with the interactions that lead to delinquency. The first pathway that I discuss involves traditional gender ideologies or beliefs about the characteristics and obligations of females and males, which are consequential for all kinds of delinquency but are especially important for violent delinquent acts, such as fighting. The second pathway targets the cost of building and maintaining identities during adolescence and its relationship to theft. The third involves the interplay among the school context, self-esteem, definitions of risk-taking, and common, "nonserious" delinquency.

Gender Ideologies and Law Violation. The structural explanations discussed previously argue that gender differences in law violation reflect the system of inequality in our society, which affords males greater political and economic power than females. Feminist scholars have argued that such inequality is supported and perpetuated by pervasive ideologies that define females and males as different in nature, obligations, and motivations (Sayers 1987; Ferree and Hess 1987). In addition, because rule violation is less tolerable by actors with diminished social status and power (Wiggins et al. 1965; Sherif and Sherif 1967), traditional gender ideologies stress conformity with rules and norms more for females than for males. Accordingly, many authors have argued that crime is counter to the image of femininity conveyed by gender ideologies and thus is treated as more "deviant" for females than for males (e.g., Chesney-Lind 1973; Harris 1977; Schur 1984).

From an interactionist perspective, gender inequality and gender ideologies shape interactions such that, from a young age, girls and boys negotiate definitions of themselves as inherently different from the other gender (Goffman 1977; Cahill 1980). They witness adult females and males holding positions of unequal political and economic power (see England and Farkas 1986). They are sanctioned for behaviors that are inconsistent with the gender roles that emerge within this context (e.g., Fagot 1977; Lamb et al. 1980). Indeed, they become aware that the construction of gender is a key aspect of almost all social interactions and that the management of gender identity is crucial to negotiating definitions of many situations (Garfinkel 1967; Goffman 1977; Burke and Tully 1977; Burke 1989; Cahill 1980).

Given these circumstances—where the construction of gender is salient across most interactions and law violation is viewed as more deviant for females than for males—girls will be less likely than boys to negotiate definitions of situations that lead to delinquency. In other words, claiming gender identity requires females more than males to avoid all forms of law violation (see also Harris 1977; Schur 1984).

Beyond this, traditional gender ideologies may have special relevance for violent delinquency. If ideologies convey an image of the "ideal" male as being independent, confident, and successful, then mandatory education creates a problematic situation for young males. Specifically, schools restrict independence by requiring conformity to rules and thereby block young males from demonstrating masculinity or, in interactionist terms, claiming gender identity. In an attempt to negotiate gender identity in this situation, young males are likely to engage in male posturing, including fighting and other kinds of violent delinquency (Greenberg 1977). This tendency may be especially acute in the case of young minority males (Miller 1958; Vigil 1985) because they receive more negative messages in school and see more unemployed and underemployed men around them than do white males (Greenberg 1977). These outcomes of structural inequality foster concern among minority males about whether they will be able to live up to the culturally valued image of men as independent and successful. Thus, minority males may experience even greater need to claim a masculine identity in their interactions and consequently engage in more fighting and other forms of male posturing. This is consistent, of course, with the argument of socialist feminist criminology that black males feel powerless because of their race and react by exaggerating the power they are afforded on the basis of their gender.

In addition to explaining the overall gender gap in delinquency, gender ideologies also explain individual differences in offending among both females and males. From an interactionist viewpoint, individuals bring to situations their prior beliefs about gender and take these into account when they negotiate definitions of new situations. Consequently, females who bring to interactions traditional beliefs about gender are likely to define situations such that delinquency seems undesirable, because they will be likely to view law violation as inappropriate for their gender. Females who are less accepting of traditional gender ideologies, in contrast, define situations such that delinquency is a more likely outcome. Among males, accepting traditional gender ideologies intensifies the contradictions that boys confront when they are blocked from expressing independence and autonomy in school. These boys may be more likely than their less traditional counterparts to engage in violence as an attempt to claim a masculine identity.

In short, gender inequality and the ideologies that support it are consequential for (1) the gender gap in all forms of delinquency, especially violent delinquency; (2) individual differences in law violation (within both genders); and (3) the higher incidence of violent delinquency of minority males than other gender and race groups. One pathway linking structural inequality with the interactions that lead to delinquency, therefore, involves beliefs about the nature, obligations, and motivations of males and females, or gender ideologies.

Identity Costs and Theft. Another pathway to delinquency stems from the unique social position of youths in contemporary society. As several sociologists have noted, mandatory education and child labor laws have segregated the daily activities of youths and adults. This separation heightens the importance placed on the peer group, and as a result a youth subculture emerges in which status is achieved through the display of symbols that are highly regarded in the subculture, including dating, cruising in cars, drinking, smoking cigarettes, and appearing physically mature (England 1960; Coleman 1962; Stinchcombe 1964; Greenberg 1977). From an interactionist perspective, displays of such symbols constitute attempts to claim valued identities in youths' everyday interactions. Because the school environment often restricts autonomy precisely at the time when youths are trying to construct definitions of themselves as independent from their parents and other adults, the identities valued in the youth subculture often involve attempts to claim adult status, such as drinking, smoking, dating, dressing "grown-up," cruising in cars, staying out late, and engaging in sexual behavior. But as Greenberg notes, the process of claiming status through such behaviors is costly—youths need money for alcohol, cigarettes, eating out, clothes, gasoline, and other props for the display of adulthood. Because youths are largely excluded from the labor market, they are forced to rely on parents to finance their attempts to claim adult identities. When their parents cannot do so, youths turn to theft.

In interactionist terms, when youths cannot get resources from parents to purchase status symbols, they are faced with a "problematic situation." They want to negotiate respected identities in their interactions with peers but need costly props to do so. They may consider and attempt a range of solutions to this dilemma. Some may seek extra money through part-time work. But if legitimate means of making money are not available, youths may turn to theft as a means of resolving their dilemma. The latter course of action is most likely when youths take the role of their peers and other significant persons and determine that theft would bring social rewards and little disapproval from others (Heimer and Matsueda 1994).

Because both females and males must develop identities with their peers, the motivational mechanisms described here explain theft regardless of gender. Although negotiating identities may require different props for girls than for boys, leading them to steal different items (Greenberg 1977: 71), the relationship between access to financial resources and theft holds across gender.

The relationship between access to resources and theft exists for both races as well. Because black teens have less access than white teens to financial resources—in part because of lower average family incomes and higher teen unemployment among blacks—one may anticipate somewhat higher rates of theft among blacks than among whites. This assumes that the costs of claiming valued identities among peers are fairly similar for youths from all socioeconomic backgrounds. It may be, however, that the costs of social status increase with socioeconomic background, so that wealthy and poor alike need more resources than they have access to, and thus both are motivated to steal (Greenberg 1977: 71). Racial inequality, therefore, may have nominal effects on theft via this motivational pathway.

In sum, access to financial resources is associated with involvement in theft for youths of both genders and races. Because all youths are motivated to negotiate valued identities with peers, all will need financial resources to support these identities; therefore, gender and racial inequality may have little impact on theft via this pathway. This argument does not imply that there will be *no* gender or race differences in theft, however. Indeed, gender inequality influences theft through the communication of traditional gender ideologies. Racial inequality also has consequences for theft via other motivational mechanisms, to which I now turn.

Self-Esteem, Risk-Taking, and Law Violation. Mandatory schooling gives rise to another pathway to law violation. Schools strip youths of autonomy and institutionalize degradation ceremonies through constant evaluation of students' academic, athletic, and other activities (Greenberg 1977). At the social-psychological level, then, the school milieu presents constant challenges to youths' self-esteem. The interactionist perspective helps to illuminate the specific mechanisms by which this occurs. First, by imposing on students myriad requirements—such as dress codes, restrictions of movement without hall passes, and written excuses for tardiness or absence—schools restrict opportunities for youths to negotiate identities as responsible, independent actors. Yet, as noted above, developing an independent, "grown-up" self-image is very important during adolescence. This means that youths are confronted with a situation that threatens positive self-image. In response, they may openly defy school authority and rules (Greenberg 1977). When youths take the roles of significant others, including their peers, this defiance of school authority allows them to assert autonomy, negotiate self-images as independent young adults, and reject the school's implicit definition of them as immature children who need to be told what to do (Marwell 1966).

Schools also threaten youths' self-esteem by supporting a variety of public degradation ceremonies, such as the grading of academic performance and evaluation of athletic performance. By communicating such evaluations to students, schools influence youths' definitions of self. For example, those deemed unathletic or poor students must confront such negative evaluations in their daily interactions with teachers and other students. Because attitudes about the self are forged through role-taking, it is no wonder that the evaluative features of the school context have a strong impact on youths' self-images and their self-esteem (A. Cohen 1955; Wylie 1979: 361; Felson 1981a; 1981b; Rosenberg et al. 1989). One way that youths seek to repair self-esteem damaged in schools is through delinquency targeted at this institution (Greenberg 1977: 73–74). Presumably, when youths with damaged self-esteem interact with others, they negotiate definitions of the school as oppressive, unfair, and perhaps even malevolent, which allows them to jointly reject the school as a valid source of information about their self-worth. This rejection gets played out through delinquency against the school, especially destroying school property and breaking school rules. This line of reasoning is consistent with research that finds that delinquency enhances self-esteem (Kaplan 1975, 1980; Kaplan et al. 1986; Rosenberg et al. 1989).

The relationship between self-esteem and delinquency can be more complex, however. Delinquency also may serve to improve esteem because risky, daring behavior allows people to negotiate valued social identities, as Goffman (1967) and Short and Strodtbeck (1965) have argued. Specifically, when individuals perceive or imagine threats to their self-image, they may engage in risky behavior, such as common delinquency, in the hopes of maintaining or improving their character in the eyes of others. Such behavior should not be interpreted as an expression of impulsivity or irrationality, but rather as a more calculated attempt to manage impressions (Goffman 1967: 238; Short and Strodtbeck 1965). Note that the desire to improve self-image is not confined to those who have suffered damage to their esteem. Indeed, through experience, youths may learn that risky behavior—including delinquency—can enhance social status, and thus they may engage in risk-taking to maintain or improve on the already favorable impressions that others hold of them. Over time, these youths come to define risk-taking positively, and these definitions can then operate fairly independently of concern for self-image.

The interactionist explanation of this pathway to delinquency suggests that gender and race influence law violation insofar as they affect evaluation in schools, self-esteem, or preference for risk-taking. The point in this process where gender is most likely consequential lies within the negotiation of "risky" lines of action. It is likely that both females and males attempt to manage impressions with others, and thus their own attitudes toward self, through risky behavior. Both genders, consequently, value risk-taking as a means to enhance esteem. Yet, as power-control theory suggests, males may define risk-taking more favorably than females because patriarchal, capitalist society encourages males to take risks while teaching females to avoid risks (Hagan et al. 1985, 1987; Hagan 1989). Because taste for risk has been linked to a variety of forms of common, nonserious delinquency (Hagan et al. 1985, 1987), the gender gaps in minor theft, school deviance, and illicit drug use may be due in part to males' holding more definitions favorable to risk-taking than females. It is also possible, however, that risk-taking may be valued equally by females and males but have very different implications for behavior across gender. Indeed, the earlier discussion of gender ideologies suggests that this may be the case. Because delinquency is considered more "deviant" for females than for males, girls may try to manage impressions with others through legal forms of risky behavior.

It also is reasonable to expect that definitions favorable to risk-taking will vary with race. Given that minority group members are denied economic and political equality, they are apt to be discouraged from valuing risk-taking, daring, and thrill-seeking, which are privileges of the powerful in capitalist society (Hagan et al. 1985). This means that blacks of both genders will be less likely than whites to commit common delinquency such as minor theft, school deviance, and illicit drug use because they are less likely to learn definitions favorable to risk-taking.

One also might expect self-esteem to be lower among blacks than among whites, because restrictions on political and economic equality would seem to take a toll on feelings of self-worth. Yet this argument is not supported by empirical work, which often finds that the self-esteem of blacks is similar to (Coleman et al. 1966) or higher than that of whites (Bachman 1970; Rosenberg and Simmons 1972). Indeed, researchers in this area maintain that positing a link between racial inequality and self-esteem assumes that minorities regularly interact with and take the role of persons of more powerful racial groups, perceive that these others evaluate them negatively, and care about those evaluations. Perhaps not surprisingly, these assumptions turn out to be erroneous (Rosenberg 1979: 175). There is no basis, therefore, for suggesting variation in offending premised on racial differences in self-esteem.

Summary. In short, the interactionist perspective provides an analysis of the social-psychological processes by which gender and racial inequality are translated into delinquency. Overall, the perspective predicts gender differences in the motivational pathways to delinquency because gender inequality structures positions and communication networks such that delinquency has somewhat different meaning for females than for males. The perspective also predicts that race will play a role in these motivational pathways because racial inequality also restricts positions and communication networks and thus definitions of situations and delinquency. The specific motivational mechanisms for delinquency will vary somewhat according to the nature and meaning of the offense. The social-psychological assumption is, therefore, that delinquency is purposeful behavior motivated by the need to establish or preserve certain identities. This assumption is consistent with structural explanations of gender-race patterns of law violation discussed earlier, which argue that inequality motivates different types of law violation according to the actor's location in the power hierarchy of society.

Toward a Model of Gender, Race, and Delinquency

The foregoing explanation involves some fairly complex social-psychological mechanisms. Although a full test of these ideas requires data that are not currently available, a partial test of the proposed motivational pathways is possible using data collected as part of the Monitoring the Future study. This is an ongoing national survey of values and lifestyles among high school seniors conducted by Bachman et al. (1990b). The data available have been collected from in-school seniors annually since 1975. The study uses a stratified cluster sample, which selects geographical areas and then samples high schools within each area and senior students within each school.[7]

The survey includes information on self-reported rates of delinquency and drug use, self-esteem, definitions favorable to risk-taking, thoughts about the appropriate work and family roles of women, academic performance, work experience, and sources of income, as well as demographic variables. These data allow me to specify and estimate a statistical model to test some key hypotheses regarding the motivational pathways leading to gender-race patterns of delinquency. I use the data from Form 2 of the 1988 Monitoring the Future survey. The sample includes 1,530 females and 1,504 males after pairwise deletion of missing data. Among the females, 237 identify themselves as black Americans; among males, 184 are black.

Specification of the Model

The interactionist perspective proposes that the gender gap in delinquency reflects not only mean differences in levels of key constructs, but more important, differences in the ways in which these constructs combine to produce law violation. In statistical terms, this means that the relationship between gender and delinquency is nonlinear because the mechanisms underlying law violation interact with gender.[8] Consequently, I estimate the structural model diagrammed in Figure 7.1 separately for females and males.

This structural model captures major dimensions of the pathways to delinquency outlined above. The structural model incorporates a measurement model (not diagrammed) to adjust for unreliability in individual questionnaire responses, which can bias estimates of the structural parameters. Appendix 7.A contains descriptions of the questionnaire items.

Recall that the important gender and race patterns culled from the structural arguments of socialist feminist criminology and power-control theory are as follows: (1) a gender gap exists in all forms of delinquency, in-

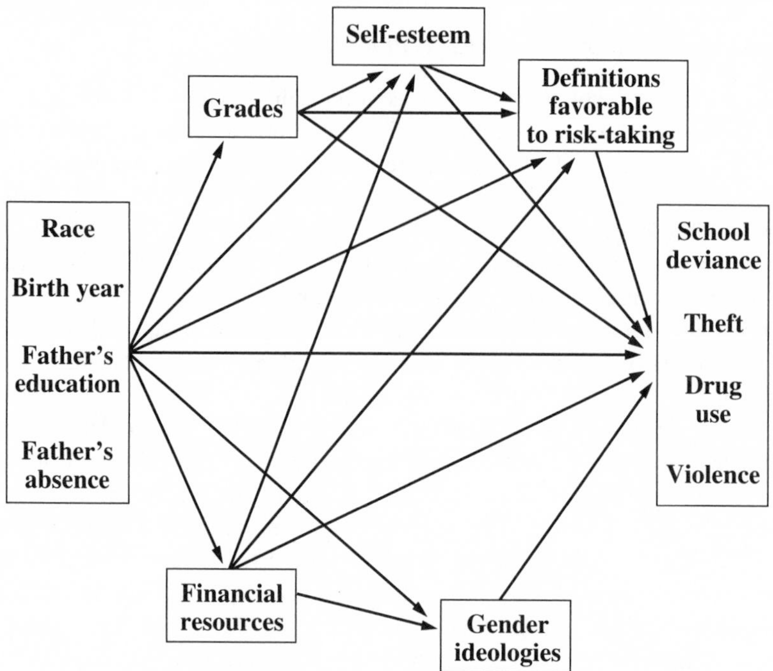

Fig. 7.1. Structural model of gender, race, and the pathways to delinquency.

cluding common, nonserious delinquency; (2) the most pronounced gender gap is in violent delinquency, with black males being more likely to engage in violence than white males; (3) there is a race difference in common, nonserious delinquency, with whites being more likely to commit these offenses (because of their greater power at the structural level). These are the patterns that my theoretical framework attempts to explain.

Because the perspective proposes that the motivations to delinquency will vary with type of offense, the structural model contains four outcome variables capturing self-reported delinquency—school deviance, theft, illicit drug use, and violence. School deviance, violence, and theft are specified as latent variables with multiple indicators and errors in measurement; drug use is a single-indicator construct consisting of scaled responses to questions about use of 11 types of drugs (see Appendix 7.A). Violence is the most serious delinquency in the model. School deviance, drug use, and theft represent common delinquency.

As Figure 7.1 shows, the social-psychological constructs capturing the interactionist process are self-esteem, definitions favorable to risk-taking, and belief about division of labor in families, which represents one dimension of gender ideologies.[9] Each of these theoretical constructs is causally before delinquency in the model. These constructs, in turn, are specified to be the products of grades in school, financial resources (i.e., spending money and number of hours worked per week for money), and a set of exogenous demographic variables. These demographic variables include black racial status, year of birth, father's education, and father's absence from the home. Black racial status is included to capture the influence of racial inequality in the process leading to law violation in both genders; the other demographic variables are important correlates of delinquency that are included to avoid bias due to omitted variables.

This model allows me to test hypotheses about the interactionist process underlying the gender-race patterns of offending noted above. Although the present data do not contain information on cognitive aspects of role-taking or specific identities (like gender identities and identities valued in the peer subculture), they do allow for a partial assessment of the ideas discussed above. First, the theoretical framework developed here proposes that grades earned in school have important consequences for delinquency among both females and males. Grades confront students with evaluations of their competence, and these evaluations are incorporated into their self-images; as a result, grades can have a profound impact on students' self-esteem. Students who receive poor grades may attempt to bolster their self-esteem through risky, daring behavior that is admired within their peer group. Such behavior may take the form of common delinquency. This suggests the following causal chain: good grades inculcate high self-esteem, which leads to less value being placed on risk-taking, which in turn reduces the likelihood of common delinquency.

Second, the interactionist perspective proposes that receiving poor grades and developing low self-esteem may directly encourage delinquency, especially that targeted at the school. The perspective argues that when the school is a source of negative information about the self, students seek to reject its authority by breaking rules or defacing school property. The test of the first two hypotheses, both of which concern the relationship between self-esteem and delinquency, allows us to begin to understand the relationship between self-conceptions more generally and motivation to break the law (Rosenberg 1979; Hewitt 1987: 117).

The third hypothesis that I assess is that females define risk-taking less positively than do males and/or are less likely to demonstrate risk-taking through illegal behaviors than males are. If this hypothesis is correct, it should be an important source of the gender gap in common delinquency.

Fourth, females who hold traditional views about division of family duties engage in less delinquency than other girls do. Such views theoretically should reflect belief in traditional gender ideologies more generally. Females holding these beliefs, then, can be expected to view delinquency as unacceptable for their gender. Fifth, when boys accept such views, they are more likely to behave violently than their counterparts who reject these views. This presumably occurs because traditional gender ideologies foster violence among males as an attempt to claim masculine identities in the face of social structures that threaten these identities. This leads to a sixth expectation, that violence will be most common among minority males, who experience additional barriers to claiming gender identity. The combination of males' increased motivation toward violence and females' decreased motivation to break the law produces a large gender gap in violent delinquency.

Another expectation assessed here is that, regardless of gender, blacks are less likely than whites to define risk-taking favorably and therefore are less likely to engage in common delinquency such as minor theft, school deviance, and drug use. The thinking here is that racial inequality itself discourages minorities from taking risks, because risk-taking is a privilege of power under capitalism.

Finally, the model allows for the test of the proposition that blocked access to legitimate financial resources—measured as spending money and hours worked per week for pay—increases the likelihood of theft. This relationship will hold for both genders and races, following the logic discussed previously.

Because the data and model permit only a partial assessment of the interactionist process, the results that follow are intended as a guide for future work. A definitive test of the theory requires data that also include measures of role-taking, specific identities, and other aspects of gender ideologies. In addition, a better assessment of the perspective would be based on longitudinal rather than cross-sectional data (see Heimer and Matsueda 1994). Longitudinal data would preclude the positing of causal relationships among social-psychological variables measured at the same time and would allow for the empirical causal ordering of variables to better match the theoretical ordering of constructs.

Estimation of the Model

I estimate the substantive and measurement models simultaneously using the maximum likelihood procedures of LISREL VII (Joreskog and Sorbom 1989). The models are estimated separately for females and males, and differences across gender in levels (means) and effects (slopes) of the latent variables are assessed using the multiple groups estimator of LISREL VII. The estimation of levels of the latent variables is achieved by fixing the scale of each variable to be equal to that of its reference indicator (see Bollen 1989). Significant differences across groups in the levels (means) of endogenous constructs can be interpreted as the gender gap that remains after differences in the means and slopes of the predictor variables have been controlled (Hayduk 1987: 315). The model fits the data reasonably well for both genders, given the large number of overidentifying restrictions ($L^2 = 387.2$, df = 204, and $L^2 = 412.75$, df = 204, for females and males respectively). Tests of invariance in the measurement of the multiple indicator constructs and sensitivity analyses demonstrate that the measurement process is comparable across groups and thus cross-gender comparisons are justified (see Bielby 1986; Thomson and Williams 1986). The results of the measurement model are presented in Appendix 7.B.

Tables 7.1 and 7.2 contain the unstandardized substantive parameter estimates for females and males, respectively. Tables 7.3 and 7.4 present the difference in likelihood ratio statistics for tests of invariance across gender in levels and efficacy of predictors. Table 7.5 presents information on the effects of race on female and male delinquency. I first discuss the most important findings regarding the motivational pathways leading to the gender gap in law violation, and then the major findings regarding the influence of race in this process.

Motivational Pathways to the Gender Gap in Delinquency. My first hypothesis posits a causal chain from grades, to self-esteem, to definition favorable to risk-taking, to delinquency. The results reported in Tables 7.1 and 7.2 provide some support for this logic. Regardless of gender, receiving high grades bolsters self-esteem (column 5). For females (Table 7.1), positive self-esteem discourages definitions favorable to risk-taking (row 5, column 8). Because definitions favorable to risk increase all forms of delinquency (column 9), high grades and positive self-esteem indirectly inhibit law violation because they discourage attitudes favorable to risk-taking, consistent with the interactionist perspective.

An unexpected difference emerges, however, when we examine this causal chain for males (Table 7.2). Specifically, among males, positive self-esteem fosters definitions favorable to risk (row 5, column 8), which in turn encourage delinquency (column 9). So, although positive self-esteem indirectly *decreases* delinquency among females, it indirectly *increases* delin-

TABLE 7.1

Unstandardized Parameter Estimates for Model of Gender, Race, and Delinquency: Females ($L^2 = 387.2$, df = 204)

	1 Black	2 Birth year	3 Father's education	4 Father's absence	5 Grades	6 Hours worked	7 Spending money	8 Self-esteem	9 Definitions of risk	10 Gender ideologies
1. Grades	−.5029*	.0861	.2410*	−.1622						
	(.1333)	(.0937)	(.0342)	(.1120)						
2. Hours worked	−.5710*	−.2032	−.1744*	.3739*						
	(.1596)	(.1122)	(.0410)	(.1341)						
3. Spending money	.7306*	.1499	.0096	.1249						
	(.1296)	(.0911)	(.0333)	(.1089)						
4. Self-esteem	.2789*	−.1283*	−.0005	.0005	.0772*	−.0149	.0700*			
	(.0687)	(.0475)	(.0177)	(.0569)	(.0130)	(.0112)	(.0138)			
5. Definitions of risk	−.7112*	.0605	.0335	−.0469	−.0664*	.0341*	.0655*	−.0957*		
	(.0923)	(.0637)	(.0236)	(.0760)	(.0176)	(.0149)	(.0186)	(.0401)		
6. Gender ideologies	.5766*	−.0775	−.0311*	.0564	.0058	−.0086	.0160			
	(.0709)	(.0489)	(.0182)	(.0585)	(.0133)	(.0115)	(.0142)			
7. School deviance	.0560	.0957*	.0428*	.1331*	−.0756*	.0219*	.0447*	−.0842*	.1812*	−.0440
	(.0711)	(.0464)	(.0173)	(.0554)	(.0132)	(.0109)	(.0137)	(.0291)	(.0253)	(.0300)
8. Theft	−.0516	.0899*	−.0185	.1116*	−.0291*	.0431*	.0189	−.1124*	.1313*	−.0851*
	(.0704)	(.0459)	(.0170)	(.0547)	(.0127)	(.0108)	(.0134)	(.0288)	(.0225)	(.0311)
9. Drug use	−.0877*	.0219	−.0063	.0373	−.0247*	.0126*	.0200*	−.0240*	.0546*	−.0181
	(.0258)	(.0168)	(.0062)	(.0200)	(.0047)	(.0039)	(.0049)	(.0105)	(.0083)	(.0110)
10. Violence	.0510	−.0518*	−.0045	.0879*	−.0174*	.0223*	.0337*	−.0428*	.0677*	−.0087
	(.0380)	(.0248)	(.0092)	(.0298)	(.0069)	(.0059)	(.0075)	(.0156)	(.0123)	(.0158)

SOURCE: All tables in this chapter are based on data from the Monitoring the Future survey (Bachman et al. 1990b).
NOTE: Standard errors are in parentheses.
*Denotes coefficient that is significant at least at $p < .05$, two-tailed test.

TABLE 7.2

Unstandardized Parameter Estimates for Model of Gender, Race, and Delinquency: Males ($L^2 = 412.75$, df = 204)

	1 Birth Black	2 Father's year	3 Father's education	4 absence	5 Hours Grades	6 Spending worked	7 Self-money	8 Definitions esteem	9 Gender of risk	10 ideologies
1. Grades	−.5310*	.1401	.2290*	−.3084*						
	(.1541)	(.0852)	(.0362)	(.1222)						
2. Hours worked	−.9735*	−.2060*	−.2114*	.2756*						
	(.1830)	(.1011)	(.0430)	(.1451)						
3. Spending money	.5469*	−.0965	.1087*	.4364*						
	(.1625)	(.0898)	(.0382)	(.1289)						
4. Self-esteem	.2239*	.0139	.0154	−.0456	.0737*	.0104	−.0075			
	(.0705)	(.0384)	(.0166)	(.0553)	(.0117)	(.0099)	(.0111)			
5. Definitions of risk	−.7240*	.0518	.0425	.0677	−.1006*	.0314*	.0255	.0958*		
	(.0951)	(.0511)	(.0221)	(.0737)	(.0159)	(.0132)	(.0148)	(.0404)		
6. Gender ideologies	.5534*	.0049	−.0038	.1061	−.0373*	−.0081	−.0027			
	(.0722)	(.0390)	(.0169)	(.0562)	(.0118)	(.0100)	(.0112)			
7. School deviance	−.0796	.0391	−.0111	.0113	−.0670*	.0541*	.0600*	−.0885*	.2193*	−.0001
	(.0731)	(.0373)	(.0161)	(.0538)	(.0121)	(.0098)	(.0109)	(.0298)	(.0273)	(.0332)
8. Theft	−.0329	.0597	−.0112	.1195	−.0459*	.0189	.0168	−.1100*	.2683*	.0154
	(.0892)	(.0455)	(.0197)	(.0658)	(.0144)	(.0118)	(.0132)	(.0360)	(.0316)	(.0404)
9. Drug use	−.1702*	−.0042	−.0038	.0650	−.0319*	.0055	.0383*	.0018	.0798*	.0176
	(.0370)	(.0189)	(.0082)	(.0272)	(.0049)	(.0054)	(.0149)	(.0123)	(.0169)	(.0060)
10. Violence	.1950*	−.0729*	−.0209	.0047	−.0212*	.0246*	.0364*	−.0655*	.1304*	.0084
	(.0568)	(.0289)	(.0125)	(.0416)	(.0091)	(.0075)	(.0084)	(.0229)	(.0195)	(.0256)

NOTE: Standard errors are in parentheses.
*Denotes coefficient that is significant at least at $p < .05$, two-tailed test.

TABLE 7.3
Difference in Likelihood Ratio Tests of Invariance Across Gender in Levels of Endogenous Variables

Endogenous variables	Gender difference L^2	df	Significance
1. Grades	1.07	1	$p>.05$
2. Self-esteem	.27	1	$p>.50$
3. Definitions favorable to risk-taking	.01	1	$p>.75$
4. School deviance	2.02	1	$p>.05$
5. Theft	1.03	1	$p>.10$
6. Drug use	.29	1	$p>.25$
7. Violence	1.03	1	$p>.10$

quency among males. The result is a significant difference across gender in the effect of self-esteem on definitions (Table 7.4, row 1), which suggests an interesting possibility that is consistent with the perspective developed here. It may be that because male status brings greater power than female status in our society, boys who feel competent are encouraged to take risks, while girls who feel competent are discouraged from taking risks. This possibility is consistent with the structural argument of power-control theory that risk-taking is encouraged primarily in powerful actors in a capitalist economy (Hagan et al. 1987).

The interactionist perspective also suggests that receiving high grades and developing positive self-esteem may directly inhibit delinquency, especially that targeted at the school. Consistent with this, Tables 7.1 and 7.2 show that, for both genders, receiving good grades increases self-esteem, which in turn inhibits delinquency, including school deviance (column 8). Moreover, the magnitudes of these effects are comparable across gender (Table 7.4, rows 2 and 3), as are mean levels of grades and self-esteem once predetermined variables are controlled (Table 7.3, rows 1 and 2). For both genders, the direct effects of self-esteem on delinquency are more pronounced than the indirect effects through definitions favorable to risk-taking.

Beyond this, the strongest predictor of all four forms of delinquency for both genders is definitions favorable to risk-taking.[10] Consistent with the interactionist perspective and power-control theory, youths who value risk-taking highly are likely to engage in school deviance, theft, and illicit drug use (Tables 7.1 and 7.2, column 9). In addition, the analysis shows that both females and males who hold definitions favorable to risk-taking also

TABLE 7.4
Difference in Likelihood Ratio Tests of Invariance Across Gender in Direct Effects (Slopes) of Predictor Variables

Effects	Gender difference L^2	df	Significance
1. Effect of self-esteem on definitions of risk	11.14	1	$p<.001$
2. Effect of grades on self-esteem	.05	1	$p>.50$
3. Effect of self-esteem on school deviance, theft, drug use, and violence	4.73	4	$p>.10$
4. Effect of definitions of risk on school deviance, theft, drug use, and violence	14.16	4	$p<.01$
5. Effect of gender ideologies on school deviance, theft, drug use, and violence	5.75	4	$p<.05$
6. Effect of race on school deviance, theft, drug use, and violence	11.51	4	$p<.01$
7. Effect of race on self-esteem	.28	1	$p>.25$
8. Effect of race on definitions of risk	.00	1	$p>.99$
9. Effect of race on gender ideology	.02	1	$p>.75$

are likely to engage in violence (column 9, row 10). Violent delinquency, therefore, also constitutes risky behavior that can bolster one's image in some social contexts (Short and Strodtbeck 1965).

More important for the present argument, however, the results show that definitions favorable to risk-taking play a different role in the process leading to delinquency among females as compared to males. Interestingly, this difference emerges because boys who value risk highly are much more likely than girls who value risk highly to break the law (Table 7.4, row 4). At the same time, there is no significant gender difference in mean level of definitions favorable to risk-taking once differences in means and slopes of other variables in the model are controlled (Table 7.3, row 3). Together these findings suggest that the gender difference in mean level of definitions favorable to risk-taking is less important than the differential impact (slopes) of these definitions on law violation. The interactionist perspective suggests that this reflects the greater societal disapproval of female than of male delinquency.

The results are counter to other expectations derived from the theoretical discussion, however. First, females who believe that married women and mothers should not work outside the home are somewhat more likely than other girls to steal, and are no more likely to break school rules, use drugs, or fight (Table 7.1, column 10). In addition, the current measure of gender ideologies has trivial effects on all forms of male delinquency, including violence (Table 7.2, column 10), which contradicts the argument that boys commit violent acts to demonstrate masculinity. Nevertheless, because the measurement of gender ideologies in this analysis captures only a small slice of the construct, it is premature to conclude that beliefs about the nature, characteristics, obligations, and roles of females and males are inconsequential for the gender gap in delinquency. Future research is necessary to explore other aspects of gender ideologies from an interactionist perspective.

The results also fail to support the argument that youths who have fewer financial resources will turn to theft to acquire the props and symbols of adulthood valued in the adolescent subculture (Tables 7.1 and 7.2). Neither having money to spend nor holding a job reduces theft (columns 6 and 7). It may be that valued symbols always exceed the legitimate means to obtain them, and therefore, even youths with abundant financial resources engage in theft.[11]

Perhaps the most important finding of this analysis, however, is that the model completely accounts for the gender gap in school deviance, theft, drug use, and violence (Table 7.3, rows 4–7). There is no significant gender difference in *any* form of delinquency once differences in means and slopes of predictor variables are taken into account. The overall pattern of results suggests that the gender gap in law violation arises in large part because definitions favorable to risk-taking have different implications for behavior across gender and also because high self-esteem discourages definitions favorable to risk-taking among females but encourages these definitions among males. Thus, the gender gap in delinquency seems to be due more to differences in the magnitudes of effects (slopes) than to differences in levels (means) of predictors, given the present model.

Indeed, when the delinquency equations are decomposed using regression standardization procedures (Winsborough and Dickenson 1971; Jones and Kelley 1984), the better part of the gender gap in violence (53.3 percent) and theft (69.7 percent) is explained by variation across gender in slopes and intercepts. For both violence and theft, differences in mean levels of the predictor variables account for a much smaller portion of the gender gap (20.9 percent and 29.6 percent, respectively). These results highlight the problem with previous research that has examined only differences in levels of predictor variables across gender. In contrast, for the forms of delinquency where the gender gap is smaller—school deviance and drug use—differences between female and male offending are largely the product of differences in the means of the predictor variables. It seems that when differences in behavioral outcomes are small, they can be accounted for by small differences in the means of predictors. Indeed, the decomposition of the equation predicting the gender gap in school deviance shows that if the predictor variables had the same means for both genders, females would be at least as deviant as males.[12]

Race, Gender, and Delinquency. The results also demonstrate that race has different consequences for female than for male delinquency (Table 7.4, row 6). This differential effect is due in large part to the fact that black males, but not black females, engage in more violence than their white counterparts (see total effects in Table 7.5).[13] Indeed, as Table 7.5 (direct effects) shows, black racial status directly fosters violence among males, but not among females. From an interactionist standpoint, this pattern can be interpreted as follows: The constraints on the positions and communication networks of African-Americans serve to restrict their social power. Black males respond to this problematic situation by negotiating behaviors that demonstrate the power that they *are* afforded on the basis of their gender. Consequently, black males are more likely than white males to engage in male posturing, including fighting and other forms of violent delinquency. This is not the case among females. Although the direct effect of race on violence is strong and positive, there is also a negative total indirect effect, which suppresses some of the total effect (Table 7.5). Black racial status directly increases violence among males, but it also inhibits violence by reducing definitions favorable to risk-taking and increasing self-esteem. The positive total effect of race on violence remains significant, however, because the positive direct effect of racial status is not completely countered by the negative total indirect effect.

Beyond this difference, the effects of race are pretty similar for females and males. For example, African-Americans of both genders are less likely than their white counterparts to steal and use drugs (Table 7.5). Moreover, this difference results from the same process regardless of gender (Table 7.4, rows 7 and 8). African-American females as well as males value risk-taking less and have higher self-esteem than their white counterparts, which reduces their involvement in delinquency (Table 7.5). This is consistent with the interactionist perspective and other empirical research.

Overall, the results with regard to race and delinquency are consistent with the structural arguments developed earlier. In general, whites, who are afforded greater social power than blacks, commit more common non-

TABLE 7.5
Effects of Black Racial Status on Delinquency

Dependent variable	Females: Total effect	Females: Direct effect	Females: Total indirect effect	Males: Total effect	Males: Direct effect	Males: Total indirect effect
1. Grades	−.5029*			−.5310*		
	(.1333)			(.1541)		
2. Hours worked	−.5710*			−.9735*		
	(.1596)			(.1830)		
3. Spending money	.7306*			.5426*		
	(.1296)			(.1625)		
4. Self-esteem	.2997*	.2789*	.0209	.1726*	.2239*	−.0513
	(.0691)	(.0687)	(.0187)	(.0702)	(.0705)	(.0170)
5. Definitions of risk	−.6781*	−.7112*	.0331	−.6751*	−.7240*	.0489
	(.0914)	(.0923)	(.0246)	(.0946)	(.0951)	(.0259)
6. Gender ideologies	.5902*	.5766*	.0137	.5797*	.5534*	.0263
	(.0699)	(.0709)	(.0129)	(.0714)	(.0722)	(.0142)
7. School deviance	−.0600	.0560	−.1159*	−.2140*	−.0796	−.1344*
	(.0688)	(.0711)	(.0369)	(.0718)	(.0731)	(.0396)
8. Theft	−.2207*	−.0516	−.1691*	−.1920*	−.0329	−.1591*
	(.0671)	(.0704)	(.0338)	(.0851)	(.0892)	(.0441)
9. Drug use	−.1228*	−.0877*	−.0351*	−.1787*	−.1702*	−.0086
	(.0248)	(.0258)	(.0127)	(.0357)	(.0370)	(.0187)
10. Violence	.0107	.0510	−.0403*	.1006*	.1950*	−.0944*
	(.0361)	(.0380)	(.0177)	(.0542)	(.0568)	(.0283)

*Denotes coefficient that is significant at least at $p < .05$.

violent delinquency. This holds regardless of gender. At the same time, black males commit more violent delinquency than whites, which can be interpreted as an attempt to demonstrate masculinity in the face of structural threats to this identity.

Conclusions

The empirical analysis reported above suggests that the interactionist perspective has potential for illuminating the dynamic relationships among gender inequality, racial inequality, and law violation. The analysis demonstrates that concern with negotiating positive self-image is indeed a key for understanding gender differences in delinquency because females and males attempt to manage their self-esteem in somewhat different ways. Specifically, girls seem most likely to develop definitions favorable to risk-taking as a response to damaged self-esteem, while boys seem more likely to acquire these definitions when they are self-assured. This difference is consistent with the notion that the capitalist economic system and its entrepreneurial ethos foster risk-taking among those who are structurally positioned to succeed in this system and who are confident about their abilities to do so. This result suggests an important avenue for exploration in future research, one that has the potential to draw links between the gender system in society and social-psychological process.

The results also suggest that, consistent with my theoretical arguments, taking risks may involve different lines of action for each gender. Indeed, what varies across gender is the *impact* on delinquency of definitions favorable to risk-taking. Mean differences in *levels* of these definitions account for little of the gender gap in law violation once other variables in the model are controlled. This is consistent with the notion that deviance is tolerated less for females, because females are the less powerful actors under the present gender system and consequently are less likely than males to manage impressions and take risks by engaging in illegal behavior. This view is directly counter to the social-control explanation of the gender gap in delinquency, which maintains that females will simply have less desire to take risks because they are restricted from doing so. Instead, the interactionist perspective argues that the gender gap emerges in part because inequality teaches girls to express their motivations through behavior that differs from that of boys. In short, it is the *meaning* of behavior that varies across gender.

In addition, the present findings show that race is indeed consequential for the gender gap in offending. The most significant point of impact is violent delinquency. According to the interactionist perspective, violent delinquency reflects the attempts of African-American males to negotiate masculine identities in the face of structural constraints that make claiming valued identities difficult. At the same time, black racial status reduces theft and drug use among both genders, largely because African-Americans value risk-taking less and have higher self-esteem than whites. This gender difference in the impact of race on violent and common delinquency suggests that theory and research that consider delinquency to be unidimensional may be missing an important part of the process. The present results indicate that there may be important differences in the meaning of violent and nonviolent offenses. Interestingly, this is reminiscent of arguments in favor of distinguishing between instrumental and expressive crimes (e.g., Chambliss 1967), which have fallen out of favor in recent years among those who maintain that there is no specialization in offending (e.g., Gottfredson and Hirschi 1990). The interactionist perspective and present results warn against ignoring the meaning that youths give to various illegal behaviors.

As mentioned earlier, the present empirical analysis is but a partial assessment of an interactionist perspective. A definitive test of this perspective must at minimum incorporate key constructs such as gender identity, identity within the peer subculture, and role-taking, as well as the meaning given to law violation. Other recent research demonstrates the importance of role-taking in negotiating definitions of oneself, anticipating the reactions of others to delinquency, and forming definitions favorable to delinquency (Matsueda 1992; Heimer and Matsueda 1994). A full test of the perspective, therefore, requires data on these outcomes of role-taking, in addition to data on gender identity, peer identity, gender ideologies, and definitions of risk.

In sum, the interactionist perspective is a useful theoretical tool for furthering our understanding of gender, race, and delinquency. Because this perspective is rooted firmly in the conflict tradition in criminology (Heimer and Matsueda 1994; Matsueda 1992), it is consistent with the political conflict model underlying the structural explanations of socialist feminist criminology and power-control theory. Further development of this perspective, therefore, has potential for building bridges between these structural explanations as well as for elucidating the links between the macro and micro processes that produce gender and race differences in delinquency.

APPENDIX 7.A *Description of Observable Variables*

Race: Dummy variable coded 1 if black, 0 if white.

Birth year: Interval level variable capturing year of birth for the high school senior respondent.

Father's education: Highest level of schooling completed by father figure. Coded as follows: 1 = completed grade school or less; 2 = some high school; 3 = completed high school; 4 = some college; 5 = completed college; 6 = graduate or professional school after college.

Father's absence: Dummy variable coded 1 if neither father or male guardian lives with the youth.

Grades: Self-reported average grades in high school, coded as 1 = D; 2 = C−; 3 = C; 4 = C+; 5 = B−; 6 = B; 7 = B+; 8 = A−; 9 = A.

Hours worked: Average number of hours worked per week over the school year.

Coded as 1 = none; 2 = 5 hours or less; 3 = 6–10 hours; 4 = 11–15 hours; 5 = 16–20 hours; 6 = 21–25 hours; 7 = 26–30 hours; 8 = more than 30 hours.

Spending money: An interval level composite variable representing amount of money respondent gets in an average week from working and other sources (allowances, etc.). Coded as 1 = none; 2 = $1–$5; 3 = $6–$10; 4 = $11–$20; 5 = $21–$35; 6 = $36–$50; 7 = $51–$75; 8 = $76–$125; 9 = $126+.

Self-esteem: Agreement with the following statements, coded as 1 = disagree; 2 = mostly disagree; 3 = neither; 4 = mostly agree; 5 = agree.
"I take a positive attitude toward myself."
"I feel I am a person of worth, on an equal plane with others."
"On the whole, I am satisfied with myself."
Also, agreement with the following statements, coded as 1 = agree; 2 = mostly agree; 3 = neither; 4 = mostly disagree; 5 = disagree.
"Sometimes I think I am no good at all."
"I feel that my life is not very useful."

Definitions favorable to risk-taking: Agreement with the following statements, coded as 1 = disagree; 2 = mostly disagree; 3 = neither; 4 = mostly agree; 5 = agree.
"I get a kick out of doing things that are a little dangerous."
"I like to test myself now and then by doing something a little risky."

Gender ideologies: The following questions, coded as 1 = not at all acceptable; 2 = somewhat acceptable; 3 = acceptable; 4 = desirable.
"Imagine you are married with no children. How would you feel about the working arrangement where the husband works full time and the wife doesn't work?"
"Imagine you are married and have one or more preschool children. How would you feel about the working arrangement where the husband works full time and the wife doesn't work?"

School deviance: Coded as 1 = none; 2 = 1 day; 3 = 2 days; 4 = 3 days; 5 = 4–5 days; 6 = 6–10 days; 7 = 11 days or more.
During the last four weeks, how many whole days of school have you missed because you skipped or "cut?"
During the last four weeks, how often have you gone to school but skipped a class you weren't supposed to?
Also, the following coded as 1 = not at all; 2 = once; 3 = twice; 4 = 3 or 4 times; 5 = 5 or more times.
During the last 12 months, how often have you damaged school property on purpose?

Theft: The following questions coded as 1 = not at all; 2 = once; 3 = twice; 4 = 3 or 4 times; 5 = 5 or more times.
"During the last 12 months, how often have you . . ."

"taken something not belonging to you worth under $50?"
"taken something not belonging to you worth over $50?"
"taken something from a store without paying for it?"

Drug use: Index of 11 questions asking for self-reported drug use in the last 12 months. The index includes one question about each of the following drugs: marijuana or hashish, inhalants, barbiturates, cocaine, heroin, other narcotics, LSD, other psychedelics, amphetamines, quaaludes, and tranquilizers. Responses are coded 1 = 0 occasions; 2 = 1–2 times; 3 = 3–5 times; 4 = 6–9 times; 5 = 10–19 times; 6 = 20–39 times; 7 = 40 or more times.

Violence: The following questions coded as 1 = not at all; 2 = once; 3 = twice; 4 = 3 or 4 times; 5 = 5 or more times.
"During the last 12 months, how often have you . . ."
"gotten into a serious fight with someone at work or school?"
"taken part in a fight where a group of your friends were against another group?"
"hurt someone badly enough to need bandages or a doctor?"

APPENDIX 7.B *The Measurement Model*

The theoretical constructs in the causal model of gender, race, and delinquency are not observed directly, but rather are assessed indirectly through respondents' answers to survey items, which are observable. The responses to interview items contain measurement error, however, and are less than perfectly reliable indicators of the latent theoretical construct. Since unreliability in measurement can attenuate substantive parameter estimates, I correct for this by incorporating a model of the measurement process. The measurement model that I specify contains 12 correlations among measurement errors, which includes 6 correlations among errors associated with indicators of self-esteem and definitions favorable to risk-taking and 6 among measurement errors in the indicators of school deviance, theft, and violence. Including these correlations significantly improves the fit of the model to the data for both females (L^2 difference = 316.53, df = 12, $p < .0001$) and males (L^2 difference = 419.39, df = 12, $p < .0001$).

Straightforward comparisons of substantive parameter estimates across sex requires invariance in the metrics of the latent constructs (Bielby 1986; Thomson and Williams 1986). As Table 7.B1 (column 1) shows, the relative magnitudes of the validity coefficients are similar across sex. The indicators that are most valid for females are in most cases the most valid for males; similarly, the indicators that are less valid for females tend to be less valid for males. Cross-group tests show that the metric loadings (unstandardized slopes) for the indicators of self-esteem (L^2 difference = 3.14, df = 4, $p > .25$), definitions favorable to risk-taking (L^2 difference = 1.87, df = 1, $p > .10$), and acceptance of gender ideologies (L^2 difference = .03, df = 1, $p < .75$) are invariant across gender. Nevertheless, there are gender differences in ratios of the metric slopes of indicators of school deviance (L^2 difference = 35.81, df = 2, $p <$

TABLE 7.B1

Parameter Estimates for the Measurement Model for Females (N = 1540) and Males (N = 1503)

Latent variable	Observed variable	1 Validity coefficient		2 Metric slope		3 Observed variance		4 Error variance		5 Observed mean	
		Male	Female	Male	Female	Male	Female	Male	Female	Male	Female
Race	Black	1.000[f]	1.000[f]	1.000[f]	1.000[f]	.115	.138	.000[f]	.000[f]	.133	.166[a]
Birth year	Year of birth	1.000[f]	1.000[f]	1.000[f]	1.000[f]	.345	.258	.000[f]	.000[f]	3.684	3.792[a]
Father's education	Level of father's education	1.000[f]	1.000[f]	1.000[f]	1.000[f]	1.944	1.940	.000[f]	.000[f]	3.960	3.868
Father's absence	Father figure absent from home	1.000[f]	1.000[f]	1.000[f]	1.000[f]	.183	.194	.000[f]	.000[f]	.240	.262
Grades	Average grades in school	1.000[f]	1.000[f]	1.000[f]	1.000[f]	3.925	3.594	.000[f]	.000[f]	5.450	5.835[a]
Hours worked	Average number of hours worked per week	1.000[f]	1.000[f]	1.000[f]	1.000[f]	5.438	5.008	.000[f]	.000[f]	4.290	4.166
Spending money	Average amount of spending money per week	1.000[f]	1.000[f]	1.000[f]	1.000[f]	4.243	3.312	.000[f]	.000[f]	3.136	2.872[a]
Self-esteem	Positive attitude toward self	.829	.806	1.000[f]	1.000[f]	.963	1.182	.285	.375	4.059	3.812[a]
	Feeling of self-worth	.741	.748	.856	.860	.884	1.015	.389	.438	4.237	4.109[a]
	Feeling of satisfaction with self	.806	.831	.937	1.005	.896	1.123	.314	.354	4.142	3.977[a]
	Thoughts that one is of some good	.545	.574	.845	.930	1.589	2.014	1.162	1.426	3.802	3.474[a]
	Feeling that one's life is useful	.574	.632	.763	.816	1.168	1.283	.815	.788	4.268	4.155[a]
Definitions of risk	Gets a kick out of doing dangerous things	.872	.942	1.000[f]	1.000[f]	1.546	1.693	.369	.169	3.313	2.782[a]
	Likes to test self by taking risks	.751	.682	.850	.739	1.506	1.764	.663	.957	3.461	2.960[a]
Gender ideologies	Accepts nonworking wife in a family with no children	.862	.905	1.000[f]	1.000[f]	.857	1.004	.226	.190	2.602	3.183[a]

TABLE 7.B1
(continued)

Latent variable	Observed variable	1 Validity coefficient		2 Metric slope		3 Observed variance		4 Error variance		5 Observed mean	
		Male	Female	Male	Female	Male	Female	Male	Female	Male	Female
	Accepts nonworking wife in a family with preschool children	.584	.591	.573	.741	.741	.790	.514	.518	1.982	2.336[a]
School deviance	Number of days cut school	.690	.662	1.000[f]	1.000[f]	1.609	1.612	1.326	1.287	1.723	1.664
	Number of days skipped class	.697	.671	.821	.784	1.062	.965	.865	.773	1.660	1.589[a]
	Rate of vandalizing school property	.347	.334	.361	.199	.831	.252	.672	.214	1.385	1.135[a]
Theft	Rate of theft of item worth less than $50	.796	.830	1.000[f]	1.000[f]	1.687	1.075	.930	.483	1.904	1.511[a]
	Rate of theft of item worth more than $50	.586	.476	.463	.240	.669	.188	.363	.137	1.277	1.079[a]
	Rate of shoplifting	.752	.782	.947	.926	1.696	1.038	1.016	.532	1.826	1.483[a]
Drug use	Scale of self-reported drug use	1.000[f]	1.000[f]	1.000[f]	1.000[f]	.204	.121	.000[f]	.000[f]	1.224	1.154[a]
Violence	Rate of serious fighting at school or work	.662	.615	1.000[f]	1.000[f]	.727	.437	.332	.293	1.399	1.231[a]
	Rate of hurting others badly	.754	.465	1.061	.373	.631	.106	.332	.082	1.314	1.055[a]
	Rate of gang fighting	.734	.654	1.283	.984	.974	.373	.332	.231	1.483	1.224[a]

[a]Denotes that means differ across groups at $p < .05$.
[f]Denotes fixed coefficient.

.001), violence (L^2 difference = 30.31, df = 2, $p < .001$), and theft (L^2 difference = 45.99, df = 2, $p < .001$). Table 7.B1 (column 2) shows that the slopes for males are steeper, indicating that for males more than females, overstating (or understating) reports of delinquency results in overestimation (or underestimation) of the true score of the three latent constructs tapping different forms of misbehavior. Consequently, I performed sensitivity analyses by varying the reference indicator of these constructs and comparing all of the substantive parameter estimates under the various normalizations (Bielby 1986). These analyses do not produce substantial departures in the substantive parameter estimates. It is reasonable, therefore, to compare the substantive parameter estimates for females with those for males.

In addition, estimates of the intercepts of the structural equations can be produced using the option for modeling levels of endogenous variables available in LISREL VII. Through this procedure, we can compare estimates of the intercepts of the structural equations (alpha) across groups, which gives an indication of the amount of variation in the gender gap in the endogenous variable that is not accounted for by the equation (Hayduk 1987; Bollen 1989). For example, a significant difference across groups in definitions favorable to risk would mean that these attitudes vary across gender even after gender differences in the exogenous variables, grades, financial resources, and self-esteem are held constant. Yet, similar to the situation described above, we can expect that if the measurement process generating the observed variable (y) varies across gender, straightforward cross-group comparisons of intercepts from the structural equations may not be justified. When modeling means, the observed variable (y) is specified to be a linear composite of the underlying latent construct, a stochastic error component, and the intercept of the observed variable. The intercept of each latent variable is identified by setting the intercept of the observed variable that serves as the reference indicator to zero. Thus, simple comparisons across groups of the intercepts in the structural equations (remaining gender gap) require that the intercepts associated with the observed variables be invariant across groups. Cross-group tests showed that these intercepts were significantly different for the observed indicators of self-esteem, taste for risk, gender ideologies, school deviance, violence, and theft (all at least $p < .05$). I perform a series of sensitivity analyses, similar to the procedure above, to get some idea of whether the estimates of the intercept of the structural equation are sensitive to varying which observable variable is specified to be the reference indicator and to have a zero intercept. These analyses produce similar estimates. Thus, it seems reasonable to use estimates of the intercepts in the equations predicting the exogenous variables to assess the gender gap in the construct.

Gender Inequality and Violence Against Women

The Case of Murder

WILLIAM C. BAILEY

RUTH D. PETERSON

To extend our understanding of crime and inequality, this chapter examines the relationship between gender socioeconomic inequality and lethal violence against women. Works in the 1960s and 1970s produced a substantial body of evidence linking various aspects of absolute and relative socioeconomic deprivation to property crime patterns. During the late 1970s and early 1980s, criminologists also began to take seriously the notion that poverty and socioeconomic inequality might be important contributors to violent crime in the United States. Indeed, recent studies have produced a fairly convincing body of evidence that socioeconomic inequality in general, and racial socioeconomic inequality in particular, are major contributors to serious crimes of violence, including murder, assault, and robbery (Bailey 1984; Blau and Blau 1982; P. Blau and Golden 1986; P. Blau and Schwartz 1984; Braithwaite 1979; Crutchfield et al. 1982; Golden and Messner 1987; Messner 1982, 1983a, 1983b; Sampson 1985; Smith and Parker 1980; K. R. Williams 1984; K. Williams and Flewelling 1988).

In addition to examining the extent to which general and racial inequality are linked to violent crime, scholars have begun to examine empirically feminist arguments that gender socioeconomic inequality is a major contributor to one form of violence against women—rape. The feminist view of rape holds that violence against women (including nonsexual violence) is an expression of a patriarchal social system whereby the subjugation of women by men is built into the organization of society (Brownmiller 1975; Clark and Lewis 1977; D. E. H. Russell 1975; Sanday 1981). Opportunity and reward systems are structured so that women are systematically disadvantaged in attaining valued socioeconomic resources upon which the perpetuation of male power depends (Ellis 1989). Moreover, for some feminists, rape and other forms of assault and coercion serve the important purpose of keeping women in their place and not challenging the existing system of gender stratification (Brownmiller 1975; Griffin 1971). Eliminating such violence requires eliminating "disparities between the sexes in sociopolitical and economic power" (Ellis and Beattie 1983: 76).

Most gender equality arguments are based on the assumption that the benefits of parity in reducing violence against women will be far-reaching (Ellis 1989; Schwendinger and Schwendinger 1983; J. Williams and Holmes 1981). However, not all are convinced that the payoff will be immediate. For example, Russell maintains that some men rape because they feel threatened by the prospect that women could obtain equality. To the extent that rape is a way for these men to express their resentment and hostility, then a narrowing of the gender gap may mean "more threatened male egos, and consequently, more rapes" (D. E. H. Russell 1975: 14). However, Russell and others expressing concern about "male backlash" do not appear to believe that the long-run and net effect of greater gender socioeconomic equality will be an increase in the level of rape. Rather, Russell expresses concern about the reactions of "some men" only.

Recent investigations by Baron and Straus (1989) and Peterson and Bailey (1992) provide support for the feminist claim that the rape problem is an added cost of socioeconomic inequality in the United States. But researchers have not investigated the possible empirical links between types of socioeconomic inequality and other forms of violence against females.[1] For example, the question remains whether general, racial, and gender socioeconomic inequality contribute significantly to female homicides. The findings from studies of general homicide and rape victimization cannot be assumed to apply to the homicide victimization of women. Since the overall homicide rate is dominated by male victimizations, it is not clear what a positive association between general and racial inequality and total homicides indicates about lethal violence against females.[2]

Similarly, although recent studies show evidence supporting the rape and gender inequality argument, this evidence sheds little light on how various dimensions of gender inequality might be associated with female killings. To the extent that rape is a "sex" crime, it may be wrong to generalize the findings of rape and gender inequality studies to female homicide. Conversely, to the extent that rape is a crime of anger and destruction, then at least certain types of female homicide might also be a consequence of gender inequality. Resolution of these issues requires that scholars ex-

TABLE 8.1
Descriptive Statistics for Predictor and Female Homicide Rate Variables

Variable	Mean	Standard deviation	Minimum	Maximum	Range
Log population	12.300	0.760	11.510	15.770	4.250
Percent black population	18.070	15.970	0.000	70.690	71.000
South (0/1)	0.360	0.480	0.000	1.000	1.000
Divorce rate	11.350	1.960	5.000	17.000	12.000
Percent family poverty	10.840	4.670	2.000	30.000	28.300
General income inequality	0.374	0.038	0.255	0.462	0.207
White-black income inequality ($1,000's)	7.090	3.310	−8.470	15.540	24.010
Percent females married	48.280	7.150	31.450	66.040	34.590
Percent females married but separated	6.845	3.848	1.404	25.220	23.816
Percent females with 4 years of college	8.220	3.460	2.850	23.760	20.910
Median income of females ($1,000's)	5.780	1.030	4.330	10.450	6.120
Percent females in managerial, professional, and administrative occupations	22.150	4.190	12.000	37.740	25.740
Percent female unemployment	6.530	2.600	2.500	17.300	14.800
Male-female gap in 4 years of college	2.520	2.090	−9.310	8.440	17.750
Male-female gap in median income ($1,000's)	6.250	2.100	2.310	14.800	12.500
Percent managers, professionals, and administrators who are female	42.490	4.270	31.000	60.510	29.510
Female-male gap in unemployment	−0.270	1.470	−6.167	4.431	10.599
Total female murder rate	6.450	4.700	0.000	26.210	26.210
Female felony murder rate	1.510	1.940	0.000	11.230	11.230
Female argument murder rate	2.130	2.230	0.000	13.730	13.730
Female family murder rate	1.990	1.820	0.000	10.460	10.460
Female friend murder rate	1.190	1.450	0.000	8.740	8.740
Female girlfriend murder rate	.730	1.140	0.000	6.050	6.050
Wife murder rate (per 100,000 married women)	2.980	3.370	0.000	20.890	20.890
Female stranger murder rate	0.450	0.710	0.000	3.710	3.710

amine directly the relationship between types of socioeconomic inequality and female homicide.

In the meantime, it is quite clear that the level of socioeconomic attainment of women varies considerably across communities in the United States, as does the *relative* status of women and men (see Table 8.1 and the following discussion). It is also clear that, like general homicides, rates of female homicide victimization vary significantly from one community to another (see Table 8.1). The purpose of our study is to investigate how variation in the socioeconomic status of women and variation in female homicides might be associated. To use the Blaus' terminology, we examine whether the female homicide problem is a further "cost" of structured socioeconomic inequality in this society.

To that end, we examine cross-sectionally the relationship between female homicide victimization rates and indicators of (1) female achievement in education, employment, occupational status, and income; and (2) male-female inequality in educational, occupational, employment, and income attainment for a sample of large cities in the United States (n = 138) for 1980. On the assumption that women are afforded greater protection against lethal assault by higher levels of educational, occupational, and income attainment, we would expect a significant inverse relationship between these areas of achievement and female homicide rates. This should be the case because a better education makes possible more lucrative employment, which in turn allows one to structure a more safe and secure environment and lifestyle. In other words, persons (including women) with better education/employment/income situations are better able to work and reside in safer communities and to avoid contexts that are more likely to lead to violent outcomes (e.g., having to rely upon public transportation).

However, if the subordinate status of women relative to men invites victimization (as appears to be the case for rape), then the male-female gap in socioeconomic status may be more important than the absolute status of women in contributing to female killings. At the same time, it is possible that some dimensions of gender inequality are more important than others in contributing to female homicides. Peterson and Bailey (1992), for example, found that the level of male-female income inequality was associated significantly with rape rates in U.S. metropolitan areas, but there was only a chance association between rates of rape and various dimensions of educational and occupational inequality. We explore these possibilities for female homicides.

Inequality and Violence Against Women

As indicated above, empirical support for the hypothesis that socioeconomic inequality contributes to violence against women stems primarily from analyses of rape. Pursuing arguments set forth by Blau and Blau (1982), some scholars have sought to determine if rape, like other types of violent crime (homicide, assault, robbery), is an added "cost" of general and racial socioeconomic inequality in the United States. The Blaus' own research indicates that forcible rape is an exception to the general finding that levels of socioeconomic inequality are associated closely with levels of metropolitan violence (Blau and Blau 1982; P. Blau and Golden 1986; P. Blau and Schwartz 1984). Subsequent studies by M. D. Smith and Bennett (1985) and Peterson and Bailey (1988) do provide evidence of a link between measures of absolute and relative deprivation and forcible rape.

Arguing that the negative findings from the Blau and Blau study were a consequence of the use of police figures for rape that are unreliable because of variation in reporting by victims and police, Smith and Bennett (1985) examined a variation on the Blau and Blau (1982) model for a sample of Standard Metropolitan Statistical Areas (SMSAs) for the 1980 period. To compensate for the possible unreliability of FBI data, they restricted their analysis to metropolitan areas (n = 88) with average rape rates (1979 to 1981) at least one standard deviation above or below the mean rate for all SMSAs. The assumption was that it would be difficult to attribute the magnitude of difference in rape rates between the two extreme groups of SMSAs to reporting practices alone.

Smith and Bennett's analysis did not reveal a significant association between the black-white income gap and rape rates. Smith and Bennett do, however, report a significant positive association between rape rates and poverty (i.e., absolute deprivation). They conclude that this finding supports the Schwendinger and Schwendinger (1983) argument that poverty breeds contempt for women. (For reasons that are not explained, the Smith and Bennett analysis does not include a measure of general economic inequality such as the Gini Index.)

In an extension of the Blau and Blau (1982) and Smith and Bennett (1985) analyses, Peterson and Bailey (1988) report some support for rape and inequality arguments. Examining average rape rates (1979 to 1981) for SMSAs (n = 243) and three dimensions of socioeconomic status, they found support for the relative deprivation hypothesis for both general income inequality (the Gini Index) and racial income inequality (the black-white gap in average family income). However, a chance-only association was observed between the level of poverty and rape.

Gender Inequality and Rape

The Smith and Bennett (1985) and Peterson and Bailey (1988) analyses shed additional light on the Blau and Blau thesis and lend credence to the argument that, like other forms of violence, rape stems at least in part from economic deprivation. However, these analyses do not examine the argument that rape rates are associated with variation in the status of women, and particularly with their economic status in relation to men's. This issue has been pursued more directly by investigators examining the feminist argument that rape is a consequence of male dominance and gender inequality.

In the first study of this type, Ellis and Beattie (1983) examined the relationship between rape rates for 26 large metropolitan areas and male-female disparities in median earnings, years of education, level of employment, participation in professional occupations, and the percentage of judges, lawyers, police, and detectives who are female. Rape rates were computed using city-level FBI figures, victim survey data for each city, and FBI figures for the standard metropolitan areas that contain the cities. Contrary to feminist arguments, Ellis and Beattie observed only a single instance of a significant positive association between the level of gender inequality and rape rates—victim survey determined rape rates and gender disparity in earnings ($r = .48$). However, when selected control factors were introduced into the analysis, this relationship was reduced to a chance level.

Baron and Straus (1984, 1987) conducted two follow-up investigations of the Ellis and Beattie study. In the 1984 analysis they examined the relationship between state-level FBI-reported rape rates for 1979 and a composite status-of-women index (SWX) reflecting four dimensions of male-female equality: economic, educational, political, and legal (Yllo 1983; Yllo and Straus 1981). A regression analysis produced a significant ($p = .014$) positive relationship between the gender equality index and rape rates. This finding is contrary to feminist arguments, but Baron and Straus conclude that it supports the male "backlash" argument for rape.

In the second investigation, Baron and Straus consider average state-level rape rates (1980 to 1982) and a revised gender-equality index (GEX) that measures male-female equality in three, rather than four, spheres of life: economic, political, and legal (Sugarman and Straus 1987). Here Baron and Straus report a statistically significant ($t = -2.77$, $p < .01$) negative relationship between rape rates and gender equality. As feminist arguments predict, higher levels of gender equality are associated with lower rape rates. Of note, Baron and Straus fail to speculate on possible reasons for the contrasting results of their two studies.[3]

In a final investigation, Peterson and Bailey (1992) examined the relationship between various dimensions of general, racial (black-white), and gender socioeconomic inequality and rape rates for U.S. metropolitan areas (n = 263) for 1980. Consistent with Blau and Blau's inequality arguments, they found that the Gini Index of general income inequality and the black-white income gap were significant predictors of rape rates throughout most of the analysis.

Importantly too, and consistent with feminist arguments, Peterson and Bailey found a very significant positive relationship between the level of male-female income inequality and rape rates. This pattern held even when gender differentials in educational attainment and occupational status were held constant. However, levels of male-female educational and occupational inequality were not associated significantly with rape rates. Peterson and Bailey argue that since power differentials in the United States are largely a consequence of income (and wealth) rather than educational attainment and occupational position, it is not surprising that the gender gap in income would be the factor most closely associated with rape.

In sum, recent investigators have explored the relationship between rape and various aspects of general, racial, and gender socioeconomic status and inequality. Although findings from these studies cannot be characterized as uniform, on balance the evidence supports claims that in the United States rape is an important cost of economic inequality in general, and of racial and gender socioeconomic inequality in particular. The question remains, however, whether such inequality contributes to other forms of violence against women, including homicide. As indicated, to the extent that rape is a sex crime, its etiology might be quite different from that of other forms of assault against women. But if rape is primarily (or even largely) a crime of hate and destruction, then gender inequality may also be an important contributor to the ultimate crime against women—murder. Empirical research has yet to explore this possibility.

Studies of Female Homicide

In recent years criminologists have focused a great deal of attention on female homicide offenders (Browne 1987; Browne and Williams 1989; Bunyak 1986; Goetting 1988a, 1988b, 1989; A. Jones 1980; Kuhl 1985; McClain 1982–1983; C. R. Mann 1988, 1990; Weisheit 1984; Wilbanks 1983a, 1983b). Female homicide victimization has also been a concern, but to a much lesser degree (Gartner 1990; Gartner et al. 1990; Gartner and McCarthy 1991; McClain 1981; Weisheit 1984; Wilbanks 1982). In both cases, the female homicide literature is largely micro and descriptive in nature. Seldom does the literature examine female homicide victimization (or offending) patterns in light of macro, structural-level considerations. Our search of the literature reveals only three recent structural analyses of female homicide victimization (all by Gartner and her colleagues), and one study of female homicide offending (Browne and Williams 1989).[4]

The Gartner et al. studies were not designed to test homicide and gender socioeconomic status and inequality arguments. Instead, the analyses are grounded largely in routine activity, lifestyle, and opportunity theses as they apply to female homicide victimization. Drawing on these perspectives, Gartner's (1990) initial investigation examined the relationship between a variety of sociodemographic and other factors and homicide rates for various gender-by-age combinations, for eighteen developing countries for selected years during the periods 1950 to 1980 (n = 126) and 1965 to 1980 (n = 72). A pooled cross-sectional and time-series analysis was employed considering the two periods.

Gartner's (1990) findings are complex. Regarding gender and homicide, they lead her to conclude that recognized motivational (material), social-integration, and cultural theories operate quite similarly for male and female homicides. For example, indicators of material deprivation (the level of welfare spending), weak social integration (the divorce rate), and exposure to official violence (the number of battle deaths resulting from war) were found to be associated significantly with female and male homicide rates. Consistent with various opportunity, lifestyle, and routine activity perspectives, however, female participation in the world of work was associated with women's being more vulnerable to murder. For women, work commonly involves spending less time at home (a more safe setting), spending more time on the streets (a less safe setting) traveling to and from the workplace, and spending more time among strangers (more dangerous persons). The net result is that employment contributes to female homicides.

Gartner et al. (1990) explore whether various sociodemographic and other selected factors are associated with the male-female *differential* in rates of homicide victimization for the same eighteen developed countries for 1950 to 1980. The analysis includes two demographic factors and selected status-of-women variables: female share of the unmarried population, female share of the labor force, occupational segregation of females, and female share of college enrollments. Consistent with routine activity, lifestyle, and opportunity theses, the analysis showed that the proportion of homicide victims who are female is associated positively with the female share of the unmarried population, the divorce rate, the illegitimacy rate, the level of female participation in the labor force, and the level of gender occupational segregation. The relative level of female killings is also associated negatively and significantly with the percentage of enrolled college students who are female.

To determine whether the relationship between the male-female homicide differential and the *roles* of women is conditioned by the *status* of women, the analysis was replicated with the eighteen nations divided into two groups. In one, the college enrollment was 35 percent or more female (n = 7); in the other, it was less than 35 percent female (n = 11). For the nations with low female college participation, the male-female homicide gap continued to be associated positively and significantly with the level of female involvement in the labor force and gender occupational segregation. For the nations with a higher level of women in college, there was a chance-only association between the homicide differential and the two gender status variables. Based on this pattern, Gartner et al. conclude that the level of female homicide (relative to male) does not necessarily increase as gender roles become less stratified. Rather, in societies that permit women higher social *status*, lower levels of gender *role* stratification do not put women at a greater risk of violence.

In a third study, Gartner and McCarthy (1991) examine female homicide victimization patterns from 1921 to 1988 in Toronto and Vancouver, Canada, in light of changes in the age structure and marital and employment status of women. As before, their predictions are grounded primarily in opportunity arguments. To examine how the relationship between female homicide and age, marital status, and employment may have shifted over time, Gartner and McCarthy divide the Toronto and Vancouver homicide data into two periods: 1921 to 1969 and 1970 to 1988. They argue that the late 1960s and early 1970s witnessed significant shifts in the status of women's lives, and in awareness of gender inequality and women's rights.

Contrary to predictions, Gartner and McCarthy found no indication that women in different age groups are more or less subject to homicide in either time period. There was also no indication that married women are afforded greater protection against homicide. The effect of employment status was found to vary for the two time periods. Before 1970, when employment was less normative for women, employed women were overrepresented among homicide victims. However, after 1969, employed women had a lower than expected homicide risk compared to the general female population. The same basic patterns held when spousal and nonintimate types of homicide were considered. The exceptions are that single and younger women were found to be overrepresented among victims of nonintimate homicides, whereas married and middle-aged women were underrepresented in these types of killings.

Like the two earlier Gartner studies, the Gartner and McCarthy analysis demonstrates that female homicide rates vary considerably over time and across locations, and suggests that different categories of women are more or less subject to violent death depending upon how various status and role factors influence criminal motivation, daily activities, and opportunities for victimization. It is important to note, however, that Gartner and her colleagues do not consider the relationship between the socioeconomic status of women and female homicide victimization. They speculate in each paper about how the economic well-being of women might influence their vulnerability to homicide but do not examine this possibility directly. Further, none of the analyses examines the feminist argument that male-female socioeconomic inequality breeds violence against women. Consequently, these studies provide little insight into whether (and how) the absolute and relative socioeconomic status of women might be associated with female homicide victimization, as seems to be true of rape (Baron and Straus 1987; Peterson and Bailey 1992). In brief, whether the gender status and inequality arguments hold for female killings remains to be determined. We now turn to an examination of this issue.

Methods and Procedures

To examine how the socioeconomic status of women may influence female homicide victimization, we examine cross-sectionally for a sample of 138 U.S. cities for 1980 the relationship between female homicide rates and various indicators of the absolute and relative (to men) socioeconomic status of women. Cities are selected as units of analysis because of their use in a number of previous structural analyses and because, compared with SMSAs and states, they minimize problems of aggregation bias (Bailey 1984). The sample of cities includes 138 of the 168 cities with a 1980 population of 100,000 or more. The 30 large cities not included in this analysis were excluded because of missing data for the female homicide variables (see discussion below). The availability of census data for 1980 permits the construction of a variety of indicators of socioeconomic status and inequality and important control variables.

Female Homicides

The dependent variables are based on the number of female homicide victims per 100,000 female population. First, a general female homicide rate is computed that includes all female killings. However, women are killed under a wide variety of circumstances and by persons with whom they have a variety of relationships. This raises the possibility that some types of female homicide may be more or less subject to the influences of socioeconomic status and inequality. Thus, separate homicide rates are computed for the most common types of female killing. These include (1) killings associated with felonies (felony murders), (2) killings growing out of arguments, (3) wife killings, (4) killings committed by boyfriends, (5) killings involving immediate family members, (6) killings involving friends and acquaintances, and (7) killings involving strangers.[5]

Required homicide data were drawn from the Federal Bureau of Investigation's (FBI) Supplementary Homicide Reports (SHR) for 1980. Two features of the SHR Program influenced our sample of cities and the types of female homicides we consider.

Missing SHR Case Information. Like the Uniform Crime Reporting (UCR) Program, the SHR Program is a voluntary program whereby police departments report crime incident information to the FBI, including demographic data about homicide victims and offenders and information about homicide circumstances and the relationship between victims and offenders. Unfortunately, the SHR Program does not provide complete national coverage. For example, the 1980 UCR reports a total of 23,044 murders and nonnegligent manslaughters, but the 1980 SHR provides data for only 21,860 murders. The UCR and SHR murder counts differ because some police departments do not participate in the SHR program, and others do not provide the FBI with SHR data for all killings. Our analysis is limited to the 138 cities with a population of at least 100,000 where the number of cases in the SHR is at least 95 percent of the UCR homicide count.[6]

SHR Circumstance and Relationship Data. As indicated, we are interested in examining the influence of gender socioeconomic status and inequality on total female homicides, *and* on the most common types of female killing. Unfortunately, crime circumstance and victim-offender relationship data are not available for all cases included in the SHR file. SHR homicide data are reported by local authorities to the FBI on a monthly basis.

However, these monthly reports often reflect only preliminary information about killings, especially for homicides that occur late in the month. As police investigations progress, more information becomes available about homicide circumstances and victim-offender relationships, but this additional information may not be passed on to the FBI. Research by Maxfield (1989) reveals that murders that are initially SHR coded as circumstances "unknown" often turn out to be felony murders, which typically involve strangers.

Among the female homicides in the 1980 SHR files for our 138 cities (n = 1,977), murder circumstance is classified as "unknown" in 361 cases (18.3 percent). The victim-offender relationship variable is recorded as "unknown" for 718 female killings (36.3 percent). In the analysis to follow (and in light of Maxfield's findings), we consider both less- and more-inclusive felony murder and stranger homicide categories. The more-inclusive felony murder category combines known and suspected (n = 532) and possible (n = 361) felony murders. The more-inclusive stranger category combines stranger (n = 135) and likely stranger (n = 718) killings.[7]

Socioeconomic Status of Women

Consistent with previous research, we consider the objective and relative socioeconomic status of women in four areas: education, income, occupational attainment, and employment (see Baron and Straus 1984, 1987; Ellis and Beattie 1983; Peterson and Bailey 1992). (Table 8.1 reports means, standard deviations, and ranges for the gender status and inequality factors.) We operationalize the level of female educational attainment as the percentage of women 25 years of age and over who have completed four or more years of college. The mean for this variable for our sample of cities is 8.2 percent, with minimum and maximum values of 2.9 percent and 23.8 percent, respectively. Women's economic status is measured by their median annual income, which ranged (in $1,000's) from 4.33 to 10.45, with a mean of 5.78 in 1980. Our occupational status variable is the percentage of females who are employed in managerial, professional, and administrative positions. The range is from 12.0 percent to 37.7 percent, with a mean of 22.2 percent. The female unemployment rate averaged 6.5 percent for the selected cities and ranged from 2.5 percent to 17.3 percent. In brief, then, the *absolute* status of women varies considerably across urban areas in the United States.

Table 8.1 also reveals that the *relative* status of women compared to that of men varies significantly across cities. For the income and education dimensions, gender inequality is measured as the male-female differential in income and completion of four or more years of college, respectively. The 1980 male-female median income gap averaged \$6,250, and ranged from \$2,310 to \$14,800. On average, 2.5 percent more men than women had completed four or more years of college, but the gender difference ranges up to 17.8 percent. Inequality in employment status is operationalized as the female-male differential in the unemployment rate. Although the average unemployment differential between females and males was not large (−.27), females experienced a much higher unemployment rate in some cities (10.6 percent) but a lower rate (4.43 percent) in others. Finally, occupational inequality is measured by the percentage of employed persons (16 years and over) in managerial and professional occupations who are females. The percentage of women in professional and managerial occupations averaged 42.5 percent for our cities and ranged from 31 percent to 61 percent.

We do not pose the foregoing measures as a complete inventory of how gender socioeconomic status and inequality can be operationalized. Rather, we are guided here by the social stratification literature and by established indicators of gender socioeconomic status and inequality (U.S. Commission on Civil Rights 1978).

Control Variables

To avoid spurious results for the gender socioeconomic factors, four demographic and three socioeconomic control variables are included in the multivariate analysis: (1) population size, log transformed to avoid skew, (2) percentage of the population that is black, (3) a 0/1 dummy variable differentiating nonsouthern from southern cities, (4) the divorce rate, an indicator of social disorganization, (5) the percentage of families with incomes below the poverty level, (6) the Gini Index of general income inequality, and (7) the gap between black and white family income, an indicator of racial socioeconomic inequality. As reported in Table 8.1, values for these control factors vary considerably across the sample of cities.

We also include two marital status factors as control variables in the analyses: percentage of women 15 years of age and older who are married, and percentage of married women who are separated from their husbands. On the basis of various lifestyle, opportunity, and routine activity theses, one might predict that married women would experience a lower level of homicide victimization than nonmarried women, especially for killings associated with other crimes (felony murders) and those involving strangers. The assumption is that married women are subject to closer supervision and more guardianship than are single women. In addition, married women may have more resources (because they share those of their mates) to structure a more safe and secure environment. It is unlikely, though, that marriage provides a protective advantage for women against domestic killings. Of note, 17 percent of female homicide victims in 1980 were wives or common-law wives killed by their husbands. Thus, married women may be more subject to domestic killings if they are in troubled relationships.

By simultaneously considering marriage and married-but-separated variables in our models, the percentage-married factor might better reflect the positive influence of guardianship and resources, while the percentage-separated variable controls for the proportion of marriages in which there is serious conflict. Similarly, including these variables in the analyses for different types of female homicide permits us to examine more directly whether female marriage rates are associated negatively with killings resulting from street crimes (felony murders) and those committed by strangers; and, conversely, whether the level of married women separated from their partners is associated with a lower rate of wife killings.

Statistical Analysis

We use multiple regression analyses to examine the relationship between the socioeconomic status of women and rates of female homicide. First we examine the relationship between types of female homicide and variation across cities in the objective socioeconomic status of women. Next we examine male-female socioeconomic inequality and the rates of female homicide.

Because of the large number of gender, control, and dependent variables being considered, space constraints preclude presenting a simple zero-order correlation matrix for all variables. However, in Table 8.2, we report the bivariate correlations between the homicide variables and each of the control and predictor variables.

Multicollinearity. Multicollinearity does not pose a problem for the gender status and gender socioeconomic inequality variables. When each of these factors is regressed *one at a time* against the other right-hand variables in our models, the resulting R^2 values do not indicate serious collinearity problems. (The results of the collinearity analysis appear in Table 8.3.) As reported, for the gender variables, the highest R^2 values for the various models are as follows: percentage of females with four or more years of college (.520); median income of women (.539); percentage of females in managerial, professional, and administrative occupations (.484); percent-

TABLE 8.2

Zero-Order Correlations Between Female Homicide Rates and Predictor and Control Variables

Predictor variable	Total killings	Felony-murders	Argument killings	Family killings	Friend killings	Girlfriend killings	Wife killings	Stranger killings
Log population	.347*	.265*	.241*	.156	.237*	.019	.093	.136
Percent black population	.637*	.373*	.523*	.460*	.530*	.260*	.374*	.384*
South (0/1)	.162	−.137	.093	.243*	.166	.145*	.163	.191*
Divorce rate	.527*	.436*	.428*	.267*	.389*	.227*	.237*	.267*
Percent family poverty	.546*	.352*	.441*	.337*	.378*	.387*	.323*	.320*
General income inequality	.528*	.356*	.335*	.337*	.268	.322*	.288*	.249*
White-black income inequality	.151	.072	.029	.136	.133	.009	.118	.120
Percent females married	−.369	−.277*	−.196*	−.127	−.305*	−.157*	−.082	−.236*
Percent females married but separated	.463*	.364*	.343*	.235*	.350*	.190*	.169*	.259*
Percent females with 4 years of college	−.158	−.123	−.228*	−.106	−.114	−.137	−.109	−.065
Median income of females	−.161	.010	−.145	−.162	−.103	−.193*	−.192*	−.047
Percent females in managerial, professional, and administrative occupations	−.111	−.064	−.186*	−.054	−.094	−.122	−.058	−.070
Percent female unemployment	.376*	.286*	.329*	.257*	.319*	.189*	.239*	.120
Male-female gap in college	−.171	−.123	−.058	−.024	−.102	−.180*	.013	−.088
Male-female gap in median income	−.278*	−.171*	−.058	−.122	−.085	−.249*	−.111	−.233*
Percent managers, professionals, and administrators who are female	.482*	.293*	.397*	.287*	.474*	.273*	.227*	.344
Female-male gap in unemployment	−.045	−.147	−.011	.135*	−.103	.076	.018	−.011

* $p < .05$.

TABLE 8.3
Summary of Multicollinearity Analysis Results for the Socioeconomic Gender and Control Variables

Predictor variable	Maximum R^2 value *
Log population	.231
Percent black population	.784
South (0/1)	.536
Divorce rate	.532
Percent family poverty	.811
General income inequality	.686
White-black income inequality	.484
Percent females married	.779
Percent females married but separated	.787
Percent females with 4 years of college	.520
Median income of females	.539
Percent females in managerial, professional, and administrative occupations	.484
Percent female unemployment	.616
Male-female gap in 4 years of college	.176
Male-female gap in median income	.730
Percent managers, professionals, and administrators who are female	.661
Female-male gap in unemployment	.496

*The maximum R^2 value is the largest R^2 that resulted when each predictor variable was regressed against the other right-hand variables in the various models being considered.

age of female unemployment (.616); the male-female gap in completing four years of college (.176); the male-female differential in median income (.730); percentage of managers, professionals, and administrators who are women (.661); and the female-male differential in unemployment (.496).

For some of the control variables, the auxiliary regressions produce more substantial maximum R^2 values: percentage of the population that is black (.784); percentage of families in poverty (.811); percentage of females who are married (.779); and percentage of females who are married but separated (.787). However, as we shall see, each of these variables proves to be a significant predictor of one or more types of female homicide.

Findings

Homicide and the Objective Status of Women

Table 8.4 presents analyses examining whether the variation in respective indicators of women's objective status is linked to the overall rate

TABLE 8.4

Total Female Homicide Rates Regressed Against Four Dimensions of Female Socioeconomic Status

Predictor variable	b[a]	se	b	se	b	se	b	se
Control variables								
Log population	.426	.424	.401	.423	.433	.423	.437	.430
Percent black population	.172*	.033	.176*	.033	.173*	.033	.170*	.036
South (0/1)	−.854	.773	−.795	.758	−.816	.759	−.837	.825
Divorce rate	.572*	.183	.508*	.196	.565*	.183	.573*	.183
Percent family poverty	−.023	.139	.061	.148	−.058	.138	−.019	.126
General income inequality	.046*	.013	.045*	.013	.048*	.013	.046*	.013
White-black income inequality	−.224*	.118	−.247*	.116	−.214*	.116	−.223*	.119
Percent females married	.080	.070	.073	.067	.069	.070	.082	.069
Percent females married but separated	−.231	.148	−.286*	.160	−.237	.149	−.233	.151
Female status variables								
Percent females with 4 years of college	−.011	.118	—	—	—	—	—	—
Median income of females	—	—	.367	.410	—	—	—	—
Percent females in managerial, professional, and administrative occupations	—	—	—	—	−.059	.094	—	—
Percent female unemployment	—	—	—	—	—	—	.017	.175
Constant	−25.919	7.929	−26.686	7.555	−24.492	7.990	−26.180	7.565
R^2	.539*		.542*		.541*		.540*	

*$p < .05$.

[a] In Tables 8.4 through 8.9, the statistic "b," the partial regression coefficient, provides a measure of trade-off between the female homicide rate in question and the predictor variable being examined.

of female killings, as various lifestyle, routine activities, and opportunity arguments would predict. Turning first to the control variables, consistent with findings of studies of general homicide, Table 8.4 reveals that the female homicide rate is associated significantly and positively with the size of the black population, the divorce rate (social disorganization), and the Gini Index of general income inequality. In contrast, there is a chance-only association between female killings and population size, the region dummy variable, and family poverty. Also contrary to expectations, each analysis shows significantly lower female homicide rates for cities with a larger gap in white-black income. As shown in Table 8.3, this pattern is not a result of collinearity problems for the racial income inequality variable.

Contrary to what female guardianship and resource arguments would predict, there is a positive relationship between the percentage of women who are married and rates of female killing. Rather than affording women a greater margin of safety, Table 8.4 suggests that marriage makes women more vulnerable to murder. The findings for the married-but-separated variable underscore this possibility. For each analysis there is a negative trade-off (b = −.231 to −.286) between the percentage of married women who are separated from their husbands and the female homicide rate. When females' median income is the status variable, the percentage-separated factor is statistically significant. For the remaining analyses the t-values for this variable (t = −1.548 to −1.598) fall just short of the conventional .05 level (t = −1.658). This pattern suggests that the more that women are separated from troubled marriages, the lower the overall female homicide rate. Marriage may afford women a level of protection against some types of victimization, but the net effect of marriage for women (when not separated from their partners) may be a greater risk of lethal violence.

Let us turn to the variables of primary interest for this analysis. Table 8.4 provides little support for arguments that as the objective socioeconomic status of women increases, they are less subject to lethal assaults. For three of the four female status variables, the coefficients are in the predicted direction. However, the coefficients are not statistically significant. The larger the proportion of women (1) with a college education (b = −.011), and (2) in managerial, professional or administrative occupations (b = −.059), the lower the homicide rate, but not significantly so. The higher the female unemployment rate, the higher the female homicide rate (b = .017), but the trade-off is only at a chance level. The coefficient for median income (b = .367) is in the opposite direction of that predicted, but it is also at a chance level.

In sum then, it does not appear from Table 8.4 that higher socioeco-

TABLE 8.5

Female Felony Murder Rates Regressed Against Four Dimensions of Female Socioeconomic Status

Predictor variable	b	se	b	se	b	se	b	se
Control variables								
Log population	.088	.210	.061	.209	.080	.209	.063	.212
Percent black population	.043*	.015	.044*	.015	.043*	.015	.047*	.017
South (0/1)	−1.453*	.381	−1.359*	.374	−1.422*	.375	−1.491	.408
Divorce rate	.259*	.090	.215*	.097	.257*	.090	.256*	.090
Percent family poverty	−.028	.065	−.010	.063	−.038	.065	−.035	.059
General income inequality	.019*	.006	.019*	.006	.019*	.006	.019*	.006
White-black income inequality	−.059	.058	−.066	.057	−.054	.057	−.059	.059
Percent females married	.063*	.032	.056*	.030	.059*	.032	.061*	.031
Female status variables								
Percent females with 4 years of college	.028	.058	—	—	—	—	—	—
Median income of females	—	—	.211	.187	—	—	—	—
Percent females in managerial, professional, and administrative occupations	—	—	—	—	.008	.046	—	—
Percent female unemployment	—	—	—	—	—	—	−.039	.085
Constant	−12.321	3.815	−12.458	3.666	−11.978	3.837	−11.599	3.646
R^2	.336*		.342*		.335*		.336*	

*p < .05.

nomic status affords women greater protection against murder. However, as noted, the total homicide rate includes killings involving a variety of types of parties and circumstances. This raises the possibility that analyses that combine all types of female homicide may mask links between female status factors and particular types of female killing. To examine whether the null pattern for the gender status variables holds across types of murder, we replicated the above analysis but considered rates for the most common types of female homicide. In Table 8.5 we report the results of female felony murders regressed against the female status and control variables. The data in Table 8.5 are based on the cases of known felony murder (n = 532 for our cities in 1980). Recall, though, that a significant number of SHR homicides are classified as "circumstances unknown"; 361 (18 percent) female homicides for our sample of cities were so classified. Because many of the "circumstances unknown" killings are probably felony murders (Maxfield 1989), we replicated the analysis reported in Table 8.5 for the combined set of reported (n = 532) and possible (n = 361) female felony murders. Use of this more inclusive felony murder variable did not alter the pattern of findings for the female status variables. Therefore, these results are not reported here.

With two exceptions, the findings for the sociodemographic control variables parallel those for total female homicides. Table 8.5 shows that rates of felony murder involving female victims are associated positively and significantly with the size of the black population, the divorce rate, and the level of general income inequality. In contrast to the pattern for total homicides, the white-black income gap is not associated significantly with female felony murders, but women residing in southern cities are significantly less likely to be murdered in connection with another felony. Also, similar to total homicides, there is no indication that marriage affords women an added measure of protection against felony murder. Rather, there is a significant positive association (b = .056 to .063) between the percentage-married variable and felony murder rates. Most important for our purposes, Table 8.5 shows that variation in the levels of educational, income, occupational, and employment status of women does not significantly influence female felony murder rates. Again, this pattern is inconsistent with various lifestyle, routine activity, and opportunity perspectives on crime.

In addition to felony murders, each year a sizable number of women are killed by friends and acquaintances (n = 360), fellow family members (n = 553), husbands (n = 167), strangers (n = 135), and probable strangers, whose relationship with the victim is unknown (n = 718). Many of these killings are preceded by arguments (n = 628), according to the SHR data.

We conducted regression analyses for these additional types of killing. The results for the female socioeconomic status variables were quite uniform and consistent with those presented in Tables 8.4 and 8.5. In none of the analyses was a significant negative (or positive) association observed between the level of female educational, income, occupational, or employment status and homicide rates. Because the findings are so uniform, and because of space constraints, we do not present the detailed regression results here. Tabular results are available upon request.

To summarize, the objective socioeconomic status of women varies considerably across U.S. cities (see Table 8.1). However, this variation does not appear to be associated with rates of total or different types of female homicide victimization. Thus our findings do not support the argument that women will be less vulnerable to homicide victimization as their *objective* socioeconomic condition improves.

Homicide and the Relative Status of Women

To examine the feminist argument that gender socioeconomic inequality breeds violence against women, we replicate the earlier analysis for each type of female murder, but substitute as our predictor variables measures of gender *inequality* in educational, income, occupational, and employment status. Table 8.6 reports the results for the analysis where we consider the relationship between total female homicide rates and the respective areas of gender inequality.

First, the findings for the control variables parallel very closely the results of analyses of the "objective" socioeconomic status of women (Table 8.4). For each model there is a significant positive association between rates and the black population, divorce, and general income inequality variables, and a significant negative association between the white-black income gap and female killings. None of the other predictors achieve statistical significance.

The results for the gender inequality variables are inconsistent with feminist arguments and parallel the earlier findings for the objective gender status variables. Here, the greater the male-female gap in median income (in $1,000's), the higher the female homicide rate (b = .047), but this association is not significant. In contrast, greater gender inequality in college education is associated with lower rates of female homicide (b = −.014). The greater the proportion of upper-level occupational positions occupied by women, the higher the female homicide rate (b = .027); and the greater the female excess in unemployment, the higher the female homicide rate

TABLE 8.6

Total Female Homicide Rates Regressed Against Four Dimensions of Male-Female Inequality in Socioeconomic Status

Predictor variable	b	se	b	se	b	se	b	se
Control variables								
Log population	.433	.425	.430	.423	.438	.425	.448	.433
Percent black population	.172*	.033	.168*	.038	.168*	.036	.172*	.033
South (0/1)	−.870	.755	−.805	.836	−.860	.756	−.927	.801
Divorce rate	.574*	.183	.577*	.184	.568*	.184	.582*	.188
Percent family poverty	−.019	.123	−.005	.137	−.028	.130	−.014	.121
General income inequality	.046*	.013	.047*	.013	.047*	.013	.045*	.013
White-black income inequality	−.227*	.115	−.222*	.116	−.226*	.114	−.226*	.114
Percent females married	.085	.066	.075	.084	.089	.070	.077	.074
Percent females married but separated	−.231	.148	−.236	.151	−.225	.150	−.243	.160
Gender inequality variables								
Male-female gap in 4 years of college	−.014	.149	—	—	—	—	—	—
Male-female gap in median income	—	—	.047	.260	—	—	—	—
Percent of managers, professionals, and administrators who are females	—	—	—	—	.027	.114	—	—
Female-male gap in unemployment	—	—	—	—	—	—	.056	.263
Constant	−26.206	7.859	−26.228	7.569	−27.709	9.988	−25.803	7.715
R^2	.540*		.540*		.540*		.540*	

*$p < .05$.

TABLE 8.7

Wife Murder Rates Regressed Against Four Dimensions of Male-Female Inequality in Socioeconomic Status

Predictor variable	b	se	b	se	b	se	b	se
Control variables								
Log population	–.321	.391	–.246	.392	–.294	.392	–.112	.397
Percent black population	.096*	.030	.081*	.032	.113*	.033	.101*	.030
South (0/1)	–.265	.647	–.098	.657	–.364	.659	–.838	.728
Divorce rate	.118	.168	.148	.169	.159	.170	.193	.170
Percent family poverty	.214*	.113	.229*	.120	.233*	.119	.189*	.111
General income inequality	.011	.011	.016	.012	.010	.011	.011	.011
White-black income inequality	.016	.105	.018	.107	–.005	.105	.002	.104
Percent females married but separated	–.380*	.128	–.378*	.127	–.400*	.126	–.436*	.127
Gender inequality variables								
Male-female gap in 4 years of college	.235*	.136	—	—	—	—	—	—
Male-female gap in median income	—	—	.222	.189	—	—	—	—
Percent managers, professionals, and administrators who are female	—	—	—	—	–.133	.100	—	—
Female-male gap in unemployment	—	—	—	—	—	—	.397*	.214
Constant	–.447	5.06	–4.471	6.101	5.123	6.652	–2.263	5.143
R^2	.236*		.226*		.228*		.238*	

*$p < .05$.

(b = .056). However, the trade-off between these gender inequality factors and homicide rates also falls short of achieving statistical significance.

The pattern of negligible results for the respective gender inequality variables is not altered when the analysis is extended to examine (1) killings associated with other felonies, (2) the killing of family members, (3) homicides involving "girlfriend" victims, and (4) women killed by strangers. However, there is not a uniform null pattern for killings involving wives, or friends and acquaintances, or homicides stemming from various types of arguments. Table 8.7 reports results for the analysis of killings involving wives.

Two of the analyses reported in Table 8.7 support gender inequality arguments; the other two do not. As expected, Table 8.7 shows significant positive associations between the rates of wife killing and the male-female gap in college attainment (b = .235, t = 1.732), and the differential in female-male unemployment (b = .397, t = 1.855). In contrast, the greater the income gap between men and women, the higher the rate of wives being killed by their husbands (b = .222, t = 1.177), but the trade-off here is only at the chance level. Similarly, the greater the proportion of professional, managerial, and administrative positions that are held by women, the lower the rate of wife killings (b = −.133, t = −1.319), but not significantly so. Also of note, in each analysis, wife killings are associated positively and significantly with the poverty and black-population variables, and negatively with the married-but-separated variable. As suggested in the earlier analyses (Tables 8.4 and 8.6), the pattern for the separation variable indicates that women who remain in troubled marriages are at a greater risk of being killed by their mates.

The results in Table 8.8 show a varied pattern for the gender inequality variables for killings in which females are victimized by friends and acquaintances. First, contrary to gender inequality arguments, the results indicate that neither the education nor the unemployment gap between women and men is associated significantly with these types of killings. In contrast, and in line with gender inequality arguments, the data show that the greater the gender gap in income, the higher the rate of women being killed by acquaintances. (The acquaintance homicide category includes women killed by friends, acquaintances, and neighbors, but excludes boyfriend-girlfriend killings.) The coefficient for the income inequality variable (b = .221, se = .095) suggests that for every $1,000 unit advantage in male income, the rate of such homicides increases by .221 persons. (As reported in Table 8.1, the average gap in 1980 median income for men and women in our sample of cities was $6,250.) This finding suggests that, other things being equal,

TABLE 8.8

Female Acquaintance Murder Rates Regressed Against Four Dimensions of Male-Female Inequality in Socioeconomic Status

Predictor variable	b	se	b	se	b	se	b	se
Control variables								
Log population	.115	.161	.125	.157	.151	.158	.093	.162
Percent black population	.044*	.012	.026*	.014	.035*	.012	.045*	.012
South (0/1)	.124	.285	.437	.31	.147	.281	.217	.296
Divorce rate	.120*	.069	.139*	.068	.108	.068	.108	.070
Percent family poverty	−.012	.043	.030	.047	−.047	.044	−.014	.042
General income inequality	−.003	.005	−.000	.005	−.000	.005	−.002	.005
White-black income inequality	−.010	.043	.003	.043	−.011	.043	−.011	.043
Percent females married	.007	.0203	.045	.028	.008	.023	.004	.024
Gender inequality variables								
Male-female gap in 4 years of college	.036	.056	—	—	—	—	—	—
Male-female gap in median income	—	—	.221*	.095	—	—	—	—
Percent managers, professionals, and administrators who are female	—	—	—	—	.083*	.042	—	—
Female-male gap in unemployment	—	—	—	—	—	—	−.101	.092
Constant	−.973	2.788	−1.856	2.737	−5.689	3.578	−1.489	2.781
R^2	.309*		.334*		.327*		.313*	

*p < .05.

if the male-female income differential were reduced to zero, the rate of women being killed by friends and acquaintances would be reduced quite substantially (.221 × 6.250 = 1.381 per 100,000 females).

The gender occupational analysis yields a very different picture. Feminist arguments suggest that the more that women are able to work their way into managerial, professional, and administrative positions, the less they should be subject to homicide. So the percentage of persons in such positions who are female should be associated negatively with female homicide rates. However, Table 8.8 shows the opposite pattern. On average, for every percentage point increase in females in these more prestigious positions, the rate of acquaintance killings *increases* by a factor of .083 (b = .083, se = .042). This finding is consistent with the "male backlash" argument regarding rape (D. E. H. Russell 1975). That is, female advancement in the world of work may result in feelings of resentment and anger in insecure men, with violence against women (in this case lethal violence) being the response of some men. Such an interpretation is not inconsistent with gender inequality arguments, but the merits of this interpretation are unclear when viewed in light of the findings for the income inequality measure. Why would greater gender parity in income reduce friendship killings, while female advancement into upper-level occupations has an opposite "backlash" effect?

Turning briefly to the control variables, the percentage of the population that is black consistently is a significant factor in female acquaintance killings. In addition, in two of the four analyses the divorce rate is a significant predictor of these types of homicide. Finally, there is no indication from the percentage-married variable that male (husband) guardianship makes women less susceptible to being killed by an acquaintance.

A sizable number of female homicides (like killings in general) result from arguments. In our final model we examine whether variation in the level of argument-related female homicides is associated with the relative socioeconomic status of women. Results of the analyses are presented in Table 8.9.

Regarding the control variables, argument-related female homicides are associated positively with the percentage of the population that is black, the divorce rate, and general income inequality. For two of the four analyses, higher rates of racial income inequality are associated with significantly lower female homicide rates. Also, throughout the analyses, the greater the percentage of women who are married (controlling for the percentage of married women who are separated), the higher the female homicide rate, and significantly so in three of the four cases. The coefficients for the

TABLE 8.9

Female Argument-Related Murder Rates Regressed Against Four Dimensions of Male-Female Inequality in Socioeconomic Status

Predictor variable	b	se	b	se	b	se	b	se
Control variables								
Log population	.061	.231	.084	.227	.086	.231	.100	.236
Percent black population	.083*	.018	.063*	.020	.081*	.019	.083*	.018
South (0/1)	−.675	.410	−.310	.449	−.681	.412	−.731	.436
Divorce rate	.251*	.099	.279*	.099	.253*	.100	.265*	.102
Percent family poverty	.042	.067	.096	.074	.024	.071	.032	.066
General income inequality	.014*	.007	.016*	.007	.015*	.007	.014*	.007
White-black income inequality	−.100	.062	−.087	.062	−.106*	.062	−.107*	.062
Percent females married	.079*	.036	.029	.045	.086*	.038	.076*	.040
Percent females married but separated	−.102	.081	−.131	.081	−.100	.082	−.115	.087
Gender inequality variables								
Male-female gap in 4 years of college	.075	.081	—	—	—	—	—	—
Male-female gap in median income	—	—	.267*	.140	—	—	—	—
Percent managers, professionals, and administrators who are female	—	—	—	—	.016	.062	—	—
Female-male gap in unemployment	—	—	—	—	—	—	.054	.143
Constant	−10.836	4.121	−11.708	4.066	−12.115	5.441	−10.880	4.201
R^2	.396*		.409*		.392*		.392*	

*$p < .05$.

separation variable are all negative (as predicted), but the t-values, which range from −1.218 to −1.613, fall short of the conventional .05 level of significance.

Three of the four analyses result in contrary findings for the gender inequality variables. There is a chance-only association between female argument-related killings and the gender differential in educational attainment, employment in professional and managerial positions, and the level of unemployment. However, and like the killing of wives, there is a significant positive association between argument killings and the male-female income gap ($b = .267$, $t = 1.907$). This finding suggests that if the gender differential in income were reduced to zero, the rate of argument killings would be reduced by about 1.7 ($.267 \times 6.25 = 1.668$) persons per 100,000 female population.

Summary and Conclusions

In this investigation we have examined an important but largely neglected question in the criminology literature—the socioeconomic determinants of female homicide victimization. For the past two decades feminist writings have pointed to gender socioeconomic inequality as a significant contributor to male violence against women in the United States and in many other parts of the world. However, research in this area has been limited in several ways. First, it has focused on a limited set of crimes against women (primarily battering, rape, incest, and pornography), while neglecting the most threatening type of violence—murder. Second, most analyses have been more descriptive than analytical. Few criminologists have provided the type of detailed structural empirical analysis of feminist arguments that has characterized the large volume of studies of the impact of general and racial socioeconomic inequality on general rates of murder, robbery, rape, and assault. Recent investigations showing gender socioeconomic inequality to be an important contributor to forcible rape are the exceptions. Unfortunately, studies of female homicide victimization have largely been descriptive in nature. With the exception of Gartner and her colleagues, scholars have not attempted to link female homicide patterns to larger structural factors.

In this investigation we have addressed this void in the literature by assessing to what extent female homicide is a "cost" of gender inequality in the United States. Recognizing that gender status and inequality are multidimensional, we examined female homicide victimization patterns in light of various indicators of the absolute and relative socioeconomic status of women. Also recognizing that female homicides are far from homogeneous, we examined the correspondence between indicators of female status and inequality for different types of female killing. Our findings are instructive.

First, our analysis did not reveal evidence of a statistically significant relationship (either positive or negative) between indicators of the *objective* educational, income, occupational, and employment status of women and total or different types of female killing. This null pattern calls into question resource and opportunity predictions that persons at higher socioeconomic levels are able to structure a safer and more secure lifestyle. Apparently, women are not less vulnerable to murder in communities where their objective socioeconomic status is at a higher level.

Second, rates for some types of female homicide were found to be unrelated to any of our indicators of *relative* socioeconomic status. Our gender inequality measures did not influence rates for total female homicides, felony murders, or killings involving family members, girlfriends, or strangers.

Third, among types of homicide, the results for rates of wife killing are most consistent with gender inequality arguments. The rate of women being killed by their husbands is significantly higher in cities where the college education gap between males and females is greater, and where women experience higher levels of unemployment than men. Wife killing is also positively associated with male-female inequality in income and negatively associated with the level of female participation in upper-level occupations. The trade-off for these latter two factors is not statistically significant. Nonetheless, the overall pattern of findings for wife killings suggests that gender inequality breeds violence against wives. Note that the feminist argument regarding violence against wives is usually made with reference to battering rather than killing. A finding that battering and wife killing may have similar root causes should not be surprising. An early analysis by Pittman and Handy (1964) demonstrated a number of parallels between the correlates of aggravated assault and murder, and the same may hold for domestic assaults and wife killings. Further, an important study reports that most domestic homicides are preceded by calls to the police for service to the address of the homicide victim or suspect during the two years preceding the killing (Breedlove et al. 1977).

Fourth, partial support for the gender inequality argument is found for acquaintance and argument-related killings. In both cases, the gender inequality hypothesis is confirmed only for the gender gap in income. Recall that Peterson and Bailey (1992) report a similar pattern for rape. Considering similar measures of gender inequality, they found that only income inequality is a significant predictor of rape rates across U.S. metropolitan areas. In accounting for this pattern, Peterson and Bailey argue that (1) a sizable proportion of rapes are crimes of power and control, and (2) in this society, power is more a matter of income (and wealth) than of educational and occupational status. As with rape, women may be more vulnerable to murder where they possess significantly less income (power) than men.

This may be especially true since many killings occur in the context of arguments. In societies that pride themselves on the values of economic opportunity and equality for all, higher levels of gender income inequality may generate greater conflict between men and women in the form of arguments. If so, the level of argument-related female homicides could be higher in these types of settings. Here, homicide can be viewed as a "normal" but not typical consequence of interpersonal conflict.

In part because of men's greater size, physical strength, and familiarity with lethal weapons, in male-female confrontations that have a lethal outcome, women more often turn out to be the victims of homicide.[8] However, feminist arguments also predict this pattern. Again, to the extent that power in this society is tied to income, when men and women have similar incomes they have similar amounts of power. Under conditions of gender parity in income and power, women are less likely to be "willing" victims and men are less likely to be "motivated" aggressors. Accordingly, there should be a lower probability of arguments (including those involving lethal violence) between men and women. These interpretations are, of course, speculative. Future researchers will have to determine whether greater levels of gender income inequality produce fewer arguments between the sexes and thereby fewer argument-related female homicides.

Fifth, our analysis revealed that higher levels of occupational gender inequality are associated with higher rather than lower rates of acquaintance killings. This finding may reflect "male backlash." While feminists are in general agreement that greater gender equality will reduce the victimization of women, some point to important costs that women incur in striving for equality. For example, D. E. H. Russell (1975) argues that as women challenge men for positions of power and authority, they may be greeted by male backlash. In this case, rape provides a way of punishing and repressing "uppity," threatening women. If this is the case for rape, it is also possible that women may be more likely to be victims of murder when they challenge men in the upper ranges of the world of work. That is, as more women move into upper-level professional, managerial, and administrative positions, the greater the potential resentment by their male colleagues and the greater the potential conflict between women in superordinate positions and male subordinates, male clients, and perhaps males in general.

Sixth, we have observed some interesting patterns regarding our marital-status variables. Gartner and her colleagues have argued that, compared with other women, married women should experience a lower overall homicide rate because of their greater economic resources and the guardianship provided by their spouses. We note, however, that these male "guardians" are a major contributor to female killings. Further, the results of our analysis are contrary to the view that married women are afforded greater protection against murder. For most kinds of female homicide, the marriage variable was related to a significantly greater risk of women being killed. However, the relationship between marriage and female killings appears to depend upon the living arrangement of marital partners. While on balance married women seem to experience a greater overall level of homicide victimization, this does not appear to be the case for married women who are separated from their husbands. The greater the proportion of married-but-separated women, the lower the rate of wives being killed by their mates, and significantly so ($p < .001$). This pattern held throughout the analysis regardless of which status or inequality variable was being considered.

Collectively, the above findings strongly suggest that certain dimensions of gender socioeconomic inequality contribute significantly to certain types of female homicide victimization in this country. In communities where there is a higher level of gender inequality in education and employment, married women are at a greater risk of being killed by their husbands. And under conditions of higher levels of gender income inequality, women are at a greater risk of being killed by acquaintances and in argument situations. Thus, consistent with feminist arguments, certain major forms of female homicide victimization appear to be consequences of gender inequality in this society. To use the Blau and Blau (1982) term, female killings in U.S. cities are an important "cost" of gender inequality.

Although instructive, we view our analysis as only a first step in better understanding the relationship between the socioeconomic status of women and female criminal victimization. First, we have considered only "univariate" female homicide rate variables. Future research should also examine the relationship between dimensions of gender inequality and circumstance-by-relationship categories of female killings. Available SHR data permit this type of analysis.

Second, because women are victims of the full array of street crimes, it would seem to be important to extend gender inequality analyses beyond the crimes of murder and rape. To illustrate, National Crime Survey (NCS) data show that women are not a small minority of crime victims (U.S. Department of Justice 1991a). For 1990, male/female victimization rates per 100,000 population were as follows: robbery (7.5/3.9), aggravated assaults (11.5/4.5), simple assaults (18.3/12.7), total assaultive crimes (29.8/17.2), total theft crimes (67.4/60.4), total crimes against persons and property (105.1/82.6). These figures make it clear that criminal victimization of females is not a trivial matter. The question therefore arises whether (and how) dimensions of socioeconomic inequality might be associated with rates of these types of female victimization. Presently neither NCS nor UCR data allow researchers to examine this question directly. However, such analyses will be possible in the near future when the FBI crime incident–based reporting system is instituted. With the adoption of this system a great deal of demographic, circumstance, and relationship information will become available for victims and offenders for a wide variety of serious and lesser crimes against persons and property.

According to J. Harper Wilson, director of the FBI Uniform Crime Reporting Program, a majority of states have established incident-based reporting systems and many others are in the process of doing so (J. H. Wilson 1991). If most states comply with the requirements of the new reporting system, researchers will have opportunities to address many new questions. In the context of this study, these will include the opportunity to construct, for various sociogeographic units, gender-specific rates of victimization and offending, and to analyze these rates in light of patterns of gender socioeconomic inequality. In the meantime, it seems fair to conclude that certain forms of gender inequality contribute significantly to at least some extreme forms of violence against women—rape and murder. The generalizability of these findings to other forms of criminal victimization against females awaits future research.

Crime, Inequality, and Justice in Eastern Europe

Anomie, Domination, and Revolutionary Change

JOACHIM J. SAVELSBERG

Social Justice, Social Problems, and Crime Under Radical Change

To the surprise of most social scientists, the late twentieth century turned into a period of radical sociopolitical change in eastern Europe.[1] It did so to a degree that has only rarely been seen in modern history. In this chapter I explore some implications of this process for theories of crime and justice and for empirical research.

We are now aware of three periods of radical sociopolitical change in modern Western history. The late eighteenth and early nineteenth centuries constitute the period of bourgeois revolution, the transformation of societies from aristocratic order to bourgeois order, democracy, and capitalism. Where revolutions did not occur, democratic reforms were initiated. One hundred years later, the period of the late nineteenth and early twentieth centuries gave birth to socialist movements and revolutions. Some expected a world revolution to result, producing universal communism and finally classless societies. A lasting communist revolution, however, occurred only in Russia. It was exported through conquest into several Central and East European countries at the end of World War II. Where radical socialist transformations did not occur, at least more or less far-reaching welfare laws and social democratic political programs were established. The late twentieth century witnesses the third step: the burial of hopes and expectations of a communist utopia, and bourgeois revolutions in socialist societies. In Europe, all eight state socialist orders were overturned within three years, first in the countries on whom communist order had been imposed, and finally in the Soviet Union.[2]

Each of these three changes implies numerous phenomena of central concern for the sociology of crime and criminal justice. Contradictions between structures of domination and newly emerging patterns of power threaten the legitimacy of governments. Existing conditions are experienced as oppressive, exploitive, and unjust. Demands for individual freedom *and* social justice are raised and forcefully articulated by social movements. They result in radical overhauls of the political, legal, and economic order.[3]

Both the path of revolution and the establishment of a new order are of interest for sociological theory. Radical transformations are never smooth processes. Their carriers are often driven by utopian hopes and general objectives but left in disarray once the old order is overcome. Vaclav Havel is frequently quoted as stating that the Czechoslovakian opposition knew that it wanted to achieve freedom but had a hard time knowing what to do with that freedom once it was achieved. Not only are expectations unspecific, but they also do not develop harmoniously with actual life chances when radical transitions occur, either before or after the revolution. Capitalism does not result in sudden wealth for all, but in struggle and adjustment of expectations for most and poverty for many. Democracy turns out to be a complicated and often frustrating process. Institutions do not simply appear and function when so ordered by constitutional changes, government decrees, or mass assemblies. Many people's expectations are disappointed. Anomie (Durkheim 1952) and strain (Merton 1938) emerge before the revolution occurs and do not disappear, at least not immediately, once it has succeeded. Anomie and strain are, in fact, sources of rebellion and revolution and may become sources of counterrebellion and counterrevolution. They are one of the links between social structural conduciveness and revolt.

But revolution and counterrevolution are not the only possible responses to anomie and strain (Merton 1938). Other well-known reactions are resignation, ritualism, emigration, and innovation (or, in other words, deviance, crime, and delinquency). The present situation provides an ideal opportunity to study these different forms of adaptation and the interrelation between them. Future research may explain which conditions in which of the eastern European countries, each of which represents different structural and cultural conditions and historical frames, will have contributed to the specific mix of strategies chosen by different segments of their populations.

Crime and Justice: Radical Change and Basic Approaches

This chapter concentrates on the strategy called innovation by Merton, or crime and delinquency.[4] Crime rates have increased suddenly in rapidly changing eastern Europe, for which the study of individual offender personalities or manipulations of the criminal justice system cannot provide explanations. It appears that these increases are not due to changes in reporting and arresting behavior. We are referred to basic sociological theory to identify the social conditions for this increase in crime rates.[5]

Yet, not only the behavioral, but also the definitorial aspect of crime changes radically. Former convicts and prison inmates, Vaclav Havel and Lech Walesa have become state presidents. Thousands of prison inmates have been rehabilitated and released. At the same time, former heads of state have been tried and executed (Ceauşescu in Romania), charged with corruption and other offenses (Zhivkov in Bulgaria, Honecker in Germany), or forced to step down. Many of their functionaries have also been tried in criminal courts. Some who "just followed orders"—for example, East German border guards who killed fleeing citizens—were charged with homicide. On January 20, 1992, a Berlin judge sentenced the first convicted border guard to a 40-month prison term. Thousands of others, privileged in the old system, lost their positions and careers in the economy, in academia, in the legal and criminal justice systems, and in the political sector. Criminal *and* social justice are being redefined. In times of revolution, crime becomes visible as what it always is: a construct of society, reflecting its structure of domination.[6]

The following sections deal with the development of crime in a changing eastern Europe, against the background of issues of social inequality and social justice. I briefly discuss the original association between social justice and criminal law under socialism and review crime trends in the prerevolutionary stage. I then take a closer look at the rapid developments after the overthrow of the old regimes.

Formal Versus Social Justice and Crime in State Socialist Society: Legal, Political, and Economic Concerns

The present situation of crime and justice cannot be adequately understood without reference to fundamental features of socialist legal, political, and economic order. The basic idea of socialist law resulted from the experience of social injustice based on extreme social inequality and exploitation in early bourgeois, capitalist societies. The legal order of bourgeois society was based on the assumption of the equality of all citizens. It was, in terms of Max Weber's legal sociology, formal-rational law, which socialist movements attempted to replace with substantive-rational law directed at social justice.

Formal-rational law of the bourgeois state created legal security, a stable foundation for "free" economic exchange, and did not intervene in societal structures. While its principle was to treat all citizens as formally equal (the *égalité* of the bourgeois revolution), it disregarded substantive social inequalities. In contract law the fiction of equality sanctioned exploitive labor contracts between entrepreneurs and proletarians. In criminal law the idea, most prominently proposed by such philosophers as Kant and Hegel, was to be just and retributive, and to punish equal and free individuals equally for equal offenses. Anatole France spoke up against this law that forbade rich and poor alike to steal bread and sleep under bridges. Scholarship recognized early that formal-rational law contributes to further social inequality and class conflict, and that it provokes calls for substantivation (Savelsberg 1992). Weber (1978: 886) observed "new demands for a 'social law' to be based on such emotionally colored ethical postulates as 'justice' and 'human dignity,' . . . directed against the pure business morality, having arisen with the modern class problem."

The question emerges, Who should define social justice, and how? When is a contract not valid; when is a crime not to be punished, or to be punished more or less? When formulating binding and general definitions of social justice is difficult (which it typically is), decision-making authority has to be distributed either to professional experts in the application of justice—for example, through extended discretion for judges and law enforcers or the community (e.g., lay judges, juries, community boards, comrade courts)—or to privileged groups with recognized special authority for the definition of social justice. In communist countries such a group is the Communist party, represented in different and changing institutionalizations of "criminal justice" throughout the history of Soviet society and its satellites.[7]

The radical pursuance of social justice through legal change implies a basic transformation of the political system. Even moderate pursuance of social justice, requiring modifications of the bourgeois legal order, has considerable consequences for the structure of the political system and may weaken democratic order. The bourgeois revolution transformed bureaucratic or regulatory law, which is public and positive, into legal order (Unger 1976). Legal order, comparable to Weber's formal rationality, is characterized by law that is not only public and positive, but also general (i.e., characterized by broadly defined categories of people and acts, to be applied without personal and class favoritism) and autonomous (in terms of substance, institutions, methods, and personnel). Unger, like Weber, sees legal order to be threatened by problematic side effects of capitalist systems.[8] He perceives these problems as a source of legal substantivation, the main characteristic of post-liberal societies. The Weimar Republic is one of the extreme manifestations of substantivation within the democratic tradition. A sudden rise of general clauses, expansive application of the "good faith" clauses and the "good morals" concept, open-ended policy directives, and shifts to purposive modes of legal reasoning and to concerns with substantive justice were justified in the name of social justice. They resulted in a weakening of legal order and threatened the generality and autonomy of law until democracy was replaced by Nazi dictatorship: "The withdrawal and weakening of the legal order was followed by the expansion of terror" (Unger 1976: 220).

The features of legal order, generality and autonomy, are secured by the separation of powers, Montesquieu's basic structural suggestion for the republican state. The dissolution of generality and autonomy implies the breakdown of the separation of powers—that is, the end of democracy. In East European societies this process was not gradual (as it was in Weimar and contemporary neo-corporatist systems) but radical. The Bolshevik revolution terminated a short period of democratic government in Russia after the overthrow of the Czarist monarchy. The imposition of communist systems on other East European countries followed several years of German occupation, which was preceded by democratic or monarchic government. The newly emerging order was dominated by the dictatorship of the proletariat, represented by the Communist party. The party monopolized the *Soviet*, *Sejm*, or *Volkskammer* and the administration as well as the judiciary in a (sometimes slightly modified) one-party system. Almost all judges in East Germany, for example, were members of the Socialist Unity party. Members of Social or Comrades' Courts as well as People's Assessors were nominated by the party or the affiliated trade unions. The party legitimized this monopoly by its claim to represent the working people and to prepare the path toward classless society in which all problems of social justice would be solved.[9] This ideology is, of course, juxtaposed to interests of the monopolistic party machine in maintaining power and of individual party members, groups, and families to secure privileged positions (Łós 1985). I hypothesize that the patterns and increases of crime before and after the revolution must be partly explained through (1) these group and individual interests and (2) the propagation of an ideology that, in the perception of major parts of the population, was not backed by the practice of governance and, as a result, was at least partly discredited. This ideology included internationalism, tolerance toward minorities, and idealism for the cause of social justice and community.[10]

The realization of social justice under communism was, of course, to be achieved through radical changes not only in the political and legal orders, but also in the economic order. Private ownership of means of production was abolished, and market mechanisms were replaced by central economic planning. Yet the socialization of means of production did not decrease the alienation of individual workers. Central planning did not lead to abundance but, given coordination problems and the lack or insufficiency of highly complex information systems, to severe shortages of goods and services. This constellation has caused widespread patterns of crime specific to socialist society (Łós 1983, 1989; Marek 1986a; Rosner 1986).

Crimes against the central plan, especially the "padding" of economic reports (forbidden by article 152-1 of the Soviet criminal code), were ubiquitous because, although the plan was impossible to fulfill, planning authorities as well as those who sought to execute the plan had a crucial interest in creating and maintaining the image of functioning production units and a functioning economy. Actors in the public sector were involved in the enterprise of constructing and maintaining a fiction, or "official lies" (Rosner 1986: 25), inconsistent with social and economic reality. Given the interest of planners and managers in maintaining this fiction, and given the subordination of enforcement agents (Shelley 1990) and planners to the same ultimate authority of the Communist party, this part of criminal law was seldom enforced.

Another set of crimes resulted from the malfunctioning of the plan: crimes against the centralized distribution of goods, criminalized by articles 153 and 154 of the Soviet criminal code. These propositions were aimed at private middlemen and "speculators." Yet, given the malfunctioning of the plan, supply was often guaranteed only through a secondary, informal, market-based economy. And again, the functional necessity of criminal behavior to prevent the complete breakdown of economic production and distribution, and the involvement of broad and influential social groups in such criminal activity, inhibited rigorous law enforcement.

Rosner (1986) illustrates that the abundance of scarcity resulted in pervasiveness of corruption. Crime became tightly woven into everyday public life: "Ordinary citizens in the USSR . . . exist in a moral standard that permits morality in private dealings with members of primary groups while excluding morality in dealings with members of secondary groups" (Rosner 1986: 38; see also p. 42).

Although criminal law prohibiting acts against the central plan and against the centralized distribution of goods and services was rarely enforced, it could always become enforced when other types of disobedience occurred—for example, political dissent. Sometimes crimes were reported in situations of personal conflicts, by neighbors or building superintendents. The result was constant fear, resulting in a "climate of evasion," "double-thinking," and "double talk," in the differentiation between an actual and a pretended world (Rosner 1986: 24–27). Other responses discussed by Rosner reinforce adaptations to anomie and strain already suggested by scarcity: resignation, that is, giving up responsibility for one's actions (e.g., by becoming an alcoholic), emigration (long restricted or prohibited), ritualism, and, again, innovation.

The structure and failures of the economic system, in combination with the legal and political order, thus led both to adaptation in the form of innovation and resignation and to a culture, socialization patterns, and psychological makeups that may not immediately disappear when state socialism and central planning are replaced by capitalism and democracy. Rosner (1986: 75ff) illustrates this for Soviet immigrants to the United States. I contend that these factors need to be taken into consideration even more when we attempt to understand the development of crime after the revolution.

State Socialism, Liberalization, Revolution, and Crime

A descriptive account of the patterns of crime in different stages of East European development is possible only with major reservations. First, the data are worse than insufficient. Victim and offender surveys are lacking.[11] Official crime data were not published at all in some countries. Other countries published sentencing statistics but not statistics of reported crimes. Only Poland and Hungary have been rather liberal in their handling and publishing of crime and justice statistics. This account is, therefore, based on different crime statistics for different time periods using various indicators from official reports and scholarly publications, and—especially for most recent years—on a systematic screening of accounts and reports in news media (*World News Digest*; *Foreign Broadcast Information Service* [*FBIS*]).

An additional difficulty is posed by the questionable validity of official crime statistics. This problem exists for all societies because crime statistics directly reflect control behavior.[12] It applies even more to communist societies, where scarcity, a nonfunctioning plan, and the lack of autonomous enforcement and judicial sectors are conducive to specific types of crime.

Crime Trends and the Validity Problem

With these caveats in mind, I present some available information on crime trends in selected countries. I add indications on the validity of these data and draw preliminary conclusions.

Poland. According to the *Statistical Yearbook of Poland*, the crime rate varied over time. Starting from fewer than 1,200 crimes (per 100,000 population) in 1954, it reached a peak of over 1,600 (in 1966), then dropped below 1,000 (1976–80).[13] After 1981, the year martial law was imposed, the crime rate increased quickly to around 1,400 per 100,000 in 1985. Thousands of political activists were imprisoned,[14] but political prosecution does not seem to have been the only cause for the increase in registered crime. More than one-quarter of the 1980 to 1986 increase is due to burglary, which almost doubled (from a rate of 110 per 100,000 in 1980 to 213 per 100,000 in 1986; see Bartnicki 1989).[15] Crime increased even more dramatically in the post-revolutionary period. In 1989, the first free elections were held in Poland, resulting in a Solidarity-led government. In March 1990, the crime rate was 28 percent higher than in March 1989. Again, a major factor was burglary, which increased by 65 percent. By June 1990, crime had increased 69 percent over the previous year.

Hungary. After a long period of relative stability, crime rates in Hungary have increased steadily since the late 1970s (Lammich and Nagy 1985). The first six years of the 1980s were characterized by an increase in crime rates, similar to the increase observed in Poland, of around 40 percent (Biénkowska 1991). After 1986, a dramatic increase of crime rates is registered (Gönczöl 1991).

Czechoslovakia. Information is available only for increases after the revolution. *Rude Pravo* published a front-page article under the title "Security in Danger." The paper cited information from the Czech Republic Ministry of the Interior, according to which the crime rate in the first quarter of 1990 was 54.4 percent higher than that in the first quarter of 1989: "While 'violent' crime increased 25 percent, property-related activity increased as much as 90 percent. The number of burglaries alone is said to have increased 164 percent" (*FBIS*, April 26, 1990, p. 17). Later in the same year, the increases for Bohemia are listed as 104 percent for theft, 201 percent for burglary, and 250 percent for robberies (*FBIS*, Sept. 5, 1990).

East Germany. Crime rates in East Germany decreased for the entire postwar period (from an average crime rate of 878 during the 1950s to 720 in 1982). The number of offenders convicted by criminal courts and the number of those placed before social courts (Wolfe 1989) was almost stable through the 1950s and 1960s, but increased by 11 percent during the first seven years of the 1970s. This trend continued during the 1980s. Objective East German criminologists explain that the increase in convictions was due to the relative increase of severe offenses (Ewald 1989). After the 1989 revolution the incidence of registered crime increased dramatically. Crime statistics showed an increase of 17.3 percent for murder and homicide, 218 percent for robbery and extortion, 13.6 percent for assault, and 51 percent for theft and embezzlement during 1990. In addition, drug crimes, prostitution, bank robberies, hooliganism, and neo-fascist violence are reported to have increased considerably (Bundesminister der Justiz 1991).

Soviet Union. State socialism, introduced by the Bolshevik revolution, lasted considerably longer in the Soviet Union than in Central and East European countries. This is reflected in the development of Soviet crime. Extremely high crime rates between 1920 and the end of World War II were followed by an almost constant decline until 1965, relative stability until 1977 (after a policy-initiated jump in 1966 resulting from a redefinition of criminal behavior), and an almost continuous increase ever since, culminating in almost doubled rates by 1989 as compared with the 1977 rates (Ivanov 1991: 188; Van Den Berg 1985: 11).

The late 1980s in the Soviet Union were characterized by increases in crime rates in some years (1985: 2.7 percent; 1988: 3.7 percent) and declines in others (1986: 4.7 percent; 1987: 9.5 percent) (Ivanov 1991; Pollard 1989: 431, 1990: 347). In its last years, the country reported considerable increases in crime rates for the same years for which crime increased steeply in Central and East European countries. The 1989 increase was 24.2 percent (Ivanov 1991: 188). Drug abuse, assault, and other violence are especially reported in journalistic sources (*Zeit Magazin*, May 10, 1991, pp. 21–31). During 1990, crime data presented by the Ministry for Internal Affairs show an increase of another 13 percent. Especially mentioned are offenses on public transportation (+28 percent), drug crimes (+ 24 percent), theft (+18 percent), murder, rape and serious assault (+18 percent), and hostage taking (in combination with hijacking of planes to force emigration, +500 percent). It is noteworthy that, according to the Ministry for Internal Affairs, the highest increases were registered in those republics seeking independence and/or experiencing interethnic conflict (Armenia: 44 percent; Estonia: 24 percent; Lithuania: 19 percent; Latvia: 17 percent) (*World News Digest*, Oct. 12, 1990, and Feb. 19, 1991). The general Soviet increase, however, cannot be exclusively explained by these special developments given these republics' relatively small proportion of the total Soviet population. In addition to the offenses listed above, racketeering and other organized crimes spread rapidly (*Zeit Magazin*, May 10, 1991, pp. 21–31).

Although these reports on selected countries do not present uniform developments, several preliminary generalizations can be made and further questions asked concerning: (1) the rather low level of registered crime in state socialist societies as compared with Western capitalist societies with democratic governments; (2) high or increasing rates under conditions of political instability in combination with repressive responses through martial law; and (3) quickly rising rates under conditions of liberalization and democratization. I discuss the validity of each of these statistical observations.

The level of registered crime was low in state socialist countries. For example, the official crime rates in Poland of 1,252 (average 1980 to 1986) and Hungary of 1,477 (same period) compare with a rate of 6,808 (same period) in the former West Germany. Are these relatively low rates in state socialist countries statistical artifacts? East European data certainly underrepresented the actual occurrence of crime because of lack of enforcement against offenses opposed to the plan and the central distribution of goods and services discussed above. At the same time, the "dark figure" in Western societies is also very high, and especially economic or white-collar offenses are vastly underreported and underenforced. Although the statistical validity issue needs more study, we may cautiously assume that crime rates were indeed somewhat lower under state socialism than in democratic countries with capitalist economies.[16] Some scholars from East European countries believe that the lower crime rate under state socialism is related to higher degrees of social justice and social integration in those countries. Buchholz, comparing the developments of East and West German crime rates, states in a particularly ideological essay:

> The development of socialist democracy (which is not restricted to representative democracy expressed only through elections) encouraged each citizen to feel a sense of responsibility for the whole, and hundreds of thousands of individuals

> were increasingly involved in all public affairs. . . . These far reaching social changes have . . . largely destroyed the basis for criminality. . . . Apart from the concern about and threat of a nuclear holocaust, the life and future of each citizen in the GDR is safeguarded. There is no existential threat and consequently no crime issuing from that source. (Buchholz 1987: 32)

Although reasons to mistrust descriptions of harmonious integration are not new, the uprising of East German and other East European peoples has fully demonstrated the ideological character of such argumentation. If crime rates were indeed low, they were so despite considerable strain experienced by the population.[17] Low crime rates would then have to be explained by other factors—for example, tight social control practiced through a dense network of secret police activities, and the considerable power difference between members of the Communist party and nonmembers.[18] Hagan's (1989) power-control theory could serve as an explanatory model along two paths. First, authoritarian states foster tightly knit informal groups that serve as a refuge from state oppression (for the Soviet Union see Shlapentokh 1989: 164–89). Such groups constitute social networks with high degrees of density and frequent interaction resulting in high social control. This explanation for low crime rates under communism is stressed by East German criminologists and sociologists (e.g., Hanf 1991). Second, power-control theory also seems confirmed when applied to state control itself. Crime rates in Soviet history increased whenever repression diminished (Shelley 1991: 266).

Yet rates of registered crime also increase to excessive levels in times of threat to the regime, which responds to the threat with especially severe oppression. This holds for the Soviet Union during the 1920s and 1930s, for Soviet republics with strong independence movements in the most recent past, and for Poland during the period of martial law (1981 to 1983) and heightened police power in subsequent years before the overthrow of the communist regime. In these periods people experience increasing strain and react with active opposition. Active opposition is defined as criminal and prosecuted by tightened criminal justice and state security control. The limits of control through power and of the power-control theory of crime (Hagan 1989) become visible in these situations when strain grows beyond previously known limits and is translated into political claims-making and active opposition. Revolt as a reaction to strain becomes more likely when oppressive power appears unstable and when its overthrow is expected. Revolt is partly expressed in lawbreaking behavior. It is further translated into growing crime rates through definitorial processes when state authorities increasingly pursue control through arrests, prosecution, and punishment. These interactive processes of structural conduciveness, strain, action, claims-making, and definition deserve further study. The East European case offers itself to such research.

We also observe considerable increases in crime rates when oppressive conditions are liberalized. This is true under communist rule, as indicated by developments in the Soviet Union and Hungary during the 1980s. It is even more true after the overthrow of communist regimes, as the numbers cited above for Hungary, eastern Germany, and Poland show.

Here again the validity question arises with particular urgency. The overthrow of political systems is accompanied by a radical change of state institutions. Should we not expect different attitudes toward these institutions by the majority of the population? Would many offenses, not reported to the police of a hated regime, now be reported to the agencies of a legitimate and, at least immediately after the change, celebrated government and political system? The answer to these questions seems to be "no" as consistent observations from different eastern European countries indicate. Although we lack studies on reporting behavior, we do have indicators on the trust with which the authorities are met under new conditions.

Recent opinion surveys in Czechoslovakia show that the population's trust in the new government is rather weak, but differs by institution. Politicians who had been leaders of the revolution enjoy high popularity (between 60 percent and 80 percent), but trust in the new political institutions (e.g., parliament, justice system) is only between 40 percent and 50 percent, and trust in the institutions seen as representing the old order is only around 30 percent (for the bureaucracy and police) or 25 percent (for large companies and unions) (Uttitz 1991: 47–48).

Also in Poland, old mistrust does not dissipate easily. Total mistrust in the police resulted from the abuses of law enforcement experienced in recent decades, especially during martial law. Reports of beatings in police custody and prisons were frequent (Lawyers' Committee for Human Rights 1987: 10); citizens had little chance for a fair defense after a 1985 bill was approved expanding use of summary procedures by permitting the government to arrest, charge, try, convict, and sentence the accused within only 48 hours. In 1986 only one-fifth of the Polish population believed that the police performed their duties well (Cole et al. 1987: 260–61). The police force was regarded as incompetent and depicted as stupid and corrupt in numerous jokes. That this attitude continues under new political conditions is likely and suggested by the considerable difficulties that the police has in recruiting new members, even under conditions of unemployment. The following statement by a Warsaw police officer is telling

(*New York Times*, Nov. 10, 1990, p. A10): "It is going to take years to rebuild the authority of the police. . . . The criminals are brave right now because they're not afraid of the police. The usual behavior of hooligans when they are caught is to yell 'I'm beaten by the police.' People come to his side immediately."

Similar accounts of continued mistrust and recruitment problems are reported from eastern Germany after the political change. In former East German cities, for example, the number of police officers was considerably reduced after unification, sometimes by 50 percent (*New York Times*, May 15, 1991, p. A6).

Both factors, the decreased control density and the population's mistrust, suggest that growing crime rates are *not* caused by increased reporting.[19] We find for eastern European countries after the revolution what Shelley concludes for the Soviet Union during the years of liberalization:

> Conversations with Soviet criminal justice statisticians, *militsiia*, prosecutorial and court personnel as well as examination of the published crime statistics suggest that the . . . rise in crime rates . . . is not a result merely of changes in reporting practices. . . . It appears to be real and particularly profound in the area of violent crime, suggesting that the anomic circumstances of *perestroika* are having criminogenic consequences (Shelley 1990: 44).

Why Do Crime Rates Increase Under Conditions of Change?

Our challenge is to explain the sudden increase in crime rates under conditions of political and economic liberalization, especially after the full transformation to democratic government and capitalist economies. The persistence of dense informal groups and networks may partly explain that the increase in crime rates is not as dramatic as the scope of emerging social problems suggests (Ewald 1991). Yet the increase is considerable. Can it be understood as an adaptation to strain? Did liberalization add to the experience of strain? Merton argues that the rate of innovation is likely to grow with the proportion of people who internalize societal goals but do not have access to legitimate means of achieving these goals. What are shared goals of the societies under consideration? Although the lack of empirical research makes this question difficult to answer, economic well-being and individual liberty are certainly among them. It can also be said that expectations concerning these goals have increased with political change. And it is likely that the legitimate means of achieving them have not increased to the same degree. For some parts of the population they have decreased, as, for example, the growing unemployment rate in eastern Germany and temporarily staggering inflation rates in Poland, Czechoslovakia, and the Soviet Union indicate. Individual liberty has probably increased for almost all members of society. But it may not have increased as fast as people's expectations. In addition, formal liberty may turn out to be different from the dreams of liberty that accompanied the revolt. For example, youth in eastern Germany opposing the 1992 war in the Persian Gulf, faced constraints to the free expression of protest that exist where such freedom is a constitutional right. Their protests were met with hostile public opinion, negative press reports, and strong opposing opinions that were not (just) official state or party positions (*Die Zeit*, Mar. 8, 1991, p. 21). Some observations thus suggest that the discrepancy between shared goals and legitimate means has indeed increased in eastern Europe.

These observations support the explanation of rising crime or innovation in eastern Europe as an adaptive strategy for dealing with strain. The discrepancy between economic expectations and economic hardship on the one hand and property crime—for example, the staggering burglary rate in Poland—on the other seem to fit the picture drawn by strain theory. Neglecting the issue of imported crime for a moment, three problems remain when the strain approach is used to explain the growing rates of crime.[20] (1) Frequent nonutilitarian crime—for example, violence against minorities—is not immediately covered by the means-ends rationale of the strain approach. (2) In the former Soviet Union, members of the most privileged group, the *nomenklatura*, seem to have been central players in growing organized crime. (3) The use of innovation rather than other action strategies is not yet explained.

I briefly deal with each of these problems in the following sections before tying the issue of criminality back to basic concerns of criminological theory.

Crime Against Minorities

Nationalist and antiminority sentiments, sometimes translated into violent crime, are reported from all eastern countries. The Russian Pamyat movement, a nationalist and anti-Semitic organization with a neo-fascist platform, has gained considerable strength. When one of its leaders was sentenced in a Soviet criminal court, the court session was forcibly interrupted by crowds of sympathizers (*World News Digest*, Oct. 12, 1990). Romanian public debate is strongly characterized by nationalist and anti-Semitic tendencies, but no violence has been reported yet (*New York Times*, June 19, 1991, p. A6). Anti-Semitic fears are also reported from Hungary

(*World News Digest*, Mar. 9, 1990). Bulgaria has experienced severe protests against its Turkish minority (*World News Digest*, Jan. 19, 1990). Most recently, pogroms against Gypsies are reported from Poland, where anti-Semitic feelings as well are expressed by high-ranking members of the reform government (*New York Times*, July 25, 1991, p. A5).

Especially detailed reports on violent actions are available for the new states of eastern Germany. According to a German government report, 30,000 Germans in the new states are involved in militant nationalist politics (*World News Digest*, Aug. 24, 1990). Recent survey research finds considerable, even though organizationally and ideologically incoherent, right-wing extremism (Stöss 1991). Neo-Nazi "skinheads" are accused of vandalizing memorial sites and gravestones (*World News Digest*, Jan. 12, 1990). Even before unification, major groups of skinheads appeared in the Leipzig demonstrations against the old regime (*World News Digest*, Feb. 16, 1990). A May 1991 article in the *New York Times* is entitled "New Hitler Youth Trouble Germany: Neo-Nazi Incidents Assuming 'Frightening Dimensions' ": "When Germany opened its borders with Poland last month, neo-Nazi groups blocked border crossings and attacked Polish travelers in their cars. On April 20, to mark Hitler's birthday, they marched in several cities in small bands and fought pitched battles with leftist gangs."

On June 28, 1991, the German weekly *Die Zeit* gave extensive coverage to the same phenomenon:

> A manhole is thrown through the windshield of the car and injures the Polish couple in face and shoulder: Görlitz, April 12, 1991. The knifeblade, 17 centimeters long, was pushed through the Pole's upper arm, the gas injured his eyes: Frankfurt/Oder, May 15, 1991. The iron bar was hit against Andrzej Staworzynski and caused head injuries. . . . Small, hidden reports like these can be found almost daily in local newspapers along the 456 kilometer long German-Polish border (*Die Zeit*, pp. 5–6, translation by author).

These phenomena are not new in eastern Germany. They existed before the revolution. Demonstrations of the Nazi salute are reported, for example, from a soccer match in 1988 that was attended by the head of the East German secret police (*New York Times*, May 1991). While they have become more visible now, it appears that they also have become much more widespread.

Nonutilitarian violence poses a challenge to strain theory (e.g., A. K. Cohen 1955). In addition, although the occurrence of racial biases and violence against minorities is common to most ethnically mixed societies, especially in historical situations of destabilization, their present development in eastern European countries poses a unique challenge. Marxist ideology has intensely proclaimed the ideals of internationalism, humanitarianism, and the idea that humans are the product of social conditions, not of innate qualities of ethnic or racial groups. Members of eastern European societies have been intensely exposed to these ideas for more than 40 and, in the case of the Soviet Union, 70 years. The rise in antiminority sentiments and aggressions thus follows a period characterized by the proclamation of ideals strictly opposed to such hostilities. We are confronted with an explanatory challenge that cannot be met in this context. More historical comparative analysis of violence against ethnic minorities under conditions of social turmoil and rapid social change and a more in-depth study of the present experience in eastern Europe are desirable. I hypothesize that the explanation in the present case can be found in the interactive effects of three factors: (1) the lack of identification with or access to social institutions that represent either a state socialist or a parliamentary democratic political order; (2) the availability of historically grown and transmitted cultural systems of racial, ethnic, or nationalist ideas; and (3) the obviously ideological and thereby devaluating use of internationalist and humanistic ideals by members of the old elite.

Elite Crime in the Soviet Union

Strain theory stresses the relation between deprivation and deviance. Strain theory is then challenged by the nomenklatura's deep involvement in organized crime, which appears to spread rapidly under conditions of liberalization in state socialist and centrally planned systems.[21] One of the predominant forms of organized crime in the liberalizing Soviet system was racketeering. Victims were small retailers as well as major joint venture entrepreneurs. Much of the newly emerging private sector seems to have been under the control of a growing "mafia." This can partly be explained by the two weak spots of private enterprise in Soviet Union. Private business depended on state authority because of its demand for raw materials and real estate. It was also charged with high taxes by the central government and municipalities. These factors combined with the particularities of the organization of formal control. The *militsiia*, the regular police, seems to have had little access to relevant information. Investigations were led by special units in the Ministry for Internal Affairs and the KGB. An Armenian investigative judge, Telman Gdljan, was dismissed after having followed the traces of an Uzbek mafia organization into the leadership of the party hierarchy. A Moscow investigative judge with the KGB who since

1990 has been a member of the freely elected Moscow city council argued: "Nothing is undertaken against the Mafia. Neither KGB nor the Ministry are concerned with organized crime. To the opposite, I was often ordered by my superiors to suspend investigations. And why? Because party bosses were involved in the affairs" (cited in *Zeit Magazin*, May 10, 1991, p. 28, my translation).

And the director of the special task force on mafia affairs wrote in *Soviet Union Today* that the rise of the mafia is caused by corrupt relations with the state apparatus. Anatolij Rubinow, writing for the opposition newspaper *Literaturnaia Gazieta*, went further: "In the Soviet Union there is only the Mafia of the Party. The Party is the real Mafia and promotes organized crime. The Ministry of the Interior blames the Mafia to disguise its own mistakes" (cited in *Zeit Magazin*, May 10, 1991, p. 28, my translation).

Be that as it may, it appears that organized crime was rising fast in the last Soviet years. I hypothesize that this increase was enhanced by an opportunity structure contributed to by three factors: conditions of scarcity, intense dependency of private enterprises on state authorities, and the lack of separation of powers.[22] The combination of scarcity, a liberalizing economy still under state control, and monopolistic political power structures is a fertile ground for organized crime. Participation by members of the nomenklatura in organized crime was further enhanced as the ideological commitment to the realization of revolutionary goals, for example, the establishment of social justice, decreased. The delegitimization of Marxist ideology provided neutralization strategies when the monopoly of power was abused for personal profit.

Other Strategies for Adapting to Change

The explanation of increasing crime rates as a reaction to anomie and strain needs further specification when alternative strategies of adaptation are taken into consideration. One such strategy is resignation, expressed, for example, in high rates of alcoholism. Another strategy is emigration. Emigration rates have increased dramatically. For example, the Soviet Union granted 270,000 exit visas in the first seven months of 1990. The total for 1988 to 1989 was 344,000 (*World News Digest*, Oct. 12, 1990).[23] In February 1991 Albanians fled en masse to Greece and Italy (*New York Times*, Mar. 8, 1991, p. A2). East Berlin, just before German unification, became a center of immigration from the east. In May 1990 alone, for example, 50,000 immigrants arrived in the city from eastern European countries (*World News Digest*, July 6, 1990). Many former East Germans moved to West German cities—110,000 people between July and December of 1990 (*Die Zeit*, Apr. 5, 1991, p. 61). The number of immigrants from eastern Europe into the Federal Republic of Germany grew dramatically.

Most recent developments indicate that—on the macroanalytical level—different strategies of adaptation to strain are not alternatives. They show parallel increases in most countries. Yet the increase in crime rates is relatively low in the former East Germany (Sessar 1991: 16), in which there are no restrictions to "emigration" (movements into the former West Germany). The German example thus suggests that the easy availability of one coping strategy may indeed reduce the rate of other strategies. On the individual or microsociological level, innovation, rebellion, emigration, ritualism, and resignation are alternative strategies. Learning and opportunity structures have to be considered to understand which categories of people choose which strategy. The East European case is a promising new field for theoretical-empirical research on the macro- and microdynamics of adaptation to strain and anomie.

East European Change: Inspiration for Criminological Theory

Revolt, in eastern Europe as elsewhere, is a typical and widely used response to contradictions between desired states and actual conditions. The East European case exemplifies that claims-making and revolt is only one strategy of adaptation to situations of anomie and strain. Other strategies, distinguished by Merton, including innovation, are empirically relevant. The case also demonstrates that reactions to strain are defined, experienced, or understood as either revolt or criminal behavior, depending on the structures of domination and the legitimacy of governments. The East European case finally illustrates that the definitions of governments and of the populace may diverge radically. Definitions of crime by criminal justice agencies may become real in terms of arrest and punishment, without becoming real in terms of public perception. The restructuralization of domination as presently experienced in eastern Europe, therefore, seems to document the fruitfulness of integrating and interrelating structural and constructionist theories of crime and social problems.

The recent history of eastern Europe also illustrates that the abolition of formal justice in the name of substantive social justice results in a loss of both. The breakdown of the separation of powers in modern societies enables dominant elites to disrespect formal rights as well as ideals of social justice for the sake of group, organizational, and individual advantages. Whereas formal and substantive justice are logically opposed to each other, social justice empirically has no chance without a minimum degree of formal justice.[24]

Finally, radical change in eastern Europe provides immense potential for sociological, criminological, and social problems research. The region is in flux, the data are preliminary, and empirical research is needed. For example, the drastic upward trend of crime during liberalization has so far led to crime rates typical for West European societies. We do not know if these rates will stabilize—that is, "normalize,"—or if they will increase to much higher levels. Subsequent crime panics may lead to authoritarian responses. Careful observation is necessary. I have further demonstrated that the East European transition provides fertile ground for theory formation, especially on (1) the interrelation between constructionist and etiological theories; (2) the relation between concentration of power and crime; (3) the relation between rapid social change and different types of adaptation to strain and anomie; (4) the relation between the use of humanistic ideals for political and ideological purposes by ruling classes and crimes of hate by deprived populations; and (5) the relation between formal and social justice. Much empirical research remains to be done to test hypotheses developed in the course of such theory formation.

The Engineering of Social Control

The Search for the Silver Bullet

GARY T. MARX

> We want to get the human out of the loop.
> —Federal Aviation Administration security official

> Science is on our side.
> —Spokesperson for Monsanto Chemical Corporation, on controversy over genetically altered hormone that increases milk production

> We don't need a sociologist, we need an engineer to solve our problems.
> —Phone company employee

With style, efficiency, high principle, and no unintended consequences, the Lone Ranger was always victorious. His silver bullet trademark is an apt metaphor for the hype accompanying current technological efforts to control crime and deviance.

In considering current developments and trends in the study of social control, I have suggested the idea of the "maximum security society" (Marx 1981, 1987, 1988); with clear indebtedness to Bentham and Foucault I have found it useful to note some parallels between control themes found in the maximum security prison and the broader society.[1]

The maximum security society is made up of six subcomponents: the engineered, dossier, actuarial, suspicious, self-monitored, and transparent societies.

George Orwell equated Big Brother with the harsh reality of a boot on a human face. The concept of the maximum security society is meant to characterize some softer social-control processes that have increased in importance and sophistication in recent decades, as the velvet glove continues to gain ascendancy over the iron fist. In contemporary society these forms of control are uncoupled and the former is clearly dominant—using the creation and manipulation of culture through the mass media, therapeutic and labeling efforts, the redistributive rewards of the welfare state, the use of deception (e.g., undercover techniques and informers), and the engineering away of infractions.

In this chapter, I expand on the notion of the engineered society.[2] The inventors and builders of the first locks, safes, moats, and castles were of course engaged in the physical engineering of social control. Today we see a continuation of the professionalization and specialization of social control that grew in the eighteenth and nineteenth centuries as new disciplines and laws appeared and the state expanded. What is new are the scale and scientific precision of those efforts and a willingness to experiment. The ratio of humans to machines as monitors and controllers continues to decrease. Controls of a remote nature have become more prominent. The cost of control per unit watched or per unit of information has decreased, and more objects and areas are probably subject to control efforts. In addition, controllers, with their specialized knowledge and sophisticated data collection techniques, are increasingly in a position to know things about subjects that the subjects do not know about themselves. Developments in electronics, computerization, artificial intelligence, biochemistry, architecture, materials science, and many related fields have led to a thriving technically based social-control and crime prevention industry.

Much traditional social analysis has unfortunately treated technology as if it were irrelevant or simply an epiphenomenon. Certainly technology is developed and applied in a social context. Decisions about what technology to develop and how to use it are socially determined based on military and commercial concerns, among others. More specifically, concerns about crime, terror, substance abuse, AIDS and other health issues, productivity, and the ironic vulnerabilities that come with our reliance on complex, interdependent technological systems (nuclear power, computer networks) help account for the development and use of extractive technologies over the past decade.

Yet technology offers new possibilities and in doing so also helps shape decisions. The increased prominence of social control through engineering is related to the availability of sophisticated and relatively inexpensive technology. If it is true that *where there is a will there is a way*, it is also often true that *where there is a way there is a will*.

Any mapping of the means by which contemporary social order is produced must give significant attention to this important topic. It in turn is a part of the broader topic of the impact of technology on society. But it offers a particularly fruitful context in which to study traditional issues of social theory and deviance and social control, as well as issues of public policy.

In the engineered society, the goal is to eliminate or limit violations by controlling the physical environment. Ideally, problems are simply designed away; when that isn't possible, deterrence is created by reducing the gain or making identification and apprehension likely. Why bother with the unpleasantness of victimization and the messiness and cost of locating violators when you can prevent violations instead? The criminal justice system is perceived as an anachronism whose agents serve only to shoot the wounded after the battle is over.

A distinction can be made between solutions involving *primary*, hard, direct prevention efforts (see strategies 1 and 4 following), which make the offense literally impossible to carry out, and *secondary*, soft, indirect prevention efforts, in which the goal is to deter. From the standpoint of social controllers the former is far superior—the physical environment is altered so that the offense cannot be carried out.

This is contrary to the mechanisms and ethos studied by Foucault (which focused on the mind of the offender and sought to transform the soul). With primary engineering strategies, it is not necessary to affect the will or calculation of the potential rule breaker. The subjective orientations of the actor (whether based on calculation, a content-filled socialization, or a contentless discipline) are simply ignored. The social-engineering example of castration as a device to control sexuality clearly contrasts with appeals to virtue to accomplish the same end. With the primary engineering strategies, the historically important reliance on the will and choices of the violator are sidestepped. Messing with the human will can be a messy business. Apart from the ethical issues, it's expensive and outcomes are uncertain. As the continuing presence of violations suggests, the endeavor always fails to some degree. From the control perspective it is far better to find technical means for making the violation impossible. But as will be noted later, for many reasons that is often not possible. Hence we see a series of secondary engineering strategies (2, 3, 5, and 6 following), which aim to affect the will.

In addition, the goal is to eliminate or reduce the role of human agents. As a federal official responsible for airline security said, "We want to get the human out of the loop." Humans are prone to inattention, fatigue, error, and corruption. They can work only for limited time periods, under severely restricted environmental conditions, and they may talk back to the bosses and organize.

The more traditional goal of deterrence is achieved by affecting the calculations of potential violators through devaluing and insulating potential targets and increasing the certainty that violations and violators will be discovered. What cannot literally be prevented may nonetheless be deterred, by eliminating the gain or by ensuring the apprehension of the violators.

I discuss six social-engineering strategies and some of their techniques and then consider some implications for theory and policy. In the best academic (although not policy) tradition, I come with questions, not answers.

Six Social-Engineering Strategies

Target Removal

The logic of prevention is clearest and most effective when a target is removed. Something that is not there cannot be taken. The move toward a cashless society is one example of target removal. Merchants who accept only credit or debit cards, or whose registers never have more than $10 in cash, are unlikely to be robbed, and public phones that accept only credit cards are unlikely to be broken into. Furniture built in to the wall cannot be stolen, and that bolted or welded to the floor is unlikely to be. Aerials that retract into the car's fender cannot be vandalized, and automobile wheels without hubcaps offer no temptation. Subways and bus exteriors with graffiti-resistant metals are difficult to deface. With new switching technology, telephones can be programmed to allow only incoming calls (and from certain numbers at that—e.g., to block a repeat crank caller) or to prevent the dialing of certain outgoing calls (e.g., long distance, dial-a-joke, dial-a-porn). Many library computers are configured so they can be used only for searches and not for e-mail or word processing. Drug eradication programs involving spraying, burning, and natural pesticides also fit here. The large pepper grinders carried by waiters in some restaurants appeared in response to widespread theft of the small grinders that once were on the tables.

Automated billing using bar codes and optical scanners on computerized cash registers (as at some supermarkets), intended to eliminate both error and employee theft (e.g., achieved by entering a lower price), is a related form of target removal.[3] In the welfare system, personal "smart cards" are replacing money and coupons, which increasingly can be used only to purchase approved food and other services directly.

A number of urban schools have created dress codes banning signs of gang affiliation and expensive clothes and jewelry. For example, students may be prohibited from wearing shirts and hats that indicate membership in nonschool organizations. Restrictions on how individuals present themselves may deter theft and eliminate symbols that can provoke assault.

Target Devaluation

The goal of target devaluation is to reduce or eliminate the value of a potential target to anyone but authorized users. The target remains, but its uselessness makes it unattractive to predators. Examples of devalued targets include products that self-destruct (some car radios when tampered with) or that leave clear proof of theft (exploding red dye packs that stain money taken in bank robberies). Some computer chips are coated with a chemical that destroys the chip if an effort is made to remove the coat. Encrypted messages can be freely sent over unprotected phone lines; anyone can intercept them, but absent the decryption code, the information is gibberish. The use of telephones, computers, and even television sets can be restricted to those with an access card, password, or the appropriate biometric pattern (e.g., handprint, fingerprint, handwriting, retinal, or voice). Items can be marked with something that makes them undesirable or impossible to use unless they are "cleansed" using a process controlled by those doing the marking. For example, to thwart the theft of live Christmas trees, some farmers spray them with a substance that causes the trees to give off a terrible odor once taken inside a house. Before a legitimate sale the spray is neutralized. "White-out" (the substance we knew well before word processing) offers another olfactory example of target devaluation. To prevent youths from sniffing it to get high, the manufacturer added mustard seed oil, which has an unpleasant odor. Some stores and shopping malls concerned about disorderly congregations of teenagers play classical music, which teenagers typically scorn.

In the case of stolen information, two authors consider the frightening possibility of brainwashing the offender with drug-induced amnesia so that the stolen information is forgotten by the offender (Montgomery and MacDougall 1986).

There is a device that, via cellular phone, can remotely cut off the engine of a stolen car. Another system, called Auto Avenger, is triggered if the door is opened while the engine is running. If not disengaged by a hidden switch, the engine will shut down after a few minutes and the system tells the thief he has fifteen seconds to get out or face a 50,000-volt shock.

Target Insulation

Target insulation is probably among the oldest of techniques for preventing violations. In the nineteenth century, some armories were built with gates designed so that the more a crowd outside pushed in on them, the tighter the gates closed (Fogelson 1989). Although the target remains, it is protected. We can separate perimeter-maintaining strategies such as fences, walls, moats, guards, and guard dogs from more specific protections such as safes, chastity belts, and placing goods in locked cases, chaining them to immovable objects, and hiding them. Recent developments in architecture and electronics offer new possibilities. There are efforts to create sanitary zones in cities where access is rigidly controlled. "Skywalks" linking downtown buildings shield their occupants from life on the street. Sections of more than 20 cities in the United States and Canada are now knit together in this fashion. In Calgary, 6 miles of skywalks connect 110 buildings. In St. Paul and Minneapolis, 65 city blocks are connected.[4] Simpler devices are one-way doors that go from enclosed, presumably secure areas to unsecured areas such as streets. For example, in some urban parking lots the exit door can be opened only from inside the lot. The goal is to channel all those who enter through a central entrance that is under surveillance. In many areas of the world, high-voltage towers wear "concrete pants" to protect against dynamite charges.

Transportation may be designed to exclude certain categories of people. Robert Moses is said to have built the parkways that led to green areas outside Manhattan with bridges that were too low for buses to get under (Caro 1974). The goal was to keep out lower-income people who would have to rely on public bus transportation. Decisions about where to locate subway stations may be made with the same goal in mind (e.g., the decision not to extend the subway to Georgetown in Washington, D.C., or to Lexington in the Boston area).

Improved locks and vaults, antitheft interlock systems for automobiles, and architectural barriers—bank buildings without first-floor windows and with "bandit barriers," the bullet-resistant glass or Plexiglas that prevents thieves from vaulting the counter—are other obvious examples of target insulation. To enter some banks in Europe, a customer first presses a button to enter a small chamber with a locked door and then is screened for metal and perhaps chemicals (in the future a video scan comparing faces with those in a suspect file might be used); if nothing suspicious is discovered, a green light flashes, the customer pushes a button, and the door to the bank opens. To leave, a reverse procedure must be followed, presumably to detain or deter any thief who manages to slip in.

Access to a building may be restricted by encryption and other codes. Thus in some large apartment complexes one no longer presses the buzzer next to the name and number. Indeed there may be no name or number. Instead, a visitor must enter a code to make the doorbell ring; the occupant may then converse with the visitor through an intercom and decide whether to admit him or her. A similar device can be obtained to screen telephone calls, such that only those with an access code can get through.

A related form of target insulation involves deception to make it appear that engineering solutions are in place, when in fact they aren't. Thus trompe l'oeil graphics may use paintings of bars on windows that at a distance look real. Flashing lights and a fake control panel, along with a decal warning that an alarm system is in operation, may be an inexpensive ploy to deter burglars. One such system (Theft Stop), which sells for $19, "creates an illusion that your home is well-protected by an expensive alarm system. Its constantly flashing lights and realistic digital keypad set on a rugged polystyrene case give the impression of high-tech circuitry." For only $9.95 one can even purchase "Man's Best Friend . . . a sound-activated electronic device that emits the forceful, intimidating barks of an enraged bulldog. Recorded on a maintenance-free microchip." Temptation may be reduced by disguising opportunities. A variety of ordinary household items with hollow interiors, from books to cans with well-known shaving cream and hairspray labels, are available for hiding valuables. A different variety of deceptive target protection is a macho-looking anti-carjacking mannequin companion that sits on the passenger's side of a car and appears to be a driving companion.

Offender Incapacitation

A classic strategy, offender incapacitation renders the potential offender harmless. There are a variety of "immobilizers," "restrainers," and "containers" that seek to prevent violations by weakening the potential offender's will or ability to commit the offense. These may act directly on the body by permanently altering it and making certain offenses impossible—psychosurgery for the violent, literal or chemical castration for sex offenders, and the practice in some Middle Eastern countries of cutting off the hands of pickpockets. Excessively aggressive behavior may be treated with tranquilizers. Drugs such as Depo-Provera may be used to reduce the sex drive. A variety of synthetic forms of progesterone are being used to block male sex hormones; remote physiological monitoring of those convicted of a crime of violence might lead to the release of chemicals in the body at the sign of a state of arousal (e.g., a peptide implant to lower the serotonin level that is related to aggression).

More indirectly, through operant conditioning a negative association with a given undesirable form of behavior may be created. After ingestion of a substance such as antabuse, an unpleasant physical reaction (gagging or vomiting) follows when alcohol is consumed. The morphine derivative trexan prevents heroin users from getting high. Methadone is used to get persons off heroin.

Nicotine patches worn on the skin have been successful in helping people to stop smoking. Abusive mothers and those who abandon their children have been subjected to sterilization or the implantation of birth control devices that last up to five years.[5] A variety of restraining or blocking devices exist, from straitjackets to nets fired over persons considered to be dangerous. Japanese police used two steel cages to contain protestors throwing firebombs and stones in response to the expansion of Tokyo's Narita airport. The police used cranes to lower the cages over towers occupied by the demonstrators. There are many other crowd-control devices, including slippery substances, tear gas, and pepper spray.

Other incapacitation efforts deal not with the body of the offender but with the instrumentalities used or involved in the offense. The goal is to render something that is essential to the violation useless. Prohibitions on the possession of weapons are an example. The use of a car can be blocked by installing an anti-drunk-driving interlock system featuring a breath analyzer attached to the automobile ignition system, or by installing clamp locks on the tires of a car whose owner owes traffic or other fines. At the Massachusetts Institute of Technology, anyone who attaches a bicycle to a handrail on a ramp for the handicapped may find a campus police chain and lock attached to it. If a $25 fine is not paid within a day, the police remove the device, impound the bicycle, and impose a $50 fine. There are devices that limit the speed of trucks and buses; "dead man" controls on vehicles such as trains require that the driver exert steady force by foot at all times while driving. Hypodermic syringes that can be used only once have been advocated as a way of stopping the spread of AIDS. Pay telephones that don't accept incoming calls or that have been converted to a rotary dial tone (which won't accept the tone signal from a pager) have been designed to prevent drug dealers from using the phones.

There are also general environmental manipulations directed at all persons within their purview. This tactic's categorical application carries the assumption that everyone is a potential offender. For example, subliminal messages may be incorporated in music played at a department store ("stealing doesn't pay," accompanied by a siren and the slamming of a jail door) or on the radio as part of an antismoking campaign. There are computer programs that permit workers to call up subliminal images (e.g., a mountain stream and the words "I am calm"). But one can also imagine programs that workers have no control over, with messages such as "work faster" or "don't join the union."

Environmental psychologists have theories about how color, light, and spatial arrangements may affect behavior, although the result is not direct incapacitation. They have advocated the increased use of Plexiglas instead of bricks and bars, better lighting, and less crowded cells as ways of reducing prison problems. Soft pastel colors are thought to have a calming effect.

Even smells may have subtle effects. In contrast to the use of smell as a deterrent, the Japanese have found that pleasant aromas reduce stress (the smell of a fresh forest) or have a rejuvenating effect (lemon and jasmine). The Shiseido Cosmetics Corporation has an "aromatic engineering program" to pump various scents into the air conditioning systems of office buildings and factories. Dietary engineering is a related area.

Offender Exclusion

Also among the oldest means of social engineering, offender exclusion is the opposite of target insulation. The offender, rather than the potential target, is restricted. Capital punishment is the most extreme form of this strategy. Other examples are exile, prison, curfews, and mobility restrictions (such as house arrests or restraining orders). At the group level, the creation of red light and drug districts away from residential areas (as in Amsterdam and Zurich) is also based on the idea of exclusion. In short, the goal of offender exclusion is to keep potential offenders away from persons or environments that may tempt them to commit violations.

Electronic location devices have recently made individual exclusion easier. These can send a message through telephone lines or transmit radio signals. In one system, if the person leaves the approved area, the signal is interrupted and a central computer notified. In a less expensive system, a probation officer makes unannounced visits to the vicinity with a receiver to see that the appropriate signal is being transmitted, indicating that the person has not left home. There will soon be an inexpensive satellite system for locating people, just as there now is for vehicles. In addition to indicating whether a person stays in a confined area, the technology can be used to send a warning that an individual is in a prohibited area (thus, abused spouses and schools have receivers that trigger an alarm if the banished person is close by).

Programs to combat truancy fit here. Whereas schools are only occasionally thought of as prisons, cities such as San Jose and Oklahoma City, which have started aggressive antitruancy programs to keep children in school, have seen a decline in burglaries (at least during school hours) (*New York Times*, Oct. 11, 1990).

In the twenty-first century we may well see new forms of "transportation"—but rather than to an undesirable location on earth, exile may be under the sea or to outer space. The ultimate exclusion may be genetic screening: persons believed to have a biological predisposition to undesirable behavior simply never appear—they aren't born. This screening could be voluntary or mandatory.

Offense, Offender, and Target Identification

When it is not possible, or when it is too expensive, to actually prevent a violation, it is at least possible to know it took place, know what happened, and perhaps to know who did it. The goal of identification is to document the occurrence of the violation and identify or even trap the violator.

Various sensors and alarms fit here. One recent invention is a battery-powered luggage alarm that fits inside a zippered purse or suitcase. When the zipper is opened an alarm goes off. A similar device does the same if a drawer, door, or briefcase is opened.

Another expanding area involves immobilization or seizure strategies. Given the great difficulty of protecting physical premises in the face of modern explosives, one system involves a super-glue that spreads onto the floor after an explosion. Persons may be able to get into a building, but the human flypaper makes it impossible for them to get out.

In an effort to combat the installation of chips that permitted free viewing of premium cable TV channels, a New York cable company sent an electronic signal that destroyed the illegally installed chips and caused the screens to go blank. When subscribers called to complain, they were told to bring their cable boxes in. These were then used as evidence in court. This clever tactic combines remote immobilization and self-identification.

Other remote identification and audit systems include computers on trucks that record details of speed, braking, shifting, etc.; ink and paper products laced with trace elements that help identify forged documents; means of showing on which photocopying machine a copy was made; a French system for spraying works of art with an invisible substance that has a distinctive odor a dog can identify years after the theft; the various password and biometric access devices for entry to buildings, rooms, or computer files (it is rumored that in one thumbprint system, if the print doesn't match, a giant robotic arm comes down and clasps the interloper's arm until a guard arrives). In some areas realtors are using electronic lock boxes (with access controlled by a personal code) to replace lock boxes containing keys on the doors of houses that are for sale. The system was developed after a Virginia realtor was charged with burglarizing houses for sale by using the standard master key previously used to gain access to the lock boxes.

Other examples are fluorescent dusting and various devices that permit the recipient of a telephone call to know where the call is coming from. A recent commercial product (DrugAlert) is a spray to detect traces of drugs on any household item. The item is wiped with a white paper towel, which is then sprayed. If drug traces are there, specific colors will appear (e.g., turquoise for cocaine, reddish-brown for marijuana). Police in New Hampshire have used this spray on the driver's licenses of people they have stopped. For an additional $299 the "Auto Avenger" will draw attention to a stolen car by releasing a plume of brightly colored smoke.

Tops on grocery items that fail to pop up when opened indicate that the goods may have been tampered with. Various personal truth technologies (polygraph, drug test, graphology, computer matching) seek to both discover infractions and verify accounts. It may even be possible to identify a person at a much later date using the DNA residue from saliva on the back of a stamp or a sealed envelope.

A more general form of identification is the stigmatic mark of the "scarlet letter," which gives evidence of past violations. A mark that is hidden or not seen will not necessarily stop an offense, but a visible mark may forewarn attentive potential victims to avoid certain persons or places. Although we no longer brand a T on the foreheads of thieves or require adulterers to wear scarlet A's, there are some modern-day equivalents. In some jurisdictions convicted drunk drivers must have special identifying license plates or signs on their cars. The requirement that individuals carry their records, or that these be checked, is equivalent. In some jurisdictions sex offenders are required to take out newspaper ads accompanied by photographs with warnings that they have been convicted of particular crimes; or their pictures may be prominently displayed around playgrounds.[6]

Another form of offender identification simultaneously identifies and punishes. There is a proposal to electrically shock those under house arrest if they attempt to leave and, if they succeed in leaving, to increase the voltage the farther they stray (Stephens and Tafoya 1985). An extreme version of this tactic was depicted in the film *Running Man*, in which prisoners had to wear collars that exploded if they went beyond a specified perimeter. Collars are available for pets that give a shock if the animal goes beyond a given area or does not respond to a call to come.

Questions for Theory and Research

In calling attention to the increased significance of social control through engineering, I am left with far more questions than answers:

- What is the ecology of engineering solutions? Are they suited to particular types of violation or violator, such as predatory crimes involving tangible identifiable property or compulsive violators? Are they less useful for offenses that require labeling, interpretation, and judgment, such as liability and contract compliance failures? Are they more appropriate for addressing forms of physical behavior directly involving the offender's body, such as drug and alcohol use, sexual abuse, and overeating, than for detecting fraud and extortion?
- Are engineering solutions likely to be found disproportionately in certain types of social setting? How do degree of industrialization and of liberal democratization relate to the prevalence of social control through engineering? Do these factors neutralize each other? For example, does industrialization push toward such control while democratization works against it? Are the most highly engineered societies those that are also highly industrialized yet the least democratic, such as South Africa before it changed?
- How do civil unrest and questioned legitimacy (as in South Africa, Northern Ireland, and Israel) or perceived high rates of crime and deviance interact with the presence of control through engineering? In Figure 10.1 I combine three variables (perceived threat of crime, degree of industrialization, and tradition of democracy) to offer an eight-cell classification for contrasts. I would predict engineering to be most used in cell C (industrialized, undemocratic, questioned legitimacy) and least in cell F (nonindustrialized, democratic, accepted legitimacy).
- Among democracies, how do distinctive national characteristics affect the extent and form of social engineering? Have the United States, Germany, and Great Britain taken it farther and faster than Italy, France, and Spain? What are the implications of a Napoleonic tradition or the experience of fascism? Does a society such as the United States, where the Bill of Rights severely limits search and seizure, place greater reliance on technical means?
- How do the various subsocieties of the maximum security society relate to each other? Is there a general "modernization" syndrome of soft repressiveness where engineering goes along with a high degree of suspiciousness, dossiers, predictive models, self-control, and transparency? Or are these functional alternatives in the sense that where there are engineering mechanisms that work, fewer of the other forms are found?
- Are there predictable cycles wherein emphasis on engineering increases, decreases, and increases again?
- How do the discovery and invention of control techniques relate to their application? Are the patterns the same as for other areas, such as the economy or medicine?
- What is the interaction between the perceived need for a social-control appli-

		Threat of crime high				*Threat of crime low*	
		Degree of industrialization				Degree of industrialization	
		high	low			high	low
Tradition of liberal democracy	strong	A	B	Tradition of liberal democracy	strong	E	F
	weak	C	D		weak	G	H

Fig. 10.1. Threat of crime, degree of industrialization, and democratic traditions.

cation and the availability of entrepreneurs to provide the technology? Can we delineate the explanatory power or causal role of the technology per se (it can fundamentally alter the context by creating new realities) without falling into a naive technological determinism?

- How do the instrumental and symbolic or political aspects interweave? How ineffective or inefficient does a means have to be for controllers to conclude that it should not be used, regardless of its possible symbolic worth? Some recent examples whose effectiveness has been questioned include the polygraph, "star wars," and the $1 million bomb detectors that the Federal Aviation Administration has mandated to be installed at 40 high-risk airports around the world.

The six "ideal types" of social-engineering strategy discussed combine a number of dimensions. While this discussion aids in descriptive classification, it also muddies some important distinctions. Another approach would be to specify dimensions and use them to create typologies. Among some major dimensions are:

1. a focus on broad environmental changes or on changes directly involving victims or offenders
2. whether changes are voluntary or involuntary
3. whether changes are visible or invisible
4. a focus on the target or the offender
5. a focus on the offense or the offender
6. to eliminate a target or render it useless to an offender
7. to eliminate or render useless an instrumentality of violation
8. to control access into or out of a system
9. use of electronic, physiological, or chemical means
10. efforts directed at a specific individual or generally
11. emphasis on literal prevention or increased certainty of identifying violations and violators
12. emphasis on controlling persons or events

Some Implications of Technological Controls for Equity

Consistent with the theme of this volume and its focus on issues of crime and inequality, let us first consider some implications of technological controls for questions of equity. I will then discuss further issues raised by the conflicting goals and unintended consequences of techno-fixes as well as the possibility of technology neutralization.

There is no clear answer to what the strategies and possibilities described here imply for equity. At least three broad positions can be identified. I view these on a continuum. The first position, in an exaggerated Marxist-Orwellian vein, views these developments critically. They occur in a context of marked inequality. The engineering of social control reflects and is designed to protect the status quo. In a version of the rich becoming richer, the more privileged become more secure and the poor less secure. A la Foucault and Habermas, the technology becomes ever more powerful and intrusive and colonizes new areas. The Leviathan state is just around the corner, or the decade. Big government and large corporations gain power not only because they design the technology but because they have the resources to use it.

The opposite of this view is an optimistic boosterism—the idea that progress can be achieved through techno-salvation. In a society where consensus and shared interests are assumed, the technologies are designed to protect us all and are seen to be essentially neutral with respect to social class. If anything, better crime control will help the poor the most because they are the most likely to be victimized. Fixed physical responses that eliminate discretion also eliminate the potential for corruption and discrimination. The video surveillance camera and heat-sensing devices do not differentiate between social classes. Data are democratically gathered from all within their purview. Accountability is thus increased and the prior ability of those with power to shield their behavior is lessened by electronic trails and tales.

A third, and I think more compelling, "realistic view" falls between these two. It recognizes that either position could in principle be correct, but it sees the current reality as being messy and contradictory. There is nothing inherent in the technology that pushes it toward or away from equity. Rather, equity depends on the context and uses of the technology. This view stresses that societies are divided and power is not homogeneous. Contradictory social and moral trends are ever present. Yes, there is a kind of radical egalitarianism associated with the broad sweep of electronic technology. But the technology develops out of social contexts that are very unequal. Conflicts in values make it difficult to reach clear moral positions. The idea of neutralization and game perspectives are also useful here: There are legitimate moves and countermoves in a free-market economy. A moving and jagged path, rather than a one-way march forward or backward, is the best model.

There are four important questions to ask when considering the implications of engineered control for equity: How does the control affect: (1) a person's chances of being put in settings in which social conditions are associated with increased risk of becoming an offender? (2) a person's chances of being victimized? (3) the chances of equal discovery across violations and violators with varied characteristics? (4) a person's chances of receiving equal treatment once a violation comes to the attention of the criminal justice system? These involve four different types of equity.

The effects of technology on equity are certainly not uniform. In general, technology cannot alter the unequal social circumstances associated with many types of offending. It is not designed to do that. To the extent that engineered solutions with their potential for access to past records and effective public communication create permanent stigmatization of offenders, the initial inequality associated with life chances may be increased.

With respect to one's chances of being a victim, to the extent that relatively effective technical solutions are treated as commodities (absent subsidies for the poor), technology may well serve to increase the victimization of the poor as crime is displaced. Those who can afford the technology (e.g., sophisticated antitheft tracking devices for automobiles and gated communities) will be able to avoid crime; those who cannot will continue to be victimized.

However, equity in the discovery of offenses may well be enhanced by the vacuum cleaner–like sweep of many technologies and their indifference to questions of race, gender, and class. There is some irony in the fact that, because of technology, the actions of elites are more visible than they have ever been; the more privileged leave electronic trails as the price for participation in the consumer society. Computer records and other forms of electronic data greatly increase the chances of discovering the violations of higher-status persons.

Similarly, there may be increased equity in processing those who are arrested. For example, the documentary record from videotaping arrest procedures may deter abusive control practices. When it does not, it may at least give greater credibility to the accounts of lower-status persons. If information-gathering technologies are widely available (e.g., to journalists and activist groups), government accountability, and by extension equal treatment, may be increased.

The commodification and privatization of justice may at the same time limit equality of treatment in some cases. To the extent that the corrections options available to a person are dependent on that person's ability to pay (as electronic home monitoring is in some jurisdictions), inequality in sentencing increases. Equity in the discovery and processing of offenses may also decline as a result of the spread of private police, who in many ways are less accountable and have more discretion than public police. Lower-status and powerless groups are not in a position to hire equivalent private control agents with technological arsenals.[7]

Conflicting Goals

In the long run, most techno-fixes are likely to work no better than ideological fixes. Human situations are too dynamic and complicated, and irony and unintended consequences are always waiting at the door when Max Weber's ghost knocks.

One issue is that there are usually multiple goals, and obtaining one may make it more difficult to obtain another. What keeps some people out keeps other people in. I illustrate with two tragic examples: (1) Fortified walls and high steel-frame fencing in the British Hillsborough soccer stadium terraces were installed to help control soccer hooliganism. But they were a major factor in the deaths of 93 fans who could not escape from the penned-in area and were crushed when the crowd surged forward. (2) In a fire in London's King's Cross subway station, 30 persons lost their lives because of deadly fumes from chemicals used in an antigraffiti paint.

The installation of new bomb detectors based on thermal neutron analysis has been held up because of concerns that they may leak radiation and lead to lawsuits. Heavy window gates or gates with double key cylinders intended to keep burglars out may keep others in, with fatal consequences if there is a fire (devices that can be opened only from the inside without a key are more expensive). One bulletproof glass system will stop repeated bullets from a 9-millimeter gun, yet it has the drawback that the window cannot be rolled down. Bulletproof vests will not stop a knife, and the vest that protects against a knife will not stop a bullet.

Efforts to combat theft and fighting by imposing school dress codes can conflict with the First Amendment right to freedom of expression. However noble the goal, the application of such categorical standards conflicts with the idea that people should be judged by their behavior, not their potential behavior or their appearance.

To require a felon released from prison to have a sign on his home and automobile saying, "Dangerous Sex Offender, No Children Allowed," may keep potential victims away. Yet it also conflicts with the goal of reintegrating violators into society once they have paid their debt.

In commercial settings where impulse-buying and access to merchandise are important, attaching expensive leather coats to a rack with a cable and lock reduces the likelihood that someone will walk off with one, but it also prevents a customer from trying one on and buying it impulsively. Electronically tagging items in retail stores achieves the same goal with less negative symbolism.

Neutralization

Another problem with technology is that it can be "neutralized." Even silver bullets tarnish. Humans are wonderfully clever at finding ways to beat technical or social systems when they have an incentive to do so. Erving Goffman's masterful essay on total institutions in *Asylums* illustrates this. To take but one example, the car interlock with a breath analyzer to prevent drunk driving can be beaten by releasing "clean" air saved in a balloon into it. When the technical system literally can't be beaten (as with encryption), then the human context in which it is embedded can sometimes be manipulated. My favorite computer crime story involves one of the largest such crimes ever perpetrated. The company had state-of-the-art security devices that were technically unbeatable. Yet a thief managed to steal millions of dollars. How? He had an affair with the woman who was responsible for the codes needed to gain access to the system. In one of the more bizarre incidents of testing mania, a competitor for the U.S. diving team passed his drug test, but the test determined that he was pregnant. A retest revealed the same thing. What happened? Using a catheter, he had substituted his girlfriend's urine for his own.

In a free-market economy most high-tech developments are also available to offenders. Thus the level of play may be improved but without a clear victory for control agents: Bulletproof vests protect criminals as well as authorities; criminals may also encrypt their communications; and a dog in heat is a wonderful antidote to a guard dog.

An important strand of the history of deviance and social control involves responding to violations with technical solutions. There is a little-studied dialectic wherein new solutions offer new challenges to violators, which in turn create a need for new solutions by social controllers. In addition to studying cultural techniques of neutralization, there is a need for studies of technologies and countertechnologies in this regard. A considerable amount of the history of deviance and social control can be understood by looking at the field as an endless spiral of violations, social-engineering responses, new violations, and new responses.

Unintended Consequences

A new series of offenses has appeared—what are called derivative second-order offenses. An example is the response of Canadian police to a radar detector used by speeders. Police have turned to "the interceptor," which detects the radar detectors of citizens by emitting a sharp buzzing noise and flashing red light when aimed at a car with a radar detector. Citizens get tickets for possession and face confiscation of the devices, whether or not they were speeding.

The old meter boxes that measured use of home electricity could be made to run backwards by running a magnet across them. These are now designed with an antimagnetic component. However, when meters began being installed inside houses, theft of power was made easier for those who knew what to do. Now the meter is located between the line and the house, making tampering more difficult.

A related issue involves the energy and resources that may be required to avoid predation. A police detective notes, "Some people park their car, and they take the radio out, then they take the hubcaps off, and remove the steering wheel. There's got to be a point where you stop and say, 'this has gotten ridiculous.' "

Ironically, security may become lax in some areas because it is assumed that a machine is on the job. Technology may offer a false sense of certainty. A Los Angeles man sentenced to house arrest and required to wear an electronic surveillance bracelet shot and killed his estranged wife. She had not reported his threats to police because she thought she was safe as long as he had the bracelet on.

Errors may occur. A problem for many police departments is the large number of false alarms caused by everything from credit card errors to system breakdowns. Credit card errors occur even with new means of signature verification. Although signature verification is a technique that might seem completely reliable, signatures are not perfectly consistent over time. If the computer standards are too rigid in verifying signatures, people will be rejected who should be authorized; if they are too flexible, forgers will not be caught.

There are dangers of escalation when ever-more-powerful means of protection require ever-more-powerful means of neutralization. In his "star wars" speech, former President Reagan argued that only techno-fixes could help us avoid war. The response to nuclear weapons after World War II was to build bigger bombs and bomb shelters, not to seek other, more peaceful, solutions. The armaments race between police and criminals in the United States has something of this quality. In many police departments automatic weapons and 9-mm pistols are now standard.

Another significant unintended consequence lurks in the potential for increased violence (whether out of anger, preventive motives, or as a means of gaining information) once an offender discovers that a target has been fortified or devalued. For example, a frustrated thief may respond to a car with a self-destructing sound system by firebombing the car. The radio is not taken, but the car is destroyed. An English colleague reports that improved armored-car alarms have reduced robberies but may have also made them more deadly, because thieves may attempt to kill the guard before the alarm button can be pressed.

One factor in the spread of "carjackings" in parking lots and on city streets and highways appears to be the increased difficulty of breaking into and "hot-wiring" cars with security systems. Another is the desire to avoid damaging the car by pulling it apart and hot-wiring it. The more problematic nature of breaking into alarmed cars and starting them without keys has led to a change of tactics. Rather than displacing the violation, the supposed deterrent causes it to escalate (Marx 1981).

In a related fashion, the use of access codes for appliances may mean that crimes of burglary are converted to crimes of robbery or kidnapping, as thieves confront property owners and coercively demand not only the property, but the code to make it work. People who take their car radios with them after parking their cars now risk having the radios stolen from their persons.

After the Irish Republican Army left bombs in rubbish bins at train stations in London, some stations eliminated the bins, but they soon found themselves "ankle deep in litter." An unintended consequence of requiring drunk drivers and child molesters to identify themselves may be vigilante attacks and harassment of these people, as well as secondary effects from labeling and stigmatization. Publicizing the names of those arrested for drunk driving or soliciting prostitutes may lead to unwarranted inferences about guilt before trial.

Some efforts may be equated with the phenomenon of iatrogenic effects in medicine. It may be possible to cure one problem but not without creating another. For example, it may be possible to cure someone of heroin addiction only by addicting him or her to methadone (some heroin addicts stay outside the health-care system because they regard methadone as more addictive than heroin).

Techno-fixes also create the possibility of displacement. A "problem" may simply be relocated. The move to a cashless society may reduce conventional robberies while encouraging the spread of computer crimes. In response to the movement of crime from one Los Angeles neighborhood to another, one officer said, "It's like squeezing Jell-O—it squirts out in other places." A variety of grates and barriers have been developed to keep the homeless away from heating vents and entrances to subway systems. To stop the homeless from sleeping on benches, the benches may be removed. These tactics do nothing to solve the problem of homelessness, but they may move it somewhere else (e.g., people will sleep on the ground). Considered more generally, displacement techniques focus on symptoms rather than causes—akin to rearranging the deck chairs on the Titanic instead of looking for icebergs.

Sometimes we assume that actions are taken for instrumental reasons when in fact a more important goal is expressive. For example, many of the target insulation and devaluation techniques, such as devices to protect cars, assume that the thief's goal is to steal an antenna or hubcaps. But to the extent that expressive motives are present, then such actions may make little difference (Katz 1988). Simplistic thinking may be involved. For example, although removing a man's testicles will reduce his sex drive, it may increase his already-present hostility toward women and society. Even without castration, many rapists are already sexually dysfunctional and may commit sexual assault without sex. Rape may occur involving objects such as sticks.

Another issue is whether techno-fixes will swamp or overload the system with more offenses and offenders than it can handle. Will more infractions be discovered than can be processed? Are there times when it is best not to know that a violation has occurred? Is it desirable to permanently stigmatize someone or to take away all possibility of a second chance? If the penalty for an offense is a permanent change to the body or a permanent public record, the offender may have no chance to change or reform. Such offenders, in response to the denial of opportunity and in anger, may become dependent on the state and increase their antisocial behavior.

Robert Frost wrote a poem that asks whether fences keep others out, or those inside within.[8] The question is well put in a play by Keith Redden (*Life During Wartime*), in which a seller of home security devices asks, "How do you protect yourself in this world that seems so chaotic, without building walls so that you're cut off from the entire world?" Similar questions regarding entry and exit can be asked about the entry chambers into banks. What happens to the person in the booth if there is a fire, an earthquake, or a power outage?

There is the problem of punishment without trial in the case of devices that do bodily or material harm. Such devices include homemade antiburglar devices that fire a gun or a crossbow when triggered by an intruder, barbed wire, electrified fences, perimeter walls with jagged glass embedded on the top, and spikes that protrude from parking lot exits.[9] Leaving aside the fact that some people may actually deserve the punishment they receive from these devices, one can also imagine scenarios in which innocent people are harmed (e.g., a passerby who is shot by a homemade burglar alarm after seeing a fire and rushing in to help, or a foreigner unfamiliar with the parking lot spikes who mistakenly drives over them in the wrong direction). In the same vein, one wonders whether the antitheft device that delivers the 50,000-volt shock to the driver of a stolen car could be lethal to a person with a weak heart, or if it could fail and deliver a much larger shock that would be lethal to anyone.

The cost to the owner of property may be great if a system malfunctions. Owners as well as thieves may be unable to use a car. Should an encryption code be destroyed or lost, the data will be lost to their proper owner as well as to interlopers. Fire alarms with ink packets that get on the hands of those who send the signal may help in deterring or identifying those who would send false alarms, but they also stain the hands of legitimate users. The removal of public benches denies others as well as loiterers a place to sit. The double-edged sword can also be seen in the impact of control techniques on the controllers: In an ironic twist of universalism, there is a highly effective crowd-control device that causes a loss of bowel control—yet because it affects controllers as well as targets, it has not been widely adopted. And Richard Nixon, in secretly tape recording others, also taped himself.

In eliminating the choice to break a rule and the negative aspects of rule violation, we also eliminate some of the positive aspects. The privilege of breaking rules (or at least a de facto policy of nonenforcement) can be an important social resource (Marx 1981). Thus much innovation is initially seen as deviance. Perhaps the social order would become less creative and dynamic, if more orderly, if social-engineering solutions were widespread.

What kind of a society would we have if order depended primarily on technical means of blocking violations? First, what would happen when the system, or elements of it, went down, as it invariably would at some point?

A social order based on techno-fixes is likely to be even more fragile than one based on overt repression. Second, even if order could be effectively maintained, what kind of a society would it be from a moral standpoint? Voluntarism and consensual behavior are central to our notion of the dignity of the individual. The regimentation involved in technical solutions to social conflicts and problems is hardly appealing. We would become more like robots than humans, and the definition of what it means to be human would certainly change. The film *Cyborg* gives us a hint of that. A society in which order is maintained through technology rather than through legitimacy presents new challenges to theorists, as well as to activists.

There is the danger noted by Leo Marx of valuing technological developments as ends in themselves, apart from a broader vision of the good society (L. Marx 1987). Technical solutions seek to eliminate negotiation and compromise and point us away from examining social conditions that generate violations, some of which could and should be changed.

In this chapter my intent is neither to deny the seriousness and costs of contemporary crime problems nor to deny the efficacy of many situational interventions.[10] There is much to be said for prevention and actions that will preclude involvement of the formal criminal justice system. Yet the search for the silver bullet represents a failure to look for the deeper causes of disorder. It is like swatting mosquitos instead of draining the swamp (though given the ecological importance of swamps, draining them is a questionable goal). It is an individualistic rather than a communal solution and ignores the value of community and responsible individual behavior. Used wisely, technical solutions have a place. But in matters of criminal justice the Lone Ranger will always be the only one with the silver bullet.

Law, Crime, and Inequality

The Regulatory State

PETER C. YEAGER

Law is to criminology as science is to technology. Law and science are the respective foundational institutions on which the enterprises of criminology and technology are built. In one way of looking, they are the theories driving the associated practices. This is even truer of criminology than of technology, because law necessarily and wholly defines the very terrain of criminology, whether considered as a specialty in behavioral analysis or in public policy.[1] As "theories" underlying vital social practices, both law and science are deeply implicated in moral questions, although these typically go unremarked upon—even unrecognized—in the conventional discourses of their practitioners.

Indeed, and more squarely to the point, the practitioners of both criminology and technology typically build their enterprises without explicit reference to the underlying logics in law and science that shape and constrain their projects. Arguably, this tendency has hindered the development of criminology more than it has stunted technological growth; in both cases it obscures many of the essential moral matters at stake.

My purpose in this chapter is to argue for the necessary and explicit consideration of law in criminological work. I do so by focusing on aspects of regulatory law, that body of statutes, regulations, and common law directed at the harmful behaviors of business enterprises. While this particular application may seem unique, the need for careful specification of law and legal process characterizes all of criminology, as I hope to make clear. Along the way, the discussion will illustrate the entwining of law and inequality, of science, technology, and regulation, and of public policy and moral considerations.

A Prolegomenon on Law, Crime, and Inequality

In criminological research, the nature of law is typically taken as nonproblematic, and criminologists are free to investigate violations as "pure" behavioral phenomena unconfounded by the form of law or processes of its enforcement. For some types of question, and to a point, this approach is sensible. For example, where the law is long settled and roundly endorsed, as in the case of much violent crime, we reasonably ask about patterns and causes of infraction, especially with a view toward finding near-term means of reducing offenses. But even here analytic limits suggest themselves. Because law is fully implicated in the structuring of group opportunities, expectations, and constraints (including those involving the legal apparatus itself), it is deeply embedded in the causal nexus of violence. Or consider the evolving criminal law definitions of violence entailed in such issues as domestic abuse, spousal rape, and drunk driving, among others. In such cases, focusing simply on the behavior of deviants will not only shortchange the analytic potential of the entire matter, but is likely to mishandle the conventional causal analysis itself.[2]

The larger point is that the general separation of criminology from law deprives us of a fuller understanding of the relations between patterns of criminality and social organization. And the losses are accounted against both social theory and public policy. It was precisely the isolation of criminological work from broader considerations of social organization, combined with the associated failure of the liberal program in criminal justice to stem the rising tide of crime in the 1970s, that led to a perception within the discipline a decade ago that criminological theory had become stagnant.[3] The subsequent failure of the conservative program of retribution to slow the growth of crime in the latter 1980s suggests not only the continuing poverty of policy, but a lack of theoretical integration in the discipline as well.[4]

In the classical tradition of social theory, the institutional analysis of law was an integral part of the enterprise. And if crime itself was epiphenomenal in the work of Marx, Weber, and Durkheim, their analyses clearly suggested that disruptive behaviors of all sorts are deeply rooted in the institutional features of social order, including legal arrangements. Durkheim, of course, most explicitly took up the question of crime and punishment. But he reversed the conventional analytic logic, explaining the former in terms of (social "needs" for) the latter. In this view, he presaged the development of the labeling school in criminology and deviancy in the 1960s, and illuminated a host of important questions in the study of crime. For example, the differential treatment at law of white-collar and conventional crimes may register the effect of a complex of social sentiments having less to do with objective criminal harm than is often thought.

For their part, Marx and Weber disagreed on many basic theoretical questions, but shared certain views on the role of law in capitalist democracies. In particular, both men underscored the importance of formal legal equality in the development of capitalism, emphasizing not only its role in facilitating trade (as in contracts), but also its role in the reproduction of socioeconomic inequality. To the extent that such inequality is implicated in patterns of crime, this argument has clear and important implications. More generally, their analyses of formal equality at law suggest that legal process plays a role in shaping the distribution of illegal outcomes.

It is noteworthy that this occurs not only in the way that punishment may be said to condition the likelihood of future infractions, as in the (opposing) logics of deterrence and labeling perspectives. It also occurs in the way that formally neutral, egalitarian legal procedures nonetheless privilege certain sorts of "inputs" over others. These inputs comprise both cultural and structural dimensions, and their differential processing at law shapes not only such instant legal decisions as determinations of guilt and punishment, but also the real rates of lawbreaking that are the targets of enforcement policies.

Cultural Constraints in Law

It is worth considering some of the ways in which law may create—or recreate—types of inequality, even where the legal processes are formally fair.[5] In the sphere of culture, or ideology, the assumptions, techniques, and language of law may shape the distribution of legal outcomes in ways that are objectionable to many observers. For example, from wide constitutional considerations to specific technical decisions, a legal system may privilege certain values (e.g., private accumulation, individual rights) over others (e.g., the commonweal, collective rights). In the legal regulation of business, this process can be seen in the application of cost- or risk-benefit logics in rule making; such utilitarian logics tend to favor the more easily measured private sector costs of compliance over the less measurable public interest at stake (e.g., in clean environments).

In conventional criminal justice, similar processes are also at work. For example, in 1987 the Supreme Court denied a novel challenge to the death penalty in *McCleskey v. Kemp*. McCleskey had challenged his sentence on the statistical evidence from criminological research (Ellsworth

1988) that capital decisions appeared to be infected with racial bias, particularly when the race of victims and interracial homicides were considered. Without challenging the research, the Court rejected the argument on the grounds that aggregate patterns were irrelevant to the constitutional question; rather, the Court ruled, to invalidate the penalty McCleskey would have to show that the jury had impermissibly considered race in his own case, an extraordinarily steep burden of proof emphasizing his specific rights and duties over the consideration of the collective experience of racial minorities.

At more "mundane" levels of criminal justice, we can compare law's relative abilities to comprehend different types of events as criminal in the first place, as well as its consequent tendencies to differentially characterize types of defendants. The technical complexity of many "white-collar" or economic events, in combination with the not uncommon ambiguity of law in relation to them, distinguishes many potential business offenses from the garden variety street crimes that are the traditional focus of criminal justice efforts. The resulting variation in law's ability to "locate" illegal activities runs well beyond the often noticed problems of detection. Substantively, it runs to the very definition of offenses, while procedurally it includes the problem of showing criminal intent in complicated commercial transactions (see, e.g., K. Mann 1985; McBarnet 1991). For example, legal definitions of fraud in complex securities or tax matters comprise considerable areas of grey, making often comfortable room for creative interpretation by corporate accountants, lawyers, and managers, while leaving enforcement personnel with the triple challenge of detection, substantive interpretation, and proving guilt in the face of vociferous professional protestations of good faith.

Notice, too, a fundamental implication of these legal relations that further—and radically—distinguishes the social control of business activities from that of conventional criminal events. Potential white-collar or business defendants are commonly involved in the active shaping of the very legal definitions being applied to their behaviors by enforcement officials. Notably, this proactive interpretive work occurs *after* the statutory decrees of legislatures, which have been debated and written in the bright light of public deliberation and media critique. Depending on the type of matter at hand, the line separating compliance from crime may be negotiated at the quieter, less visible stages of agency rule making, investigation of potential wrongdoing, and even sanctioning (Mann 1985; McBarnet 1991; Yeager 1991). In contrast, defendants in conventional criminal cases typically find themselves in more passive (hence, disadvantaged) roles in relation to the law, left only to argue facts (and occasionally procedure) against the implacable definitional and moral judgments of the criminal code.

Related to these distinctive legal processes, as both cause and effect, is the attachment of moral ambiguity to notions of white-collar offending. In the first instance, this ambiguity is founded upon the highly technical nature of many business operations and transactions. Amidst the overlapping complexities of modern production and rule systems (e.g., scientific, accounting, and legal), the moral character of events is often either difficult to define or simple to obscure. Moreover, given the generally high social value placed on private sector production (of both goods and jobs) in market economies, government regulation itself is often considered morally suspect, at least by the regulated and particularly at the margins of perceived costs and benefits. As a result, not only is the line defining legal compliance subject to shift, but events clearly on the wrong side of legal boundaries may appear open to ethical debate.

Where it occurs, this result has the effect, of course, of encouraging white-collar lawbreaking by enlarging the repertoire of justifications. Another effect, arguably, is to promote more favorable treatment of such offenders by the bar and the regulatory agency or court. One may contrast, for example, Mann's (1985) evidence for the zealous advocacy of white-collar defendants by their attorneys, and for the more careful consideration of moral responsibility by their sentencing judges in complex cases, with the standard typifications of clients and assumptions of guilt made by counsel and judges in their efficient plea bargaining of "normal crime" (Blumberg 1967; Sudnow 1965). Naturally, the relation between counsel and client is influenced by its institutional features, such as whether the attorney is paid by the client or is court-appointed and compensated by public revenues, the attorney's case load, and the like. But it is also true that the *moral characterization of events* will color legal professionals' judgments of the *moral character of defendants*, and thereby tend to contribute to relatively favorable outcomes for white-collar as against conventional criminal suspects.

Social Structures, Legal Structures

In addition to the cultural aspects of sociolegal relations, there are structural factors in social organization that shape the outcomes of legal process. Again, the general operation of these factors tends to privilege white-collar defendants over conventional suspects by increasing the likelihood of favorable legal outcomes for the former; it also tends to favor the larger, better-organized among the white-collar class of defendants—for example, large corporations over individual operators or small firms (cf. Galanter 1974). The structural factors I have in mind include the *organization of enterprise*, at the levels of both markets and firms, the *organization of legal institutions*, and the relationships between these two sets of structures.

The organization of business activities affects both the occasion of offending, its detectability, and—upon detection—its sanctioning. At the level of industrial organization, or market structures, the nature of standard business operations may even limit the legal definitions of otherwise objectionable behavior. For example, in federal antitrust law the Sherman Act clearly prohibits price-fixing conspiracies, in which competitor firms actively collude in the setting of prices, debiting both efficiency in the economy and consumers' wallets. But the law does not reach the identical results of "conscious parallelism," in which the few large corporations that dominate a highly concentrated industry simply match each other's highly visible price changes, often by nothing more sinister than "following the leader" through media reports of pricing decisions (Clinard and Yeager 1980: 136–37). Companies in such oligopolistic industries, therefore, may in effect legally fix prices, while their (typically smaller) brethren in less concentrated industries must risk criminal prosecution to achieve the same noncompetitive advantage.

Larger, more powerful organizations in industries of all sorts may enjoy other law-defining advantages not shared by smaller competitors. I have in mind cases in which government standards are set on the basis of the current practices of leading producers, often the larger, more resource-rich firms. In this event, competitor firms are forced to invest capital to meet the new standards, or fall into violation. In a variant of this outcome, government may even set standards based on the dominant or typical practices in the industry, leaving only the marginal (from an economic viewpoint) laggards to come to standard or face prosecution. I illustrate these possibilities in a later section with the example of environmental regulation. Here I pause only to mark the difference from the conventions of standard criminality: the behaviors of ordinary offenders are typically not used to define crime, even if at certain margins they do influence processes of enforcement (as, for example, with prostitution in many jurisdictions).

The institutional locus and substantial resources of large corporations may also shield them from the full effect of law at the stage of enforcement against violations. This occurs when, for example, enforcement agents eschew stringent sanctioning and instead bargain for compliance over time, whether because they wish to avoid the result of plant closures and large job losses often threatened by regulated firms, or because they wish to avoid a protracted court battle with a powerful corporate adversary whose legal resources may overmatch even the federal government's (see, e.g., Clinard and Yeager 1980; Yeager 1991).[6]

At the level of the firm, the nature of internal organization also shapes legal outcomes. This is clearly the case with the related matters of detectability and deterrence. Not only may the evidence of business offenses be buried deeply within the ordinary complexities of conventional business practices, but individual responsibility for them may be equally difficult to locate amidst the structural complexities of hierarchy and the division of labor, especially as these are manifested in very large organizations. As a result, even when companies are prosecuted for offenses, responsible officials often are not. And where officials are prosecuted, they tend to be selected from the middle ranks of management rather than from the top levels of executive policymakers, who are often shielded from culpability by the legal requirement that knowledge of the offense and criminal intent be proven. They are shielded by subordinates who have been pressured by top management to achieve results in a difficult environment, but who are reluctant to report operating difficulties and consequent illegal activities for fear of being labeled incompetent (see, e.g., Clinard and Yeager 1980: chaps. 3, 12; Hagan et al. 1989: chap. 1; Stone 1975; Yeager 1990).

For all of these reasons, then, corporations—especially the largest firms that dominate economic output and profits—enjoy a privileged relationship to law relative to that of individuals. These "juristic persons" enjoy both greater opportunity to define law's commands in the first place, and greater immunity from the full weight of sanctioning in the second place. Much as Galanter (1974) has argued, these advantages are the cumulative results of the powers accruing to organization and large resources.[7] Relative to conventional, individual criminal offenders, corporate organizations are less likely to be harshly sanctioned. And within the firm, relative to lower-level business managers, top executives are less likely to be prosecuted. On the argument that corporate offenses in the aggregate may be more socially harmful than street crime (e.g., Clinard and Yeager 1980), one may therefore well agree that "where desert is greatest, punishment will be least" (Braithwaite and Pettit 1990: 182). But we need not make this arguable assumption about relative harm, or desert. The argument for inequality in law need simply assert clear, widespread inequities in the application of sanctions to the offenses of organizations and individuals, a claim well supported by the criminological literature cited above.

Implied in all of the above is the key role of legal institutions. The financing and structuring of these apparatuses only enhance the advantages of large firms. Among other factors, the chronic shortage of resources for regulatory law enforcement often forces regulators either to overlook many corporate offenses entirely, or to sanction even serious offenses softly, in order to avoid costly and protracted legal battles with powerful adversaries. When stiff penalties are applied in white-collar cases, they may therefore be disproportionately reserved for less powerful entities. As Braithwaite and Pettit have argued, "The bureaucratic realities of criminal justice administration inevitably result in systemic pressures towards lenient treatment of sophisticated criminals and tough treatment of unsophisticated ones" (1990: 183).

In addition, law facilitates this result to the extent that it provides privileged routes of access for powerful organizations. This is the case in many arenas of white-collar regulation, where the law provides special forums and procedures through which regulated parties can negotiate not only the terms of compliance (e.g., timetables, extent), but even the original definition of compliance, as I noted earlier. Moreover, where multiple agencies share jurisdiction over corporate offenses, as with many regulatory agencies and the U.S. Department of Justice, processes of bureaucratic "turf" protection and the use of conflicting legal logics may similarly dilute enforcement efforts (see, e.g., Bequai 1977; Yeager 1991). All of these processes work especially well in the context of highly complex regulatory matters (as in environmental and securities regulation), where corporate resources are sufficiently impressive that law enforcement officials choose to negotiate rather than risk a confrontation with a powerful adversary in court, and where the morality of law itself may be challenged, as in the intended imposition of regulatory requirements in the face of economic stagnation and decline. In later sections, I illustrate the operation of these various processes in regulatory law.

Inequality and Public Policy

Finally, it may be said that legal inequality exists when the aforementioned structures and processes result in systematic failures of public policies to meet their stated promises. Here, the state essentially fails to distribute fairly rights and duties to society's various competing interests. And where there exists a gap between formal law and its application in practice, it typically favors more organized and powerful interests in the political economy, while disfavoring the "public interest."

But notice that this occurs not at the simple behest of a farsighted guiding elite, as an instrumental Marxist argument might have it. Nor is it a matter of life cycles of regulatory agency capture by regulated parties

(Bernstein 1955), or of a simple split in the distribution of public policy rewards: symbolic ones to diffuse publics and tangible ones to organized, powerful ones (cf. Edelman 1964). Instead, this inequality is rooted in the deep structures of sociolegal relations and sustained by associated ideological features of Anglo-American law. It is important to add, however, that these structures and beliefs, while relatively stable in our political economy, are periodically subject to shifts, especially in times of crisis in social organization. This is why, for example, today's symbol may become tomorrow's substance, as illustrated in the history of environmental regulation in the United States.

Environmental Law: The Public Regulation of Private Pollution

To demonstrate aspects of these processes at law that both reflect and reproduce inequality in social organization, I focus on the case of the federal Clean Water Act, first passed in its modern manifestation in 1972 as amendments to the Federal Water Pollution Control Act (Yeager 1991).[8] This key piece of social legislation represented a significant shift in the government's efforts to control one of the most threatening "externalities" of modern productive systems: industrial water pollution. In addition to its clear importance in public policy, this law illustrates a number of the structural features and processes that often result in inequitable implementation in state regulation of business, even while such law realizes a measure of social good.

It demonstrates, for example, the ways in which complex regulatory programs can unintentionally shape the balance of interests that are recognized in rule making in federal agencies. While this matter is always salient in democratic decision-making structures formally premised on public deliberation, it is all the more so in the context of the Clean Water Act: because of the difficulty entailed in defining *a priori* the appropriate trade-offs between clean water and other values in public policy (e.g., a healthy economy), the Congress designed public deliberation and participation into virtually every phase of rule making and enforcement in the law. Among other reasons, the legislature was concerned precisely to prevent the sort of regulatory "capture" of policymaking by business that Bernstein (1955) and others had long described.

In addition, this case is something of a "peak" example of the social regulation of business in the United States. Not only was the statute highly ambitious in its means and goals for clean water, but much of it was also implemented during the activist "environmental decade" of the 1970s and overseen by the Carter administration, which in its early years was particularly aggressive in its social regulatory policies. As further measure of environmental regulation's continuing salience in law, it proved to be the only area of social regulation to produce a serious political backlash to the Reagan administration's deregulatory policies in the 1980s. By early 1983 the federal Environmental Protection Agency (EPA) was awash in public scandal amid charges that its rule making and enforcement had become corrupted by a pattern of secret negotiations with industry representatives, exclusion of public interest voices from policy deliberations, and improper influence exerted from the upper reaches of the executive branch. By April most of the president's appointees to leadership positions in the agency, including top administrator Anne Burford, had resigned under fire, as the administration sought to resolve this crisis in legitimacy by publicly embracing the philosophy of environmental protection, if not its rigorous application at law.

In general, this political history demonstrates two, apparently opposing, conclusions. On the one hand, it shows the special place of environmental protection in public policy. Once institutionalized as a recognizable state policy, and more importantly as a fundamental public right, pollution control—more than any other important areas of social regulation—has proved resistant to wholesale evisceration because significant majorities have perceived a vital problem whose solution is simply beyond the voluntary capabilities of the private sector. On the other hand, as I attempt to show below, the Reagan administration's policies only amplified and made overt dynamics that commonly restrict regulatory law, limiting its benefit in public policy.

The 1972 Clean Water Law

The 1972 amendments to the Federal Water Pollution Control Act comprised a detailed, ambitious, and unprecedented environmental program providing for the control of both industrial and municipal water pollution. The law included a radically new system of pollution controls and penalties for infractions, broad public participation in the law's administration, and "whistle blower" protection for employees reporting violations of law, among numerous other provisions in 88 pages of legislation (Yeager 1991: 167–70).

The centerpiece was a national permit program mandating technology-based standards of water pollution control for all industrial facilities. The law's logic was to "level the playing field" for polluting plants: all facilities within definable industry categories were, at a minimum, to achieve the same levels of pollution reduction; this requirement would eliminate the advantages to some firms of the "pollution havens" historically provided by states fearful of industry flight from stiff controls. The law required EPA to formulate two progressively stringent levels of pollution reductions by writing specific regulations for each industry category, then applying them equally to all plants in each category by means of pollution discharge control permits setting out the required reductions and timetables.

The agency was to accomplish its rule making and permitting tasks such that by mid-July 1977 all industrial plants were to have achieved a level of pollution reduction that reflected "the application of the best practicable control technology [BPT] currently available," and by mid-1983 a greater level indicating the use of "the best available technology [BAT] economically achievable."[9]

With respect to toxic pollutants, which pose the greatest risks to the environment and human health, the law was uncompromising: In its first section, the statute states that "it is the national policy that the discharge of toxic pollutants in toxic amount *be prohibited*."[10] Instead of the technology-based (and cost-constrained) standards to be applied to conventional pollutants (such as sediments and pH concentrations), the 1972 amendments sought to regulate toxic discharges on the more stringent criteria of their broad environmental effects on water and water-based organisms, and up the food chain to human health, making no mention of the limits of control technologies or costs.[11] Within fifteen months of the law's passage EPA was to publish a list of toxic pollutants (both singly and in toxic combinations—a very large task indeed) and to finalize the multitude of discharge regulations controlling them "with an ample margin of safety" to protect the environment. Industrial firms were to be in compliance with the new limits no more than one year after their promulgation, or by mid-1975.[12] The Congress's stated goal in the statute was the *elimination* of all industrial water pollution by 1985.

On the matter of enforcement, the law also represented a dramatic change from previous controls. It provided for maximum criminal penalties of $25,000 per day of discharge violation and up to one year's incarceration ($50,000 and two years for repeat offenders).[13] That such fines can build up to significant amounts was illustrated in 1976 when the federal government fined the large, multinational Allied Chemical Corporation (now Allied Corporation) $13.24 million for criminal discharges of the toxic pesticide Kepone and other chemicals into Virginia's James River. The statute also provided for citizens' rights to sue violating companies if the government took no action, and to sue EPA itself on the grounds that the agency had failed to perform nondiscretionary duties under the law (e.g., promulgation of statutes on a timely basis).[14]

The 1987 amendments strengthened the government's enforcement options, enlarging both criminal and civil penalties and for the first time providing that EPA could issue its own administrative fines for violations. The water pollution law now distinguishes three types of criminal violation. It provides the same minimum and maximum penalties for *negligent* offenses that the 1972 amendments did. For *knowing* violations, however, the specified fines now range between $5,000 and $50,000 per day and/or up to three years' incarceration, with the maximums set at $100,000 and at six years for second convictions. The maximum penalties for violations involving *knowing endangerment* of persons are now $250,000 and/or 15 years' incarceration for individuals, and $1,000,000 for organizational offenders. Second convictions for such offenses double the maximums. The new administrative penalties range from $10,000 per day or per violation, but only up to a maximum total penalty of $125,000, which in some cases arguably will be less than the corporate savings realized by offending. Finally, the 1987 amendments increased the maximum civil penalties from $10,000 to $25,000 per day for each violation.

Rule Making: The Structuring of Inputs in Law

While true of law generally, the process of implementation is particularly dynamic and uncertain when the statutory guidance is culturally novel—threatening long-established patterns and relations—and technically complex from the standpoints of law, science, administration, or any combination of these. The complexity of law ensures the vital play of discretionary judgment, while its novelty promises a key role to relations of power in the exercise of that judgment. Thus the implementation of law is inherently contingent and always problematic. And it is certainly both in the case of the Clean Water Act.

For EPA, the scope of its duties under this single statute was immense, let alone in combination with all of the other environmental laws under its jurisdiction (e.g., the Clean Air Act, the Resource Conservation and Recovery Act, the Noise Pollution Control Act, etc.). The law required the agency to make complex and politically sensitive (because of the high costs of the new controls) determinations of BPT and BAT for all types of industry within a year of its passage, and to issue water pollution control discharge permits implementing the regulations to tens of thousands of individual polluting facilities within two years. Whereas the statute had identified 28 basic categories of industry to be so regulated, EPA eventually identified more than 500 subcategories for which separate technology-based control regulations had to be formulated (Yeager 1991: 179). Given the resource constraints that always limit regulatory agency effectiveness (Clinard and Yeager 1980), it is not surprising that the agency quickly fell behind its regulatory schedule, particularly with respect to the top-priority toxic pollutants. Now sixteen years past the original deadline for compliance with toxic controls, American industry remains far from compliance (Yeager 1991: 216–42).

Moreover, the regulatory process comprised numerous decision points, from the writing of regulations, through the numerous appellate court challenges to them made by both industry and environmental law groups, to the issuance of individual permits implementing them, to the hearing of thousands of corporate appeals of the terms of the permits (Yeager 1991: 190–91, 206). Given the importance to ultimate pollution control of these many decisions, and the discretion necessarily involved in them, Congress had provided for wide public input in each. But in the nature of things, the content of the input has always been slanted toward industry's arguments, however subtly.

This is because the very substance of law conditions the structuring of inputs into policymaking and the weighting of factors in decision making, in effect differentially distributing points of access to (and relative advantage in) regulation to the various interests in its outcomes. In the case of the Clean Water Act, it was the specific emphasis on extant technologies that shaped the distribution of access as well as the limits of policy success. In particular, this emphasis tended to favor the input of industry over that of competing environmental interests, given the combination of industry's control over vital technical knowledge and the agency's dependence on that knowledge for complex and numerous regulatory rulings.

In addition, the focus on technologies was complemented by the law's "end-of-line" approach to pollution control: the law and the agency implemented the position that the government could seek to control pollution only outside of the factory, at the end of the discharge pipe. The law would not seek to force specific changes in manufacturers' production practices, nor would the state seek to develop new, less-polluting productive methods itself; it would simply identify allowable pollution levels based on the better (BPT) and best (BAT) control technologies already demonstrated in the various industries. In thus privileging the autonomy of industrial processes, the law was fundamentally self-limiting.

The Substance and Structures of Deliberation

The emphasis on private sector technological potentials shaped deliberations at every stage of rule making. The results were a shift in the moral tone of these deliberations and a policy impact short of the legislature's intent.

Because the law concentrates on identifying and asserting the best control technologies being utilized within industries, rather than on the harm to receiving waters and human health, debates over the terms and application of standards tend to both disproportionately attract and favor the input of industry over environmentalists. Couched in the dry terms of the limits of engineering technologies rather than in the environmentally and emotionally compelling language of the limits of nature, all of the key decisions present themselves as purely technical, depoliticized matters that seldom evoke the moral drama of rights discourse that had originally motivated the 1972 law (Yeager 1991: 199–200).

In addition to favoring industries' input on the basis of their control of the relevant technical knowledge, this "demoralization" of regulatory deliberations has the effect of increasing the weight given to cost considerations at every stop. In other words, the focus on technical potentials only enhances the tendency in utilitarian calculations of industry costs and public benefits to favor the "hard" estimates of the former over the "soft" determinations of the latter.

An illustrative contrast is found in a comparison of the Clean Air and Clean Water acts (Yeager 1991: 192–99).[15] Unlike the technology-based approach of the water law, the Clean Air Act takes a primarily media-quality-based approach to regulation, an approach that sets pollution levels in the air (the medium) explicitly on the basis of considerations of harm to human health and welfare (McGarity 1983). As a result of this difference, at least in part, both the federal appellate courts reviewing agency regulations and agency personnel themselves have been more likely to constrain the reach of law under the water amendments, while the appellate courts have been more likely to uphold and even expand the agency's authorities under the Clean Air Act.

For example, when EPA administratively amended the water law by inserting clauses in its BPT regulations that allowed an individual plant to be excepted from the stated limits upon showing that its circumstances were "fundamentally different from" those considered in the rule making, the Supreme Court upheld the decision against environmentalists' challenge that it was unauthorized by the statute.[16] In addition, the appellate courts were often willing to impose on the agency a greater consideration of the costs of controls to industrial water polluters. For example, in two cases remanding regulations for the intendedly more stringent BAT discharge standards, two federal courts of appeal ruled that EPA had shown inadequate consideration of costs to industry in the record.[17] In general, appellate court remands of EPA regulations under the water law were the rule: of the eighteen cases decided by the federal courts of appeal across the country (after consolidation of many separate industry challenges), all but three resulted in court remand for further consideration by EPA of such factors as economic and technological feasibility (Yeager 1991: 190–91).

While these decisions are not necessarily unreasonable *prima facie*, together they stand in notable contrast to the appellate courts' treatment of Clean Air Act cases. For example, EPA's models for calculating pollution reduction loads to meet air quality standards have readily survived judicial review, even when industrial petitioners "have pointed to other models that appear to depend upon fewer brash assumptions" (McGarity 1983: 216).[18] In addition, the courts have gone beyond the agency in mandating stringent regulation, for example by requiring EPA to mount a regulatory program to "prevent significant deterioration" of airsheds already well under national air quality limits. Not explicitly mandated by Congress, the courts took as their principal authority for this major program the simple, broad statement of purpose in the law: "to protect and enhance the quality of the Nation's air resources" (see also Melnick 1983: 71–112). Salient here were precisely moral notions connected to human health and its opposite: harm.

This description is not to imply the greater relative success of the Clean Air Act; indeed, the nation's airsheds are woefully out of compliance in many major metropolitan areas. As it happens, equity considerations more favorable to industry interests came into play in air pollution enforcement proceedings at the federal district court level (Melnick 1983: 353–55). Here industry lawyers were often able to persuade federal judges, themselves more closely tied to local interest and conditions, to modify (reduce) requirements under the standards and to extend deadlines for compliance with them. Thus, there exists a dynamic tension between the "absolutist" support for environmental protection in the appellate courts, and the more utilitarian concern for equity considerations—the balancing of environmental and economic considerations at the local level that shaded matters toward the economic—at the stage of enforcement.

But with the Clean Water Act, this same dynamic tension (which threatened to undercut even reasonable environmental goals) exists at all stages of implementation—standard setting, judicial review, the granting of permits to individual plants, and enforcement—rather than in the split between the various phases of lawmaking. Therefore, the points at which the law's purposes might be compromised were multiplied in the case of the water amendments. Among other consequences, this "structuring" of legal process complicates the role played by representatives of the public interest in ways not anticipated by the framers of law. At the least, it stretches the always spare resources of public interest organizations even thinner over the whole, often convoluted course of lawmaking, and moreover denies them the hortatory support of unambiguously embraced regulatory standards at law (as by the appellate courts for the Clean Air Act). In effect, this result amplifies industry's knowledge advantage by multiplying the decision points and undermining the original moral force of the law.

As McGarity has observed about technology-based standards, in contrast to those based on media quality: "The regulated firms may feel more comfortable with a process that gives them room to bargain with the agency in low visibility proceedings that depend heavily on industry-supplied information, especially when the agency may be sympathetic toward their plight" (1983: 208). Because the water law was implemented by often inexperienced discharge permit writers in EPA regional offices and various state agencies (under EPA delegation), who issued tens of thousands of permits against tight deadlines to often complaining businesses, and under a variety of legal frameworks (e.g., to meet deadlines, permits were issued under preliminary regulations, and even in the absence of regulations), the playing field was all the more likely to be tilted.

In addition, the evidence on public participation in the regulation of industrial water pollution suggests structured imbalances in input. At the broad levels of legislation and appellate court review, environmental interests have enjoyed a rough parity with industry groups in bringing their positions to bear on policymakers' deliberations. In the actual formulation and application of industry-wide standards to dischargers, however, the balance swings toward the regulated.

For example, the most successful public interest environmental law firm, the Natural Resources Defense Council (NRDC), has only infrequently been able to participate in the agency discussions leading to industry discharge standards. By 1977, the NRDC docket listed the council as having fully participated in the formulation of just five of the numerous sets of regulations EPA had written by then. Here, passion and commitment are not in short supply; material resources are. And the narrower the decision matter, the more limited is the voice of environmentalists. An NRDC official noted that his group was rarely able to participate in such matters as EPA's formal adjudicatory hearing procedures, in which individual polluters seek favorable alterations in the terms of their permits (to allow greater discharges or longer compliance timetables) in courtlike proceedings before administrative law judges, or other (less formal) permit modification proceedings. These key determinations, which define law in individual cases while shaping the reach of public policy, were left largely to the deliberations of agency and industry experts. And even when his organization intervened, as in a case challenging several offshore oil permits, it was often "ill-equipped" from a resource standpoint to engage in such numerous "wars of experts."[19]

A congressional study of federal regulation has also noted this imbalance in participation in agency decision making, suggesting that the processes identified here for EPA are characteristic of business regulation more generally:

> At agency after agency, participation by the regulated industry predominates—often overwhelmingly. Organized public interest representation accounts for a very small percentage of participation before Federal regulatory hearings. In more than half of the formal proceedings, there appears to be no such participation whatsoever, and virtually none at informal agency proceedings. In those proceedings where participation by public groups does take place, typically it is a small fraction of the participation by the regulated industry. One-tenth is not uncommon; sometimes it is even less than that. This pattern prevails in both rule-making proceedings and adjudicatory proceedings, with an even greater imbalance occurring in adjudications than in rule making (U.S. Senate 1977, vol. 3: vii; see also chap. 2).[20]

In sum, the processes thus far described constrain law not only independently, but synergistically. The tendency of technology-based standards to evoke equity considerations at all stages underscores the importance of representative public input at each of them, at the same time that their highly technical nature renders such participation increasingly difficult as laws are transformed into applicable rules and applied to firms. Similarly, the heavy regulatory burden the water amendments placed on EPA forced it to enlarge on the law's discretionary realms—such as writing permits on the basis of incomplete standards to meet the agency's own timetables set by Congress. The resulting proliferation of decision points increased the need for wide public inputs while again making such participation more difficult to ensure and provide. Such processes typically constrain law's effectiveness to levels below even those that are economically achievable.

Of Public Policy and Private Production: The Limits of the "Chinese Wall"

In the Weberian sense, these processes also represent the increasing *rationalization* of law, the apparent depoliticization of legal decision making that takes the form of ever more abstruse technical determinations made by specialists in law, science, engineering, economics, and the like. This is the "disenchantment" of law, the displacement from legal process of substantive (or moral) criteria, and their replacement by "rational" calculations of means and ends (Ewing 1987).

It is noteworthy that this development in law attends the historic decline of congressional power and the corresponding concentration of state power in an increasingly depoliticized executive branch (see, e.g., Alford and Friedland 1985; Esping-Andersen et al. 1976; Halberstam 1979). This development has the effect of putting many critical policy decisions beyond the view and reach of potentially interested publics, as just described.

While these parallel developments therefore undermine the democratic legitimacy of the modern state, legal decisions become ideologically justified on the basis of a technocratic legitimacy (see, e.g., Gold et al. 1975 (November); Stryker 1989). Officials present policy determinations as rational formulations, neutrally (i.e., nonpolitically) reached through a process based on technical expertise, particularly legal and scientific knowledge beyond the ken of most citizens.

These forces of rationalization reached environmental law nowhere more completely than in the regulation of toxic pollutants.[21] As I earlier noted, Congress had taken its most stringent stance on this aspect of the law, going so far in the statutory language as to divorce toxic pollution controls from the sorts of cost considerations that were to be made for conventional pollutants, and providing for industrial compliance with these uncompromising standards by 1975. Ironically, however, this topmost priority—put by Congress in the language of moral imperatives—was in effect relegated to the regulatory "backseat" by the federal government, which in the early years focused instead on the more tractable problems of the much less threatening conventional pollutants. The consequence was that by the end of the 1980s American industry was still discharging billions of pounds of toxic wastes into the nation's surface waters, part of more than 22 billion pounds of toxic discharge into the land, air, and water, a level EPA itself called "startling and unacceptably high."[22] Most important, much of this polluting was being done legally by virtue of long delays in formulating and implementing the relevant discharge standards, and by virtue of fundamental change in the nature of the standards since the original statement of congressional intent. Only by 1990—fifteen years past the original deadline—were the final regulations for toxic water pollution being put into place, presaging further years of permitting procedures for industrial facilities and companies' eventual achievement of ultimate compliance schedules.

In part, the law's shortfall—in terms of both oft-missed regulatory timetables and ultimate stringency—was conditioned by the scientific complexity and large uncertainties attaching to toxics regulation. Some 65,000 chemicals are manufactured in the United States every year, and for many there is simply little knowledge of the toxic effects, either alone or in their myriad combinations (Schneider 1985: 15; Conservation Foundation 1982: 119–22). In 1977 EPA estimated that the nation's drinking water contained between 3,000 and 5,000 different chemicals, and in the waterways some several hundred thousand chemical compounds were far outstripping scientists' ability to determine their toxic effects (for humans and other organisms) and at what levels of concentration such effects occur (U.S. House of Representatives 1977: 24).

Adding to the weight of these uncertainties was EPA's need to create a defensible regulatory record, one that could withstand the inevitable court challenges by industry to the rules; lawsuits were especially likely given the perceived high costs of toxics controls. In the face of the numerous appellate court challenges to industry-wide toxics standards, reviewing courts were unlikely to object to the government's specific expert determinations and judgments, but often remanded regulations to the agency on the charge that EPA had not produced an adequate record of decision making. Indeed, during a number of the final rule-making procedures for toxic water pollution in the 1980s, EPA voluntarily withdrew proposed regulations under industry challenges to the record, anticipating that the courts would force such a decision in the absence of agency reconsideration (Yeager 1991: 221).

But also contributing to this dilution of law were the effects of the "Chinese Wall"–like separation in our political economy between the prerogatives of private industry and the purposes of public policy. This separation manifested itself in a number of ways in the regulatory process, including the effects of industrial control over relevant production information and technologies. For example, by 1977—two years after the statutory deadline for industry compliance with toxic regulations—EPA's own personnel testified in congressional hearings that its permit system had produced very little information on the types and loads of toxic chemicals being discharged by industry (U.S. House of Representatives 1977:

18). The lack of regulatory baselines was the joint product of the agency's general inattention to toxics to that point—it proved politically expedient to concentrate on conventional pollutants, where early results were more easily produced—and industry's disinterest in volunteering such information, often on the argument that it would reveal trade secrets. Intentionally or otherwise, companies often withheld or even misrepresented their toxics data, not infrequently to the later surprise of the agency.[23] As further evidence of the "knowledge gap" between industry and government, it was not until the 1987 amendments to the Federal Water Pollution Control Act that Congress mandated a national study of toxics in U.S. water due to point discharges, the results of which were finally reported in the summer of 1989.[24]

But if the knowledge gap was slowly closing, there remained a more fundamental constraint on the legal control of industrial water pollution: the reluctance of government to intrude forcefully on the traditional production prerogatives of private industry. In theory, under the 1972 amendments EPA could establish pollution limits on the basis of publicly funded model plants that might demonstrate new technologies or, somewhat less stringently, on the basis of the single best plant in an industry. But as a practical matter, the agency did not do so, instead basing its regulations on the controls that the technologically more advanced firms in industry categories had in place, or (less stringent yet) on the dominant industry practices.

Again in theory, this constraint should have mattered less for the toxics because by statute they were to have been regulated not on the basis of industrial technologies, but on the less cost-conscious basis of toxic risks to the environment and human health, as earlier noted. However, the daunting uncertainties inherent in the statute's mandate for toxics—scientific/technical, administrative, and ultimately political (stemming, e.g., from the high costs of controls to business)—drove EPA to amend the 1972 law administratively, with the ultimate imprimatur of the federal courts,[25] Congress (in 1977 amendments to the law), and even the organized environmental public interest groups.[26] The key feature of the change was to have toxics regulated by the same two-stage technological determinations (of better and best technologies) that were being made for conventional pollutants. On the one hand, the result is understandable: It allowed the agency to proceed sure-footedly on the basis of real technologies rather than on its questionable abilities to penetrate the obscure mysteries of nature. On the other hand, it was certain to limit the control of toxics, arguably even short of manageable cost constraints.

For a number of industrial categories, EPA rejected the second-stage "best available technology" altogether, settling for the less stringent "best practicable technology" for the control of toxics. For example, after initially proposing BAT for the leather tanning industry, in response to industry criticisms the agency issued a final rule in 1982 setting controls at BPT because, it said, *the proposed BAT controls had not yet been demonstrated in the industry and were not economically achievable*.[27] In that same year EPA revoked its proposed BAT regulations for the petroleum refining industry and instead promulgated final regulations setting the controls on toxics as BPT (Bureau of National Affairs 1983). That powerful industry had successfully resisted the agency's original proposal to greatly restrict the flow of wastes by mandating recycling and reuse of waste streams, control that—unlike typically end-of-pipe and less effective BPT—apparently intruded too forcefully on the industry's traditional production practices.

Three final points are worth mention in this connection. First, in addition to the implied reduction in environmental protection, this subtle policy shift—made long after the public and impassioned stands for the elimination of toxic pollution—necessarily results in higher compliance rates because many businesses, often the larger firms with advanced technologies, are commonly asked to make relatively few changes to comply with standards. Second, there was no small measure of historic irony in this approach. Just as the very first, turn-of-the-century federal water pollution laws had been passed to protect commerce by creating clear river routes for industrial transportation, rather than to meet the public health needs of citizens, so too did the present-day technological "needs" of industry tend to relegate environmental health criteria to the shadows of public policy.[28]

Finally, although the Reagan administration's efforts in the 1980s to protect industry from expensive regulation certainly slowed the development of toxic controls, the more fundamental constraints were the systemic, "mundane" ones associated with basic legal processes (e.g., appellate court review of standards), the ideological separation of public policy from private production techniques, and the key political and economic roles that leading producers play in the society. Thus, the law registered the structural and cultural limits deeply embedded in the architecture of our political economy; the instrumental limits of direct political control were relatively less salient in the development of this area of law.[29]

Enforcement: The Structures of Legal Bias

To the public mind, enforcement is the centerpiece of legal regulation, whether for conventional criminal offenses or for business infractions. Both symbolically and practically, enforcement is a capstone, a final indicator of the state's seriousness of purpose and often a key determinant of the permeability of the barrier between compliance and lawlessness. But given real resource constraints and competing priorities in law enforcement, official discretion is always the silent partner of control policies. The key questions, therefore, concern the social forces that shape the use of that discretion, and whether its use produces regulatory efficiency and justice.

The questions are especially pertinent to environmental regulation generally, and water pollution law in particular. The federal environment laws passed in the 1970s were intended to radically reshape industry's view of what had long been standard production procedure: the free use of the environment as a waste receptacle. In the effort to so reshape sentiment and behavior, enforcement policy has been both linchpin and target—all the more so in the case of the water pollution amendments, given the stringency of the penalties provided by the Congress. In addition to the high maximum criminal penalties earlier noted, the statute provided that enforcement was mandatory against all violations. At a minimum, the law directed EPA to respond to any water pollution violations with either formal administrative orders to comply or a civil suit for injunctive relief or monetary penalties or both.[30] Criminal penalties could be pursued in cases of willful or knowing failures to comply.

Despite the clear congressional intent, early on EPA administratively amended the law by reading substantial enforcement discretion into it. The real options used by the agency ranged from the relatively rare criminal and civil actions, through administrative orders, to warning letters, phone calls to offending firms, and even the formal decision to take no action at all against many offenses (Yeager 1991: 186). While federal district courts had split on the question of mandatory enforcement, in 1977 a federal appellate court determined that enforcement was discretionary under the law despite the clarity of the legislative language.[31]

That discretionary enforcement has not since been seriously at issue is a measure of the strength of the institutional logic that demanded it. Among other things, the policy allows the government to conserve scarce enforcement resources by first seeking compliance through simple negotiation and warnings, all that may be needed in some cases. In addition, the policy allows the agency to conserve another precious commodity: credibility. If formal orders or court actions were used for all violations—even the minor, isolated, or inadvertent—over time the sanctions would tend to lose their legally compelling stature, diluted by overuse. Relying on substantial sanctions only for the more serious cases maintains the law's symbolic force. An internal memorandum to EPA's enforcement division from the agency's assistant administrator for enforcement and general counsel made just this point in 1974: "It is *crucial* that the permits be credible. This means that we do not want 'nitpicking' enforcement. Above all, use your head. Ask yourself whether a good, environmentally sympathetic federal district court judge would be impressed that the enforcement action you are taking seems reasonable on the facts."[32]

But the other side of the coin of legal discretion is the question whether (and how) discretionary decision making becomes systematically distorted, biased in favor of some interests over others as a consequence of structured imbalances in power and influence. This inequity may occur not only because of the commonly observed reluctance of many regulators to take on powerful opponents in court, noted in the first section above. It may also occur simply through the routine operations of ostensibly neutral legal procedures, procedures that nonetheless reflect and reproduce inequalities in the wider political economy.

Structural Bias in Environmental Law Enforcement

There is substantial evidence that a structural bias exists in social regulation generally, and for environmental law more specifically. For example, my research on EPA's enforcement practices against industrial violations of the water law found evidence that larger, more powerful firms have both direct and indirect advantages at law over their smaller brethren (Yeager 1987, 1990: chap. 7). The direct advantages have to do, first, with what might be called the regulatory economies of scale that allow larger companies to more easily manage expensive regulatory costs (because they are spread over larger volumes of production) and, second, with the aforementioned reluctance of regulators to aggressively sanction more powerful adversaries. The indirect advantages involve the larger companies' greater access to technical agency procedures, which firms can use to generate exceptions to the regulatory requirements imposed on them, thereby bringing the law more into line with their intent or capacity to comply. As a result, two consequences obtain, both of them vitally important to public policy. First, technology-driven standards such as those required under the Clean Water Act tend to be regressive, disproportionately burdening small companies with expensive implementation duties and more stringent enforcement. Second, given the ability of many large polluters to successfully negotiate more lenient pollution standards with the government, the nation receives less environmental protection than is economically feasible.

For example, my research found that larger firms were more successful in appealing the terms of their pollution control permits to the EPA's adjudicatory hearing procedure, in which an administrative law judge hears technical arguments regarding the appropriateness of the controls for individual facilities. Presumably this advantage is owing to these companies' greater technical resources in law and engineering. For enforcement, the result of successful appeals is twofold: violation rates are lower for these firms because the controls have been relaxed, and enforcement for offenses is suspended during the pendency of the hearings, which often took years rather than months because of the extraordinary backlog of hearings requests that developed at the agency.

These findings are in line with Kolko's (1963) classic analysis of the federal Meat Inspection Act of 1906 and receive further corroboration in two recent studies of environmental regulation. Lynxwiler and his colleagues (1983) found similar advantages at law for larger companies in their study of the use of enforcement discretion by field inspectors from the Federal Office of Surface Mining Reclamation and Enforcement (see also Shover et al. 1986). The study found that larger mining companies, because of their greater resources and technical expertise, were able to negotiate more successfully the characterization of violations with the government inspectors, who generally viewed the larger firms as both more cooperative with regulatory expectations (in part because of their ability to negotiate at the highest technical levels with government experts), and more likely than smaller firms to challenge stringent enforcement through legal appeals. One important result was that the smaller companies tended to be assessed higher fines than larger corporate violators because inspectors tended to *interpret* the violations of the former as more serious offenses, quite apart from more objective measures of the harm occasioned by them.

Especially apposite to this discussion are the conclusions Keith Hawkins (1983, 1984) reached in his intensive investigation of field inspectors attempting to enforce water pollution regulations in Britain. He analyzed the enforcement process as involving an exchange relationship in which forbearance in enforcement is traded for good faith efforts at compliance. Importantly, his research suggests that because the regulated behavior is vitally linked to the (re)production of core political economic values, its status is at worst morally ambivalent, with the result that the law itself shares the same characterization. In such a context, enforcement agents in the field find it necessary to negotiate compliance rather than to stringently enforce it. Hawkins also notes the field agents' perception that enforcement must be patient and "reasonable" lest it produce uncooperative attitudes toward compliance on the part of the regulated.

Therefore, compliance negotiations usually go forward as scientific and technical matters (rather than as moral affairs) between regulators and the regulated, and tend to exclude the concerns and viewpoints of environmental interests. Most relevant here is that Hawkins finds this process to be skewed in favor of larger, more powerful companies, which are more likely to have the relevant expertise at hand, and which enforcement agents are therefore more likely to see as socially responsible and as generally more cooperative regarding the aims of the agency.

In sum, similar structured biases at regulatory law have been indicated in investigations conducted at different levels of analysis (from field studies of enforcement interactions to structural analyses of enforcement procedures), in different cultural contexts (albeit within the broader context of Western, capitalist political economies with a largely shared legal heritage), and in different regulatory areas. Generally, the findings suggest that in the effort to maintain even modest levels of accomplishment and credibility, social regulators must essentially bargain enforcement with the regulated. And in bargaining over what is to be the reality of regulation, law inescapably reflects and reproduces the favored status of major producers.

The Paradoxes of Powerful Penalties

In important part because of the issues noted above, the use of more serious sanctions—civil and criminal charges—against industrial water polluters is relatively infrequent, especially against large corporate polluters. The general approach of the agency has been to use the "jawboning" sanctions of warning and administrative orders to negotiate and compel compliance. By policy, civil and criminal penalties were reserved for serious violations within the control of management; the agency considered criminal cases to be appropriate only in situations of willful or negligent misconduct, and especially in cases of bad faith in which the company was flaunting its opposition to the agency's authority (Yeager 1991: 254–55). In my research on EPA's Region II enforcement practices in New Jersey, civil and criminal cases were infrequent: Referrals to the Justice Department for such penalties constituted only 0.6 percent of the agency's responses to violations (Yeager 1991: 279).

But if the formal enforcement policy was rational in the face of limited resources and novel legal requirements, the *enacted* policy was further constrained by a sort of nonrationality associated with competing institutional logics for handling offenses.

Part of the problem lies in the bureaucratic competition that often evolves when two agencies—in this case EPA and the Department of Justice—share jurisdiction over policy matters. At least from the standpoint of some Justice Department prosecutors, the agency refrains from referring some prosecutable cases because EPA does not wish to share credit for the case with the department; instead, it uses its administrative sanctions to negotiate compliance so that the agency will get sole enforcement credit, and subsequently have a stronger regulatory record to show its superiors and congressional oversight committees when annual budgets are requested. According to the chief assistant U.S. attorney for Los Angeles, for example:

> In fact, many cases by the non-criminal investigative agencies—by that I mean the regulatory agencies—never get presented to the U.S. Attorney's Office. A very significant reason why they don't . . . is because the agency gets no credit for a criminal prosecution. The agency gets credit for civil action [or other compliance-generating actions] that it can file and that its lawyers can handle, but the agency gets no statistical credit at budget time for a criminal case that has been prosecuted.
>
> The best example is that for the last three years the United States Attorney in Los Angeles . . . has been trying to get the United States government more actively involved in environmental prosecutions. . . . But when the EPA takes a look at a case, very often we never even hear about it. They will handle it either administratively or civilly and they will not bring the U.S. Attorney's Office into it for criminal prosecution.[33]

Besides bureaucratic "turf" protection, another factor may inhibit the agency's use of criminal referrals. A principal advantage of the 1972 amendments over previous water pollution control legislation was that they explicitly eliminated the difficult burden of proof of showing harm to the environment. Under the new law, infractions were to be demonstrated by a simple showing of a violation of a plant's discharge permit, regardless of the level of damage, a measure included to encourage the more vigorous enforcement of environmental standards. However, by 1976 EPA had discovered that U.S. attorneys were often declining to file its enforcement cases unless there was evidence of actual environmental damage. Dismayed at this executive "amendment" of the statute, the agency asked the Justice Department to inform all U.S. attorneys "of the correct interpretation of our statutes and the importance of prosecuting our enforcement cases without requiring proof of harm."[34]

The department responded that its official policy recognized that proof of environmental harm was not an essential element in water act prosecutions, and that it did not support U.S. attorneys' automatically rejecting referrals from EPA for lack of such proof. However, the department wrote EPA that in its experience, "the only assured way of receiving meaningful relief is a showing by the Government of some adverse effect of the defendant's pollutants, and some courts require it. This is a fact which cannot be ignored." The department therefore told EPA that it declined to issue a "'hard and fast' directive of any sort" to its prosecutors around the country, leaving the "degree of harm" issue a relevant factor in the discretionary decision to prosecute cases.[35]

Again, there remains the question of how the combined discretion of the two government agencies is used. And on this there is some evidence—albeit quite limited—that the government hesitates to prosecute the larger corporations for water law offenses. For example, in 1978 a seasoned EPA attorney in the Office of Water Enforcement said, "We're afraid to go after [the big corporations]. We prefer to go after the little guys."[36] And in my study of enforcement in Region II, all of the few referrals to the Justice Department for civil or criminal penalties involved smaller companies; none involved large corporations, even those with long records of noncompliance (Yeager 1991: 281). Moreover, there remains the general point that this sort of bureaucratic insulation from prosecution does not ordinarily characterize standard enforcement practices for conventional offenses.

There is some evidence that in response to continuing high rates of noncompliance and ongoing public pressure for greater enforcement of environmental law, the federal government increased somewhat its use of criminal and civil penalties by the latter 1980s (Adler and Lord 1991: 792–97, 843–45, 860–61). For example, recent data (for all types of environmental offenses combined) show that between 1985 and 1989 EPA increased its annual number of criminal investigations from about 60–65 to about 85–90. In 1985, the agency referred 43 percent of such cases to the Justice Department for prosecution; in 1989 it referred 65 percent. Similarly, Justice increased its prosecution rate for such referrals: from 46 percent in 1983 to 62 percent in 1989. Under the water pollution law, average fines per count of violation increased threefold for corporations (from $10,750 in 1983–84 to $34,375 in 1989) and for individuals (from $1,586 in 1983–84 to $4,880 in 1988), while those serving jail or prison terms increased from 0 percent to about 25 percent.

On the other hand, the assessed Clean Water Act penalties remained well below statutory maximums, and their deterrent effects are yet to be determined. Moreover, Adler and Lord (1991: 796) report circumstantial evidence that large companies continue to avoid criminal penalties. They note, for example, that of the companies prosecuted under the nation's federal environmental laws since 1984, only 6 percent were among the country's 500 largest industrial corporations in 1989, and that less than 2 percent of these 500 firms have ever been prosecuted for environmental offenses despite their dominant collective share of industrial production. And there is also government evidence that enforcement officials do not regularly collect civil monetary penalties that equal the economic benefits firms enjoy through noncompliance with pollution control laws, despite EPA's formal policy since 1984 that they do so (U.S. General Accounting Office 1991).

Finally, there is another, quite unusual dynamic at play in the enforcement of this law against industrial polluters. At the height of the deregulatory efforts of the Reagan administration in the mid-1980s, EPA's own enforcement efforts were virtually paralyzed. But at a level not before seen in the history of American regulatory law, this stunted federal enforcement generated private enforcement cases in significant numbers. For the first time under any regulatory statute, citizens' and environmentalist groups began to file substantial numbers of enforcement lawsuits against industrial violators under the citizen suit provision of the water pollution law amendments. This private sector enforcement activity even came to rival the federal government's own efforts: of the 108 citizen actions initiated against water polluters in 1983, 62 eventuated in actual citizen lawsuits, compared with 77 suits filed by the Justice Department for EPA under the water law regulations during fiscal year 1983 (Yeager 1991: 320–21). And the record suggests the efficacy of this private action. Using EPA's own publicly available corporate self-monitoring reports, in most cases citizens succeeded in having corporate defendants settle cases rather than contesting them, sometimes for considerable penalties, such as the $1.5 million penalty paid by the Bethlehem Steel Corporation in 1987, the largest to that point in the history of citizen enforcement under the law.

Conclusions

This research on the environmental regulation of business suggests a number of conclusions regarding criminological theorizing and public policy. Among other things, it suggests that social regulation both reflects and reproduces inequalities in political economy, certainly within the social structure of business organization. Arguably, too, it suggests that business defendants generally experience advantages at law not available to conventional criminal defendants. These advantages have to do with the structures and complexities of much regulation, which have the effect of shielding many (especially) corporate offenders from the full weight or moral force of law. At the level of policy, the consequence is often a public benefit that falls short of legislative intentions and even of the limits of feasibility.

In terms of criminological theorizing, this work and other research on white-collar crime more generally clearly indicate the problem of "counting what we cannot see" (e.g., Mann 1985; McBarnet 1991). To the extent that our empirical work relies on officially generated counts of offenses, typically indicated only by official enforcement responses, it will unwittingly incorporate any biases that are built into the legal processes that structure both the likelihood of offenses among regulated parties and the sanctions aimed (or not) at them. Compared with this vital empirical and theoretical challenge, the old but still current debate about just what constitutes white-collar crime is the much simpler problem to solve (see, e.g., Yeager 1990).

The accumulating work on the social regulation of business also clearly indicates the importance of historically informed studies of specific regulatory programs. In the first place, depending on the precise nature of the legal requirements—for example, whether the associated costs and benefits are distributed to diffuse or specific constituencies, and the relative political power of each (see, e.g., Stryker 1991; J. Q. Wilson 1980)—government regulation will be more or less effective in reaching stated public purposes; conversely, it will be more or less vulnerable to compromise by regulated interests. And these variations will be further shaped by changes in the broader society, such as economic and political trends that generate greater or lesser degrees of class organization around important questions of public policy.

In the second place, regulatory regimes vary considerably in terms of the legal processes used to implement them. These processes are ordained both formally (e.g., by statute) and informally (e.g., by administrative "amendment"), and are key in generating the profiles of offenders that are available to public view.

In the case of the Clean Water Act, the evidence of citizen enforcement illustrates the importance of both of these points. This relatively unique outcome in the 1980s suggests the historical specificity of the new environmental controls and the social forces underlying them, while at the same time indicating a novel sanctioning option dynamically related to official patterns of enforcement of a more traditional sort.

This argument has important implications for the prospects for a general theory of crime such as that recently proposed by Gottfredson and Hirschi (1990). In general, to the extent that inequalities are variably "structured into" legal processes and thereby produce different patterns of offenses and sanctions, criminological theorizing is likely to be confined to typological explanations for various subtypes of crime. This point applies to types of conventional offending as well as to more complex regulatory laws.

Research on regulatory law also has implications for Gottfredson and Hirschi's specific neo-classical argument (see also Hirschi and Gottfredson 1987). In their general theory, these authors tend to marginalize the role of opportunity:

> Since crimes involve goods, services, or victims, they have other constituent properties as well: they all require opportunity, and are thought to result in punishment of the offender if he or she is detected. Such properties cannot account for the general tendency of particular individuals to engage in crime, and they are therefore not central to a theory of criminality (Hirschi and Gottfredson 1987: 959).

Their theory instead privileges the role of motivation in the explanation of crime, in particular the classical view of motivation as involving the self-interested pursuit of pleasure and avoidance of pain. But this argument ignores the ways in which motivation and opportunity may be entailed in each other, perhaps especially as wealthy, organized interests endeavor to shape law itself (cf. Coleman 1987).

This would seem to be especially the case for the legal regulation of business behavior, where the relation between law and the regulated is highly dynamic. In particular, not only may perceptions of law increase (or decrease) the psychological availability of illegal acts, but the relevant (regulated) parties may be actively involved in shaping both the law and the regard in which it is held. In addition to increasing psychological availability, this action may also reduce the deterrent effects of law, whether considered in terms of the conventional logic of the calculus of pain and gain, or in more expressive moral terms. To the extent that such processes occur, both motivation and opportunity will be dynamically produced and reproduced.

In the case of environmental law, for example, core features in the regulatory process reduce the moral salience of offending, and to that extent expand the "moral opportunities" for lawbreaking. The regulated parties commonly participate actively in shaping the moral dialogue that produces such expanded opportunities. It is in this sense that opportunities are socially constructed rather than "naturally" given in the environment, as in the simple availability of goods to steal or gullible citizens to fleece.

Inequality and Republican Criminology

JOHN BRAITHWAITE

In this chapter I show that the struggle for equality and checking of power is central to republican political theory. Although a republican normative theory of criminal justice does not prescribe maximum equality in criminal sentencing, it prescribes a principle of parsimony in sentencing that would have the effect of producing more egalitarian punishment practices than competing models, such as just deserts. Just as with republican normative theory, republican explanatory theory is strongly focused on inequality (as a cause of crime). Theories are most valuable when they help us to see a problem differently and to see changed and effective ways of responding to it. Republican criminology achieves this because it replaces pessimism that nothing works in reducing crime with an optimistic vision. Republican theory enables us to see that: (a) the most serious crime problems in contemporary societies are precisely the crime problems we are in the best position to reduce; and (b) the changes needed to effect these reductions have gathered considerable momentum in Western societies such as Australia since the mid-1970s. These changes are not so much in criminal justice policies as they are in the support for an effectiveness of social movements with egalitarian criminal justice agendas. Republican criminological praxis involves active support for social movements such as feminism, the environmental movement, the consumer movement, and the social movement against drunk driving and drug-promoting industries such as the alcohol, tobacco, and pharmaceutical industries.

This chapter explains that republicans have moral commitments to both political and economic equality and community involvement in disapproving of criminality. The objective is to show how it follows from these commitments that political support for certain progressive social movements is the best way for republicans to respond to the crime problem. After setting out the basics of a republican normative framework, empirical foundations for the efficacy of this kind of response are hypothesized—that reintegrative shaming prevents crime and that stigmatization causes crime. Next we address the worry that even if these empirical foundations are right, they are foundations for a repressive response that is a threat to freedom. It is concluded that *republican* shaming constitutes freedom rather than threatens it. I show that shaming of our most serious crimes has been historically muted because these types of criminality have been sheltered from shame by concentrations of power. Then I show how progressive social movements are finally mobilizing community disapproval against our protected criminal species. Having made a case for the greater efficacy of community mobilization over criminal justice system mobilization, I then return to why republican normative commitments argue for political support for social movements such as feminism. Finally, I advance a model of the synergy republicans ought to seek between community mobilization against crime and state enforcement.

In my book with Philip Pettit, *Not Just Deserts*, we began a detailed fleshing out of why and how our criminology is republican (Braithwaite and Pettit 1990). Whereas this book advances a normative theory of criminal justice, *Crime, Shame and Reintegration* advances an explanatory theory of crime (Braithwaite 1989a). These theories may be found to be wrong in some important respects. My purpose here is not to defend them, but to go beyond the two books to show how the republican criminologist will view the state and the nature of the struggle against crime in a different way. *Not Just Deserts* is a normative analysis of how to design criminal justice policies. Yet in a way this emphasis is misplaced because the republican criminologist must see the best strategies for dealing with crime as outside the criminal justice system. In this chapter I seek to remedy the preoccupation with criminal justice institutions and to set forth what should be at the center of the political agenda of republican criminology.

For the benefit of readers who are unfamiliar with *Not Just Deserts*, I first explain the basic idea of that book—that the pursuit of dominion is a useful normative framework for criminologists. Then I explain the basic idea of *Crime, Shame and Reintegration*—that reintegrative shaming is the key to crime control.

What is Republicanism?

Republican normative commitments direct us to take both political and economic inequality (Montesquieu 1977, chaps. 3–4; Pettit 1989) and community disapproval (Braithwaite and Pettit 1990; Pocock 1977) seriously. Sunstein (1988) advances four commitments as basic to republicanism: (1) deliberation in governance in order to shape as well as balance interests (as opposed to deal making between prepolitical interests); (2) political equality; (3) universality, or debate to reconcile competing views, as a regulative ideal; and (4) citizenship, community participation in public life.

Consistent with these commitments, in *Not Just Deserts* Pettit and I seek to define in a more foundational way the political objective republicans pursue. We develop a consequentialist theory that posits the maximization of dominion as the yardstick against which to measure the adequacy of policy. What is this dominion that we wish to maximize?

Dominion is a republican conception of liberty. Whereas the liberal conception of freedom is the freedom of an isolated atomistic individual, the republican conception of liberty is the freedom of a social world. Liberal freedom is objective and individualistic. Negative freedom for the liberal means the objective fact of individuals' being left alone by others. For the republican, however, freedom is defined socially and relationally. You only enjoy republican freedom—dominion—when you live in a social world that provides you with an intersubjective set of assurances of liberty. You must subjectively believe that you enjoy these assurances, and so must others believe. As a social, relational conception of liberty, by definition it also has a comparative dimension. To fully enjoy liberty, you must have equality-of-liberty prospects with other persons. If this is difficult to grasp, think of dominion as a conception of freedom that, by definition, incorporates the notions of *liberté*, *égalité*, and *fraternité*; then you have the basic idea.[1]

This conception of dominion as a target for the criminal justice system has two attractive political features for progressive criminologists. First, we show that it motivates a minimalism in state criminal justice interventions. This is the principle of parsimony: If in doubt, do less by way of criminal justice intervention.

Second, at the same time, dominion requires a highly interventionist state policy to secure equality-of-liberty prospects. This is the relational element built into the definition. When women or Aborigines enjoy lesser liberty prospects, affirmative action and redistributive tax and economic policies are commended by the theory. So we have a theory that can require minimalism in criminal justice policy alongside interventionism in economic policy.

The principle of parsimony does important theoretical work. Pettit and I show that it motivates a theoretically driven incrementalism in criminal justice policy—actually a decrementalism. Republicans, we argue, are required to struggle politically alongside the budget-cutting economic rationalists for progressive reductions in criminal justice interventions. The right level of punishment is not determined by the just deserts of offenders. The right level of punishment, according to the theory, is as low as we can take it without clear evidence emerging that crime has increased as a result of cuts to the system.

Not Just Deserts argues that a consequence of implementing this approach will be more equitable punishment practices than we have seen, or could ever see, by following competing philosophies—notably just deserts. We argue that even though the policy of just deserts is based on equal punishment for equal wrongs and republicanism is not, it is republicanism that in practice can deliver more egalitarian punishment practices. Because just deserts tend to be successfully imposed on the poor and unsuccessfully on the rich, a parsimonious policy will be more equitable than a policy of pursuing just deserts. Minimalist policies will tend to be more equitable because of the structural theorem that says where desert is greatest, punishment will be least.

The Explanatory Idea

The notion that shaming controls crime is an old one. But so is the seemingly contradictory notion that stigmatization makes crime problems worse. The only originality of *Crime, Shame and Reintegration* is in positing a theoretical resolution of this contradiction. Reintegrative shaming is posited as a shaming mechanism that prevents crime, stigmatization as a mechanism that increases the risks of crime by the shamed actor. Moreover, the partitioning of shaming mechanisms into two types with these opposite effects is advanced as a missing link in criminological theory. It enables us to integrate previously irreconcilable theories—control, subcultural, labeling, opportunity, and learning theories.

Reintegrative shaming is disapproval extended while a relationship of respect is sustained with the offender. Stigmatization is disrespectful, humiliating shaming where degradation ceremonies are never terminated by gestures of reacceptance of the offender. The offender is branded an evil person and cast out in a permanent, open-ended way. Reintegrative shaming, in contrast, might shame an evil deed, but the offender is cast as a respected person rather than an evil one. Even the shaming of the deed is finite in duration, terminated by ceremonies of forgiveness-apology-repentance.

A crucial preventive effect of reintegratively shaming criminals occurs when the offender recognizes the wrongdoing and shames him- or herself. Hence, a particular type of crime will be less common in a community when that type of crime is subjected to extensive and intensive reintegrative shaming. Extensive stigmatization, in contrast, will have equivocal effects on crime. On the one hand, it will reduce crime through the general deterrent effects of social disapproval. On the other hand, specific deterrence will be worse than a failure because stigmatization will foster the rejection of one's rejectors and the formation of subcultures of resistance to the law.

A Repressive Idea?

Seeking to bring crime under control by community shaming seems more benign than relying on the punitive state. Shaming is not as oppressive as imprisonment. Nevertheless, shame can be a tool of extraordinarily powerful oppression. The most common and profound concerns that come to mind are not about shaming crime, but about shaming forms of deviance that are not criminal—unconventional political and religious views or unconventional sexuality, for example. And the types of shaming of criminals that are most often raised as unconscionable are examples of stigmatization rather than reintegrative shaming. Reintegrative shaming, as a communicative, dialogic form of shaming that seeks to persuade offenders to disapprove of their own criminal conduct is not equivalent to ridiculing wrongdoers as persons by putting them in the stocks.

Even though reintegrative shaming is more respecting of persons than stigmatization, it can be oppressive. Just because it avoids the worst repressive excesses of the punitive state and the stigmatizing community, that is not to deny that reintegrative shaming is a dangerous game. Victims of violence, after all, are often ashamed of their victimization (Stanko 1990: 55, 67). Republicans cannot support reintegrative shaming as the dominant crime control strategy unless they have a clear moral position on what should and should not be shamed. Saying that all that is being advocated is the shaming of criminal conduct is not good enough, because this warrants the shaming of a soldier who refuses to fight in an evil war against Iraq. Pettit and I argue that conduct should never be criminalized unless we can be confident that its criminalization will increase dominion (the republican conception of liberty) in the community (Braithwaite and Pettit 1990). Our contention is that republicans must reserve the reprobation of criminal conduct for conduct that passes this test. Republicans are therefore required to actively support the reintegrative shaming of conduct whose criminalization uncontroversially protects dominion (such as criminal acts of violence). They are also required to actively oppose the shaming of deviant conduct that poses no threat to dominion.

Republicanism is a consequentialist theory that motivates a strong concern about rights (Braithwaite and Pettit 1990). Yet rights have meaning only as claims that rich individuals and corporations can occasionally assert in courts of law unless community disapproval can be mobilized against those who trample on the rights of others. Liberals and republicans can agree that gay men and lesbian women have a right to be deviant outside the constraints of the criminal law. Yet because liberals are squeamish about mobilizing community disapproval against those who trample on the rights of others, liberalism lacks a practical political program for protecting gays from harassment by the police and other citizens. The liberal idea of a practical political program is that gays should be able to take the police to court when they harass them. Although the republican supports this, it must be viewed as a rather empty gesture. For the republican, rights to diversity acquire genuine power only when socializing institutions and community campaigns foster in citizens a concern to be rights-respecting. Liberal rights can be sterile legalist gestures; republican rights are active cultural accomplishments. Strong gay and lesbian rights movements are the medium for securing these accomplishments.

Another way to think about the dangers of shaming is in terms of Scheff and Retzinger's (1991) framework about the bipolar evils of isolation and engulfment. Engulfment, they claim, was responsible for the violence of Nazi Germany. According to Scheff and Retzinger, societies in which the group is everything (the individual is engulfed) as well as societies of rampant individualism (the individual is isolated) risk endemic violence. Engulfment entails individuals' giving up parts of self in order to be accepted by others; it means fusion of individual needs with the needs of the group, as opposed to differentiation of individual needs from the needs of the group.

We all know what a family that isolates its children is like and what one that engulfs its children is like. Interdependency, mutual respect, love, community are needed to avoid isolation in families. But paradoxically, interdependency and mutual respect are needed to avoid engulfment as well. An engulfing family, the members of which have traditionally gone into the professions, might ridicule or label as a drop-out a member who decides to be an artist. The individuating family, in contrast, while communicating honest disappointment and disagreement with a choice of art over medicine, also communicates satisfaction that the child is capable of thinking for him- or herself, capable of breaking the mold set by parents and siblings. The individuating family uses interdependency and mutual respect as resources to ensure individuality; social bonds enable the constitution of a secure individual self that cannot be engulfed by a fascist or totalitarian state.

At the level of normative theory, individuating social bonds are one reason for rejecting a liberal conception of freedom (the freedom that isolated individuals perfectly enjoy) in favor of a republican conception of freedom (the freedom citizens enjoy in a social world where other citizens grant them social assurances of liberty) (Braithwaite and Pettit 1990: 55–69). A social world where individuals are what Scheff and Retzinger call "in attunement" with other human beings is not just a happy medium between isolation and engulfment. It is a world of social assurances and rights that secure individuation. Families in such an attuned social world will mobilize strong disapproval to protect one member from an act of violence by another; they will mobilize disapproval against a member who undermines another member's right to be deviant in ways that do not threaten dominion. What then is the crucial mechanism that guarantees individuation in families? Reintegrative shaming is that mechanism. Shaming is as essential to guaranteeing freedom as it is to preventing crime.

The republican does not struggle politically for a world in which shaming is used in a way that trades a reduction in freedom for a reduction in crime. Such a trade-off manifests a liberal way of thinking about crime. The republican struggles for a world where shame is used both to increase freedom and to reduce crime. The widespread liberal belief that a high crime rate is a price we pay for free society, that freedom and crime are locked into some hydraulic relationship, is wrong. Republican theory opens our eyes to this theoretical error.

A Useful or a Utopian Idea?

The explanatory theory of *Crime, Shame and Reintegration* is not alone in concluding that tinkering with criminal justice policies will not make a great difference to the crime rate (see, e.g., Gottfredson and Hirschi 1990: 272–73). Like Gottfredson and Hirschi's, my theory concludes that what families do is much more important to the causation and prevention of crime than what police forces do. Does this mean that the republican criminologist shares with theorists of this ilk a structurally impotent psychologism? Does this mean accepting the patriarchal family as our salvation? After all, *Crime, Shame and Reintegration* hypothesizes that it is women much more than men who are susceptible to being both effective subjects and objects of reintegrative shaming (see Hagan et al. 1979). Does it follow, then, that we should struggle to keep women locked into the moral guardianship role within families, which they have demonstrably performed more effectively than men?

A proper republican answer to all three questions, I will argue, is no. For the republican, the family is not a man's castle, but part of a community of citizens. The family is not and should not be immune from outside disapproval resulting from the deliberative processes of an active democracy. The concern for equality of prospects for dominion that republicanism requires means that the republican must struggle against patriarchy (Pettit 1989). Patriarchy is an institutional order that secures systematically lesser prospects of dominion for women than for men. Thus patriarchy must be resisted by the republican. Furthermore, I argue later that patriarchy is a cause of crime.

Patriarchy surely means a gendered patterning of reintegrative shaming. But it is hardly an effective strategy of resistance for women to jettison the obligations they feel to disapprove the wrongdoing of family members as they continue to nurture those family members in bonds of love. For one thing, if my analysis is correct on what is required to secure rights, reintegrative shaming is needed to assure women of their right to equal prospects of dominion. The republican solution is to struggle for equality of obligation to engage in reintegrative shaming. The republican priority is to change men in this respect, not women.

On how to do this, the republican political theorist is anything but individualistic, even though the objective is to change individuals and families. As Sunstein (1988) has argued, active citizenship, community participation in public life, is fundamental to republican ideology. The republican must take seriously social movements of citizens, organized influence from below, as vehicles for progressive change. Such social movements are precisely the vehicles that can and do deliver the changes that will bring a lower crime rate. There is little prospect of top-down solutions to the problem of families that raise violent boys because they fail to disapprove of violent episodes when they first occur. If the state mandated parent effectiveness training, these families probably would not attend. Even if they did attend and understand, they still might not confront members who perpetrate violence (Wilson and Herrnstein 1985: 386–87).

Social Movement Activism

Deeper cultural changes are needed. For these, we must look to social movements like feminism. To the extent the state can make a contribution, it can do so by cutting the budgets of police and prison services somewhat and handing these resources over to feminist women's refuges. The women's movement may be the most important social movement engaged in the struggle for a society more free of crime, but it is not the only one.[2] Before briefly discussing some of these other social movements, I will make some general points about where our greatest crime problems lie and why social movements are especially well placed to have an impact on these crimes.

In Australia, the types of crimes that cause the greatest harm to persons are domestic violence (Hopkins and McGregor 1991; Scutt 1983), occupational health and safety and other corporate crimes of violence such as those of the pharmaceutical industry (Braithwaite 1984; Braithwaite and Grabosky 1985: 1–41), and drunk driving (Homel 1988). The property offenders who cause the majority of criminal losses are white-collar criminals (Braithwaite 1979; Grabosky and Sutton 1989; Wilson and Braithwaite 1978).

There is a common structural reason why these particular offense types are Australia's greatest crime problems. All have enjoyed a historical immunity from public disapproval because of certain structural realities of power. The worst of Australia's white-collar criminals have been not only unusually respectable men, but also men who have been hailed as great entrepreneurial heroes. Violent men have enjoyed historical immunity even from the disapproval of the police when they engaged in acts of domestic assault (Hatty and Sutton 1986; Scutt 1983: chap. 9; Wearing 1990). This has been because of shared values between the offenders and the police about the prerogatives of men to engage in violence in the personal kingdoms of their homes. Since police who answer calls about domestic violence are the main window through which public disapproval might enter the domestic domain, this patriarchal collusion has been effective until very recently in preventing domestic violence from becoming a public issue.

Australian patriarchy takes the culturally specific form of a male mateship culture in which gender-segregated drinking is important (Sergeant 1973).[3] Women were not to be found in public bars in Australia until the 1970s. Pub and club drinking followed by driving is something that most Australian males have done many times, something which they regard as important to sustaining patterns of mateship, and something which they find difficult to regard as shameful. As a consequence of the strong support drunk driving has enjoyed in such a patriarchal context, informal disapproval by friends and formal disapproval by the courts has been historically muted.

These then are the bases for my claim that the particular crime problems that do most harm in Australia have been allowed to continue because of the muted or ambivalent disapproval they elicit, where this limited disapproval arose because of patterns of power. However, since the mid-1970s all of these forms of crime have been targeted by social movements concerned to engender community disapproval about them. The most important of these was the women's movement. Domestic violence was an important issue for the Australian women's movement in the late nineteenth century (Allen 1986). At first the resurgent women's movement of the early 1970s did not give any significant priority to domestic violence (Hopkins and McGregor 1991). By the mid-1970s, this was changing. Major conferences, including rather important conferences organized by feminists at the Australian Institute of Criminology, drew attention to the issue, as did subsequent criminological research (Hatty 1985; O'Donnell and Craney 1982; Scutt 1983; Stubbs and Powell 1989). The most important momentum, however, came from the feminist refuge movement, strategically supported by "femocrats" working within the state (Hopkins and McGregor 1991).

This social movement has had a considerable impact. Media current affairs programs now carry a regular fare of stories exposing the evils of domestic violence. Police education curricula, responding to feminist critiques (Hatty and Sutton 1986; Scutt 1982), have begun to push the line that domestic violence is a crime and a priority concern for Australian police services (McDonald et al. 1990; see also Stubbs and Powell 1989). Domestic violence is now much more out in the open in Australia. While private condoning of domestic violence continues, the public voices heard today are the voices of condemnation. And this is progress.

The social movement against white-collar crime in Australia has not been as vigorous as that in the United States (Ayres and Braithwaite 1992: chap. 1; Cullen et al. 1987; Katz 1980). However, in the 1970s and 1980s, the Australian consumer movement took up the issue with a vigor that had not been seen in previous decades. The specific issues that provoked high-profile public campaigns ranged from nursing home malpractice to used car fraud, tax scams, unsafe consumer products, and finance company rip-offs and misrepresentations. The Australian criminological research community has also given the issue a priority higher than it has been given in any other country.

In the area that has been of greatest interest to me, corporate crime in the pharmaceutical industry (Braithwaite 1984), social movement activism took some big strides in the 1980s. The Australian Consumers' Association and the Australian Federation of Consumer Organizations took much more interest in the issue. A national peak council, The Consumers' Health Forum, was established in 1985, which also gave considerable priority to malpractice in the pharmaceutical industry. These groups linked up with Health Action International and the International Organization of Consumers' Unions to deal with the transnational character of the problems they were confronting. Consumer Interpol began in the 1980s to send out alerts from Penang in Malaysia about dangerous pharmaceuticals that had been dumped in other parts of the world so that national consumer groups could draw attention to the problem if the product was being distributed in their own country. A particularly important development in the 1980s was the establishment in Adelaide of the Medical Lobby for Appropriate Marketing. This group organized letter-writing campaigns and adverse publicity among doctors when pharmaceutical companies were found to be making promotional claims about drugs that were untrue or that covered up side effects, particularly when it was third world consumers who were being victimized. The international reach of the social movement against pharmaceutical industry malpractice indicates a strength that social movement activism enjoys as an approach to transnational crime, a strength not shared by state law enforcement. Intriguingly, the pharmaceutical industry's counterstrategy today is to recruit the social movement against AIDS to resist "unreasonable regulation of the industry" in the forlorn hope that this will speed the desperate search for a cure of AIDS.

The late 1970s and early 1980s saw a social movement against occupational health and safety offenses organized by the trade union movement. Today this movement has almost run out of steam because its vision was limited in most states to achieving legislative reforms. When these were achieved in the mid-1980s, the movement lost focus and direction. Even so, in the state of Victoria over 14,000 workplace health and safety representatives have been appointed and trained by the trade union movement, giving an ongoing, if rather quiescent, grass-roots basis for a continuing movement (Carson et al. 1990).

The environmental movement has cultivated a strong surge in community support since the mid-1970s (McAllister 1991). In terms of organization, resources, and ideological coherence, it is certainly the most politically impressive social movement in Australia. It has, however, been less focused on violations of environmental laws by business than environmental movements in other countries. Instead, it has been more concerned with Australia's biggest environmental problem—soil erosion caused by agricultural practices—and with struggles to declare national parks beyond the reach of the logging and mining industries. Nevertheless, the organization of community disapproval against environmental degradation has changed to the point where powerful business leaders can no longer afford to be shameless about acts of environmental despoliation (McAllister 1991). Moreover, substantial internalization of genuine respect for the environment is evident among many in the business elite.

Both the consumer movement and conservative women's groups such as the Country Women's Association were among several community organizations that made small contributions to the social movement against alcohol abuse in Australia during the 1970s and 1980s. Australia lacked the focused, organized anti-drunk-driving movement that emerged in the late 1970s in the United States—Remove Intoxicated Drivers (RID), Mothers Against Drunk Driving (MADD), and Students Against Drunk Driving (SADD) (Jacobs 1989: xv)—though there is a MADD chapter in Australia. Although the Australian movement against drunk driving was more diffuse than the American movement, this diffuseness may not have been a weakness since changes in Australian attitudes in this area have been dramatic. This movement has less of a grass-roots quality than the others we have discussed; many of the key players were employees of the state or activists from the professions. The medical profession, the road safety research community, and the alcohol and drug education and research community played the leadership roles in this social movement which, for all its diffuseness, attracted widespread public support. Random breath testing to detect drunk driving was supported by only 37 percent of the people of New South Wales in 1973 but by 91 percent in 1983, the year of its introduction (Homel 1988: 114). The punishment of drunk driving is less severe in Australia than in many, perhaps most, other countries, with resort to imprisonment being extremely rare, but the intensity of detection efforts through the use of random breath testing in the states of New South Wales and Tasmania exceeds that to be found anywhere else in the world (Homel 1988). Perhaps because of this, the evidence of the effect of random breath testing (and the associated public campaigning against drunk driving in these states) is of a substantial impact in reducing alcohol-related road fatalities (Homel 1988), in contrast to the equivocal results of evaluation studies on the effect of more halfhearted American experiments (Ross 1982; 1984). Surprisingly, in the late 1980s we had survey evidence suggesting that drunk driving is somewhat more shameful in Australia than the

United States, though considerably less so than in Norway (Berger et al. 1990: 461).

In spite of some spirited opposition from the pub and club industry in New South Wales (Homel 1988: 117), which suffered from reduced alcohol sales, nervous politicians held firm with the reforms. In the end, the alcohol industry was in a sense co-opted by the movement against drunk driving via the introduction and aggressive marketing for the first time in Australia of low-alcohol beers. The marketing campaigns for the new products were notable for their reference to the risks of drunk driving, as in Toohey's "breathe easy" advertising campaign for low-alcohol beer.

Beyond Statist Criminology

All of the social movements I have described became strong only from the mid-1970s onward. What an irony this is for criminology when the mid-1970s was precisely the historical moment for the disillusionment of the "nothing works" era to set in. In the late 1970s, criminologists deserted utilitarianism in droves to join the "just deserts" movement that ultimately became a "get tough" movement (S. Cohen 1985; Cullen and Gilbert 1982). Perhaps nothing does work particularly well if our vision is limited to statist responses to the crime problem.[4] Republican criminology opens our eyes to the limited relevance of statist criminology—the sort the state gives money to—to practical ongoing struggles to reduce the crime rate.

If I am right, it is the most severe crime problems Australians confront that social movements have been making the greatest progress against over the past fifteen years. I do not suggest that the progress has been decisive or overwhelming: patriarchy is not about to breathe its last gasp; the environment continues to collapse; even if some pharmaceutical companies have adopted a markedly more responsible attitude today, most corporate cowboys do not yet seem overwhelmed by remorse; drunk driving is not a problem of the past.

If some progress is being made in the places that count most, statist criminology is tied to statist statistical methodologies that leave it blind to such changes. The methodologies of statist criminology churn out data that are artifacts of the very patterns of power at the heart of my argument. Crimes of domestic violence were not counted very seriously by patriarchal police forces before the social movement against domestic violence, which gained momentum in the mid-1970s. Similarly, victim surveys conducted by the Australian government provided a doubtful baseline because interviews were conducted in the households where domestic violence occurred, presumably in many cases within sight or sound of the persons who committed the violent acts. In fact, statist methodologies show that the problem is getting worse because the social movement against domestic violence has made police more sensitive to domestic violence and has provided support to women who wish to lodge complaints against violent spouses (Hopkins and McGregor 1991).

This is also true of white-collar crime and of crime generally; when a form of crime becomes more shameful, the community discovers more instances of that form of crime. So if bank robbery is shameful and insider trading is not, the community will have the impression that bank robbery is the more common and more serious of these two problems. This when we know the fact of the matter to be that "the best way to rob a bank is to own it."

Taking state statistics on white-collar crime seriously is a similarly foolish enterprise. Criminologists such as Hirschi and Gottfredson (1987) have done just this and reached startling conclusions, such as that white-collar criminals in the United States are disproportionately black! Statist criminology is an edifice built on methodological foundations that render it incapable of knowing the things most worth knowing about crime.[5]

One response to directing shame against specific forms of crime is that this is a utopian enterprise, because shaming is not an effective mechanism of social control in modern, urbanized, heterogeneous societies. Elsewhere I have argued that there is no unidirectional historical trend either toward or away from the effectiveness of shame-based social control (Braithwaite 1991a). Like Elias (1982) and Goffman (1956), I contend that there are some features of interdependency in modern urban societies that actually increase our vulnerability to shame, and others that reduce it.

It is more important to address the specific forms of crime that are the locus of my argument here. I have already said that criminological research gives us no way of knowing whether there is more or less domestic violence today than in the past. What we can say with some confidence, however, is that domestic violence has become more shameful in the nineteenth and twentieth centuries. The following description of the shamelessness of male violence in fifteenth-century England could not be regarded as an accurate description of the situation in that country today.

> Wife-beating was a recognized right of man and was practiced without shame by high as well as low. Similarly, the daughter who refused to marry the gentleman of her parents' choice was liable to be locked up, beaten, and flung about the room, without any shock being inflicted upon public opinion. (Trevelyan 1985: 196)

This fact is not only recorded in the history books, but in the courts as well. Even after World War II, there is evidence of English lower courts finding domestic assault to be legitimate as a punishment for a wife who had disobeyed her husband (Stratmann 1982: 121), and indeed it was a matter of right rather than shame in English law until 1891 that a husband could beat his wife. At least in public forums, the beating of wives and daughters today surely does invoke more shame. Public outcry would surely ensue if a ducking stool for the disciplining of nagging wives were installed in any English town today.

More generally, the American evidence shows that concern about white-collar crime and mistrust of business has increased substantially since the mid-1970s (see the studies cited by Cullen et al. 1987: 43). When Edwin Sutherland (1983) wrote in 1949 that white-collar crime flourished because of a lack of organized community resentment against respectable criminals, he may have been right. But contemporary American and Australian data, as well as data from many other countries, suggests that this is no longer true (Grabosky et al. 1987).

Community attitudes toward white-collar crime today should be a worry for the republican, but not for lack of shame; rather my concern is that attitudes can be so stigmatic and punitive. In a study of eight countries (the United States, the United Kingdom, Finland, Sweden, Norway, Denmark, the Netherlands, and Kuwait), Scott and Al-Thakeb (1977) found that in every country the recommended sentence for the manufacture and sale of potentially harmful pharmaceuticals was more severe than for auto theft, larceny (felony), burglary, aggravated assault, and robbery. When this study was replicated some years later in Australia, respondents were even more punitive on this item ("The offender is an executive of a drug company who allows his company to manufacture and sell a drug knowing that it may produce harmful side effects for most individuals"), recommending an average of nine years' imprisonment for the offense (Broadhurst and Indemaur 1982). Some respondents in an Australian Institute of Criminology survey even recommended capital punishment for serious environmental and industrial safety offenses (Grabosky et al. 1987). When I visited Ralph Nader's office in 1990, they had recently lost the services of a person who supported the death penalty for business executives who sold consumer products that caused loss of life. He believed that such convicted corporate criminals should not be executed in the normal way, but in a defective electric chair. I am pleased to report that Ralph Nader was not persuaded by this idea.

Similarly, as I reported above, in Australia at least, community attitudes have become more intolerant of drunk driving. So it seems that the types of crime that are our most serious problems in Australia have become more shameful during the last fifteen years. Levi's (1988) study and recent annual reports of the Australian Commissioner for Taxation even suggest that for tax evasion, an offense low in moral opprobrium the world over, but seemingly even less shameful in Australia than in a number of other countries (Grabosky et al. 1987: 37), the extraordinary moral crusade of the 1970s and 1980s against tax dishonesty has improved tax compliance among the wealthy and brought to an end the era when wealthy Australians openly bragged about tax evasion.[6]

While we need much more systematic data on these questions, we have enough to suggest that social movements can affect attitudes in a way that increases social disapproval and causes pangs of conscience in those contemplating breaking the law. The empirical point applies equally to types of offenses that republicans should not regard as a high priority. Take drug use, an offense that Pettit and I contend republicans should not regard as a crime at all (Braithwaite and Pettit 1990: 97–99). The conventional wisdom of criminology might lead one to believe that drug use is an unsolvable problem. This view seems unduly pessimistic in light of what I would hypothesize to be the contribution the temperance movement made to the dramatic reduction in English-speaking countries of drunkenness and excessive drinking during the nineteenth century right up until its Pyrrhic victory in securing prohibition in the United States. In Australia, the long period of falling alcohol consumption from the mid-nineteenth century corresponds with the rise of the temperance movement, and the long rise in alcohol consumption from the 1930s to the 1970s corresponds with the decline and virtual demise of the old temperance movement (Powell 1988).[7] The decline of alcohol consumption since the mid-eighties (McAllister et al. 1991) may be associated with the rise of a new social movement against the alcohol industry grounded in the consumer and health education movements. In the late nineteenth and early twentieth centuries, the temperance movement was a movement of both Christians and feminists who were involved in the women's franchise campaign and who were deeply concerned about prostitution in public houses and domestic violence (Beresford 1984; Gusfield 1963; Tyrell 1984). Just as contemporary Alcoholics Anonymous meetings rely heavily on self-shaming in a nurturant collectivity (Trice and Roman 1970), so the nineteenth-century American temperance movement gave pride of place to the reintegrative power of the reformed (Powell 1988: 46). Similarly, the Australian temperance movement of the first half of the nineteenth century was oriented to persuading the wayward to "sign the pledge," rejecting at that time the idea of reform through government intervention (Beresford 1984: 3).

Within the narrow ahistoricism of contemporary social science, researchers wax pessimistic at the results of drug education programs of very short duration because of the rather small or insignificant preventive effects they secure (Ogborne 1988; Wragg 1987; 1990). Yet any plausible model of how social movements might transform community attitudes to drugs (and consumption patterns of drugs) would surely involve gradual cumulative change over a historical period of many years such as we have observed with male consumption of tobacco since World War II. A change strategist operating with a model of gradual change over a long historical haul would take comfort from American data on small but significant annual reductions in consumption of drugs such as marijuana and cocaine in recent years (Bachman et al. 1988; 1990a). This research shows that during the years when the social disapproval and perceived health risk of marijuana and cocaine use were declining, usage increased; during the years when social disapproval and perceived risk increased, usage decreased for both drugs (Bachman et al. 1990a: 176). The change strategist would not become pessimistic because the changes are small; her project only makes sense with a reform timetable measured in decades rather than years.[8] But this may be of limited interest to statist criminology, which is loath to fund projects grounded in historical vision. Parliamentary terms and periods of incumbency at the head of government research units do not readily accommodate historical farsightedness.

Confronting the Paralysis of Pessimism

A further basis for pessimism about the capacity of social movements to reduce crime arises from devotion to what Hindess (1982) calls a "capacity-outcome" approach to understanding struggles. According to such an understanding, it is naive to believe that disorganized social movements can secure any more than symbolic victories against powerful organized interests. The capacity-outcome approach assumes that in order to determine the likely outcome of a struggle all one need do is identify what resources or capacities are available to the contending parties; the outcome can then be read off in *a priori* fashion. Hence, if the alcohol industry is a powerful and affluent industry with many political friends and the temperance movement is an economically disorganized collection of women, you can read off the outcome—the alcohol industry will win. Yet the mechanics of history are not so simple. The environmental and consumer movements perhaps do lose more battles than they win, but often enough they win against industries with superior resources. Hopkins and McGregor's (1991) analysis of the Australian movement against domestic violence addresses the structure-agency issue, the extent to which the agency of social movements can prevail against structures of domination:

> An American study found that the existence of local feminist groups was a more important predictor of community programmes for battered women throughout the USA than per capita income, political liberalism or the existence of state domestic violence legislation (see Tierney 1982: 211). The movement against domestic violence does seem to be a case of, in this instance, women making their own history. (Hopkins and McGregor 1991: 138)

It seems that social movements can make progress in moral crusades that appeal to the sense of justice of people. Progressive change is possible by asking citizens to challenge a hegemony that unjustly acquiesces in a certain type of crime's being less serious because it is perpetrated by men in a position of some national or familial power. The appeal of such crusades can be broad because what is demanded is really so little and so consistent with the rhetoric of Western justice systems. It is a demand simply that we should not afford criminals an advantage in our perceptions of the evil of their deeds simply because they are powerful. It is a plea for the uncontroversial notion of treating equal crimes with equal seriousness. This is certainly part of what makes progress against the odds more possible for social movements when they demand that the criminal law be taken seriously.

Progress may be easier here than in so many of the other domains where social movements struggle. The truly difficult part of the republican criminologist's political agenda is to find or build social movements to mobilize against the excesses of the criminal justice system. Just as the symbolic power of the criminal law makes mobilization against criminal justice neglect comparatively easy, this symbolic power makes mobilization against criminal justice excess difficult.

One of the more sophisticated versions of the capacity-outcome approach to struggles is Edelman's (1964) account that diffuse, disorganized publics win symbolic victories, while organized interests receive tangible rewards. So, for example, the social movement against white-collar crime gets the symbolic victory of enacting new laws to regulate business, but the powerful players of the industry win the tangible victory of ensuring that the new laws are enforced only against marginal operators whom the powerful corporations are quite pleased to have harassed (Carson 1975; Hopkins and Parnell 1984; O'Malley 1980). Although this model has explanatory power in some criminal justice domains, it would be more of a concern to the republican if her job were primarily to secure tougher state enforcement. But in fact, when confronted with a domain where the criminal law is not being taken seriously enough, the republican is more concerned with symbolic victories than with tangible changes to state policies. The republican analysis is that crime rates are more responsive to patterns of community disapproval of crime than to state enforcement patterns. So it is the symbolic victory for the hearts and minds of citizens that is more important than securing tangible changes to state criminal justice practices. This is not to say that republicans are unconcerned about reforming criminal justice practices (the nature of such concerns is developed at length in Braithwaite and Pettit 1990), it is just to say that the republican pursues the objective of reducing crime with more of an eye to community organization than to criminal enforcement.

Although all of these social movements seem to have succeeded in turning community attitudes against the conduct of concern to them, the crime control dividends may have been less than expected because a significant proportion of the campaigning has been stigmatic. These social movements have failed to grasp the crucial difference between reintegrative shaming and stigmatization. Hence, stigmatic features of the social movement against alcohol have motivated a culturally specific form of resistance within Australian male mateship culture—the denunciation of antialcohol activists as "wowsers" (Dunstan 1974). Recent community disapproval of illicit drug use has been stigmatic in a way that has enabled drug subcultures to assure drug users that their rejectors are worthy of rejection. In contrast, the Australian antitobacco movement has been at pains not to stigmatize users while disapproving of their practices. Even here, though, a stigmatizing fringe to the movement has fueled subcultures of resistance in the form of smokers' rights movements, which are supported by the tobacco industry.

Similarly, while the social movement against white-collar crime in the United States has dramatically changed community attitudes to disapproval, many white-collar criminals have acquired an immunity to this disapproval. They also reject their rejectors. An important study by Benson (1990) found that convicted white-collar criminals were more likely to feel mad than bad about their offending. The reason, I have argued, is that the stigmatic features of the social movement against white-collar crime in the United States have fueled business subcultures of resistance to regulatory laws (Braithwaite 1989b). Consequently, the social movement regularly fails to bring offenders to a position of shame about their crime.

Instead, offenders feel angry about being unfairly picked on by antibusiness prosecutors.

Similarly, many violent men in Australia reject their rejectors as man-haters. One reason they may be able to do this is that there is a fringe of the Australian women's movement who are in fact man-haters. While the Australian women's movement in general eschews the stigmatization of men, managing to communicate disapproval within a continuum of respect for men, occasional stigmatic excess has provided symbolic ammunition for chauvinist cultures of resistance that sustain the moral ambiguity of domestic violence.

The Egalitarian Thrust of Republican Support for Social Movements

In this section I briefly sketch five additional reasons why republican political theory counsels the consideration of support for the social movements I have mentioned. These are (1) the republican commitment to economic and political equality; (2) the commitment to active participation of citizens in community life; (3) the effect of inequality on crime, not only through the historical muting of disapproval toward crimes of the powerful but also, for example, through the effect of patriarchy on the structuring of humiliation; (4) the way social movements can inculcate pride in being law-abiding and rights-respecting as well as shame at violating these norms; and (5) the way social movements can encourage the evolution of cooperation in regulatory regimes while preventing the evolution of capture and corruption.

The republican supports social movements that represent the egalitarian aspirations of less powerful groups because a concern with political and economic equality is basic to republicanism (Pettit 1989; Sunstein 1988). For Philip Pettit and me, this concern defines republicanism—the republican wants to maximize the dominion of citizens, defined in a social or relational way as equality-of-liberty prospects (Braithwaite and Pettit 1990: 64–65). Women living under the thumb of a patriarch or men living in abject poverty cannot enjoy equality-of-liberty prospects with the wealthy. Because republicans also support the active participation of citizens in community life, they have two reasons for supporting the women's or consumer movements besides their concern about crime prevention—an equality-based reason and a participation-based reason.

A third consideration is the belief that inequality is a direct cause of crime. Inequality of power has allowed our most serious crime problems to fester because the powerful have been able to sustain immunity from community disapproval. Elsewhere I have argued that for more direct theoretical reasons, economic inequality, inequality in political power (slavery, totalitarianism), racism, ageism, and patriarchy are causes of crime (Braithwaite 1991b). There is both a noninstrumental and an instrumental side to this argument. First, much crime, particularly violent crime, is motivated by the humiliation of the offender and the offender's perceived right to humiliate the victim. Inegalitarian societies, it is argued, are structurally more humiliating than egalitarian societies. For example, it is structurally more humiliating to be a black in South Africa than in Tanzania. The more instrumental analysis of the motivation of crime also rejects Sutherland's (1983) interpretation that poverty cannot be a cause of crime because it is the rich and not the poor that commit greater numbers of more serious crimes. According to my more instrumental analysis, inequality worsens crimes of *poverty* motivated by *need* for goods for *use* and crimes of *wealth* motivated by *greed* enabled by goods for *exchange* (Braithwaite 1979, 1991b). Inequality worsens both crimes of the exploited and crimes of exploitation.

Social movements affect crime not only by mobilizing shame against criminal behavior, but also by mobilizing pride in prosocial patterns of behavior that provide alternatives to crime. For example, the state contributed to the campaign against drunk driving in Australia with television advertisements showing role models for responsible male drinking. One member of the drinking group would in a nonthreatening way "be a mate" by insisting that he drive home a drinking companion who had consumed too much. Tom Scheff has rightly criticized *Crime, Shame and Reintegration* for not giving enough importance to pride as a complement to shame (Scheff and Retzinger 1991: 175). It may be that pride in being law-abiding, caring, responsible, and rights-respecting has more marked effects than shame does on the thought of being criminal or trampling on the rights of others. I give more prominence to shaming in *Crime, Shame and Reintegration* only because the partitioning of shaming resolves the central theoretical contradictions of criminology. At the same time, pride does seem to be an even more important emotion for the women's movement to cultivate than shame—pride in being a woman, pride in resisting patriarchal domination, pride in persuading men to respect the rights of women, and pride among the men who are so persuaded.

Finally, Ian Ayres and I have argued that business regulation schemes can be more effective if they are transformed from bipartite games between the state and a regulated industry to tripartite games in which the third player is a community group with an active interest in the particular regulatory domain (Ayres and Braithwaite 1992). Republican empowerment of community groups in regulatory deliberation can improve the cost effectiveness and decency of regulatory institutions. Tripartite regulation, it is argued, can secure the advantages of the evolution of cooperative regulation (Scholz 1984) while preventing the evolution of capture and corruption. This analysis is of more general criminal justice import than one might think. This is because the republican believes that many social problems that are currently dealt with by criminal law would be better dealt with by regulatory law (Braithwaite and Pettit 1990). Hence, for example, the republican is interested in abandoning bipartite state criminal control of prostitution in favor of multiparty dialogic regulation that gives both the women's movement and sex workers' unions seats at the negotiating table when regulatory arrangements are put in place (Ayres and Braithwaite 1992).

I have sketched only summary references to these other works that give further reasons why the political program of republican criminology is support for empowering social movements of the powerless. I do this only to give some sense of the theoretical interconnections within the wider corpus of my work and why they converge on the political program of support for the social movements I have discussed.[9]

Synergy Between State and Social Movement Activism

Thus far I have overplayed the juxtaposition between preventing crime through state enforcement and preventing crime by mobilizing social movements. I have done this to make as effective a break as possible with the entrenched *étatisme* of conventional criminological thinking. But in fact, my view is that social movements are more effective when they eschew both a total preoccupation with changing state policies and a total preoccupation with grass-roots consciousness raising (see also Grabosky 1990). Social movements are effective when their strategies recognize the synergy between these two thrusts.

The purpose of my book with Ian Ayres is to show how a creative synergy can be sustained between state regulation of business and public interest group activism. First, we argue for state empowerment and resourcing of weak and disorganized public interest groups so that they can become credible participants in tripartite regulation. From the public interest group point of view, they must lobby for their empowerment by the state. The synergy between femocrats and the refuge movement in Aus-

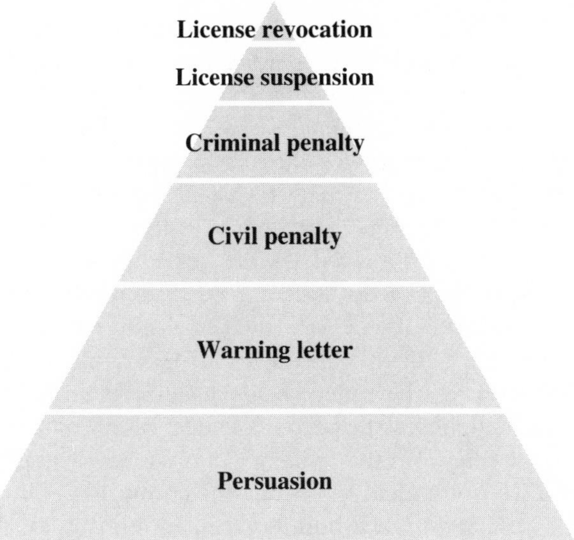

Fig. 12.1. Example of an enforcement pyramid. The proportion of space at each layer represents the proportion of enforcement activity at that level.

tralia is a strategic model of how this can be done (Hopkins and McGregor 1991; Yeatman 1990).

It is also important that progressive social movements lobby for credible state sanctioning capacities against crimes of the powerful. This is not because social movements should seek to achieve results by relying on the state to deter crime. Unfortunately, this is precisely the miscalculation social movements often make. A credible capacity for sanctioning the powerful is necessary for enabling dialogic regulation, regulation based on reasoning about what sort of conduct should cause us to be proud or ashamed.

In *Responsive Regulation*, Ayres and I make this point with the idea of the enforcement pyramid (Ayres and Braithwaite 1992; see also Braithwaite 1985). An example of a pyramid is given in Figure 12.1. In this model, the state signals that it has a range of sanctioning possibilities through which it can escalate if the firm does not cooperate with dialogic regulation. The agency has the capacity to escalate right up to corporate capital punishment (license revocation). The paradox of the model is that by carrying a big stick, the state is able to speak softly. More crucially for the present argument, by carrying a big stick, the state is also able to require the firm to hear the voices of its critics from public interest groups. Tripartite dialogic regulation at the base of the enforcement pyramid is enabled by the capacity of the state to escalate in punitiveness. Paradoxically, if we lop the top off such an enforcement pyramid, the state may have less capacity to do this. By weakening the criminal enforcement capability of the state, we end up with a more litigious, less cooperative regulatory regime in which public interest movements can have effects only by going to court.

We can translate the same basic model to the arena of domestic violence. My theoretical position is that violence within families is least likely when those families themselves succeed in persuading their members to internalize an abhorrence of violence, to take pride in respecting the rights of women and caring for others. But sometimes families will fail in accomplishing this. Then they must be able to look for support outside. A battered woman might seek help from a refuge. With a refuge worker, she might then seek help from the civil law (an order restraining a man from entering his own house) and ultimately the criminal law (imprisonment of the man). Just as with the business regulation pyramid, the capacity of the victim of domestic violence to show the offender how continued violence will lead inevitably to more and more dire outside intervention is empowering for the victim. If the victim is afraid to signal this power that the state enables her to have, another member of the family may have the courage to do so. Family members or domestic violence workers are likely to get the attention of violent men only when they can signal to the offender with genuine credibility that he is on a slippery slope leading to more and more forceful state intervention until the violence stops. Equally important to mobilizing outside legal support is outside support that gives women and their children the economic power to leave a violent household and to credibly threaten to leave should future violence occur. Obviously, state policies are essential here, and the women's movement is the crucial political force for securing those state policies.

The hope is not that state enforcement will be so powerful and so regularly used that it will deter rational offenders. The hope is that state enforcement will be sufficiently credible to empower informal processes of social control, to enable dialogic regulation of violence. State criminal enforcement capabilities are a resource that women, children, and domestic violence workers can use to demand that violent offenders take seriously their disapproval of acts of violence. Of course, state criminal enforcement capability is also important for securing the incapacitation of some men who are beyond reform or civil restraint and for signifying the shamefulness of crime. Neither of these latter reasons for criminal enforcement

Fig. 12.2. Example of a domestic violence enforcement pyramid.

justifies, however, widespread or automatic resort to imprisonment. They justify only the capability for and the occasional use of imprisonment.

Philip Pettit and I have derived from the republican objective of maximizing dominion a presumption in favor of being parsimonious in the use of the criminal law (Braithwaite and Pettit 1990: 87). What the enforcement pyramid shows, however, is a paradox about the way the world works. The very capacity to escalate state intervention enables social control to work better at less coercive levels. While republicans should be faithful to the simple principle of parsimony by supporting reductions in the maximum prison sentence that can be imposed for assault, it would not serve the objective of parsimonious punishment to abolish imprisonment altogether as a sentence for assault. One reason for this is that a consequence of throwing away the big stick is that middle-sized sticks would be used more often. This at least follows if I am right that the tough sanctions at the peak of the enforcement pyramid channel social control down to the dialogic base of the pyramid.

For the republican, then, credible criminal enforcement capability strengthens the hand of communitarian crime control; it does not supplant it. We can conceptualize an enforcement pyramid for domestic violence as in Figure 12.2.[10] The republican envisages that a long historical process of community and state involvement in shaming acts of domestic violence will result in most citizens' internalizing the shamefulness of violence. Consequently, most social control will work at the base of the enforcement pyramid by self-sanctioning with pangs of conscience. If this fails, the history of community shaming of violence will persuade the perpetrators that others will disapprove of them after they have committed an act of violence. Note that no one has to confront the offender directly with shame at this level; an offender who understands the culture will know that those who find out about the violence will be gossiping disapprovingly. As I was at pains to argue in *Crime, Shame and Reintegration*, on most of the occasions when gossip hits its target, it will do so without being heard by the target; it will be effective in the imagination of a culturally knowledgeable subject. If the offender is incapable of imagining the disapproval others feel about the violence, then someone must make clear that disapproval. If family members are too intimidated to do it, then a domestic violence worker must do it. If disapproval, dialogue, and counseling do not work, then the formal law must be invoked: first a court order restraining the freedom of movement of the offender (perhaps associated with arrest after a specific outburst [see Hopkins and McGregor 1991; Sherman and Berk 1984]) and if that fails, criminal enforcement. The republican, therefore, does not call simply for informalism rather than formalism; she calls for a formalism that empowers informalism. The effect of successful implementation of an enforcement pyramid is, however, that most social control is communitarian control rather than state control and that most of the day-to-day successes are achieved by dialogic regulation, with state regulation stepping in to mop up the failures. This is also the story of Homel's (1988) work on the reduction of drunk driving in Australia—the formalism of random breath testing empowered the informalism of dialogic regulation within drinking groups or by bar attendants.

The real power of reintegrative shaming is at the level of prevention: conscience building. With the very worst cases of deep-seated violence, reintegrative shaming is quite likely to fail, but then so is everything else. When things come to this pass, we must do our best with clumsy protective measures for victims. But the heart of a political program that I suspect is shared by feminism and republicanism is to struggle for cultural and economic changes that prevent violence long before it becomes unpreventable.

Summary

1. The partitioning of shaming into reintegrative and stigmatizing modalities is the key theoretical move for criminology to take.

2. Social movements like the women's movement can affect the level of crime not only by shaming crimes of violence but also by inculcating pride in solving problems nonviolently, pride in caring for others and pride in respecting the rights of women.

3. Australia's most serious crime problems are domestic violence, white-collar crime, and drunk driving. These have been allowed to become our major crime problems because of historical failures of the community and the state to mobilize shame against these offenses. This historical failure is explained by the structural position of men and the structural position of those in command positions in the economy.

4. Since the mid-1970s, social movements have worked with the state and the mass media in a progressively more effective way to raise voices against the muted and ambiguous disapproval these offense types have attracted. Social movements such as the women's, environmental, and consumer movements can be more effective in campaigns to get the state and the community to take seriously the crimes of powerful people than in many of the other domains in which they struggle.

5. The republican way of thinking about crime therefore encourages the view that since the mid-1970s in Australia we may have been making slow but significant progress with the crime problem. This is not being achieved without setback and reversal. The excesses of financial deregulation caused a surge in certain types of corporate crime in the mid-1980s. The stigmatizing of men by some sections of the women's movement has fostered resistance and backlash to feminist thought in some quarters, most tragically among Aboriginal women (Ridgeway 1986). The stigmatization of business executives by some sections of the consumer and environmental movements has at times engendered business subcultures of resistance to regulatory law. But on balance, there has been progress.

6. There is no inexorable march with modernization and urbanization toward a society where reintegrative shaming cannot work. It is likely that in many Western countries, like Australia, domestic violence, drunk driving, environmental crime, corporate crimes of violence, and other types of white-collar crime have become more shameful in recent times.

7. This empirical view of historical shifts in patterns of community disapproval can be detached from republican normative commitments. My theory would be that illicit drug use can never be successfully controlled

by a state deterrence policy; it can be better controlled by a social movement against drug use, as long as that movement does not stigmatize drug users. The nineteenth- and early twentieth-century temperance movement is not in every way a model of the social movement I have in mind. However, it may be that its dialogism and its disapproval of drug abuse contributed to the dramatic decline in alcohol consumption that occurred during its heyday. The contemporary antismoking movement is another in which my analysis would place confidence as a strategy for change. Social movements do not have to be ideologically coherent, and they certainly do not have to accept republicanism, to be effective in changing patterns of disapproval for crime.

8. Progress with crime does not depend on cultural changes that are especially dramatic. It does not require our transformation into a society of busybodies, constantly prying into the affairs of other individuals. Such an individualistic vision would be politically impotent and an authoritarian threat to dominion. Progress requires us to support progressive social movements whose agendas include the disapproval of our most serious crimes. These social movements have effects at the microlevel. Consequently, shaming will work most of the time in the consciences and imaginations of potential wrongdoers who dislike the thought of people gossiping about them. We are not required to confront others daily with our disapproval (except our children, who are still learning how to imagine what others will disapprove of). This is not to deny that every now and then during a lifetime, most of us will encounter violent people who lack conscience, who fail to imagine the depth of disapproval others feel toward their violence. These people we certainly must confront. For most of us, this is not a month-to-month demand on our republican obligations. The month-to-month demand is to be active in one progressive social movement or another. Republicans do not have to be busybodies of daily private life so much as activists of public life, participants in a collective struggle for a republican culture.

9. Social movements can reduce crime not only by mobilizing disapproval of crime but also by attacking the structural roots of crime. Patriarchy is a structural cause of domestic violence, feminism a social movement that addresses this cause. Corruption in business-government relations is one reason why regulatory agencies cover up corporate crimes; consumerism (in the Nader public-citizen mold) is a social movement concerned with addressing this structural basis of crime.

10. Reintegrative shaming directed at the kinds of crime that republicans struggle to have recognized as crime is not repressive. Reintegrative

shaming is as necessary to increasing freedom as it is to reducing crime. Liberals are wrong to conclude that a high crime rate is a price we pay for freedom. A high crime rate is one of the consequences of the limited conception of freedom in liberalism.

11. Republicans believe in individuation, because dominion is something individuals enjoy as individuals. For republicans, both individual isolation and engulfment by the group are evils. Individuation in a social world is secured by a system of social assurances, including rights. Republican rights are best secured by reintegrative shaming of those who are not rights-respecting. Liberal rights, in contrast, are empty legal gestures of limited practical use to securing individuation in a social world infused with relations of power.

12. The republican is interested in exploring synergies between social movement action and state action that will increase dominion for citizens. In the domain of crime control, the task is not so much to get the state to do the job but for the state to empower citizens and movements of citizens who are ultimately our best hope for a reduction in crime.

Reference Matter

Notes

Chapter 3

1. Chiricos (1987: 195) notes that the objectives of these surveys of the U-C research literature are similar to those of the more quantitatively oriented "meta-analysis" techniques that have been developed in recent decades (Glass et al. 1981; Hunter et al. 1982). However, a precondition for the quantitative meta-analysis of regression studies—that exactly the same instruments be used to measure the independent and dependent variables in regression studies—generally is not satisfied. Chiricos does, though, report several summaries of algebraic directions and levels of statistical significance of the U-C relationship in the studies he surveys. Thus, his study may be regarded as a "quasi-meta-analysis."

2. Regarding Chiricos's (1987) conclusion that the U-C relationship has become more strongly positive in post-1970 data, it is noteworthy that Land et al. (1990), after controlling for other indicators of deprivation/affluence in analyses of homicide rates at the city, metropolitan area, and state levels, found consistently negative (although not always statistically significant) estimated cross-sectional unemployment regression coefficients for 1960, 1970, and 1980. A similar analysis of other violence rates by McCall, Land, and Cohen (1992) also found a negative unemployment relationship more often than a positive one for robbery, and positive but never statistically significant effects for rape and assault. Given the comprehensiveness of the samples analyzed (all cities, metropolitan areas, and states for which the crime rate data are available in the three census years), it would appear that the evidence is more supportive of an inference of a weak negative U-C relationship from 1960 through 1980.

3. The system-activity effect is essentially the "business-cycle" effect studied by social scientists in the nineteenth and early twentieth centuries before the development of national unemployment statistics (see Vold 1979: 165–78, for a review). It is noteworthy, furthermore, that the more recent and more relatively rigorous of these studies, such as Thomas's (1925) study of England and Wales for the period 1857 to 1913 and Henry and Short's (1954) study of the United States in the early

twentieth century, generally infer a decline for some types of crimes during an economic downturn.

4. The assumption of normality is not necessary, in general.

5. The multiplier is 4.1627.

6. A time series of 45 observations approaches the length (50 or more observations) conventionally considered a minimum for application of ARIMA techniques (see, e.g., McCleary and Hay 1980: 20).

7. Numerical estimates were obtained by application of the SAS/ETS ARIMA Procedure (SAS Institute 1988).

8. Results of other empirical tests of the nonstationarity hypothesis for the unemployment series, 1946 to 1982, are reported in Cantor and Land (1991). The results reported there are somewhat mixed. This is not surprising given that the unemployment rate series experienced a series of oil price shocks and recessions in the mid-1970s to early 1980s, which produced an upward drift pattern indicative of exploding variance (which is consistent with the behavior of a random walk model). The downward pattern of the unemployment series in the mid- to late 1980s, however, appears to have been sufficient to restore the clear stationarity of the series.

9. To conserve space, the estimated autocorrelation and partial autocorrelation functions are not reported here, but are available from the authors on request.

10. For all Index crime rates for which our ARIMA analyses implied an AR(1) or AR(2) time-series behavior in first-differences, results from estimation of regression model (1) are reported in Table 3.1. But for aggravated assault, for which we found AR(2) behavior only in second-differences, results of estimation of regression model (2) are given in the table. The regression models were estimated by application of the AUTOREG Procedure of SAS/ETS (SAS Institute 1988).

11. The regression models also were estimated for the total Index violent crime rate (murder, rape, assault, robbery), the total Index property crime rate (burglary, larceny-theft, motor vehicle theft), and the total Index crime rate. We find that both the negative contemporaneous and the positive differenced unemployment coefficients are significant in all three models, largely because of the dominance in each aggregated Index series of those component crime rate series that exhibit significant coefficients for both effects in Table 3.1.

12. Cantor and Land (1985: 322) note that the effects of a large population of chronically unemployed individuals on criminal motivation should be found in persistent and/or growing levels of crime rates rather than in short-term fluctuations. This seems particularly the case among the nation's underclass, overly represented in the black population, whose lives are affected only minimally by anything other than very strong macroeconomic changes (Auletta 1983).

13. There also are several technical limitations to the Cappell and Sykes (1991) study. First, they use Index crime rate data series extending back to before World War II—years in which the number of jurisdictions reporting to the UCR system was small and variable, with corresponding limitations on accuracy of the time series. Second, the aggregate Index crime rate they use as a dependent variable does not include larceny. Third, it is not clear whether, or how, autocorrelated errors were accommodated in the statistical estimation techniques they utilized.

14. Interestingly, in an alternative model specification that allows for both simultaneous reciprocal effects of the crime and imprisonment rates in year t and correlated errors between the two equations of the model, Cappell and Sykes find a negative estimated effect coefficient for the first-differenced unemployment rate on the crime rate in year t. In addition, this specification produces positive estimated reciprocal effects of the crime and imprisonment rates. But Cappell and Sykes reject this model as misspecified.

15. Because Cappell and Sykes's preferred model is recursive with independent errors, it follows that each of the crime and prisoner commitment rate equations can be estimated separately.

16. In contrast to many other time-series studies, the age structure variable does not attain statistical significance in the Cappell and Sykes crime rate equations. This may be due either to the particular model specifications they analyzed or to the definition of the variable (most studies constrain the youth age range to, say, ages 15 to 29 rather than 15 to 44).

17. To conserve space, the statistical estimates are not reported here, but are available from the authors on request.

Chapter 4

1. Not all the studies that claim (or are categorized) to be ethnographic are in fact ethnographic in a participant-observation sense. Those who are doing in-depth interviewing of subjects where the subjects live often consider what they are doing ethnographic. Yet, it is more accurate to understand that they are interviewing, not doing ethnography.

2. For a more detailed discussion of the methods involved in the gang study see my *Islands in the Street: Gangs in American Urban Society* (Sánchez Jankowski 1991).

3. Much of the crime motivated in this way parallels that of persons in the previous state-socialist countries of Eastern Europe and the former Soviet Union who engage in the secondary economy or black market (illegal) jobs to supplement their incomes. See Grossman 1989.

This and all subsequent quotations in this chapter that are not otherwise identified are from my current, ongoing research.

4. Because the evidence for this paper comes from participant-observation in racial/ethnic minority communities, this proposition will need to be empirically tested by comparing individuals who are from ethnic groups that have not faced persistent discrimination and those that have.

5. See Massey 1990 and Massey and Denton 1993 for data indicating the inordinately high rate of segregation that exists between European (white) Americans and Mexican- and African-Americans.

6. Mercer Sullivan (1989: 110, 120) also found in his ethnographic study of youth in Brooklyn that situations were important in determining whether violence would be used in an economic crime.

7. None of these fears need be exclusive of the others. It is quite possible for them to be separate or for the individual to have more than one fear.

8. The work of Lillian Rubin, although not participant-observation, has provided enormous insight and evidence on this subject. See Rubin 1976.

9. Communicating to members of the community that one has a gun and is willing to use it if threatened is often the modus operandi in large urban areas, especially in low-income areas. There are numerous examples. One involves elderly people in Detroit who go outside in their bathrobes with guns on Devil's night (the night before Halloween) in an effort to protect their property from the tradition that young people engage in of burning buildings and homes (usually abandoned). For a description of this, see Chafets 1990.

10. The present research is only two years into a multiyear design.

11. David Matza referred to such processes of rationalization in his discussion of techniques of neutralization. See Matza 1990 and Matza and Sykes 1957: 664–70.

12. James Q. Wilson and Edward Herrnstein are good examples of those who tend to believe that the relationship between inequality and crime is too complex to understand and is thus to be avoided (see J. Q. Wilson and Herrnstein 1985). Jencks also noticed this in the work of Wilson and Herrnstein (see Jencks 1992: 11).

Chapter 5

1. Jolin and Gibbons (1987: 240), for example, have described Gove's "physical prime" explanation of the timing of crime as "an incisive discussion of age (and gender) relationships in deviant behavior of various kinds."

2. The authors are engaged in a more extensive exploration of the relationship between physical prime and crime prime. The age curve for physical strength is typical of the age curves for numerous other physical indicators: None show any resemblance to the age curve for physically demanding crimes (Steffensmeier and Allan 1990).

3. The percentages reflect what the percentage of adult arrests would be if juvenile and adult populations were equal in size. The actual percentage of adult arrests is much greater for both blacks and whites. The formula used is: $[AR/(AR + JR)] \times 100$, where AR is the race-specific arrest rate for adults, and JR is the race-specific arrest rate for juveniles. Rates were calculated using youth population aged 10 to 17 and adult population aged 18 to 64. Unfortunately, the unavailability of detailed race- and age-specific arrest data compel us to use simple adult versus juvenile comparisons.

4. Pennsylvania Crime Commission 1991.

5. These data are part of a larger project conducted by the senior author aimed at gathering information on age and other offender characteristics (e.g., gender) of white-collar and corporate offenders.

Chapter 6

I am grateful for financial assistance in support of my research to the Social Science and Humanities Research Council of Canada and to the Ministry of the

Solicitor General of Canada through its Contributions Grant to the Centre of Criminology, University of Toronto. I wish to express my gratitude to Tony Doob for help with the data, and to Donna Andrew, Tina Loo, and Barbara Todd for their helpful suggestions about an earlier version of this essay.

1. The following paragraphs are based principally on the following work: Beattie 1986: chap. 5; Cockburn 1977; Gatrell 1980; Gatrell and Hadden 1972; Hay 1982; Lawson 1986; Philips 1977; Sharpe 1983.

2. See in particular, Beattie 1986: chap. 5; Hay 1982; Lawson 1986. For insightful analyses of the relationships between long-term trends in judicial data and the trade cycle in the nineteenth century—and the wider contexts within which that needs to be interpreted—see Gatrell and Hadden 1972 and Gatrell 1980.

3. For discussion of the problems raised by indictments as guides to criminality, see Beattie 1981; Cockburn 1975; Gatrell 1980; Hay 1982; Innes and Styles 1986. A particular reason for caution in interpreting judicial data in this period is the small number of cases that typically came to trial—a few dozen at each session of a court, rarely more than a few hundred in a year, even in London. Even small absolute changes can seem significant in those circumstances, especially when they are expressed as percentages. It has also been pointed out that if the ratio of indictments to offenses was as low in the early modern period as both contemporaries and historians assume it to have been, a small change in prosecutors' determination to press charges would show more effect on the level of indictments than a much larger shift in the behavior of offenders (King 1984: 27–43).

4. The most recent estimate places the population of the City at about 94,000 in 1700, and of the metropolis as a whole at 490,000 (Finlay and Shearer 1986: 39, 42–49).

5. For the courts of the metropolis and the structure of the Old Bailey sessions, see Beattie 1988: 216–18.

6. The distinction between petty and grand larceny (thefts of a shilling or more) was very significant indeed. Grand larcenies were felonies that in some circumstances might have been capital offenses, though by this period they were almost always punished in some other way. Petty larceny was a noncapital felony and had its own distinct punishment: whipping, usually in public. For the history of the punishment of grand larceny, including the matter of benefit of clergy which is central to it, see Beattie 1986: 141–48.

7. It is difficult to get an accurate count of such cases because they were dealt with entirely informally by the magistrates. The lord mayor's practice as a magistrate is however revealed in his "Charge Book" (in the Corporation of London Record Office), which records the business conducted at his daily sittings at the Guildhall. These records are not complete for this period, but those that have survived suggest that in 1694, for example, the lord mayor committed at least 25 women and 12 men to Bridewell for a variety of pilfering offenses, none of whom was subsequently indicted and put on trial. Some were described simply as "idle, disorderly, and pilfering" persons, a vague charge that amounted to vagrancy. But most were charged with something much more specific than that: with "pilfering a pewter

basin" from a named victim, for example, or for taking a "small piece of bone lace" or "half a crown" or "stealing a piece of ribbon." In other words, they were charged with offenses for which it would appear they might well have been indicted.

8. For the process by which capital offenses were constructed in England in the early modern period, see Radzinowicz 1948; Beattie 1986: chaps. 3 and 4.

9. On robbery in the early eighteenth century, see Beattie 1986: 148–61; Linebaugh 1991: chap. 6.

10. The character of simple larcenies is not disclosed in the indictments—which merely charge that something of a certain value has been stolen and taken away. But the nature of the theft can be learned from the depositions taken by the magistrate and occasionally in printed trial accounts. The depositions that survive are included among the manuscripts relating to the Old Bailey in the Corporation of London Record Office. Brief printed accounts of trials in London were published in this period in a series that was popularly known as the *Sessions Papers*. Few of these have survived from before 1714, but they are complete from that date on. For their character and value, see Langbein 1978; 1983.

11. For the development of shops, particularly in the second half of the century, see Hoh-cheung Mui and Mui 1989; and for changing patterns of consumption, see McKendrick et al. 1982.

12. For the view that, despite massive immigration, there was a sufficiently large settled population in most London parishes to maintain a sense of social cohesion, see Boulton 1987a, 1987b: chaps. 9–11.

13. For the effects of war and peace on prosecution levels, see Beattie 1986: chap. 5; Hay 1982.

14. Malcolm Feeley and Deborah Little have also found that women accounted for a high proportion of the felons accused at the Old Bailey in this period. Their data—derived from the printed record of the Old Bailey—show women to have formed between 28 percent and 43 percent of defendants from the late seventeenth century through the eighteenth (Feeley and Little 1991).

15. These calculations are based on the sessions rolls and assize files of Surrey and Sussex for the years in which they are complete—ten years between 1690 and 1720 in each county. For these records, see Beattie 1975.

16. It may well be that the differences in the level of prosecution of women in rural and urban environments reflect in part differences in the availability of courts. Peter King has shown that in towns in Essex that had their own quarter sessions, women were prosecuted at a much higher rate than in urban centers without their own local courts—i.e., in which prosecutors had to take cases to the county courts. This suggests that victims were much more likely to go to the trouble and expense of complaining to the authorities when a court was near at hand than when a prosecution would involve them in a long journey and possibly a long stay away from home; and that since women were more likely to be accused of the most minor forms of property crime, they were less likely than men to be proceeded against in a rural parish or in a town without its own court. That seems entirely plausible, though it is not likely in itself to explain the exceptionally high level of prosecution of women in London. Even in the Essex towns with their own sessions, women ac-

counted for no more than 31 percent of the accused (King 1984: 141–46). Evidence for a high level of prosecutions against women in urban settings in this period is also provided by a study of Leiden, in which women accounted for 47 percent of property charges in the period 1678 to 1794 (Kloek 1990).

17. A preliminary investigation suggests that this level of women's involvement as accused at the Old Bailey may have been higher than that experienced earlier in the century. In four years checked at random between 1665 and 1684, the proportion of women among accused felons from the City of London at the Old Bailey ranged between 21 percent and 43 percent. This supports the notion that a relatively high level of female indictment was an urban phenomenon, but that the levels reached in the 1690s and early eighteenth century were unusual, even in London.

18. For a discussion of the effects of war and other possible distortions on the gender distribution of defendants at the Old Bailey in the eighteenth century, see Feeley and Little 1991: 738–40.

19. For the range of women's work in this period, see Earle 1989: 339–41. The median stay of domestic servants in one post in Earle's sample was one year; many stayed less than six months (Earle 1989: 339); and for servants later in the century, see Kent 1989: 111–28.

20. For the particular difficulties of single women in London, see George 1964 [1925]: 159, 165, 172, 207.

21. This figure is based on the Old Bailey records for the two years 1694 and 1704 in which a total of 162 women were indicted for property offenses from the City of London. Of these, 80 percent were identified as spinsters; 16 percent as married; 3 percent as widows. These figures can only be regarded as approximate, since the identification of a woman's marital status in the indictment is not entirely trustworthy. Women who reported themselves as married or who were thought to be married were generally indicted as "AB, spinster, otherwise known as AB, wife of CB." This ambiguous designation almost certainly reflects a concern in the court with the rule that forbade the conviction of a married woman for a felony committed with her husband unless it could be shown that she instigated the offense and did not simply follow his lead. Whether a woman accused of a felony was in fact married or not might thus become an important issue, and the double designation left open the possibility that if marital status were raised as a defense that point could be tried in court. (See on this, Wiener 1976; Baker 1977; and especially Edwards 1977, whose lead I have followed here.) I have looked at other court documents—depositions, examinations, and recognizances in particular—in an attempt to verify the marital status of accused women. For the most part, women indicted as both spinster and wife were indeed married, and I have so taken them here. And, while at least one woman charged as a spinster was said in a deposition to have been married, I have counted the spinsters as single women. It is of course possible that many of the women identified as spinsters were in common-law relationships. Clearly, too much credence should not be given to the precise proportions reported above. But the broad picture they reveal seems right.

Chapter 7

The data in this chapter were made available by the Inter-University Consortium for Political and Social Research. I thank Robin S. Stryker, Ross L. Matsueda, Sandra Wong, and Charles Mueller for helpful comments and Kathy Anderson for her careful and capable research assistance.

1. Interestingly, these assumptions suggest gender differences across all categories of law violation but smaller class differences when all forms of delinquency are summed and treated as a composite variable, consistent with findings from much research (see Tittle and Meier 1990).

2. This work focuses exclusively on black-white differences in offending. While minority groups other than African-Americans are overrepresented in crime statistics, treatment of the joint influence of other racial statuses and gender is beyond the scope of this chapter.

3. Elliott and Ageton (1980) report that blacks are not disproportionately involved in predatory crimes against persons, including sexual assault, aggravated assault, simple assault, and robbery. Yet, since these events are relatively rare occurrences and the number of blacks in their sample is modest, Elliott and Ageton may be unable to detect a pattern in the sample that does exist in the population. The finding of greater involvement in violence by numerous studies using victimization and official data suggest that this indeed may be the case (e.g. Hindelang 1978; Tracy et al. 1990).

4. Hindelang et al. (1981) report that the validity scores of self-reported delinquency are somewhat lower for blacks than for whites. This difference seems to be largely the result of underreporting among blacks of more serious offenses, including violent delinquency, rather than severe underreporting of common delinquency (p. 178).

5. This is not meant to convey the image of males as violent and females as nonviolent, which as Simpson (1991: 125) points out, ignores statistics on black female crime. Rather, these statements mean only that the *likelihood* of violence is greater among marginalized males than females.

6. Moreover, these gender and racial differences in definitions of situations serve to recreate existing inequalities. Although this paper does not focus explicitly on the role of individuals in reproducing the broader social organization, our interactionist theory of delinquency assumes that this is an important part of the process. This argument must be addressed in future work.

7. The stratified sampling procedure was as follows: First, 74 geographical areas in the United States were selected, including the 12 largest metropolitan areas and representative areas from all regions of the country (following the procedure used by the University of Michigan's Survey Research Center in its nationwide interview studies). Second, a probability sample of high schools within each geographical area was selected such that the chance of a school's being sampled was proportional to the size of its senior class. Third, up to 400 senior students were sampled within each school. Bachman and his colleagues note that completed questionnaires were

obtained from 75 percent to 83 percent of all students sampled. The major reason for nonresponse was absenteeism. The investigators determined that the bias in estimates introduced due to absenteeism was quite small, however (Bachman et al. 1990b: x). These data are representative, therefore, of in-school seniors in the United States in 1988 (Bachman et al. 1990b). While the theoretical perspective emphasizes the role of the school in motivating delinquency, the omission of youths who are not in school may introduce bias in the parameter estimates. Unfortunately, the Monitoring the Future sampling frame does not allow for controlling the effects of sample selection bias.

8. Interestingly, most empirical research has assessed only hypotheses about differences in levels of controls or motivations and has not considered that the magnitudes of the effects of these factors may vary with gender (e.g., Jensen and Eve 1976; Hagan et al. 1985, 1987). Some studies have produced evidence of gender differences in the magnitudes of effects (e.g., Canter 1982; Cernkovich and Giordano 1987). Nevertheless, these findings seem to have not been adequately incorporated into our theorizing about crime and gender, which continues to focus on differences in levels of theoretical constructs and assumes that, beyond this, the process leading to delinquency is invariant across gender.

9. Gender ideologies encompass a variety of beliefs about the nature, characteristics, obligations, and roles of females and males. The construct incorporated in this model captures only a narrow slice of gender ideologies, specifically, those pertaining to whether it is desirable for married women and mothers to work outside the home. Unfortunately, data on other critical dimensions of gender ideologies are not available from Form 2 of the Monitoring the Future survey.

10. This statement is based on a comparison of standardized parameter estimates within each gender. The standardized estimates of the effects of definitions favorable to risk-taking on school deviance are .39 for females and .43 for males. The comparable estimates for the effects of definitions on theft are .21 for females and .30 for males. The standardized estimates of the effects of definitions on drug use are .19 for females and .19 for males, and the estimates of the effects of definitions on violence are .22 for females and .24 for males.

11. Nevertheless, this does not explain the finding that among females, those who work more hours a week are actually *more* likely to steal (Table 7.1, column 6), or the finding that for both genders, working more hours and having more spending money each *increases* the likelihood of school deviance, violence, and drug use (rows 7–10). One interpretation of these findings is that the resource constructs actually capture a portion of variability in social-class stratification not accounted for by including father's education in the model. Consistent with power-control theory, this would suggest that youths from more advantaged backgrounds are more likely to become involved in minor law violation. Another possible interpretation of the relationship between work and delinquency is that youths with jobs simply have more opportunities to break the law. They may experience opportunities to steal on the job (Daly 1989), encounter conflicts on the job that result in violence, have more money to purchase drugs and perhaps even more reason to

engage in school deviance, if by comparison to the work environment the school seems to unjustly restrict their autonomy.

12. When the female equation is estimated using the male mean or grand mean as a predictor, the predicted value for female school deviance is larger than that for male school deviance. Similarly, when the male equation is estimated at the female mean, the predicted value for male school deviance is less than that for female school deviance. The predicted values for school deviance are listed below:

1. evaluated at the female mean	females = 1.66	males = 1.57
2. evaluated at the male mean	females = 1.79	males = 1.72
3. evaluated at the grand mean	females = 1.72	males = 1.66

13. While Hindelang et al. (1981) report that the validity scores of self-reported delinquency are somewhat lower for blacks than for whites, they argue that the validity scores for blacks are acceptable. Nevertheless, their research suggests that the negative impact of race on delinquency in the current study may reflect some underreporting by blacks. If underreporting were substantial in the case of violent delinquency, however, this would mean that the large positive effect of race on male violence is a conservative estimate.

Chapter 8

1. The issue of gender inequality and the battering of women by husbands and other intimates has received considerable attention in the professional literature during the past two decades. To a lesser extent, criminologists and feminist scholars have also devoted attention to the crimes of incest, pornography, and sexual harassment. However, with the exception of a few studies of rape, we have not been able to locate empirical analyses that examine the relationship between variation in levels of gender inequality and rates of violence against women.

2. To illustrate, 1990 FBI figures show that 78 percent of murder victims were males. Similarly, for 1980 (the year considered in this analysis) 77 percent and 23 percent of homicide victims were male and female, respectively. For homicide offending the sex ratio is even more uneven. The vast majority of persons arrested for murder (i.e., offenders) in 1980 (87 percent) and 1990 (90 percent) were male.

3. Baron and Straus's 1987 analysis was also reported in a 1989 book, *Four Theories of Rape in American Society: A State Level Analysis*. Because the two analyses are identical, there is no need to discuss the 1989 work here. We do note, however, that even in this larger work, Baron and Straus do not attempt to reconcile the conflicting results of the 1984 and 1987 investigations.

4. Browne and Williams (1989) examine, for states, the relationship between the rate of female-perpetrated mate killings and the availability of legal and extralegal resources for abused women for the periods 1976–1979 to 1980–1984. The analysis is based upon the observations that (1) a significant proportion of women who kill their mates are victims of battering; (2) the resources available to battered women increased significantly over the 1976 to 1984 period; but (3) the availability of such

resources varied considerably from state to state. Their expectation was that rates of female-perpetrated mate killings would be highest, over time and cross-sectionally, for states that provide fewer legal and extralegal resources for women seeking escape from abusive partners. Contrary to expectations, Browne and Williams found a chance-only association between the rates of female mate killing and a composite index measuring the level of state legislation available to battered women. As predicted, however, a "resources-for-abused-women index" proved to be a significant predictor of these types of killing, both in terms of rate reductions from 1976–1979 to 1980–1984, and variation in rates across jurisdictions. Browne and Williams conclude that legal and nonlegal interventions can provide nonviolent alternatives to female victims of male partner abuse.

5. For its Supplementary Homicide Reports (SHR), the FBI codes murders and nonnegligent manslaughters into 25 crime circumstance categories, and 29 victim-offender relationship categories. In this analysis we examine only the more common types of female killing. Of the circumstance categories, only felony murders and argument-related killings have large enough frequencies (n = 100 or more) to be considered here. Similarly, we only consider female homicides for the five noted victim-offender categories that have at least 100 killings.

6. We replicated the analysis to follow for the sample of cities where the UCR and SHR homicide counts were identical for 1980 (n = 96). The results of the analysis for this smaller sample are identical to those for our larger sample of 138 cities. Therefore, to extend degrees of freedom we chose to consider the larger sample.

7. To control for possible yearly fluctuations in homicide rates, we considered examining female homicides for a three-year period (1979–1981) rather than just for 1980; but we ruled out this possibility because of missing data problems for 1979 and 1981. Significantly fewer large cities participated in the SHR program in 1979; and for "reporting" cities, the level of missing crime circumstance data is higher for 1981 than for 1980. In addition, for 1980, census data are available for the predictor and control variables.

8. For example, the 1990 UCR show that of single victim–single offender killings involving males and females, women were more than twice as likely to be homicide victims (67.5 percent) than offenders (32.5 percent).

Chapter 9

Research on this topic was supported by an Andrew W. Mellon Grant from the Western European Area Studies Center at the University of Minnesota. U. Ewald (Berlin) gave valuable comments on an earlier draft. J. Oreskovich assisted in the difficult search for empirical information. G. Olmscheid also identified hidden sources. K. Gönczöl (Budapest), K. Kulcsár (Ottawa), I. Szelenyi (UCLA), and D. Galarraga and K. Rose (Justice Statistics Clearinghouse, U.S. Department of Justice, Bureau of Justice Statistics) provided helpful advice, references, and data. I thank all of these individuals and institutions for their support.

1. For some exceptions see Collins and Waller 1991.

2. I leave out Yugoslavia as a special case.

3. It is surprising and worth speculation, though not my topic, that research on these processes emerges only hesitantly, especially in the United States.

4. The choice of adaptation by innovation can, of course, be understood only in relation to the other alternative strategies. Groups and individuals neglect those strategies when they choose crime to manage the strain to which they are exposed.

5. The developments in Eastern Europe also serve as a reminder that, in the United States, solutions to the crime problem will hardly be achieved through the manipulation of aspects of the criminal justice system but only through basic social change.

6. In addition, we are reminded that the definitions of dominant groups are not accepted by major groups in society when perceptions of justice diverge too dramatically between dominant and subordinate groups. Definitions of crime may then become real in their consequences in the sense of punishment but not in the perception of the majority of the population.

7. One of the probably last books propagating communist Soviet law is Alexeyev's *Socialism and Law: Law in Society* (1990, especially pp. 95–103). On the criminal-law control of "political offenses" for the stabilization of party dominance, see the collection of documents in Matthews (1989: 81–127). See also Berman and Quigley (1969) for a good collection of basic laws on the structure of the Soviet state.

8. Unger mentions undesired outcomes of market processes, concentrations of private power, and the vicissitudes of class struggle resulting in needs of administrations and courts for ad hoc balancing of interests that often does not fit general rules (Unger 1976: 192–223).

9. On the Soviet judiciary, see Baradat (1989: 160–73).

10. Nonet and Selznick (1978) praise reflective (substantive-rational) law as superior to autonomous (formal-rational) law. Yet they also point to the dangers that reflective law is relatively unstable and could be misused as repressive law. It remains a challenge to apply the legal and organizational dimensions developed by Nonet and Selznick to the concept of socialist law.

11. First studies on the former East Germany are now being conducted by C. Pfeiffer, P. Wetzels, and W. Bielsky (Criminological Research Institute of Lower Saxony, Hannover); H. Kury (Max Planck Institute for Foreign and Comparative Criminal Law, Freiburg) in cooperation with H. Kräupel (University of Jena); and H.J. Kerner and K. Boers (University of Tübingen) in cooperation with K. Sessar (University of Hamburg), U. Ewald, and E. Lautsch (Institute for Criminology, Berlin).

12. Mixed into the statistical measurement of control behavior is, to an unknown degree, the actual level and development of criminal behavior (for important specifications see Archer and Gartner 1984: 29ff).

13. For more detailed information on crime, punishment, and criminology in Poland before the imposition of martial law, see Gaberle and Weigand 1980.

14. During martial law (December 1981 through July 1983), thousands of political activists were imprisoned (Ascherson 1987: 173). After the lifting of martial law,

new provisions were enacted to extend tightened political control. Article 282a of the criminal code, enacted six days after the lifting of martial law, stated: "Whoever undertakes activities with the intent of inciting public disturbance or unrest will be sentenced to up to three years imprisonment" (cited in Lawyers' Committee for Human Rights 1987: 15).

15. Despite the increase of crime rates between 1980 and 1986 by almost 43 percent, the conviction rate grew only slightly during the same period (Biénkowska 1991; on the more punitive shift of criminal courts toward the end of this period, see Marek 1986b and Górny 1987).

16. Walter and Fischer (1988) demonstrate in a comparative study of juvenile delinquency in the cities of Budapest and Hamburg that the difference is probably not as pronounced as crime statistics suggest.

17. The strain on the population was most dramatically demonstrated by the spontaneous mass emigration of East Germans to the West that followed the opening of borders (i.e., before internal economic conditions had changed) (cf. Opp 1993).

18. This does not mean that the security of employment and at least modest living conditions may not also have contributed to relatively low crime rates. At the same time, social inequality was much greater than suggested by official ideology (cf. on Hungary: Kolosi 1988; I. Szelenyi 1983, 1991; S. Szelenyi 1987). Implications of social inequality for juvenile delinquency in the Soviet Union are discussed in Connor (1970, 1972) and Finckenauer (1988).

19. Another argument that comes to mind for the artificiality of the statistical measurements can also be dismissed: that the increased rates are caused by criminal procedures against members of the previously dominant class and their agents. Arrests have so far been rare, significant only as they were directed against leading members of the old regime, but not in terms of numbers.

20. At least part of the increasing property crime rate seems to be due to improved opportunities, partly committed by Western organized crime or by East Europeans hired by Western criminal organizations (see, for example, *New York Times*, June 6, 1991, p. 12, on art theft in East Germany and Czechoslovakia). More research would be needed to identify the quantitative relevance of this factor.

In addition to the following factors, social equality under the old conditions has been vastly exaggerated (I. Szelenyi 1983) and no radical changes of social structure and social inequality have been registered to date (I. Szelenyi 1991). But clear conclusions are difficult to draw since the data are insufficient and much more empirical research is needed on the development of social inequality as well as crime.

21. The following observations concern especially the Soviet Union during the late Gorbachev era. Information on developments after the collapse of communism in the former Soviet Union is not yet available (written in 1991).

22. Hann (1985) discusses the disastrous consequences of highly centralized control of resources for the economic development of the private sector for the case of Polish agriculture.

23. Here again we have to deal with a validity problem of statistical data. We are not certain to what degree emigration rates express changing pressures toward

emigration or changing government policies in granting visas. In the Soviet case the policy changes have certainly contributed considerably to the recent surge in emigration.

24. The related argument can be formulated for Western societies. Formal justice has empirically little chance if concerns of substantive social justice are radically neglected (Savelsberg 1992).

Chapter 10

1. An alternative formulation for organizing the self and the social environment is suggested by Pizzorno (1991). Four modes of achieving order based on coercion or inducement and short- and long-term effects are identified: leviathan, market, discipline, and value integration.

2. The transparent society is treated in G. Marx (1981, 1987, 1988) and elements of the dossier society in Marx and Reichman 1984 and in Laudon 1986.

3. Strictly speaking, this isn't target removal; it is discretion elimination. The possibility for theft remains if an item is simply not rung up, although video cameras are intended to identify and deter such action.

4. See for example, *Time*, Aug. 1, 1988, and Whyte 1985.

5. A related aspect is the increased availability of technical birth control protections. Thus as a first, the city of Cambridge, Mass., passed a law requiring that condom-dispensing machines be placed in public places such as hotels, bars, and movie theaters. In a controversial plan, the superintendent of New York schools has advocated giving out birth control devices in schools. Though of a different order, there is even a patch worn on the upper arm that provides increased testosterone to men who need it.

6. The goal of such public notices is presumably to warn others to stay away from the offender, but they also may be intended to have some deterrent value by humiliating the offender. Advertisements or posters also may increase the likelihood of apprehension if the offender commits another violation; for example, a condition of probation may be that the person stay away from a given area.

7. For a striking example of the class nature of recent efforts to achieve security through architecture and space-age military technology, see Davis's 1990 account of Los Angeles and its future.

8. The unintended consequences of the electronic monitoring movement more generally are considered in R. Corbett and G. Marx (1991).

9. For example, a thief in Mobile, Alabama, was killed in a trap set by a homeowner. The trap consisted of two hunting rifles in separate locations. One pointed down a staircase. The rifle fired when the thief stepped on a wire rigged to the trigger. A neighbor called police when he heard a shot fired and then entered himself; fortunately, the second gun did not fire at him (*New York Times*, Dec. 28, 1989).

10. See, for example, Clarke 1992 and Birkbeck and LaFree 1993.

Chapter 11

1. Consider, for example, that the effective human use of gravity did not depend on the formulation of a science or law or gravity.

2. Forty years later, Aubert's reminder is still necessary: "It is frequently impossible to discover the sociopsychological origins and functions of criminal behavior without insight into the social processes behind the enactment of the corresponding parts of the criminal legislation. . . . The nature of the norms thus legally sanctioned may, for instance, to some extent determine whether the criminals tend to be rebels, psychopaths, or rational profit seekers." (1952 [1977: 168–69])

3. See, for example, Dinitz (1979) and Meier (1980). By the end of the 1970s, prominent spokespersons within the discipline were commonly lamenting its lack of intellectual fervor. Dinitz (1978: 234) pronounced the liberal impulse in criminology and corrections "spent," while Cressey (1978: 177) argued that "the typical modern criminologist is a technical assistant to politicians bent on repressing crime, rather than a scientist seeking valid propositions stated in a causal framework."

4. Cressey's view, cited above, in particular suggests not only that criminological theory often fails to drive public policy in useful directions, but that the politics of policy making may "drive" intellectual work, an especially unfortunate result for both thought and action. None of this, however, is to imply an utter lack of promise in criminological theorizing. Indeed, the recent and provocative contributions of Braithwaite (1989a), Hagan et al. (1989), and Gottfredson and Hirschi (1990) indicate hopeful ferment in the field. But the voices remain distinctive and arguably incompatible, and criminology remains in search of unifying themes.

5. The idea of "fairness" brings to mind the distinction between *inequality* and *inequity*. Not all inequalities are considered inherently inequitable, or unfair. For example, many believe that differential rewards in occupational hierarchies are fundamentally fair in the context of a meritocracy. In general, we tend to consider fair those distributive systems that make *valid* distinctions between *kinds* (whether of merit, contribution, need, etc.). Such judgments are moral in nature and vary across time and place. To illustrate the distinction in the context of criminal justice, notice that we not only consider it fair (even obligatory) that the law scales punishments to crime severity and the offender's past record, but we also often accept as fair differential punishment by jurisdiction *for the same crime*. We do so essentially on Durkheimian grounds regarding the variable degree of offense to the different "collective consciences" of local communities.

I suspect that in much research on crime and law, "inequality" is used when what is really at stake is the moral concern with inequity or unfairness. In this essay, I generally stay with the convention of using the language of inequality, rather than the less familiar language of equity, but mean clearly to imply social judgments of fairness or—rather less salient but still moral in character—*reasonableness*.

6. Larger firms are typically in a better position to make the jobs-saving argument to regulators because they generally operate larger plants than small companies do. As it happens, in the history of water pollution controls in the United

States, only relatively few, economically marginal plants have been closed, arguably in part because of expensive regulations (Yeager 1991: 249).

7. Hagan et al. (1989: chap. 2) have nicely illustrated the other side of "the corporate advantage." Among other things, in their research they found that *corporate* victims were more successful than *individual* victims of crime in obtaining convictions of *individual* offenders, and that the larger the firm, the greater the likelihood of conviction. They interpret these results as suggesting that large corporations enjoy the advantages of formal rationality (e.g., emotional distance, planning) and large resources (e.g., private security), and that therefore, "in Weberian terms, . . . there is an 'elective affinity' between corporate actors and agencies of criminal justice" not shared in by individual victims of crime (1989: 62).

8. Federal Water Pollution Control Act Amendments of 1972, Public Law 92-500; 33 U.S.C. 1251 *et seq*. The law was amended in 1977 (Pub.L. 95-217; 33 U.S.C. 1251 *et seq*. [1982 ed.]), and again in 1987 (Pub.L. 100-4; 33 U.S.C. 1251 *et seq*. [Supp. V 1987]).

9. Pub.L. 92-500, 301.

10. Pub.L. 92-500, 101 [a] [3]; emphasis added.

11. The law authorized EPA to promulgate toxic effluent standards that "shall take into account the toxicity of the pollutant, its persistence, degradability, the usual or potential presence of the affected organisms in any waters, the importance of the affected organisms and the nature and extent of the effect of the toxic pollutant on such organisms," 307 [a] [2]. Unlike the statements for establishing BPT and BAT, no mention at all is made of the costs of control (see Schroeder 1983: 27–28).

12. Pub.L. 92-500, 307 [a] [1, 2, 4, 5, 6].

13. Pub.L. 92-500, 309. As discussed below, the penalties were strengthened in the 1987 amendments to the law; Pub.L. 100-4, 33 U.S.C. 1251 et seq. Criminal penalties are set out at 33 U.S.C. 1319[c][1,2,3], civil penalties at 33 U.S.C. 1319[d], and administrative penalties at 33 U.S.C. 1319[g].

14. Pub.L. 92-500, 505.

15. Like the Clean Water Act, the Clean Air Act underwent major changes in amendments passed during the 1970s. The two major sets of amendments were the Clean Air Act Amendments of 1970, Pub.L. 91-604, 84 Stat. 1676; and the Clean Air Act Amendments of 1977, Pub.L. 95-95, 91 Stat. 685, 42 U.S.C. 7401, *et seq*.

16. See *Natural Resources Defense Council v. EPA*, 537 F.2d 642 (2nd Cir. 1976); *E.I. duPont de Nemours & Co. v. Train*, 430 U.S. 112, 128 (1977).

17. See *Hooker Chemicals & Plastics Corp. v. Train*, 537 F.2d 620 (2nd Cir. 1976); *American Petroleum Institute v. EPA*, 540 F.2d 1023 (10th Cir. 1976).

18. See, e.g., *Republic Steel Corp. v. Costle*, 621 F.2d 797 (6th Cir. 1980); *Alabama Power Co. v. Costle*, 13 ERC 1993, 2032 (D.C. Cir. 1979); *Mission Industries, Inc. v. EPA*, 547 F.2d 123 (1st Cir. 1976).

19. Interview, 1981.

20. The congressional study of imbalances in public participation was based on information on rule making and adjudicatory proceedings from eight regulatory agencies, overseeing both economic and social regulation: Federal Communications Commission, Federal Power Commission, Federal Trade Commis-

sion, Interstate Commerce Commission, Civil Aeronautics Board, Food and Drug Administration, Nuclear Regulatory Commission, and Securities and Exchange Commission. For no apparent reason other than simple sampling and resource constraints, this aspect of the study did not include EPA. Nonetheless, the report clearly suggests that the findings of imbalances in participation were generalizable across federal agencies of all sorts.

21. For an extended discussion of these and related issues in toxics regulation under the Clean Water Act, see Yeager 1991: 216–50.

22. Studies released by the federal government in 1989 revealed for the first time the massive amounts of toxics being released into the environment (Yeager 1991: 245–46). EPA reported in April 1989 that American industry had released or disposed of at least 22.5 billion pounds of hazardous substances in 1987, including 9.7 billion pounds of toxics released into surface waters, 3.2 billion pounds injected into underground wells, 2.7 billion pounds into landfills, and 2.7 billion pounds into the air. See also the articles by Philip Shabecoff in the *New York Times*: "Industrial Pollution Called Startling" (Apr. 13, 1989, p. D21); "U.S. Pinpoints Waterways Polluted by Toxic Chemicals" (June 14, 1989, p. A24).

23. See, for example, U.S. House of Representatives (1977: 19). Evidence from related regulatory arenas also suggests that data on industrial chemicals are often unreliable because of either inadequate and falsified industry tests, inadequate agency oversight of such chemicals and private sector testing, or a combination of the two. Such problems have been identified, for example, in connection with the federal Food and Drug Administration's new drug approval process, EPA's testing of pesticide ingredients, and the National Cancer Institute's cancer testing system (see, e.g., Schneider 1985).

24. Pub.L. 100-4, 304 [1].

25. See *Natural Resources Defense Council v. Train* (D.D.C. 1976; 8 ERC 2120). In this 1976 case, the federal district court for the District of Columbia approved a consent decree (known as the Flannery Decree after the presiding judge) establishing the new regulatory framework and timetables for compliance for the control of toxic water pollution. The court ordered that the regulations be finalized no later than the end of 1979, with industry to achieve compliance no later than June 30, 1983. But because of factors such as those already described, many additional extensions became necessary, and the decree was modified by the court in 1979, 1982, 1983, 1984 (twice), 1985, 1986, and 1987 (Yeager 1991: 222).

26. Pub.L. 95-217; see 33 U.S.C. 1251 *et seq.* (1982 ed.).

27. This sort of result is connected to a practical problem in the core logic of the 1972 amendments. The risk in the two-stage sequence of controls—from BPT to BAT shortly thereafter—was that many companies would invest heavily to implement first-stage controls that would prove incompatible with the more advanced controls (BAT) for toxics. When this occurred, it strengthened industry's argument that the latter were therefore not achievable economically (see, e.g., Tripp 1977). Interestingly, this problem had been precisely recognized in advance of the law's passage by members of the House of Representatives, but their arguments for a more effective system of controls went unheeded (Yeager 1991: 158–59).

28. See the discussion in Yeager (1991), especially at chap. 3 and pp. 225–26.

29. See generally the discussion in Yeager (1991), chaps. 6 and 8.

30. Section 309 [a] [3] of the 1972 amendments simply states that, upon a finding of any violation of the law or of a discharge permit, the EPA administrator "*shall* issue an order requiring such person to comply, . . . or he *shall* bring a civil action" (emphasis added). The legislative history of the act is also unusually clear that enforcement was to be mandatory. See Yeager (1991: 186–87).

31. *Sierra Club v. Train*, 557 F. 2d 485, 489 (5th Cir. 1977).

32. EPA Headquarters Enforcement Memorandum, "Compliance Monitoring, Administrative Orders, and Court Actions Under Section 309 of the Federal Water Pollution Control Act Amendments of 1972," March 20, 1974 (emphasis in the original).

33. Statement of Richard E. Drooyan, chief assistant U.S. attorney, Los Angeles, in *Proceeding of Symposium 87: White Collar/Institutional Crime: Its Measurement and Analysis* (Sacramento: California Department of Justice, Bureau of Criminal Statistics and Special Services, 1988), p. 69.

34. EPA Headquarters Enforcement Memorandum, regarding correspondence between EPA and the Justice Department on problems in enforcement, December 3, 1976.

35. Ibid.

36. Conversation with author, EPA Headquarters, spring 1978.

Chapter 12

This chapter is in part stimulated by discussions of my earlier work with Ngaire Naffine, the late June Fielding, and Betsy Stanko. Unfortunately, I have taken only pathetically small steps down the three paths suggested by these scholars. My thanks to Ross Homel, Andrew Hopkins, Toni Makkai, David Nelkin, and Philip Pettit for extremely helpful comments on an earlier draft of this work.

1. For the philosophers who are shocked by such a casual definitional gestalt, here is a formal definition. A person enjoys full dominion, we say, if and only if:

> a. She enjoys no less a prospect of liberty than is available to other citizens.
>
> b. It is common knowledge among citizens that this condition obtains, so that she and nearly everyone else knows that she enjoys the prospect mentioned; she and nearly everyone else knows that the others generally know this too, and so on.
>
> c. She enjoys no less a prospect of liberty than the best that is compatible with the same prospect for all citizens (Braithwaite and Pettit 1990, 64–65).

2. Needless to say, I am not impressed by the theoretical or empirical bite of Adler's (1975) arguments on the effect of the women's movement in causing the rise of a new female criminal (see Adler 1975; Box and Hale 1983; Scutt 1980; Smart 1979; Steffensmeier and Steffensmeier 1980).

3. It should also be noted that this social formation accounts for Australia's other major violence problem, beyond domestic violence. This is male-on-male violence,

macho responses to insult or humiliation, mostly by young working-class males, in the context of drinking at pubs, clubs, and other entertainment venues (Tomsen et al. 1991).

4. Purists who claim that statism does not exist in the English language can read it as a translation from the French (*étatisme*), a language more accommodating to republican writing.

5. According to republican criminology, among the many things that are critical to know, two of the distinctively republican things are: (1) Is it true that when we come to view a certain type of crime as shameful, we are less likely to engage in it? (2) Is it true that an effect of the campaigning of social movements has been to make some of the most serious types of crime more shameful?

6. The high point of this moral crusade was the extraordinary event of a National Tax Summit. Business, union, and community leaders were invited to the chamber of parliament to address the prime minister on what needed to be done to return to a fair tax system that citizens would respect.

7. As Gusfield says of the nineteenth-century heyday of the American temperance movement, "Sobriety was virtuous and in a community dominated by middle-class Protestants, necessary to social acceptance and to self-esteem." In contrast, by the mid-twentieth century or earlier, "Abstinence has lost much of its ability to confer prestige and esteem" (Gusfield 1963: 4).

8. A fully fleshed out theory of this sort would have to give an account of how entrepreneurs can create new waves of drug use until an effective community reaction takes hold—marijuana in the 1960s, heroin in the 1960s, cocaine in the 1980s, amphetamines and LSD in the 1960s with a resurgence in the 1990s. Does community reaction occur wave by wave, drug by drug? Is there a hopeful new ideological turn in community reaction today, where *all* drugs, tobacco and alcohol included, are being bundled together as harmful things to put into your body? Are parents today who fail to educate their children about the generic undesirability of drugs at risk of being cast as negligent parents? Are smoking parents now vulnerable to community expectations that they have an obligation to confess their own stupidity to their children?

9. The republican commitment also implies support for the crime victims' movement more generally (Braithwaite and Pettit 1990: 91–92). But this is a more difficult question I must leave for another paper.

10. I am grateful to the late June Fielding for suggesting in a seminar that the enforcement pyramid idea might be extended to the domain of crimes against women.

Bibliography

Adler, Freda. 1975. *Sisters in Crime: The Rise of the New Female Criminal*. New York: McGraw-Hill.

Adler, Robert W., and Charles Lord. 1991. "Environmental Crimes: Raising the Stakes." *George Washington Law Review* 59: 781–861.

Ageton, Susan, and Delbert Elliott. 1974. "The Effects of Legal Processing on Self-Concept." *Social Problems* 22: 87–100.

Akers, Ronald. 1985. *Deviant Behavior: A Social Learning Approach*. 3d ed. Belmont, CA: Wadsworth.

Alder, Christine. 1985. "Theories of Female Delinquency." In A. Borowski and J. M. Murray, eds., *Juvenile Delinquency in Australia*. North Ryde, Australia: Methuen.

Alexeyev, Sergei. 1990. *Socialism and Law: Law in Society*. Moscow: Progress Publishers.

Alford, Robert R., and Roger Friedland. 1985. *Powers of Theory: Capitalism, the State, and Democracy*. New York: Cambridge University Press.

Allan, Emilie, and Darrell Steffensmeier. 1989. "Youth, Underemployment, and Property Crime: Differential Effects of Job Availability and Job Quality on Juvenile and Young Adult Arrest Rates." *American Sociological Review* 54: 107–23.

Allen, Judith. 1986. "Desperately Seeking Solutions: Changing Battered Women's Options Since 1880." In Suzanne E. Hatty, ed., *National Conference on Domestic Violence*. Vol. 1. Australian Institute of Criminology Seminar Proceeding No. 12, Canberra.

Alschuler, Albert. 1979. "Plea Bargaining and Its History." *Law & Society Review* 13: 211–45.

Anderson, E. 1978. *A Place on the Corner*. Chicago: University of Chicago Press.

———. 1990. *Streetwise: Race, Class and Change in an Urban Community*. Chicago: University of Chicago Press.

Archer, Dane, and Rosemary Gartner. 1984. *Violence and Crime in Cross-National Perspective*. New Haven, CT: Yale University Press.

Ascherson, Neal. 1987. *The Struggles for Poland*. London: M. Joseph.

Aubert, Vilhelm. 1952. "White-Collar Crime and Social Structure." *American Journal of Sociology* 58 (November): 263–71. Reprinted in G. Geis and R.F. Meier, eds., *White-Collar Crime: Offenses in Business, Politics, and the Professions*, pp. 168–79. New York: The Free Press, 1977.

Auletta, K. 1983. *The Underclass*. New York: Vintage.

Ayres, Ian, and John Braithwaite. 1992. *Responsive Regulation Transcending the Deregulation Debate*. New York: Oxford University Press.

Bachman, Jerald G. 1970. *Youth in Transition*, Vol. 2: *The Impact of Family Background and Intelligence on Tenth Grade Boys*. Ann Arbor, MI: Institute for Social Research.

Bachman et al. 1988. [Bachman, Jerald G., Lloyd D. Johnston, Patrick M. O'Malley, and Ronald H. Humphrey]. "Explaining the Recent Decline in Marijuana Use Differentiating the Effects of Perceived Risks, Disapproval, and General Lifestyle Factors." *Journal of Health and Social Behavior* 29: 92–112.

———. 1990a. [Bachman, Jerald G., Lloyd D. Johnston, and Patrick M. O'Malley]. "Explaining the Recent Decline in Cocaine Use Among Adults: Further Evidence that Perceived Risks and Disapproval Lead to Reduced Drug Use." *Journal of Health and Social Behavior* 31: 173–84.

———. 1990b. [Bachman, Jerald G., Lloyd D. Johnston, and Patrick M. O'Malley]. *Monitoring the Future: A Continuing Study of the Lifestyles and Values of Youth, 1988*. Ann Arbor, MI: Institute for Social Research.

Bailey, William C. 1984. "Poverty, Inequality and City Homicide Rates: Some Not So Unexpected Findings." *Criminology* 22: 531–50.

Baker, J. H. 1977. "Male and Married Spinsters." *American Journal of Legal History* 21: 255–59.

Balbus, Isaac D. 1973. *The Dialectics of Legal Repression: Black Rebels Before the American Criminal Courts*. New York: Russell Sage Foundation.

Banfield, Edward C. 1968. *The Unheavenly City*. Boston: Little, Brown.

Baradat, Leon P. 1989. *Soviet Political Society*. Englewood Cliffs, NJ: Prentice-Hall.

Baron, Larry, and Murray A. Straus. 1984. "Sexual Stratification, Pornography, and Rape in the United States." In N. M. Malamuth and E. Donnerstein, eds., *Pornography and Sexual Aggression*, pp. 185–209. New York: Academic Press.

———. 1987. "Four Theories of Rape: A Macrosociological Analysis." *Social Problems* 34: 467–89.

———. 1989. *Four Theories of Rape in American Society: A State-Level Analysis*. New Haven, CT: Yale University Press.

Bartnicki, S. P. 1989. "Crime in Poland: Trends, Regional Patterns, and Neighborhood Awareness." In David J. Evans and David T. Herbert, eds., *The Geography of Crime*, pp. 135–60. London: Routledge.

Beattie, J. M. 1975. "The Criminality of Women in Eighteenth-Century England." *Journal of Social History* 8, no. 4: 80–116.

———. 1981. "Judicial Records and the Measurement of Crime in Eighteenth-Century England." In Louis A. Knafla, ed., *Crime and Criminal Justice in Europe and Canada*. Waterloo, ON: Wilfrid Laurier Press.

———. 1986. *Crime and the Courts in England, 1600–1800*. Princeton, NJ: Princeton University Press.

———. 1988. "London Juries in the 1690s." In J. S. Cockburn and Thomas A. Green, eds., *Twelve Good Men and True: The Criminal Trial Jury in England, 1200–1800*. Princeton, NJ: Princeton University Press.

———. 1992. "London, Crime and the Making of the 'Bloody Code,' 1689–1718." In Timothy Hitchcock and Robert Shoemaker, eds., *'Stilling the Grumbling Hive': The Response to Social and Economic Problems in England, 1688–1750*. Gloucester: Allan Sutton.

Beier, A. L. 1986. "Engine of Manufacture: The Trades of London." In A. L. Beier and Roger Finlay, eds., *London 1500–1700: The Making of the Metropolis*. London: Longman.

Beier, A. L., and Roger Finlay. 1986. "The Significance of the Metropolis." In A. L. Beier and Roger Finlay, eds., *London 1500–1700: The Making of the Metropolis*. London: Longman.

Beirne, Piers, and James Messerschmidt. 1991. *Criminology*. New York: Harcourt Brace Jovanovich.

Bell, P. J., and R. A. Davis. 1991. *Time Series: Theory and Methods*, 2d ed. New York: Springer-Verlag.

Benson, Michael. 1990. "Emotions and Adjudication: A Study of Status Degradation Among White-Collar Criminals." Unpublished paper, Department of Sociology, University of Tennessee.

Bequai, August. 1977. "White-Collar Plea Bargaining." *Trial Magazine* (July): 38–41.

Beresford, Q. 1984. "Drinkers and the Anti-Drink Movement in Sydney, 1870–1930." Ph.D. diss., Australian National University.

Berger et al. 1990. [Berger, Dale E., John R. Snortum, Ross J. Homel, Ragnar Hauge, and Wendy Loxley]. "Deterrence and Prevention of Alcohol-Impaired Driving in Australia, the United States and Norway." *Justice Quarterly* 7: 453–65.

Berk et al. 1980. [Berk, R. A., K. J. Lenihan, and P. H. Rossi]. "Crime and Poverty: Some Experimental Evidence from Ex-Offenders." *American Sociological Review* 45: 766–86.

Berman, Harold J., and John B. Quigley, Jr., eds. 1969. *Basic Laws on the Structure of the Soviet State*. Cambridge, MA: Harvard University Press.

Bernstein, Marver H. 1955. *Regulating Business by Independent Commission*. Princeton, NJ: Princeton University Press.

Bickford, A., and D. Massey. 1991. "Segregation in the Second Ghetto: Racial and Ethnic Segregation in American Public Housing, 1977." *Social Forces* 69: 1011–36.

Bielby, William T. 1986. "Arbitrary Metrics in Multiple Indicator Models of Latent Variables." *Sociological Methods and Research* 15: 3–23.

Biénkowska, Ewa. 1991. "Crime in Eastern Europe." In Frances Heidensohn and Martin Farrell, eds., *Crime in Europe*, pp. 43–54. London: Routledge.

Birkbeck, Christopher, and Gary LaFree. 1993. "The Situational Analysis of Crime and Deviance." *Annual Review of Sociology* 19: 113–38.

Black, Donald. 1970. "Police Control of Juveniles." *American Sociological Review* 35: 63–77.

———. 1983. "Crime as Social Control." *American Sociological Review* 48: 34–45.

Black, Donald, and Albert J. Reiss. 1967. "Patterns of Behavior in Police-Citizen Transactions." *Studies in Crime and Law Enforcement in Major Metropolitan Areas, Field Surveys III*, Vol. 2, *President's Commission on Law Enforcement in Major Metropolitan Areas*. Washington, DC: U.S. Government Printing Office.

Blassingame, John. 1977. *The Slave Community*. New York: Oxford University Press.

Blau, Judith R., and Peter M. Blau. 1982. "The Cost of Inequality: Metropolitan Structure and Violent Crime." *American Sociological Review* 47: 114–29.

Blau, Peter M., and Reid M. Golden. 1986. "Metropolitan Structure and Criminal Violence." *The Sociological Quarterly* 27: 15–26.

Blau, Peter M., and Joseph E. Schwartz. 1984. *Crossing Social Circles: Testing a Macrostructural Theory of Intergroup Relations*. Orlando, FL: Academic Press.

Blumberg, Abraham S. 1967. "The Practice of Law as a Confidence Game: Organizational Cooptation of a Profession." *Law & Society Review* 1 (June): 15–39.

Blumer, Herbert. 1969. *Symbolic Interactionism: Perspective and Method*. Englewood Cliffs, NJ: Prentice-Hall.

Blumstein, Alfred, Jacqueline Cohen, and Daniel Nagin. 1978. *Deterrence and Incapacitation: Estimating the Effects of Criminal Sanctions on Crime Rates*. Washington, D.C.: National Academy of Sciences.

Blumstein et al. 1986. [Blumstein, Alfred, Jacqueline Cohen, Julius Roth, and Christy Visher, eds.]. *Criminal Careers and "Career Criminals."* Washington, DC: National Academy Press.

Bollen, Kenneth A. 1989. *Structural Equations with Latent Variables*. New York: Wiley and Sons.

Bonger, Willem A. 1916. *Criminality and Economic Conditions*. Boston: Little, Brown and Company.

———. 1939. *Race and Crime*. Montclair, NJ: Patterson Smith.

Boulton, Jeremy. 1987a. "Neighbourhood Migration in Early Modern London." In Peter Clark and David Souden, eds., *Migration and Society in Early Modern England*. London: Hutchinson.

———. 1987b. *Neighbourhood and Society: A London Suburb in the Seventeenth Century*. Cambridge, Eng.: Cambridge University Press.

Bound, J., and R. Freeman. 1992. "What Went Wrong: The Erosion of Earnings and Employment of Young Black Men in the 1980s." *Quarterly Journal of Economics* 107, no. 1: 201–32.

Box, G. E. P., and G. M. Jenkins. 1976. *Time Series Analysis: Forecasting and Control*. 2d ed. San Francisco: Holden-Day.

Box, Steven, and Chris Hale. 1985. "Liberation and Female Criminality in England and Wales." *British Journal of Criminology* 23: 35–49.

———. 1984. "Liberation/Emancipation, Economic Marginalization, or Less Chivalry." *Criminology* 22: 473–97.

Braithwaite, John. 1979. *Inequality, Crime and Public Policy*. London: Routledge and Kegan Paul.

———. 1984. *Corporate Crime in the Pharmaceutical Industry*. London: Routledge and Kegan Paul.

———. 1985. *To Punish or Persuade: Enforcement of Coal Mine Safety*. Albany: State University of New York Press.

———. 1989a. *Crime, Shame and Reintegration*. Melbourne: Cambridge University Press.

———. 1989b. "Criminological Theory and Organizational Crime." *Justice Quarterly* 6: 333–59.

———. 1991a. "Shame in Western History." Unpublished manuscript, Australian National University.

———. 1991b. "Power, Poverty, White-Collar Crime and the Paradoxes of Criminological Theory." *Australian and New Zealand Journal of Criminology* 24: 40–58.

Braithwaite, John, and Peter Grabosky. 1985. *Occupational Health and Safety Enforcement in Australia*. Canberra: Australian Institute of Criminology.

Braithwaite, John, and Philip Pettit. 1990. *Not Just Deserts: A Republican Theory of Criminal Justice*. Oxford: Oxford University Press.

Breedlove et al. 1977. [Breedlove, R. K., J. W. Kennish, D. M. Sanker, and R. K. Sawtell]. "Domestic Violence and the Police: Kansas City." In *Domestic Violence and the Police: Studies in Detroit and Kansas City*, pp. 22–33. Washington, DC: Police Foundation.

Brewer, John. 1989. *Sinews of Power: War, Money, and the English State, 1688–1783*. New York: Knopf.

Broadhurst, R., and D. Indemaur. 1982. "Crime Seriousness Ratings: The Relationship of Information Accuracy and General Attitudes in Western Australia." *Australian and New Zealand Journal of Criminology* 15: 219.

Brockwell, Peter J., and Richard A. Davis. 1991. *Time Series: Theory and Methods*. 2d ed. New York: Springer-Verlag.

Browne, Angela. 1987. *When Battered Women Kill*. New York: The Free Press.

———. 1990. "Assaults Between Intimate Partners in the United States." Washington, DC: Testimony before the United States Senate, Committee on the Judiciary.

Browne, Angela, and Kirk R. Williams. 1989. "Exploring the Effect of Resource Availability on the Likelihood of Female Perpetrated Homicides." *Law and Society Review* 23: 75–94.

Brownmiller, Susan. 1975. *Against Our Will: Men, Women and Rape*. New York: Simon and Schuster.

Buchholz, Erich. 1987. "Reasons for the Low Rate of Crime in the German Democratic Republic." *Crime and Social Justice* 29: 26–42.

Bundesminister der Justiz. 1991. "Kriminalität in den neuen Bundesländern." *Recht* 3: 40.

Bunyak, Jane R. 1986. "Battered Wives Who Kill: Civil Liability and the Admissibility of Battered Women's Syndrome Testimony." *Law and Inequality* 4: 606–36.

Bureau of Justice Statistics. 1985. "The Prevalence of Imprisonment." *U.S. Department of Justice Special Report*. Washington, DC: Government Printing Office.

Bureau of National Affairs. 1983. "Special Report: Effluent Guidelines Rulemaking Nears End; Litigation, Compliance Extensions Expected." *BNA Environment Reporter: Current Developments* 13: 1629–31.

Burke, Peter J. 1989. "Gender Identity, Sex, and School Performance." *Social Psychology Quarterly* 52: 159–69.

Burke, Peter J., and Judy C. Tully. 1977. "The Measurement of Role/Identity." *Social Forces* 55: 881–97.

Bursik, R. J., Jr. 1988. "Social Disorganization and Theories of Crime and Delinquency: Problems and Prospects." *Criminology* 26: 519–52.

———. 1989. "Political Decision-Making and Ecological Models of Delinquency: Conflict and Consensus." In S. Messner, M. Krohn, and A. Liska, eds., *Theoretical Integration in the Study of Deviance and Crime*. Albany: State University of New York Press.

Buskirk, Elsworth, and Steven Segal. 1989. "The Aging Motor System: Skeletal Muscle Weakness." In W. W. Spirduso and A. M. Eckert, eds., *Physical Activity and Aging*, pp. 19–34. Champaign, IL: Human Kinetics.

Byrne, J., and R. J. Sampson. 1986. "Key Issues in the Social Ecology of Crime." In J. Byrne and R. J. Sampson, eds., *The Social Ecology of Crime*, pp. 1–22. New York: Springer-Verlag.

Cahill, Spencer E. 1980. "Directions for an Interactionist Study of Gender Development." *Symbolic Interaction* 3: 123–38.

Campbell, Anne. 1984. *Girls in the Gang*. New York: Basil Blackwell.

Canter, Rachelle J. 1982. "Family Correlates of Male and Female Delinquency." *Criminology* 20: 149–68.

Cantor, D., and L. E. Cohen. 1980. "Comparing Measures of the Homicide Trends: Methodological and Substantive Differences in the Vital Statistics and Uniform Crime Report Time Series (1933–1975)." *Social Science Research* 9: 121–45.

Cantor, D., and K. C. Land. 1985. "Unemployment and Crime Rates in the Post-World War II United States: A Theoretical and Empirical Analysis." *American Sociological Review* 50: 317–23.

———. 1987. "Unemployment and Crime Rates: A Bivariate Seasonal ARIMA Analysis of Monthly Data, 1969–1985." Revision of a paper presented at the Annual Meeting of the American Society of Criminology, Cincinnati, OH, November 1984. Department of Sociology, Duke University, Durham, NC.

———. 1991. "Exploring Possible Temporal Relationships of Unemployment and Crime: Comment on Hale and Sabbagh." *Journal of Research in Crime and Delinquency* 28: 418–25.

Cappell, C. L., and G. Sykes. 1991. "Prison Commitments, Crime and Unemployment: A Theoretical and Empirical Specification for the U.S., 1933–85." *Journal of Quantitative Criminology* 7: 155–99.

Caro, R. 1974. *The Power Broker: Robert Moses and the Fall of New York*. New York: Vintage Books.

Carroll, Leo, and Pamela Irving Jackson. 1983. "Inequality, Opportunity, and Crime Rates in Central Cities." *Criminology* 21: 170–94.

Carson, W. G. 1975. "Symbolic and Instrumental Dimensions of Early Factory

Legislation: A Case Study in the Social Origins of Criminal Law." In R. Hood, ed., *Crime, Criminology, and Public Policy*. Glencoe, IL: Free Press.

Carson et al. 1990. [Carson, Kit, W. G. Creighton, C. Henenberg, and R. Johnston]. *Victorian Occupational Health and Safety: An Assessment of Law in Transition*. Melbourne: La Trobe University.

Centerwall, Brandon. 1984. "Race, Socioeconomic Status and Domestic Homicide, Atlanta, 1971–2." *American Journal of Public Health* 74: 813–15.

Cernkovich, Stephen A., and Peggy C. Giordano. 1987. "Family Relationships and Delinquency." *Criminology* 25: 295–322.

Chafets, Ze'ev. 1990. *Devil's Night: And Other True Tales of Detroit*. New York: Random House.

Chambliss, William. 1967. "Types of Deviance and Effectiveness of Legal Sanctions." *Wisconsin Law Review*, pp. 703–19.

Chambliss, William J., and Robert B. Seidman. 1971. *Law, Order and Power*. Reading, MA: Addison-Wesley.

Chesney-Lind, Meda. 1973. "Judicial Enforcement of the Female Sex Role: The Family Court and the Female Delinquent." *Issues in Criminology* 8: 51–69.

———. 1987. "Female Offenders: Paternalism Reexamined." In Laura Crites and Winifred Hepperle, eds., *Women, the Courts and Equality*. Beverly Hills, CA: Sage.

Chilton, Roland. 1986. "Age, Sex, Race and Arrest Trends for Twelve of the Nation's Largest Central Cities." In J. Byrne and R. Sampson, eds., *The Social Ecology of Crime: Theory, Research and Public Policy*. New York: Springer-Verlag.

Chilton, Roland, and Susan K. Datesman. 1987. "Gender, Race, and Crime: An Analysis of Urban Arrest Trends, 1960–1980." *Gender and Society* 1: 152–71.

Chilton, Roland, and Jim Galvin. 1985. "Race, Crime and Criminal Justice." *Crime and Delinquency* 31: 3–14.

Chiricos, T. G. 1987. "Rates of Crime and Unemployment: An Analysis of Aggregate Research Evidence." *Social Problems* 34: 187–212.

Cicourel, Aaron. 1968. *The Social Organization of Juvenile Justice*. New York: Wiley and Sons.

Clark, Lorenne M. G., and Debra J. Lewis. 1977. *Rape: The Price of Coercive Sexuality*. Toronto: Women's Educational Press.

Clark, Peter, and David Souden. 1987. *Migration and Society in Early Modern England*. London: Hutchinson.

Clarke, Ronald, ed. 1992. *Situational Crime Prevention: Successful Case Studies*. New York: Harrow and Heston.

Clinard, Marshall B., and Peter C. Yeager. 1980. *Corporate Crime*. New York: The Free Press.

Cloward, Richard, and Lloyd Ohlin. 1960. *Delinquency and Opportunity: A Theory of Delinquent Gangs*. New York: The Free Press.

Cockburn, J. S. 1975. "Early Modern Assize Records as Historical Evidence." *Journal of the Society of Archivists* 5, no. 4: 215–31.

———. 1977. "The Nature and Incidence of Crime in England, 1559–1625: A Preliminary Survey." In J. S. Cockburn, ed., *Crime in England, 1550–1800*. London: Methuen.

Cohen, Albert K. 1955. *Delinquent Boys.* Glencoe, IL: Free Press.

———. 1966. *Deviance and Control*. Englewood Cliffs, NJ: Prentice-Hall.

Cohen, Jerome Alan. 1968. *The Criminal Process in the People's Republic of China*. Cambridge, MA: Harvard University Press.

Cohen, Lawrence E., and Marcus Felson. 1979. "Social Change and Crime Rate Trends: A Routine Activity Approach." *American Sociological Review* 44: 588–608.

Cohen, Stanley. 1985. *Visions of Social Control: Crime, Punishment and Classification*. Cambridge, MA: Polity.

Cole et al. 1987. [Cole, George F., Stanislaw J. Frankowski, and Marc G. Gertz]. *Major Criminal Justice Systems*. Beverly Hills, CA: Sage.

Coleman, James. 1962. *The Adolescent Society.* Glencoe, IL: Free Press.

Coleman et al. 1966. [Coleman, J. S., E. Q. Campbell, C. J. Hobson, J. McPartland, A. M. Mood, F. D. Weinfeld, and R. L. York]. *Equality in Educational Opportunity*. Office of Education, U.S. Department of Health, Education and Welfare. Washington, D.C.: U.S. Government Printing Office.

Coleman, J. W. 1987. "Toward an Integrated Theory of White Collar Crime." *American Journal of Sociology* 93: 406–39.

Collins, Randall, and David Waller. 1991. "What Theories Predicted the State Breakdowns and Revolutions of the Soviet Bloc?" Paper presented at the 86th Annual Meeting of the American Sociological Association, Cincinnati, OH.

Colvin, Mark, and John Pauly. 1983. "A Critique of Criminology: Toward an Integrated Structural-Marxist Theory of Delinquency Production." *American Journal of Sociology* 89: 513–51.

Connor, Walter D. 1970. "Juvenile Delinquency in the USSR: Some Quantitative and Qualitative Indicators." *American Sociological Review* 35: 283–97.

———. 1972. *Deviance in Soviet Society*. New York: Columbia University Press.

Conservation Foundation. 1982. "Water Resources." In *State of the Environment 1982*, pp. 89–144. Washington, DC: Conservation Foundation.

Corbett R., and G. Marx. 1991. "No Soul in the New Machine: Technofallacies in the Electronic Monitoring Movement." *Justice Quarterly* 8, no. 3: 399–414.

Cressey, Donald R. 1978. "Criminological Theory, Social Science, and the Repression of Crime." *Criminology* 16 (August): 171–92.

Crutchfield, Robert D. 1989. "Labor Stratification and Violent Crime." *Social Forces* 68: 489–512.

Crutchfield et al. 1982. [Crutchfield, Robert D., Michael R. Geerken, and Walter R. Gove]. "Crime Rate and Social Integration: The Impact of Metropolitan Mobility." *Criminology* 20: 467–78.

Cullen, Frank, and Karen E. Gilbert. 1982. *Reaffirming Rehabilitation*. Cincinnati: Anderson.

Cullen et al. 1987. [Cullen, Frank T., William J. Maakestaad, and Gray Cavender]. *Corporate Crime Under Attack: The Ford Pinto Case and Beyond*. Cincinnati: Anderson.

Currie, Elliot. 1986. *Confronting Crime*. New York: Pantheon.

Curtis, Lynn A. 1975. *Violence, Race, and Culture*. Lexington, MA: D.C. Heath.

Daley, S., and R. Mieslin. 1988. "New York City, the Landlord: A Decade of Housing Decay." *New York Times*, February 8.

Daly, Kathleen. 1989. "Gender and Varieties of White-Collar Crime." *Criminology* 27: 769–93.

Datesman, S., and F. Scarpitti. 1977. "Unequal Protection for Males and Females in the Juvenile Court." In T. N. Ferdinand, ed., *Juvenile Delinquency: Little Brother Grows Up*. Beverly Hills, CA: Sage.

Davis, M. 1990. *City of Quartz*. New York: Random House.

Dickson, P. G. M. 1967. *The Financial Revolution in England*. London: Longman.

Dinitz, Simon. 1964. *The Symbolic Uses of Politics*. Urbana: University of Illinois Press.

———. 1978. "Nothing Fails Like a Little Success." *Criminology* 16 (August): 225–38.

———. 1979. "Economic Crime." Mimeo.

Duncan et al. 1972. [Duncan, O. D., D. L. Featherman, and B. Duncan]. *Socioeconomic Background and Achievement*. New York: Seminar Press.

Dunstan, Keith. 1974. *Wowsers*. Melbourne: Cassell.

Durkheim, Emile. 1952. *Suicide: A Study in Sociology*. London: Routledge and Kegan Paul.

Earle, Peter. 1989. "The Female Labour Market in London in the Late Seventeenth and Early Eighteenth Centuries." *Economic History Review* 42, no. 3, 2nd ser.: 328–53.

Edelman, J. M. 1964. *The Symbolic Uses of Politics*. Urbana: University of Illinois Press.

Edwards, Valerie C. 1977. "The Case of the Married Spinster: An Alternative Explanation." *American Journal of Legal History* 21: 260–65.

Elias, Norbert. 1978. *The Civilizing Process: The History of Manners*. Trans. Edmund Jephcott. Oxford: Basil Blackwell.

———. 1982. *State Formation and Civilization: The Civilizing Process*. Oxford: Basil Blackwell.

Elliott, Delbert, and Susan Ageton. 1980. "Reconciling Race and Class Differences in Self-Reported and Official Estimates of Delinquency." *American Sociological Review* 45: 95–110.

Ellis, Lee. 1989. *Theories of Rape: Inquiries into the Causes of Sexual Aggression*. New York: Hemisphere.

Ellis, Lee, and Charles Beattie. 1983. "The Feminist Explanation of Rape: An Empirical Test." *Journal of Sex Research* 19: 74–93.

Ellsworth, P. C. 1988. "Unpleasant Facts: The Supreme Court's Response to Empirical Research on Capital Punishment." In K. C. Haas and I. Inciardi, eds., *Challenging Capital Punishment*. Newbury Park, CA: Sage.

England, Ralph W. 1960. "A Theory of Middle Class Juvenile Delinquency." *Canadian Journal of Criminal Law, Criminology and Police Science* 50: 535–40.

England, Paula, and George Farkas. 1986. *Households, Employment, and Gender: A Social, Economic, and Demographic View*. New York: Aldine de Gruyter.

Engle, R. F., and C. W. J. Granger. 1987. "Cointegration and Error Correction: Representation, Estimation and Testing." *Econometrica* 55: 251–76.

Esping-Andersen et al. 1976. [Esping-Andersen, Gösta, Roger Friedland, and Erik Olin Wright]. "Modes of Class Struggle and the Capitalist State." *Kapitalistate* (Summer): 186–220.

Ewald, Uwe. 1989. "Kriminalitätsentwicklung in der DDR und die Notwendigkeit eines neuen Konflikt- und Kriminalitätsverständnisses im modernen Sozialismus." Unpublished manuscript, Berlin.

———. 1991. "The Social Transformation Process in the Former German Democratic Republic with Respect to Crime." Paper presented at the 50th Annual Meetings of the American Society of Criminology, San Francisco.

Ewing, Sally. 1987. "Formal Justice and the Spirit of Capitalism: Max Weber's Sociology of Law." *Law & Society Review* 21, no. 3: 487–512.

Executive Office of the President. 1991. *Economic Report of the President*. Washington, DC: U.S. Government Printing Office.

Fagan et al. 1987. [Fagan, J., F. Piper, and Y. Cheng]. "Contributions of Victimization to Delinquency in Inner Cities." *Journal of Criminal Law and Criminology* 78: 586–613.

Fagot, Beverly I. 1977. "Consequences of Moderate Cross-Gender Behavior in Preschool Children." *Child Development* 48: 902–7.

Farnworth, Margaret, and Michael Leiber. 1989. "Strain Theory Revisited: Economic Goals, Educational Means and Delinquency." *American Sociological Review* 54: 263–74.

Federal Bureau of Investigation. 1991. *Uniform Crime Reports 1990*. Washington, DC: U.S. Government Printing Office.

Feeley, Malcolm. 1979. *The Process Is the Punishment*. New York: Russell Sage Foundation.

Feeley, Malcolm, and Deborah Little. 1991. "The Vanishing Female: The Decline of Women in the Criminal Process, 1687–1912." *Law and Society Review* 25, no. 4: 719–57.

Felson, Marcus. 1983. "Ecology of Crime." In *The Encyclopedia of Crime and Justice*. New York: Macmillan.

Felson, Richard B. 1981a. "Ambiguity and Bias in the Self-Concept." *Social Psychology Quarterly* 44: 64–69.

———. 1981b. "Social Sources of Information in the Development of the Self." *Sociological Quarterly* 22: 69–79.

Ferdinand, Theodore, and Elmer Luchterhand. 1970. "Inner-City Youth, The Police, the Juvenile Court and Justice." *Social Problems* 17: 510–27.

Ferree, Myra Marx, and Beth B. Hess. 1987. "Introduction." In Beth B. Hess and Myra Marx Ferree, eds., *Analyzing Gender*. Beverly Hills, CA: Sage.

Finch, Caleb, and Edward Schneider, eds. 1985. *Handbook of the Biology of Aging*. New York: Van Nostrand Reinhold.

Finckenauer, James O. 1988. "Juvenile Delinquency in the USSR: Social Structural Explanations." *International Journal of Comparative and Applied Criminal Justice* 12: 73–80.

Fingerhut, L. A., and J. C. Kleinman. 1989. *Firearm Mortality Among Children and Youth*. Advance Data from Vital and Health Statistics, National Center for Health Statistics, no. 178.

———. 1990. "International and Interstate Comparisons of Homicide Among Young Males." *Journal of the American Medical Association* 263: 3292–95.

Fingerhut et al. 1991. [Fingerhut, L., J. Kleinman, E. Godfrey, and H. Rosenberg]. "Firearms Mortality Among Children, Youth, and Young Adults 1–34 Years of Age, Trends and Current Status: United States, 1979–88." *Monthly Vital Statistics Report* 39 (11): 1–16.

Finlay, Roger, and Beatrice Shearer. 1986. "Population Growth and Suburban Expansion." In A. L. Beier and Roger Finlay, eds., *London 1500–1700: The Making of the Metropolis*. London: Longman.

Fisher, F. J. 1948. "The Development of London as a Centre of Conspicuous Consumption in the Sixteenth and Seventeenth Centuries." *Transactions of the Royal Historical Society* 30, 4th ser.: 37–50.

———. 1954. "The Development of the London Food Market, 1540–1640." In E. M. Carus-Wilson, ed., *Essays in Economic History*. Vol. 1. London: Arnold.

Flowers, Ronald. 1988. *Minorities and Criminality*. Westport, CT: Greenwood.

Fogelson, R. 1989. *America's Armories*. New York: Harvard University Press.

Freeman, R. B. 1983. "Crime and Unemployment." In J. Q. Wilson, ed., *Crime and Public Policy*, pp. 89–106. San Francisco: ICS Press.

Freeman, Richard. 1991. "Crime and the Economic Status of Disadvantaged Young Men." Paper presented to Conference on Urban Labor Markets and Labor Mobility, Airlie House, Warrenton, VA.

Friedman, Lawrence. 1979. "Plea Bargaining in Historical Perspective." *Law and Society Review* 13, no. 2: 247–60.

Gaberle, Andrzej, and Ewa Weigand. 1980. "Kriminologie und Kriminalitätsentwicklung in Polen." *Monatsschrift für Kriminologie und Strafrechtsreform* 63: 82–97.

Galanter, Marc. 1974. "Why the 'Haves' Come Out Ahead: Speculations on the Limits of Legal Change." *Law & Society Review* 9 (Fall): 95–160.

Garfinkel, Harold. 1967. *Studies in Ethnomethodology*. Englewood Cliffs, NJ: Prentice-Hall.

Garofalo, James. 1987. "Reassessing the Lifestyle Model of Criminal Victimization." In M. R. Gottfredson and T. Hirschi, eds., *Positive Criminology*, pp. 29–36. Newbury Park, CA: Sage.

Gartner, Rosemary. 1990. "The Victims of Homicide: A Temporal and Cross-National Comparison." *American Sociological Review* 55: 92–106.

Gartner, Rosemary, and Bill McCarthy. 1991. "The Social Distribution of Homicide in Urban Canada, 1921–1988." *Law and Society Review* 25: 287–311.

Gartner et al. 1990. [Gartner, Rosemary, Kathryn Baker, and Fred Pampel]. "Gender Stratification and the Gender Gap in Homicide Victimization." *Social Problems* 37: 593–612.

Gastil, Raymond D. 1971. "Homicide and a Regional Culture of Violence." *American Sociological Review* 36: 412–27.

Gatrell, V. A. C. 1980. "The Decline of Theft and Violence in Victorian and Edwardian England." In V. A. C. Gatrell, Bruce Lenman, and Geoffrey Parker, eds., *Crime and the Law: The Social History of Crime in Western Europe Since 1500*. London: Europa.

Gatrell, V. A. C., and T. B. Hadden. 1972. "Criminal Statistics and Their Interpretation." In E. A. Wrigley, ed., *Nineteenth-Century Society: Essays in the Use of Quantitative Methods for the Study of Social Data*. Cambridge, Eng.: Cambridge University Press.

George, M. Dorothy. 1964 [1925]. *London Life in the Eighteenth Century*. New York: Harper & Row.

Gillespie, R. W. 1978. "Economic Factors in Crime and Delinquency: A Critical Review of the Empirical Evidence." In House of Representatives, *Unemployment and Crime: Hearings Before the Subcommittee on Crime of the Committee on the Judiciary*, pp. 601–26. Washington, DC: U.S. Government Printing Office.

Giordano, Peggy C. 1978. "Girls, Guys, and Gangs: The Changing Social Context of Female Delinquency." *Journal of Criminal Law and Criminology* 69: 126–32.

Giordano et al. 1981. [Giordano, Peggy C., Sandra Kerbel, and Sandra Dudley]. "The Economics of Female Criminality: An Analysis of Police Blotters, 1890–1975." In Lee H. Bowker, ed., *Women and Crime in America*. New York: Macmillan.

Glasgow, Douglas G. 1981. *The Black Underclass: Poverty, Unemployment, and the Entrapment of Ghetto Youth.* San Francisco: Jossey-Bass.

Glass et al. 1981. [Glass, G. V., B. McGaw, and M. L. Smith]. *Meta-Analysis in Social Research*. Beverly Hills, CA: Sage.

Glueck, Sheldon, and Eleanor T. Glueck. 1934. *Five Hundred Delinquent Women.* New York: Alfred A. Knopf.

———. 1950. *Unraveling Juvenile Delinquency*. Cambridge, MA: Harvard University Press.

Goetting, Ann. 1988a. "Patterns of Homicide Among Women." *Journal of Interpersonal Violence* 3: 3–20.

———. 1988b. "When Females Kill One Another: The Exceptional Case." *Criminal Justice and Behavior* 15: 179–89.

———. 1989. "Patterns of Marital Homicide: A Comparison of Husbands and Wives." *Journal of Comparative Family Studies* 20: 341–54.

Goffman, Erving. 1956. "Embarrassment and Social Organization." *American Journal of Sociology* 62: 264–71.

———. 1959. *The Presentation of Self in Everyday Life*. Garden City, NY: Doubleday.

———. 1961. *Asylums: Essays on the Social Situation of Mental Patients and Other Inmates*. Garden City, NY: Anchor Books.

———. 1967. "Where the Action Is." In *Interaction Ritual*. New York: Pantheon Books.

———. 1977. "The Arrangement Between the Sexes." *Society and Theory* 4: 301–31.

Gold et al. 1975. [Gold, David A., Clarence Y. H. Lo, and Erik Olin Wright]. "Recent Developments in Marxist Theories of the Capitalist State." *Monthly Review* (October): 29–43; (November): 36–51.

Gold, Martin. 1966. "Undetected Delinquent Behavior." *Journal of Research in Crime and Delinquency* 3: 27–46.

Golden, Reid M., and Steven F. Messner. 1987. "Dimensions of Racial Inequality and Rates of Violent Crime." *Criminology* 25: 525–41.

Gönczöl, Katalin. 1991. Personal communication.

Good, D. H., M. A. Pirog-Good, and R. C. Sickles. 1986. "An Analysis of Youth Crime and Employment Patterns." *Journal of Quantitative Criminology* 2: 219–36.

Goodman, Paul. 1960. *Growing Up Absurd*. New York: Vintage.

Górny, Jerzy. 1987. "Die Gefängnispopulation in Polen." *Monatsschrift für Kriminologie und Strafrechtsreform* 70: 34–41.

Gottfredson, Michael, and Michael Hindelang. 1981. "Sociological Aspects of Criminal Victimization." *Annual Review of Sociology* 7: 107–28.

Gottfredson, Michael, and Travis Hirschi. 1986. "The True Value of Lambda Would Appear to Be Zero: An Essay on Career Criminals, Criminal Careers, Selective Incapacitation, Cohort Studies, and Related Topics." *Criminology* 24: 213–34.

———. 1990. *A General Theory of Crime*. Palo Alto, CA: Stanford University Press.

Gove, Walter. 1985. "The Effect of Age and Gender on Deviant Behavior: A Bio-Psychosocial Perspective." In Alice Rossi, ed., *Gender and the Life Course*, pp. 115–44. Hawthorne, NY: Aldine.

Gove, Walter R., and Robert D. Crutchfield. 1982. "The Family and Juvenile Delinquency." *The Sociological Quarterly* 23: 301–19.

Grabosky, Peter. 1990. "Crime Control and the Citizen: Non-Governmental Participants in the Criminal Justice System." Paper presented at the East Meets West Conference on International Trends in Crime, Bali, Indonesia.

Grabosky, Peter, and Adam Sutton, eds. 1989. *Stains on a White Collar*. Sydney: Federation Press.

Grabosky et al. 1987. [Grabosky, Peter, John Braithwaite, and Paul R. Wilson]. "The Myth of Community Tolerance Toward White-Collar Crime." *Australian and New Zealand Journal of Criminology* 20: 33–44.

Granger, C. W. J. 1980. *Forecasting in Business and Economics*. New York: Academic Press.

Granger, C. W. J., and Newbold, P. 1986. *Forecasting Economic Time Series*. 2d ed. New York: Academic Press.

Grant Commission on Work, Family, and Citizenship. 1988. *The Forgotten Half: Non-College Youth in America*. Washington, DC: The William T. Grant Foundation Commission on Youth and America's Future.

Greenberg, David F. 1977. "Delinquency and the Age Structure of Society." *Contemporary Crises: Crime, Law, and Social Policy* 1: 189–223.

———. 1985. "Age, Crime, and Social Explanation." *American Journal of Sociology* 89: 552–84.

Griffin, Susan. 1971. "Rape, the All-American Crime." *Ramparts* 10: 26–35.

Grogger, Jeff. 1991. "The Effect of Arrest on the Employment Outcomes of Young Men." Unpublished manuscript, University of California at Santa Barbara.

Grossman, Gregory. 1989. "Informal Personal Incomes and Outlays of the Soviet Urban Population." In Alejandro Portes, Manuel Castells, and Lauren A. Benton, eds., *The Informal Economy: Studies in Advanced and Less Developed Countries*, pp. 150–72. Baltimore: Johns Hopkins University Press.

Gusfield, J. 1963. *Symbolic Crusade*. Urbana: University of Illinois Press.

Gutierrez, Ramon A. 1991. *When Jesus Came, the Corn Mothers Went Away: Marriage, Sexuality, and Power in New Mexico, 1500–1846*. Stanford, CA: Stanford University Press.

Hackney, Sheldon. 1969. "Southern Violence." In H. D. Graham and T. R. Gurr, eds., *Violence in America*, pp. 479–500. New York: Signet Books.

Hagan, John. 1974. "Extra-Legal Attributes and Criminal Sentencing: An Assessment of a Sociological Viewpoint." *Law & Society Review* 8: 357–83.

———. 1985. "Toward a Structural Theory of Crime, Race and Gender: The Canadian Case." *Crime and Delinquency* 31: 129–46.

———. 1989. *Structural Criminology*. New Brunswick, NJ: Rutgers University Press.

———. 1991. "Destiny and Drift: Subcultural Preferences, Status Attainments, and the Risks and Rewards of Youth." *American Sociological Review* 56: 567–82.

———. 1992. "Class Fortification Against Crime." *Canadian Review of Sociology and Anthropology* 29: 126–40.

Hagan, John, and Celesta Albonetti. 1982. "Race, Class and the Perception of Criminal Injustice in America." *American Journal of Sociology* 88: 329–55.

Hagan, John, and Kristin Bumiller. 1983. "Making Sense of Sentencing: A Review and Critique of Sentencing Research." In A. Blumstein, J. Cohen, S. E. Martin, and M. H. Tonry, eds., *Research on Sentencing: The Search for Reform*. Vol. 2. Washington, DC: National Academy Press.

Hagan, John, and Alberto Palloni. 1988. "Crimes as Social Events in the Life Course: Reconceiving a Criminological Controversy." *Criminology* 26: 87–100.

———. 1990. "The Social Reproduction of a Criminal Class in Working Class London, Circa 1950–80." *American Journal of Sociology* 96: 265–99.

Hagan et al. 1978. [Hagan, John, A. R. Gillis, and Janet Chan]. "Explaining Official Delinquency: A Spatial Study of Class, Conflict and Control." *Sociological Quarterly* 19: 386–98.

———. 1979. [Hagan, John, John Simpson, and A. R. Gillis]. "The Sexual Stratification of Social Control." *British Journal of Sociology* 30: 25–38.

———. 1985. [Hagan, John, A. R. Gillis, and John Simpson]. "The Class Structure of Gender and Delinquency: Toward a Power-Control Theory of Common Delinquent Behavior." *American Journal of Sociology* 90: 1151–78.

———. 1987. "Class in the Household: A Power-Control Theory of Gender and Delinquency." *American Journal of Sociology* 92: 788–816.

———. 1989. [Hagan, John, Celesta Albonetti, Duane Alwin, A. R. Gillis, John Hewitt, Alberto Palloni, Patricia Parker, Ruth Peterson, and John Simpson]. *Structural Criminology*. New Brunswick, NJ: Rutgers University Press.

Hagedorn, John. 1988. *People and Folks: Gangs, Crime and the Underclass in a Rustbelt City*. Chicago: Lake View Press.

Halberstam, David. 1979. *The Powers That Be*. New York: Knopf.

Hale, C. 1991. "Unemployment and Crime: Differencing Is No Substitute for Modeling." *Journal of Research in Crime and Delinquency* 28: 426–29.

Hale, C., and D. Sabbagh. 1991. "Testing the Relationship Between Unemployment and Crime: A Methodological Comment and Empirical Analysis Using Time Series Data from England and Wales." *Journal of Research in Crime and Delinquency* 28: 400–17.

Hanawalt, Barbara A. 1979. *Crime and Conflict in English Communities 1300–1348*. Cambridge, MA: Harvard University Press.

Hanf, Thomás. 1991. "Gewaltlosigkeit als Thema des Transformationsprozesses." Unpublished manuscript, Berlin.

Hann, C. M. 1985. *A Village Without Solidarity: Polish Peasants in Years of Crisis*. New Haven, CT: Yale University Press.

Hannerz, Ulf. 1969. *Soulside: Inquiries into Ghetto Culture and Community*. New York: Columbia University Press.

Harris, Anthony. 1976. "Race, Commitment to Deviance and Spoiled Identity." *American Sociological Review* 41: 432–42.

———. 1977. "Sex and Theories of Deviance: Toward a Functional Theory of Deviant Type-Scripts." *American Sociological Review* 42: 3–16.

———. 1991. "Race, Class and Crime." In Joseph Sheley, ed., *Criminology*. Belmont, CA: Wadsworth.

Harris, Louis. 1973. *The Anguish of Change*. New York: W. W. Norton.

Hatty, Suzanne E., ed. 1986. *National Conference on Domestic Violence*. Australian Institute of Criminology Seminar Proceeding No. 12, Canberra.

Hatty, Suzanne, and Jeanna Sutton. 1986. "Policing Violence Against Women." In Suzanne E. Hatty, ed., *National Conference on Domestic Violence*. Vol. 2. Australian Institute of Criminology Seminar Proceeding No. 12, Canberra.

Hawkins, Darnell, ed. 1986. *Homicide Among Black Americans*. Lanham, MD: University Press of America.

Hawkins, Keith. 1983. "Bargain and Bluff: Compliance Strategy and Deterrence in the Enforcement of Regulation." *Law and Policy Quarterly* 5: 35–73.

———. 1984. *Environment and Enforcement: Regulation and the Social Definition of Pollution*. New York: Oxford University Press.

Hay, Douglas. 1982. "War, Death and Theft: The Record of the English Courts." *Past and Present* 95 (May): 117–60.

Hay, Douglas, and Francis Snyder. 1989. "Using the Criminal Law, 1750–1850: Policing, Private Prosecution, and the State." In Douglas Hay and Francis Snyder, eds., *Policing and Prosecution in Britain, 1750–1850*. Oxford: Oxford University Press.

Hayduk, Leslie A. 1987. *Structural Equation Modeling with LISREL*. Baltimore, MD: Johns Hopkins University Press.

Hayes, Linsey, et al. 1989. *The Female Offender in Delaware: Populations Analysis and Assessment*. Alexandria, VA: National Center on Institutions and Alternatives.

Hayner, Norman. 1942. "Variability in the Criminal Behavior of American Indians." *American Journal of Sociology* 47: 602–13.

Hecht, J. Jean. 1981. *The Domestic Servant Class in Eighteenth-Century England*. Rev. ed. Westport, CT: Hyperion.

Heimer, Karen, and Ross L. Matsueda. 1994. "Role-Taking, Role-Commitment, and Delinquency: A Theory of Differential Social Control." *American Sociological Review* 59: 365–90.

Henry, A. F., and J. F. Short, Jr. 1954. *Suicide and Homicide: Some Economic, Sociological and Psychological Aspects of Aggression*. New York: The Free Press.

Hewitt, John P. 1987. *Self and Society: A Symbolic Interactionist Social Psychology*. Boston: Allyn and Bacon.

Hill, Gary D., and Maxine P. Atkinson. 1988. "Gender, Familial Control, and Delinquency." *Criminology* 26: 127–47.

Hill, Gary D., and Elizabeth M. Crawford. 1990. "Women, Race and Crime." *Criminology* 28: 601–23.

Hindelang, Michael J. 1971. "Age, Sex, and the Versatility of Delinquent Involvements." *Social Problems* 18: 522–35.

———. 1976. *Criminal Victimization in Eight American Cities*. Cambridge, MA: Ballinger.

———. 1978. "Race and Involvement in Common Law Personal Crimes." *American Sociological Review* 43: 93–109.

———. 1979. "Sex Differences in Criminal Activity." *Social Problems* 27: 143–56.

Hindelang et al. 1978. [Hindelang, Michael, Michael Gottfredson, and James Garofalo]. *Victims of Personal Crime: An Empirical Foundation for a Theory of Personal Victimization*. Cambridge, MA: Ballinger.

Hindelang et al. 1981. [Hindelang, Michael J., Travis Hirschi, and Joseph G. Weis]. *Measuring Delinquency*. Beverly Hills, CA: Sage.

Hindess, Barry. 1982. "Power, Interests and the Outcomes of Struggles." *Sociology* 16: 498–511.

Hinds, M. 1990. "Number of Killings Soars in Big Cities Across U.S." *New York Times*, July 18, p. 1.

Hirsch, A. 1983. *Making the Second Ghetto: Race and Housing in Chicago, 1940–1960*. Chicago: University of Chicago Press.

Hirschi, Travis. 1969. *Causes of Delinquency*. Berkeley: University of California Press.

Hirschi, Travis, and Michael Gottfredson. 1983. "Age and the Explanation of Crime." *American Journal of Sociology* 89: 552–84.

———. 1987. "Causes of White-Collar Crime." *Criminology* 25: 949–74.

Hogan, Dennis, and Evelyn Kitagawa. 1985. "The Impact of Social Status, Family Structure, and Neighborhood on the Fertility of Black Adolescents." *American Journal of Sociology* 90: 825–55.

Hoh-cheung Mui and Lorna H. Mui. 1989. *Shops and Shopkeeping in Eighteenth-Century England*. Kingston and Montreal: McGill-Queen's University Press.

Holtzman, H. 1983. "The Serious Habitual Property Offender as 'Moonlighter': An Empirical Study of Labor Force Participation Among Robbers and Burglars." *Journal of Criminal Law and Criminology* 73: 1774–92.

Homel, Ross. 1988. *Policing and Punishing the Drinking Driver: A Study of General and Specific Deterrence*. New York: Springer-Verlag.

Hopkins, Andrew, and Heather McGregor. 1991. *Working for Change: The Movement Against Domestic Violence*. Sydney: Allen and Unwin.

Hopkins, Andrew, and N. Parnell. 1984. "Why Coal Mine Safety Regulations in Australia Are Not Enforced." *International Journal of Sociology and Law* 12: 179–84.

Horowitz, Ruth. 1983. *Honor and the American Dream*. New Brunswick, NJ: Rutgers University Press.

———. 1987. "Community Tolerance of Gang Violence." *Social Problems* 34: 437–50.

Horowitz, R., and A. Pottieger. 1991. "Gender Bias in Juvenile Justice Handling of Seriously Crime-Involved Youth." *Journal of Research in Crime and Delinquency* 28: 75–100.

Howson, Gerald. 1970. *Thief Taker General: The Rise and Fall of Jonathan Wild*. London: Hutchinson.

Hunter, J. E., F. L. Schmidt, and G. B. Jackson. 1982. *Meta-Analysis*. Beverly Hills, CA: Sage.

Iams, H. H., and A. Thornton. 1975. "Decomposition of Differences: A Cautionary Note." *Sociological Methods and Research* 3: 341–52.

Innes, Joanna. 1987. "Prisons for the Poor." In Douglas Hay and Francis Snyder, eds., *Labour, Law, and Crime*. London: Tavistock.

Innes, Joanna, and John Styles. 1986. "The Crime Wave: Recent Writing on Crime and Criminal Justice in Eighteenth-Century England." *Journal of British Studies* 25, no. 4: 380–435.

Ivanov, Lev. 1991. "Charakteristik der Kriminalitätstendenzen in der Sowjetunion 1961–1989." *Monatsschrift für Kriminologie und Strafrechtsreform* 74: 182–91.

Jacobs, James. 1977. *Statesville: The Penitentiary in Mass Society*. Chicago: University of Chicago Press.

———. 1989. *Drunk Driving: An American Dilemma*. Chicago: University of Chicago Press.

Jacobs, Jane. 1961. *The Death and Life of Great American Cities*. New York: Random House.

James, G. 1991. "New York Killings Set Record in 1990." *New York Times*, p. A14.

Jaynes, Gerald, and Robin Williams, Jr., eds. 1989. *A Common Destiny: Blacks and American Society*. Washington, DC: National Academy Press.

Jencks, Christopher. 1988. "Deadly Neighborhoods." *The New Republic*, June 13.

———. 1991. "Is Violent Crime Increasing?" *The American Prospect*, Winter: 98–109.

———. 1992. *Rethinking Social Policy: Race, Poverty, and the Underclass*. Cambridge, MA: Harvard University Press.

Jensen, Gary F., and Raymond Eve. 1976. "Sex Differences in Delinquency: An Examination of Popular Sociological Explanations." *Criminology* 13: 427–48.

Jensen et al. 1977. [Jensen, Gary, Joseph Stauss, and V. William Harris]. "Crime, Delinquency and the American Indian." *Human Organization* 36: 252–57.

Jensen, Gary, and Kevin Thompson. 1990. "What's Class Got to Do with It? A

Further Examination of Power-Control Theory." *American Journal of Sociology* 95: 1009–1023.

Jolin, Annette, and Don Gibbons. 1987. "Age Patterns in Criminal Involvement." *International Journal of Offender Therapy* 31: 237–60.

Jonassen, C. 1949. "A Reevaluation and Critique of the Logic and Some Methods of Shaw and McKay." *American Sociological Review* 14: 608–14.

Jones, Ann. 1980. *Women Who Kill*. New York: Holt, Rinehart and Winston.

Jones, D. W. 1972. "London Merchants and the Crisis of the 1690s." In Peter Clark and Paul Slack, eds., *Crisis and Order in English Towns, 1500–1700*. Toronto: University of Toronto Press.

Jones, Frank L., and Jonathan Kelley. 1984. "Decomposing Difference Between Groups: A Cautionary Note on the Measurement of Discrimination." *Sociological Methods and Research* 12: 323–43.

Jones, Nolan. 1975. "Differential Legal Treatment Between Blacks and Whites as a Function of Social Context." *Journal of SBS* Spring–Summer: 49–63.

Joreskog, Karl G., and Dag Sorbom. 1989. *LISREL VII: Analysis of Linear Structural Relationships by Maximum Likelihood and Least Squares Methods*. Chicago: National Educational Resources.

Kaplan, Howard B. 1975. *Self-Attitudes and Deviant Behavior*. Pacific Palisades, CA: Goodyear.

———. 1980. *Deviant Behavior in Defense of Self*. New York: Academic.

Kaplan et al. 1986. [Kaplan, Howard B., Steven S. Martin, and Robert J. Johnson]. "Self-Rejection and Explanation of Deviance: Specification of Structure Among the Latent Constructs." *American Journal of Sociology* 92: 384–411.

Kasarda, J., and M. Janowitz. 1974. "Community Attachment in Mass Society." *American Sociological Review* 39: 328–39.

Katz, J. 1980. "The Social Movement Against White-Collar Crime." In E. Bittner and S. L. Messinger, eds., *Criminology Review Yearbook, Vol. 2*. Beverly Hills, CA: Sage.

———. 1988. *Seductions of Crime: The Sensual and Moral Attractions of Doing Evil*. New York: Basic.

Keller, Suzanne. 1987. "Social Differentiation and Social Stratification: The Special Case of Gender." In Celia S. Heller, ed., *Structured Social Inequality: A Reader in Comparative Social Stratification*, pp. 329–49. New York: Macmillan.

Kent, D. A. 1989. "Ubiquitous but Invisible: Female Domestic Servants in Mid-Eighteenth Century London." *History Workshop* 20: 111–28.

King, Peter. 1984. "Crime, Law, and Society in Essex, 1740–1820." Ph.D. diss., Cambridge University.

Kitch, M. J. 1986. "Capital and Kingdom: Migration to Later Stuart London." In A. L. Beier and Roger Finlay, eds., *London 1500–1700: The Making of the Metropolis*. London: Longman.

Kleck, Gary. 1981. "Racial Discrimination in Criminal Sentencing: A Critical Evaluation of the Evidence on the Death Penalty." *American Sociological Review* 46: 783–804.

Klein, Dorie. 1973. "The Etiology of Female Crime: A Review of the Literature." *Issues in Criminology* 8: 3–30.

Kloek, Els. 1990. "Criminality and Gender in Leiden's *Confessieboeken*, 1678–1794." *Criminal Justice History* 11: 1–29.

Kohfeld, Carol W., and John Sprague. 1988. "Urban Unemployment Drives Urban Crime." *Urban Affairs Quarterly* 24: 215–44.

Kolko, Gabriel. 1963. *The Triumph of Conservatism: A Reinterpretation of American History, 1900–1916*. New York: The Free Press.

Kolosi, Tomas. 1988. "Stratification and Social Structure in Hungary." *Annual Review of Sociology* 14: 405–19.

Kornhauser, R. 1978. *Social Sources of Delinquency*. Chicago: University of Chicago Press.

Kotlowitz, Alex. 1991. *There Are No Children Here*. New York: Doubleday.

Krohn, Marvin, James Curry, and Shirley Nelson-Kilger. 1983. "Is Chivalry Dead?: An Analysis of Changes in Police Dispositions of Males and Females." *Criminology* 21: 417–37.

Kuhl, Anna F. 1985. "Battered Women Who Murder: Victims or Offenders?" In Imogene L. Moyer, ed., *The Changing Roles of Women in the Criminal Justice System*, pp. 197–216. Prospect Heights, IL: Waveland Press.

LaFave, W. R. 1965. *Arrest: The Decision to Take a Suspect into Custody*. Boston: Little, Brown.

LaFree, Gary. 1980. "The Effect of Sexual Stratification by Race on Official Reactions to Rape." *American Sociological Review* 45: 842–54.

Lamb et al. 1980. [Lamb, Michael E., M. Ann Easterbrook, and George W. Holden]. "Reinforcement and Punishment Among Preschoolers: Characteristics, Effects, and Correlates." *Child Development* 51: 1230–36.

Lammich, Siegfried, and Ferenc Nagy. 1985. "Kriminalitätsentwicklung und Strafpraxis in Ungarn nach dem Inkrafttreten des StGB von 1978." *Monatsschrift für Kriminologie und Strafrechtsreform* 68: 176–86.

Land et al. 1990. [Land, K., P. McCall, and L. Cohen]. "Structural Covariates of Homicide Rates: Are There Any Invariances Across Time and Space?" *American Journal of Sociology* 95: 922–63.

Landers, Daniel, ed. 1984. *Sport and Elite Performers*. Champaign, IL: Human Kinetics.

Langan, Patrick. 1991. "America's Soaring Prison Population." *Science* 251: 1568–73.

Langbein, John J. 1978. "The Criminal Trial Before the Lawyers." *University of Chicago Law Review* 45, no. 2: 263–316.

———. 1983. "Shaping the Eighteenth-Century Criminal Trial: A View from the Ryder Sources." *University of Chicago Law Review* 50, no. 1: 1–136.

Lasley, James. 1989. "Drinking Routines/Lifestyles and Predatory Victimization: A Causal Analysis." *Justice Quarterly* 6: 529–42.

Laudon, K. 1986. *Dossier Society*. New York: Columbia University Press.

Lawson, Peter. 1986. "Property Crime and Hard Times in England, 1559–1624." *Law and History Review* 4, no. 1: 95–128.

Lawyers' Committee for Human Rights. 1987. *Repression Disguised as Law: Human Rights in Poland*. New York: Lawyers' Committee for Human Rights.

Lehmann, Nicholas. 1991. *The Promised Land: The Great Black Migration and How it Changed America*. New York: Alfred Knopf.

Leighton, B. 1988. "The Community Concept in Criminology: Toward a Social Network Approach." *Journal of Research in Crime and Delinquency* 25: 351–74.

Lemert, Edwin. 1951. *Social Pathology*. New York: McGraw-Hill.

Levi, Margaret. 1988. *Of Rule and Revenue*. Berkeley: University of California Press.

Lewis, Diane K. 1981. "Black Women Offenders and Criminal Justice." In Marguerite Q. Warren, ed., *Comparing Female and Male Offenders*. Beverly Hills, CA: Sage.

Lichter, Daniel T. 1988. "Racial Differences in Underemployment in American Cities." *American Journal of Sociology* 93: 771–92.

Liebow, E. 1967. *Tally's Corner*. Boston: Little, Brown.

Linebaugh, Peter. 1991. *The London Hanged: Crime and Civil Society in the Eighteenth Century*. London: Allen Lane.

Ljung, G. M., and G. E. P. Box. 1978. "On a Measure of Lack of Fit in Time Series Models." *Biometrika* 65: 297–303.

Lockwood, D. 1980. *Prison Sexual Violence*. New York: Elsevier.

Loftin, Colin, and Robert H. Hill. 1974. "Regional Subculture and Homicide: An Examination of the Gastil-Hackney Thesis." *American Sociological Review* 39: 714–24.

Logan, J., and H. Molotch. 1987. *Urban Fortunes: The Political Economy of Place*. Berkeley: University of California Press.

Long, S. K., and A. D. Witte. 1981. "Current Economic Trends: Implications for Crime and Criminal Justice." In K. N. Wright, ed., *Crime and Criminal Justice in a Declining Economy*. Cambridge, MA: Oelgeschlager, Gunn and Hain.

Łós, Maria. 1983. "Economic Crimes in Communist Countries." In Israel L. Barak-Glantz and Elmer H. Johnson, eds., *Comparative Criminology*, pp. 39–57. Beverly Hills, CA: Sage.

———. 1985. "The Myth of Popular Justice Under Communism: A Comparative View of the USSR and Poland." *Justice Quarterly* 2: 447–71.

———. 1989. *Communist Ideology, Law and Crime*. New York: St. Martin's Press.

Lovejoy, Arthur O. 1942. *The Great Chain of Being: The Study of the History of an Idea*. Cambridge, MA: Harvard University Press.

Lowry et al. 1988. [Lowry, Philip, Susan Hassig, Robert Gunn, and Joyce Mathison]. "Homicide Victims in New Orleans: Recent Trends." *American Journal of Epidemiology* 128: 1130–36.

Lynxwiler et al. 1983. [Lynxwiler, John, Neal Shover, and Donald A. Clelland]. "The Organization and Impact of Inspector Discretion in a Regulatory Bureaucracy." *Social Problems* 30 (April): 425–36.

McAllister, Ian. 1991. "Community Attitudes to the Environment, Forests and Forest Management in Australia." Canberra: Resources Assessment Commission.

McAllister et al. 1991. [McAllister, Ian, Rhonda Moore, and Toni Makkai]. *Drugs in Australian Society: Patterns, Attitudes and Policy*. Melbourne: Longman Cheshire.

McBarnet, Doreen. 1991. "Whiter than White-Collar Crime: Tax, Fraud Insurance and the Management of Stigma." *British Journal of Sociology* 42, no. 3: 323–44.

McCall et al. 1992. [McCall, P. L., K. C. Land, and L. E. Cohen]. "Violent Criminal Behavior: Is There a General and Continuing Influence of the South?" *Social Science Research* 21: 286–310.

McClain, Paula D. 1981. "Black Female Homicide Offenders and Victims: Are They from the Same Population?" *Death Education* 6: 265–78.

———. 1982–1983. "Black Females and Lethal Violence: Has Time Changed the Circumstances Under Which They Kill?" *Omega* 3: 13–25.

McCleary, R., and R. A. Hay, Jr. 1980. *Applied Time Series Analysis for the Social Sciences*. Beverly Hills, CA: Sage.

McCord, M., and H. Freeman. 1990. "Excess Mortality in Harlem." *New England Journal of Medicine* 322: 173–75.

McDonald et al. 1990. [McDonald, B., J. Elliott, T. Logan, N. Norris, C. Norris, J. Shostak, and S. Kusher]. *The New South Wales Police Recruit Education Programme: An Independent Evaluation*. Sydney: N.S.W. Police Department.

McEachern, A. W., and Riva Bauzer. 1967. "Factors Related to Disposition in Juvenile Police Contacts." In Malcolm Klein and Barbara Myerhoff, eds., *Juvenile Gangs in Context: Theory, Research and Action*. Englewood Cliffs, NJ: Prentice-Hall.

Macfarlane, Stephen. 1986. "Social Policy and the Poor in the Later Seventeenth Century." In A. L. Beier and Roger Finlay, eds., *London 1500–1700: The Making of the Metropolis*. London: Longman.

McGarity, Thomas O. 1983. "Media-Quality, Technology, and Cost-Benefit Balancing Strategies For Health and Environmental Regulation." *Law and Contemporary Problems* 46 (Summer): 159–233.

McKendrick et al. 1982. [McKendrick, Neil, John Brewer, and J. H. Plumb]. *The Birth of a Consumer Society: The Commercialization of Eighteenth-Century England*. London: Europa.

Maddala, G. S. 1988. *Introduction to Econometrics*. 2d ed. New York: McGraw-Hill.

Maguire, K., and T. J. Flanagan. 1990. *Sourcebook of Criminal Justice Statistics–1989*. Washington, DC: U.S. Government Printing Office.

Mann, Coramae Richey. 1988. "Getting Even? Women Who Kill in Domestic Encounters." *Justice Quarterly* 5: 33–51.

———. 1990. "Black Female Homicide in the United States." *Journal of Interpersonal Violence* 5: 176–201.

Mann, Kenneth. 1985. *Defending White-Collar Crime: A Portrait of Attorneys at Work*. New Haven, CT: Yale University Press.

Marek, Andrzej E. 1986a. "Organized Crime in Poland." In Robert J. Kelley, ed., *Organized Crime: A Global Perspective*, pp. 159–71. Totowa, NJ: Rowman and Littlefield.

———. 1986b. "Resozialisierung und wechselnde Strategien der Bestrafung: Einige Anmerkungen in Bezug auf Polen." *Monatsschrift für Kriminologie und Strafrechtsreform* 69: 138–46.

Marwell, Gerald. 1966. "Adolescent Powerlessness and Delinquent Behavior." *Social Problems* 14: 35–47.

Marx, G. 1981. "Ironies of Social Control: Authorities as Contributors to Deviance Through Escalation, Nonenforcement and Covert Facilitation." *Social Problems* 28, no. 3: 221–46.

———. 1987. "Are We Becoming a Maximum Security Society?" Paper presented at the International Conference on Technology and Criminal Justice, Montreal.

———. 1988. *Undercover Police Surveillance in America*. Berkeley: University of California Press.

Marx, G., and N. Reichman. 1984. "Routinizing the Discovery of Secrets," *American Behavioral Scientist* 27, no. 4: 423–52.

Marx, L. 1987. "Does Technology Mean Progress?" *Technology Review*, January.

Massey, Douglas S. 1990. "American Apartheid: Segregation and the Making of the Underclass." *American Journal of Sociology* 96: 329–57.

Massey, Douglas S., and Nancy A. Denton. 1993. *American Apartheid: Segregation and the Making of the Underclass*. Cambridge, MA: Harvard University Press.

Mather, Lynn. 1979. *Plea Bargaining or Trial? The Process of Criminal Case Disposition*. Lexington, MA: Lexington Books.

Matsueda, Ross L. 1988. "The Current State of Differential Association Theory." *Crime and Delinquency* 34: 277–306.

———. 1992. "Reflected Appraisals, Parental Labeling, and Delinquency: Specifying a Symbolic Interactionist Theory." *American Journal of Sociology* 97: 1577–1611.

Matsueda, Ross L., and Karen Heimer. 1987. "Race, Family Structure and Delinquency: A Test of Differential Association and Social Control Theories." *American Sociological Review* 52: 826–40.

Matthews, Mervyn, ed. 1989. *Party, State, and Citizen in the Soviet Union: A Collection of Documents*. Armonk, NY: M. E. Sharpe.

Matza, David. 1990. *Delinquency and Drift*. New Brunswick, NJ: Transaction Books.

Matza, David, and Gresham Sykes. 1957. "Techniques of Neutralization: A Theory of Delinquency." *American Sociological Review* 22: 664–70.

Mauer, M. 1990. *Young Black Men and the Criminal Justice System: A Growing National Problem*. Washington, DC: The Sentencing Project.

Maume, David J., Jr. 1989. "Inequality and Metropolitan Rape Rates: A Routine Activity Approach." *Justice Quarterly* 6: 513–27.

Maxfield, Michael G. 1989. "Circumstances in Supplementary Homicide Reports: Variety and Validity." *Criminology* 27: 671–95.

Mead, George Herbert. 1934. *Mind, Self, and Society*. Chicago: University of Chicago Press.

Meier, Robert F. 1980. "The Arrested Development of Criminological Theory." *Contemporary Sociology* 9 (May): 374–76.

Mello, M. 1984. "Florida's 'Heinous, Atrocious, or Cruel' Aggravating Circumstance: Narrowing the Class of Death-Eligible Cases Without Making It Smaller." *Stetson Law Review* 13: 523–54.

Melnick, R. Shep. 1983. *Regulation and the Courts: The Case of the Clean Air Act.* Washington, DC: Brookings Institution.
Merton, Robert. 1938. "Social Structure and Anomie." *American Sociological Review* 3: 672–82.
Merton, Robert K., and M. F. Ashley Montagu. 1940. "Crime and the Anthropologist." *American Anthropologist* 42: 384–408.
Messerschmidt, James W. 1986. *Capitalism, Patriarchy, and Crime.* Totowa, NJ: Rowman and Littlefield.
Messner, Steven F. 1982. "Poverty, Inequality, and the Urban Homicide Rate: Some Unexpected Findings." *Criminology* 20: 103–14.
———. 1983a. "Regional Differences in the Economic Correlates of the Urban Homicide Rate: Some Evidence on the Importance of the Cultural Context." *Criminology* 21: 477–88.
———. 1983b. "Regional and Racial Effects on the Urban Homicide Rate: The Subculture of Violence Revisited." *American Journal of Sociology* 88: 997–1007.
———. 1989. "Economic Discrimination and Societal Homicide Rates: Further Evidence on the Cost of Inequality." *American Sociological Review* 54: 597–611.
Messner, Steven, and Kenneth Tardiff. 1985. "The Social Ecology of Urban Homicide: An Application of the Routine Activities Approach." *Criminology* 23: 241–67.
Messner, S., and R. Sampson. 1991. "The Sex Ratio, Family Disruption, and Rates of Violent Crime: The Paradox of Demographic Structure." *Social Forces* 69: 693–714.
Miethe, T. D., and C. A. Moore. 1985. "Socioeconomic Disparities Under Determinate Sentencing Systems: A Comparison of Preguideline and Postguideline Practices in Minnesota." *Criminology* 23: 337–63.
Miller, Eleanor. 1986. *Street Woman.* Philadelphia: Temple University Press.
Miller, Walter. 1958. "Lower Class Culture as a Generating Milieu of Gang Delinquency." *Journal of Social Issues* 14: 5–19.
Minnis, Mhyra. 1963. "The Relationship of the Social Structure of an Indian Community, Its Adults and Juvenile Delinquency." *Social Forces* 41: 395–403.
Mitchell, B. R., and Phyllis Deane. 1962. *Abstract of British Historical Statistics.* Cambridge, Eng.: Cambridge University Press.
Modell, John. 1976. "Social Change and the Transition to Adulthood in Historical Perspective." *Journal of Family History* 1: 7–32.
Monahan, Thomas. 1957. "Family Status and the Delinquent Child: A Reappraisal and Some New Findings." *Social Forces* 35: 250–55.
Montagu, A. 1980. "The Biologist Looks at Crime." *Annals of the American Academy of Political and Social Sciences* 217: 46–57.
Montesquieu, Baron de. 1977. *The Spirit of Laws.* Ed. D. W. Carrithers. Berkeley: University of California Press.
Montgomery, R., and E. MacDougall. 1986. "Curing Criminals." *The Futurist,* Jan.–Feb.
Montoye, Henry. 1975. *Physical Activity and Health: An Epidemiologic Study of an Entire Community.* Englewood Cliffs, NJ: Prentice-Hall.

Moore et al. 1978. [Moore, Joan, with Robert Garcia, Carlos Garcia, Luis Cerda, and Frank Valencia]. *Homeboys: Gangs, Drugs and Prison in the Barrios of Los Angeles*. Philadelphia: Temple University Press.

Munford et al. 1976. [Munford, R. S., Ross Kazev, Roger Feldman, and Robert Stivers]. "Homicide Trends in Atlanta." *Criminology* 14: 213–21.

Myers, Martha. 1991. "Economic Threat and Racial Disparities in Incarceration: The Case of the Postbellum Georgia." *Criminology* 28: 627–56.

Myers, Martha, and John Hagan. 1979. "Private and Public Trouble: Prosecutors and the Allocation of Court Resources." *Social Problems* 26: 439–51.

Myers, Martha, and S. Talarico. 1987. *The Social Contexts of Criminal Sentencing*. New York: Springer-Verlag.

Nagel, Ilene, and John Hagan. 1982. "Gender and Crime: Offense Patterns and Criminal Court Sanctions." In Norval Morris and Michael Tonry, eds., *Crime and Justice*. Vol. 4. Chicago: University of Chicago Press.

National Research Council. 1989. *A Common Destiny: Blacks and American Society*. Washington, DC: National Academy Press.

Neugarten et al. 1965. [Neugarten, Bernice, J. W. Moore, and J. C. Lowe]. "Age Norms, Age Constraints, and Adult Socialization." *American Journal of Sociology* 70: 710–17.

Newman, Donald. 1966. *Conviction: The Determination of Guilt or Innocence Without Trial*. Boston: American Bar Association.

Newman, Oscar. 1972. *Defensible Space*. New York: Macmillan.

Newton, G. D., and F. E. Zimring. 1969. *Firearms and Violence in American Life*. Washington, DC: U.S. Government Printing Office.

Nonet, Philippe, and Philip Selznick. 1978. *Law and Society in Transition: Toward Responsive Law*. New York: Octagon.

Nye, F. Ivan. 1958. *Family Relationships and Delinquent Behavior*. New York: Wiley and Sons.

O'Donnell, J., and J. Craney, eds. 1982. *Family Violence in Australia*. Melbourne: Longman Cheshire.

Office of Management and Budget. 1974. *Social Indicators 1973*. Washington, DC: U.S. Government Printing Office.

Ogborne, Allan C. 1988. "School-based Educational Programs to Prevent the Personal Use of Psychoactive Drugs for Non-medical Purposes." *Australian Drug and Alcohol Review* 7: 305–14.

O'Malley, P. 1980. "Theories of Structural Versus Causal Determination Accounting for Legislative Change in Capitalist Societies." In R. Tomasic, ed., *Legislation and Society in Australia*. Sydney: Allen and Unwin.

Opp, Karl-Dieter. 1993. "Spontaneous Revolutions: The Case of East Germany in 1989." In Heinz Kurz, ed., *United Germany and the New Europe*. Cheltenham, Eng.: Edward Elgar.

Paley, Ruth. 1989. "Thief-takers in London in the Age of the McDaniel Gang, c. 1745–1754." In Douglas Hay and Francis Snyder, eds., *Policing and Prosecution in Britain, 1750–1850*. Oxford: Oxford University Press.

Parcel, Toby L., and Charles W. Mueller. 1983. *Ascription and Labor Markets*. New York: Academic.

Parmelee, Maurice. 1918. *Criminology*. New York: Macmillan.

Paternoster, Raymond, and A. Kazyaka. 1988. "Racial Considerations in Capital Punishment: The Failure of Evenhanded Justice." In K. C. Haas and J. A. Inciardi, eds., *Challenging Capital Punishment: Legal and Social Science Approaches*. Newbury Park, CA: Sage.

Pawlak, E. 1977. "Differential Selection of Juveniles for Detention." *Journal of Research in Crime and Delinquency* 14: 152–65.

Pennsylvania Crime Commission. 1991. *Organized Crime in Pennsylvania: A Decade of Change—1990 Report*. Darrell Steffensmeier, Project Director, and Emilie Allan, Associate Director. Conshohocken, PA: Pennsylvania Crime Commission.

Peristiany, J. 1965. *Honor and Shame: The Values of Mediterranean Society*. Chicago: University of Chicago Press.

Petersilia, Joan. 1983. *Racial Disparities in the Criminal Justice System*. Santa Monica, CA: Rand.

———. 1985. "Racial Disparities in the Criminal Justice System: A Summary." *Crime & Delinquency* 31: 15–34.

Peterson, Ruth D., and William C. Bailey. 1988. "Forcible Rape, Poverty, and Economic Inequality in U.S. Metropolitan Communities." *Journal of Quantitative Criminology* 4: 99–119.

———. 1992. "Rape and Dimensions of Gender Socioeconomic Inequality in U.S. Metropolitan Areas." *Journal of Research in Crime and Delinquency* 29: 162–77.

Peterson, Ruth, and John Hagan. 1984. "Changing Conceptions of Race: The Sentencing of Drug Offenders in an American City, 1963–76." *American Sociological Review* 49: 56–71.

Pettit, Philip. 1989. "Liberty in the Republic." John Curtin Memorial Lecture, Research School of Social Sciences, Australian National University.

Philips, David. 1977. *Crime and Authority in Victorian England*. London: Croom Helm.

Piliavin, Irving, and Scott Briar. 1964. "Police Encounters with Juveniles." *American Journal of Sociology* 70: 206–14.

Pittman, David J., and William Handy. 1964. "Patterns in Criminal Aggravated Assault." *Journal of Criminal Law, Criminology and Police Science* 55: 462–70.

Pitt-Rivers, Julian. 1968. "Honor." In *International Encyclopedia of the Social Sciences*, pp. 503–11. New York: Macmillan.

Pizzorno, A. 1991. "On the Individualistic Theory of Social Order." In P. Bourdieu and J. Coleman, eds., *Social Theory for a Changing Society*. Boulder, CO: Westview Press.

Plant, J. S. 1957. "The Personality of an Urban Area." In P. Halt and A. Reiss, eds., *Cities and Society*. New York: The Free Press.

Pocock, J. G. A., ed. 1977. *The Political Works of James Harrington*. New York: Cambridge University Press.

Pole, J. R. 1978. *The Pursuit of Equality in American History*. Berkeley: University of California Press.

Pollard, Alan P., ed. 1989. *USSR: Facts and Figures Annual*. Vol. 13. Gulf Breeze, FL: Academic International Press.

———. 1990. *USSR: Facts and Figures Annual*. Vol. 14. Gulf Breeze, FL: Academic International Press.

Powell, Keith C. 1988. *Drinking and Alcohol in Colonial Australia 1788–1901 for the Eastern Colonies*. National Campaign Against Drug Abuse, Monograph Series No. 3. Canberra: Australian Government Publishing Service.

Prothrow-Stith, D. 1991. *Deadly Consequences*. New York: Harper Collins.

Quetelet, Adolphe. 1831. *Research on the Propensity to Crime of Different Ages*. Brussels: Hayez.

Quinney, Richard. 1970. *The Social Reality of Crime*. Boston: Little, Brown.

———. 1977. *Class, State and Crime*. New York: David McKay.

Radelet M. L., and G. L. Pierce. 1985. "Race and Prosecutorial Discretion in Homicide Cases." *Law and Society Review* 19: 587–621.

Radzinowicz, Sir Leon. 1948. *A History of English Criminal Law and Its Administration*. Vol. 1. London: Macmillan.

Rainwater, Lee. 1970. *Behind Ghetto Walls: Black Families in a Federal Slum*. Chicago: Aldine.

Reasons, Charles. 1972. "Crime and the Native American." In Charles Reasons and Jack Kaykendall, eds., *Race, Crime and Justice*. Pacific Palisades, CA: Goodyear.

Recktenwald, W., and B. Morrison. 1990. "Guns, Gangs, Drugs Make a Deadly Combination." *Chicago Tribune*, July 1, Section 2, p. 1.

Reed, John S. 1971. "To Live and Die in Dixie: A Contribution to the Study of Southern Violence." *Political Science Quarterly* 86: 429–43.

Reed, Gary E., and Peter C. Yeager. 1991. "Organizational Offending and Neoclassical Criminology: A Challenge To Gottfredson and Hirschi's General Theory of Crime." Paper presented to Annual Meeting of the American Society of Criminology, San Francisco.

Reese, William, and Russell Curtis. 1991. "Paternalism and the Female Status Offender: Remanding the Juvenile Justice Double Standard for Desexualization." *The Social Science Journal* 28: 63–83.

Reiss, A. J., Jr. 1986. "Why Are Communities Important in Understanding Crime?" In A.J. Reiss, Jr., and M. Tonry, eds., *Communities and Crime*, pp. 1–33. Chicago: University of Chicago Press.

Reiss, Albert J., and David Bordua. 1967. "Organization and Environment: A Perspective on the Municipal Police." In David Bordua, ed., *The Police: Six Sociological Essays*. New York: Wiley and Sons.

Reiss, Albert J., and Jeffrey Roth, eds. 1993. *Understanding and Preventing Violence*. Washington, D.C.: National Academy Press.

Ridgeway, Beverly. 1986. "Domestic Violence: Aboriginal Women's Viewpoint." In Suzanne E. Hatty, ed., *National Conference on Domestic Violence*. Vol. 1. Australian Institute of Criminology Seminar Proceeding No. 12, Canberra.

Riley et al. 1988. [Riley, Matilda White, Anne Foner, and Joan Waring]. "Sociology of Age." In *Handbook of Sociology*. New York: Macmillan.

Robins, Lee. 1966. *Deviant Children Grown Up*. Baltimore, MD: Williams and Wilkins.

Rogers, Nicholas. 1991. "Policing the Poor in Eighteenth-Century London: The Vagrancy Laws and Their Administration." *Histoire sociale/Social History* 24, no. 47: 127–47.

Romero, Leo, and Luis Stelzner. 1985. "Hispanics and the Criminal Justice System." In Pastora San Juan Cafferty and William C. McCready, eds., *Hispanics in the United States*. New Brunswick, NJ: Transaction Books.

Rosenberg, Morris. 1979. *Conceiving the Self*. New York: Basic Books.

Rosenberg, Morris, and Roberta G. Simmons. 1972. *Black and White Self-Esteem: The Urban School Child*. Roe Monograph Series. Washington, DC: American Sociological Association.

Rosenberg et al. 1989. [Rosenberg, Morris, Carmi Schooler, and Carrie Schoenbach]. "Self-Esteem and Adolescent Problems." *American Sociological Review* 54: 1004–18.

Rosner, Lydia S. 1986. *The Soviet Way of Crime: Beating the System in the Soviet Union and the U.S.A.* South Hadley, MA: Bergin & Garvey.

Ross, H. Lawrence. 1982. *Deterring the Drinking Driver: Legal Policy and Social Control*. Lexington, MA: Lexington Books.

———. 1984. "Social Control Through Deterrence: Drinking and Driving Laws." *Annual Review of Sociology* 10: 21–35.

Ross, Harold, and Paula McClain. 1990. *Race, Place and Risk: Black Homicide in Urban America*. Albany: State University of New York Press.

Rossi et al. 1974. [Rossi, Peter, Emily Waite, Christine Bose, and Richard Berk]. "The Seriousness of Crimes: Normative Structure and Individual Differences." *American Sociological Review* 39: 224–37.

Rowe, Allan, and Charles Tittle. 1977. "Life Cycle Changes and Criminal Propensity." *Sociological Quarterly* 18: 223–36.

Rubin, Lillian. 1976. *Worlds of Pain: Life in the Working-Class Family*. New York: Harper & Row.

Russell, Diana E. H. 1975. *The Politics of Rape: the Victim's Perspective*. New York: Stein and Day.

Russell, William Felton, as told to William McSweeny. 1966. *Go Up to Glory*. New York: Coward-McCann.

Sampson, Robert J. 1985. "Race and Criminal Violence: A Demographically Disaggregated Analysis of Urban Homicide." *Crime and Delinquency* 31: 47–82.

———. 1986. "Effects of Socioeconomic Context on Official Reaction to Juvenile Delinquency." *American Sociological Review* 51: 876–86.

———. 1987. "Urban Black Violence: The Effect of Male Joblessness and Family Disruption." *American Journal of Sociology* 93: 348–82.

———. 1990. "The Impact of Housing Policies on Community Social Disorganization and Crime." *Bulletin of the New York Academy of Medicine* 66: 526–33.

———. 1991. "Linking the Micro and Macrolevel Dimensions of Community Social Organization." *Social Forces* 70: 43–64.

Sampson, R. J., and W. B. Groves. 1989. "Community Structure and Crime: Testing Social-Disorganization Theory." *American Journal of Sociology* 94: 774–802.

Sampson, R. J., and John Laub. 1990. "Stability and Change in Crime and Deviance over the Life Course: The Salience of Adult Social Bonds." *American Sociological Review* 55: 609–27.

Sampson, R. J., and J. Lauritsen. 1994. "Violent Victimization and Offending: Individual, Situational, and Community-level Risk Factors." In A. J. Reiss, Jr., and J. Roth, eds., *Understanding and Preventing Violence: Social Influences*. Vol. 3. Committee on Law and Justice, National Research Council. Washington, DC: National Academy Press.

Sánchez Jankowski, Martín. 1991. *Islands in the Street: Gangs in American Urban Society*. Berkeley: University of California Press.

Sanday, Peggy. 1981. *Female Power and Male Dominance: On the Origins of Sexual Inequality*. London: Cambridge University Press.

SAS Institute. 1988. *SAS/ETS User's Guide, Version 6*. 1st ed. Cary, NC: SAS Institute.

Savelsberg, Joachim J. 1992. "Law That Does Not Fit Society: Sentencing Guidelines as a Neo-Classical Reaction to the Dilemmas of Substantivized Law." *American Journal of Sociology* 97, no. 5: 1346–81.

Sayers, Janet. 1987. "Science, Sexual Difference, and Feminism." In Beth B. Hess and Myra Marx Ferree, eds., *Analyzing Gender*. Beverly Hills, CA: Sage.

Scheff, Thomas, and Suzanne Retzinger. 1991. *Emotions and Violence: Shame and Rage in Destructive Conflicts*. Lexington, MA: Lexington Books.

Schmidt, P., and A. D. Witte. 1984. *An Economic Analysis of Crime and Justice*. New York: Academic Press.

Schneider, Keith. 1985. "The Data Gap: What We Don't Know About Chemicals." *Amicus Journal* 6 (Winter): 15–24.

Scholz, John T. 1984. "Deterrence, Cooperation and the Ecology of Regulatory Enforcement." *Law and Society Review* 18: 179–224.

Schroeder, Christopher. 1983. "Introduction: Federal Regulation of the Chemical Industry." *Law and Contemporary Problems* 46 (Summer): 1–40.

Schur, Edwin M. 1984. *Labeling Women Deviant*. New York: McGraw-Hill.

Schwartz, Richard, and Jerome Skolnick. 1964. "Two Studies of Legal Stigma." In Howard Becker, ed., *The Other Side: Perspectives on Deviance*. New York: The Free Press.

Schwendinger, Herman, and Julia Siegel-Schwendinger. 1985. *Adolescent Subcultures and Delinquency*. New York: Praeger.

Schwendinger, Julia, and Herman Schwendinger. 1983. *Rape and Inequality*. Beverly Hills, CA: Sage.

Scott, J. C., and F. Al-Thakeb. 1977. "The Public's Perceptions of Crime: A Comparative Analysis of Scandinavia, Western Europe, the Middle East and the United States." In C. Huff, ed., *Contemporary Corrections*. Beverly Hills, CA: Sage.

Scutt, Jocelynne. 1980. "Crime and Sexual Politics." In E. Windschuttle, ed., *Women, Class and History*. Melbourne: Fontana.

———. 1982. "Domestic Violence: The Police Response." In C. O'Donnell and J. Craney, eds., *Family Violence in Australia*. Melbourne: Longman Cheshire.

———. 1983. *Even in the Best of Homes*. Melbourne: Penguin.

Sellin, Thorsten. 1935. "Race Prejudice in the Administration of Justice." *American Journal of Sociology* 41: 312–17.

———. 1976. *Slavery and the Penal System*. New York: Elsevier.

Sennett, Richard, and Jonathan Cobb. 1972. *The Hidden Injuries of Class*. New York: Vintage.

Sergeant, Margaret. 1973. *Alcoholism as a Social Problem*. Brisbane: University of Queensland Press.

Sessar, Klaus. 1991. "Crime Rate Trends Before and After the End of the German Democratic Republic: Impressions and First Analyses." Paper presented at 50th Annual Meeting of the American Society of Criminology, San Francisco, CA.

Shapiro, Susan. 1984. *Wayward Capitalists*. New Haven, CT: Yale University Press.

Sharpe, J. A. 1983. *Crime in Seventeenth-Century England: A County Study*. Cambridge, Eng.: Cambridge University Press.

———. 1984. *Crime in Early Modern England, 1550–1750*. London: Longman.

Shaw, Clifford, and Henry McKay. 1942. *Juvenile Delinquency and Urban Areas*. Chicago: University of Chicago Press.

———. 1949. "Rejoinder." *American Sociological Review* 14: 614–17.

———. 1969. Rev. ed. *Juvenile Delinquency and Urban Areas*. Chicago: University of Chicago Press.

Shelley, Louise I. 1990. "The Soviet Militsiia: Agents of Political and Social Control." *Policing and Society* 1: 39–56.

———. 1991. "Crime in the Soviet Union." In Anthony Jones, Walter D. Connor, and David E. Powell, eds., *Soviet Social Problems*, pp. 252–69. Boulder, CO: Westview Press.

Sherif, Musafer, and Carolyn Sherif. 1967. "Group Processes and Collective Interaction in Delinquent Activities." *Journal of Research in Crime and Delinquency* 4: 43–62.

Sherman, L., and R. Berk. 1984. "The Specific Deterrent Effects of Arrest for Domestic Assault." *American Sociological Review* 49: 261–72.

Shibutani, Tamotsu. 1961. *Society and Personality*. Englewood Cliffs, NJ: Prentice-Hall.

———. 1986. *Social Processes*. Berkeley: University of California Press.

Shlapentokh, Vladimir. 1989. *Public and Private Life of the Soviet People: Changing Values in Post-Stalin Russia*. New York: Oxford University Press.

Shock, Nathan, et al. 1984. *Normal Aging: The Baltimore Longitudinal Study of Aging*. Washington, DC: Department of Health and Human Services.

Shoemaker, Robert. 1992. "Reforming the City: The Reformation of Manners Campaign in London, 1690–1738." In Timothy Hitchcock and Robert Shoemaker, eds., *'Stilling the Grumbling Hive': The Response to Social and Economic Problems in England, 1688–1750*. Gloucester: Allan Sutton.

Short, J. F., Jr. 1963. "Introduction to the Abridged Edition." In F. Thrasher, ed., *The Gang: A Study of 1,313 Gangs in Chicago*, pp. xv–liii. Chicago: University of Chicago Press.

———. 1985. "The Level of Explanation Problem in Criminology." In R. Meier, ed., *Theoretical Methods in Criminology*, pp. 51–74. Beverly Hills, CA: Sage.

Short, James F., and Fred L. Strodtbeck. 1965. *Group Process and Gang Delinquency*. Chicago: University of Chicago Press.

Shover, Neal. 1985. *Aging Criminals*. Beverly Hills, CA: Sage.

Shover et al. 1986. [Shover, Neal, Donald A. Clelland, and John Lynxwiler]. *Enforcement or Negotiation: Constructing a Regulatory Bureaucracy*. Albany: State University of New York Press.

Simpson, Sally S. 1991. "Class, Caste, and Violent Crime: Explaining Difference in Female Offending." *Criminology* 29: 115–35.

Skogan, Wesley. 1986. "Fear of Crime and Neighborhood Change." In A. J. Reiss, Jr., and M. Tonry, eds., *Communities and Crime*, pp. 203–29. Chicago: University of Chicago Press.

———. 1990. *Disorder and Decline: Crime and the Spiral of Decay in American Neighborhoods*. New York: The Free Press.

Skogan, W., and M. G. Maxfield. 1981. *Coping with Crime: Individual and Neighborhood Reactions*. Beverly Hills, CA: Sage.

Skolnick, Jerome. 1966. *Justice Without Trial*. New York: Wiley and Sons.

Smart, Carol. 1976. *Women, Crime, and Criminology: A Feminist Critique*. London: Routledge and Kegan Paul.

———. 1979. "The New Female Offender: Reality or Myth?" *British Journal of Criminology* 19: 50–59.

———. 1984. *The Ties That Bind: Law, Marriage and the Reproduction of Patriarchal Relations*. London: Routledge and Kegan Paul.

Smith, Douglas. 1986. "The Neighborhood Context of Police Behavior." In Albert J. Reiss and Michael Tonry, eds., *Communities and Crime*. Chicago: University of Chicago Press.

Smith, Douglas, and Craig Uchida. 1988. "The Social Organization of Self-Help." *American Sociological Review* 53: 94–102.

Smith, Douglas, and Christy Visher. 1982. "Street Level Justice: Situational Determinants of Police Arrest Decisions." *Social Problems* 29: 167–77.

Smith et al. 1990. [Smith, D., J. Devine, and J. Sheley]. *Crime and Unemployment: Effects Across Age and Race Categories*. Working paper, Department of Sociology, Tulane University, New Orleans, LA.

Smith, M. Dwayne, and Nathan Bennett. 1985. "Poverty, Inequality and Theories of Forcible Rape." *Crime and Delinquency* 31: 295–305.

Smith, M. Dwayne, and Robert Nash Parker. 1980. "Types of Homicide and Regional Rates." *Social Forces* 59: 136–47.

Snipp, Mathew. 1992. "Sociological Perspectives on American Indians." *Annual Review of Sociology* 18: 351–72.

Souden, David. 1984. "Migrants and the Population Structure of Later Seventeenth Century Provincial Cities and Market Towns." In Peter Clark, ed., *The Transformation of English Provincial Towns, 1600–1800*. London: Hutchinson.

Spear v. Ariyoshi. 1985. Consent Decree, Civil No. 84-1104, U.S. District Court, District of Hawaii, June 12, 1985.

Spirduso, Waneen. 1982. "Physical Fitness in Relation to Motor Aging." In Rodney Stark, ed., *Sociology* (3d ed.) Belmont, CA: Wadsworth.

Spohn et al. 1981–82. [Spohn, C., J. Gruhl, and S. Welch]. "The Effect of Race on Sentencing: A Reexamination of an Unsettled Question." *Law & Society Review* 16: 71–88.

Stanko, Elizabeth. 1990. *Everyday Violence*. London: Pandora.

Stark, Evan. 1990. "The Myth of Black Violence." *New York Times*, July 18, p. A21.

Steffensmeier, Darrell. 1983. "Organization Properties and Sex-Segregation in the Underworld: Building a Sociological Theory of Sex Differences in Crime." *Social Forces* 61: 1010–32.

———. 1986. *The Fence: In the Shadow of Two Worlds*. Totowa, NJ: Rowman and Littlefield.

Steffensmeier, Darrell, and Emilie Allan. 1990. "Gender, Age, and Crime." In Joseph Sheley, ed., *Criminology: A Contemporary Handbook*, pp. 67–94. Belmont, CA: Wadsworth.

Steffensmeier, Darrell J., and Michael J. Cobb. 1981. "Sex Differences in Urban Arrest Patterns, 1934–79." *Social Problems* 29: 37–50.

Steffensmeier, Darrell J., and Renee Hoffman Steffensmeier. 1980. "Trends in Female Delinquency: An Examination of Arrest, Juvenile Court, Self-Report and Field Data." *Criminology* 18: 62–85.

Steffensmeier et al. 1989. [Steffensmeier, Darrell, Emilie Allan, Miles Harer, and Cathy Streifel]. "Age and the Distribution of Crime." *American Journal of Sociology* 94: 803–31.

Stephens, G., and W. Tafoya. 1985. "Crime and Justice: Taking A Futuristic Approach." *The Futurist*, February.

Stewart, O. 1964. "Questions Regarding American Indian Criminality." *Human Organization* 23: 61–66.

Stinchcombe, Arthur. 1963. "Institutions of Privacy in the Determination of Police Administration Practice." *American Journal of Sociology* 69: 150–60.

———. 1964. *Rebellion in a High School*. Chicago: Quadrangle Books.

Stone, Christopher. 1975. *Where the Law Ends: The Social Control of Corporate Behavior*. New York: Harper & Row.

Stöss, Richard. 1991. "Right-Wing Extremism in East and West Germany." Paper presented at the Conference on the Radical Right in Western Europe. West European Area Studies Center, University of Minnesota, Minneapolis, MN.

Stratmann, P. 1982. "Domestic Violence: The Legal Responses." In C. O'Donnell and J. Craney, eds., *Family Violence in Australia*. Melbourne: Longman Cheshire.

Stryker, Robin. 1989. "Limits on Technocratization of the Law: The Elimination of the National Labor Relations Board's Division of Economic Research." *American Sociological Review* 54 (June): 341–58.

———. 1991. "Government Regulation." In E. F. Borgatta and M. L. Borgatta, eds., *Encyclopedia of Sociology*. New York: Macmillan.

Stryker, Sheldon. 1980. *Symbolic Interactionism*. Menlo Park, CA: Benjamin-Cummings.

Stubbs, Julie, and Diana Powell. 1989. *Domestic Violence: Impact of Legal Reform in N.S.W.* Sydney: New South Wales Bureau of Crime Statistics and Research.

Styles, John. 1983. "Sir John Fielding and the Problem of Criminal Investigation in Eighteenth-Century England." *Transactions of the Royal Historical Society* 33, 5th ser.: 127–50.

Sudnow, David. 1965. "Normal Crimes: Sociological Features of the Penal Code in a Public Defender Office." *Social Problems* 12, no. 3: 255–76.

Sugarman, David B., and Murray A. Straus. 1987. "Indicators of Gender Equality for American States and Regions." *Social Indicators Research* 20: 1–42.

Sullivan, Mercer. 1989. *"Getting Paid": Youth Crime and Work in the Inner City.* Ithaca, NY: Cornell University Press.

Sunstein, Cass. 1988. "Beyond the Republican Revival," *Yale Law Journal* 97: 1539–90.

Sutherland, Edwin. 1937. *The Professional Thief.* Chicago: University of Chicago Press.

———. 1983. *White-Collar Crime: The Uncut Version.* New Haven, CT: Yale University Press.

Sutherland et al. 1992. [Sutherland, Edwin, Donald Cressey and David Luckenbill]. *Principles of Criminology.* Dix Hills, NY: General Hall.

Suttles, G. 1968. *The Social Order of the Slum.* Chicago: University of Chicago Press.

Sykes, Gresham, and John Clark. 1975. "A Theory of Deference Exchange in Police Civilian Encounters." *American Journal of Sociology* 81: 584–600.

Sykes, Gresham M., and Francis T. Cullen. 1992. *Criminology.* New York: Harcourt, Brace Jovanovich.

Szelenyi, Ivan. 1983. *Urban Inequalities Under State Socialism.* Oxford: Oxford University Press.

———. 1991. "Social Inequality in Hungary." Lecture held at the 2nd Sociology Research Institute, Department of Sociology, University of Minnesota, Minneapolis, MN.

Szelenyi, Szonya. 1987. "Social Inequality and Party Membership." *American Sociological Review* 52: 559–73.

Taylor, R., and J. Covington. 1988. "Neighborhood Changes in Ecology and Violence." *Criminology* 26: 553–90.

Taylor et al. 1984. [Taylor, R., S. Gottfredson, and S. Brower]. "Black Crime and Fear: Defensible Space, Local Social Ties, and Territorial Functioning." *Journal of Research in Crime and Delinquency* 21: 303–31.

Thomas, D. S. 1925. *Social Aspects of the Business Cycle.* New York: E. P. Dutton.

Thomson, Elizabeth, and Richard Williams. 1986. "Normalization Issues in Latent Variable Modeling." *Sociological Methods and Research* 15: 24–43.

Thornberry, Terrence P., and R. L. Christenson. 1984. "Unemployment and Criminal Involvement: An Investigation of Reciprocal Causal Structures." *American Sociological Review* 49: 398–411.

Thrasher, Frederick. 1927. *The Gang.* Chicago: University of Chicago Press.

———. 1963. *The Gang: A Study of 1,313 Gangs in Chicago.* Rev. ed. Chicago: University of Chicago Press.

Tierney, K. 1982. "The Battered Women Movement and the Creation of the Wife-beating Problem," *Social Problems* 29: 208–20.

Tittle, Charles. 1988. "Two Empirical Regularities (Maybe) in Search of an Explanation: Commentary on the Age/Crime Debate." *Criminology* 26: 75–85.

Tittle, Charles R., and Robert F. Meier. 1990. "Specifying the SES/Delinquency Relationship." *Criminology* 28: 271–99.

Tittle et al. 1978. [Tittle, Charles, Wayne Villemez, and Douglas Smith]. "The Myth of Social Class and Criminality: An Empirical Assessment of the Empirical Evidence." *American Sociological Review* 43: 643–56.

Toby, Jackson. 1957. "The Differential Impact of Family Disorganization." *American Sociological Review* 22: 505–12.

Tomsen et al. 1991. [Tomsen, Stephen, Ross Homel, and Jenny Thommeny]. "The Causes of Public Violence: Situational 'Versus' Other Factors in Drinking Related Assaults." In D. Chappell, R. Grabosky, and H. Strang, eds., *Australian Violence: Contemporary Perspectives*. Canberra: Australian Institute of Criminology.

Tracy et al. 1990. [Tracy, Paul E., Marvin D. Wolfgang, and Robert M. Figlio]. *Delinquency Careers in Two Birth Cohorts*. New York: Plenum.

Trevelyan, G. M. 1985. *A Shortened History of England*. Harmondsworth: Penguin.

Trice, H. M., and P. M. Roman. 1970. "Delabeling, Relabeling and Alcoholics Anonymous." *Social Problems* 17: 538–46.

Tripp, James T. B. 1977. "Tensions and Conflicts in Federal Pollution Control and Water Resource Policy." *Harvard Journal on Legislation* 14 (February): 225–80.

Turk, Austin. 1969. *Criminality and the Legal Order*. Chicago: Rand McNally.

Turner, Ralph H. 1962. "Role-taking: Process vs. Conformity." In Arnold M. Rose, ed. *Human Behavior and Social Processes*. Boston: Houghton Mifflin.

Tyree, Andrea, and Jean Malone. 1991. "How Can It Be That Wives Hit Husbands as Much as Husbands Hit Wives and None of Us Knew It?" Paper to American Sociological Association Annual Meeting, Cincinnati.

Tyrell, I. 1984. "International Aspects of the Women's Temperance Movement in Australia: The Influence of the American W.C.T.U., 1882–1914." *Journal of Religious History* 12: 184–304.

Uhlman, Thomas. 1979. *Racial Justice: Black Judges and Defendants in an Urban Trial Court*. Lexington, MA: Lexington Books.

Unger, Roberto M. 1976. *Law in Modern Society: Toward a Criticism of Social Theory*. New York: The Free Press.

U.S. Commission on Civil Rights. 1978. *Social Indicators of Equality for Minorities and Women*. Washington, DC: United States Government Printing Office.

U.S. Department of Justice. 1985. *The Risk of Violent Crime*. Washington, DC: U.S. Government Printing Office.

———. 1988. *Survey of Youth in Custody, 1987*. Washington, DC: Bureau of Justice Statistics.

———. 1990. *Profile of Felons Convicted in State Courts, 1986*. Washington, DC: Bureau of Justice Statistics.

———. 1991a. *Criminal Victimization in the United States, 1990*. Washington, DC: Bureau of Justice Statistics.

———. 1991b. *Profile of Jail Inmates, 1989*. Washington, DC: Bureau of Justice Statistics.

———. 1991c. *Women in Prison*. Washington, DC: Bureau of Justice Statistics.

U.S. General Accounting Office. 1991. *Environmental Enforcement: Penalties May Not Recover Economic Benefits Gained by Violators*. Washington, D.C.: U.S. General Accounting Office (GAO/RCED-91-166).

U.S. House of Representatives. 1977. *Implementation of the Federal Water Pollution Control Act: Summary of Hearings on the Regulation and Monitoring of Toxic and Hazardous Chemicals Under the Federal Water Pollution Control Act (P.L. 92-500)*, July 19, 20, 21, 28, 29, 1977. Report prepared by the Environment and Natural Resources Policy Division of the Congressional Research Service, Library of Congress, for the Committee on Public Works and Transportation, Serial no. 95-25. Washington, DC: U.S. Government Printing Office, September.

U.S. Senate. 1977. *Study on Federal Regulation*. Committee on Governmental Affairs, Vols. 1–6. Washington, DC: U.S. Government Printing Office.

Uttitz, Pavel. 1991. "Motive und Einstellungen tschechoslowakischer Wähler: Die Juni-Wahl und die Entwicklung bis Ende des Jahres 1990." *Zentralarchiv-Informationen* 28: 40–51.

Van Den Berg, Ger P. 1985. *The Soviet System of Justice: Figures and Policy*. Dordrecht: Martinus Nijhoff.

Vigil, James Diego. 1985. *Barrio Gangs*. Austin, TX: University of Texas Press.

Visher, Christy. 1983. "Gender, Police Arrest Decisions and Notions of Chivalry." *Criminology* 21: 5–28.

Vold, G. B. 1979. *Theoretical Criminology*. New York: Oxford University Press.

Von Hentig, Hans. 1945. "The Delinquency of the American Indian." *Journal of Criminal Law* 36: 84.

Wacquant, Loic. 1991. "The Specificity of Ghetto Poverty: A Comparative Analysis of Race, Class, and Urban Exclusion in Chicago's Black Belt and the Parisian Red Belt." Paper presented at the Chicago Urban Poverty and Family Life Conference, University of Chicago.

Wallace, R., and D. Wallace. 1990. "Origins of Public Health Collapse in New York City: The Dynamics of Planned Shrinkage, Contagious Urban Decay and Social Disintegration." *Bulletin of the New York Academy of Medicine* 66: 391–434.

Walsh, Marilyn. 1977. *The Fence: A New Look at the World of Property Theft*. Westport, CT: Greenwood.

Walter, Michael, and Wolfgang Fischer. 1988. "Strukturen registrierter Jugendkriminalität und Formen ihre Bewältigung in Budapest und Hamburg." *Monatsschrift für Kriminologie und Strafrechtsreform* 71: 228–45.

Warr, M., and M. C. Stafford. 1983. "Fear of Victimization: A Look at the Proximate Causes." *Social Forces* 61: 1033–43.

Wearing, Rosemary. 1990. "A Longitudinal Analysis of the 1987 Crimes (Family Violence) Act in Victoria." Report to Criminology Research Council, Canberra.

Weber, Max. 1978. *Economy and Society*. Berkeley: University of California Press.

Weis, Joseph G. 1976. "Liberation and Crime: The Invention of the New Female Criminal." *Crime and Social Justice* 6: 17–27.

Weisheit, R. A. 1984. "Female Homicide Offenders: Trends over Time in an Institutional Population." *Justice Quarterly* 1: 471–89.

Welch et al. 1985. [Welch, Susan, John Gruhl, and Cassia Spohn]. "Convicting and Sentencing Differences Among Black, Hispanics, and White Males in Six Localities." *Justice Quarterly* 2: 67–80.

Whyte, W. 1985. *The Social Life of Small Places*. New York: Random House.

Wiener, Carol. 1975. "Sex Roles and Crime in Late Elizabethan Hertfordshire." *Journal of Social History* 8, no. 4: 38–60.

———. 1976. "Is a Spinster an Unmarried Woman?" *American Journal of Legal History* 20: 27–31.

Wiggins et al. 1965. [Wiggins, J. A., F. Dill and R. D. Schwartz]. "On 'Status-Liability.'" *Sociometry* 28: 197–209.

Wilbanks, W. 1982. "Murdered Women and Women Who Murder: A Critique of the Literature." In Nicole Hahn Rafter and Elizabeth Anne Stanko, eds., *Judge, Lawyer, Victim, Thief: Women, Gender Roles, and Criminal Justice*, pp. 157–80. Boston: Northeastern University Press.

———. 1983a. "Female Homicide Offenders in the U.S." *International Journal of Women's Studies* 6: 302–10.

———. 1983b. "The Female Homicide Offender in Dade County, Florida." *Criminal Justice Review* 8: 9–14.

———. 1986. "Criminal Homicide Offenders in the U.S.: Black vs. White." In D. Hawkins, ed., *Homicide Among Black Americans*, pp. 43–56. Lanham, MD: University Press of America.

William, Terry. 1989. *The Cocaine Kids*. Reading, MA: Addison-Wesley.

William, Terry, and William Kornblum. 1985. *Growing Up Poor*. Lexington, MA: Lexington Books.

Williams, Joyce, and Karen Holmes. 1981. *The Second Assault: Rape and Public Attitudes*. Westport, CT: Greenwood.

Williams, Kirk R. 1984. "Economic Sources of Homicide: Reestimating the Effects of Poverty and Inequality." *American Sociological Review* 49: 283–89.

Williams, Kirk R., and Robert Flewelling. 1988. "The Social Production of Criminal Homicide: A Comparative Study of Disaggregated Rates in American Cities." *American Sociological Review* 53: 421–31.

Wilmore, Jack, and David Costill. 1988. *Training for Sport and Activity*. Dubuque, IA: William C. Brown.

Wilson, J. Harper. 1991. Director, Uniform Crime Reporting Program. Personal communication, January 17.

Wilson, James Q. 1968. *Varieties of Police Behavior*. Cambridge: Harvard University Press.

———. 1980. "The Politics of Regulation." In James Q. Wilson, ed., *The Politics of Regulation*, pp. 357–94. New York: Basic Books.

Wilson, James Q., and Richard Herrnstein. 1985. *Crime and Human Nature*. New York: Simon and Schuster.

Wilson, Paul R., and John Braithwaite, eds. 1978. *Two Faces of Deviance: Crimes of the Powerless and Powerful*. Brisbane: University of Queensland Press.

Wilson, William Julius. 1986. "The Urban Underclass in Advanced Industrial Society." In Paul E. Peterson, ed., *The New Urban Reality*. Washington, DC: Brookings Institution.

———. 1987. *The Truly Disadvantaged: The Inner City, the Underclass, and Public Policy*. Chicago: University of Chicago Press.

———. 1989. "The Ghetto Underclass: Social Science Perspectives." *Annals of the American Academy of Political and Social Science* 501: January.

———. 1991. "Studying Inner-City Social Dislocations: The Challenge of Public Agenda Research." *American Sociological Review* 56: 1–14.

Wilson et al. 1988. [Wilson, W. J., R. Aponte, J. Kirschenman, and L. Wacquant]. "The Ghetto Underclass and the Changing Structure of American Poverty." In F. Harris and R. W. Wilkins, eds., *Quiet Riots: Race and Poverty in the United States*, pp. 123–54. New York: Pantheon.

Winsborough, H. H., and P. Dickenson. 1971. "Components of Negro-White Income Distributions." *Proceedings of the American Statistical Association*, Social Statistics Section: 6–8.

Wolfe, Nancy Travis. 1989. "Social Courts in the GDR and Comrades' Courts in the Soviet Union: A Comparison." In David Childs, Thomas Boylis, and Marilyn Rueschemeyer, eds., *East Germany in Comparative Perspective*, pp. 60–80. London: Routledge.

Wolfgang, M., and F. Ferracuti. 1967. *The Subculture of Violence*. London: Tavistock.

Wolfgang et al. 1972. [Wolfgang, Marvin D., Robert M. Figlio, and Thorsten Sellin]. *Delinquency in a Birth Cohort.* Chicago: University of Chicago Press.

Wolfgang et al. 1985. [Wolfgang, Marvin, Robert Figlio, Paul Tracy, and Simon Singer]. *The National Survey of Crime Severity*. Washington, DC: U.S. Department of Justice, Bureau of Justice Statistics.

Wolfgang, Marvin, and Marc Riedel. 1973. "Race, Judicial Discretion, and the Death Penalty." *Annals of the American Academy of Political and Social Science* 407: 119.

Wolfgang et al. 1987. [Wolfgang, Marvin, Terrence Thornberry, and Robert Figlio]. *From Boy to Man: From Delinquency to Crime*. Chicago: University of Chicago Press.

Wragg, Jeffrey. 1987. "The Development of a Model for Drug Education Programme Implications Derived from Past Education Studies and Known Causative Factors." *Drug Education Journal of Australia* 1: 1–5.

———. 1990. "The Longitudinal Evaluation of a Primary School Drug Education Program: Did It Work?" *Drug Education Journal of Australia* 4: 33–44.

Wright, John, ed. 1989. *The Universal Almanac*. New York: Andrews and McMeel.

Wrigley, E. A. 1967. "A Simple Model of London's Importance in Changing English Society and Economy 1650–1750." *Past and Present* 37: 21–46.

Wylie, Ruth C. 1979. *The Self-Concept*. Vol. 1. *A Review of Methodological Considerations and Measuring Instruments*. Rev. ed. Lincoln: University of Nebraska Press.

Yeager, Peter C. 1987. "Structural Bias in Regulatory Law Enforcement: The Case of the U.S. Environmental Protection Agency." *Social Problems* 34, no. 4: 330–44.

———. 1990. "Analyzing Corporate Offenses: Progress and Prospects." In W. C. Frederick and L. E. Preston, eds., *Business Ethics: Research Issues and Empirical Studies*, pp. 165–92. Greenwich, CT: JAI Press.

———. 1991. *The Limits of Law: The Public Regulation of Private Pollution*. New York: Cambridge University Press.

Yeatman, A. 1990. *Bureaucrats, Technocrats and Femocrats*. Melbourne: Allen and Unwin.

Yllo, Kersti. 1983. "Using a Feminist Approach to Quantitative Research: A Case Study." In D. Finkelhor, R. J. Gelles, G. T. Hotaling, and M. A. Straus, eds., *The Dark Side of Families*. Beverly Hills, CA: Sage.

Yllo, Kersti. 1983. "Using a Feminist Approach to Quantitative Research: A Case Study." In D. Finkelhor, R. J. Gelles, G. T. Hotaling, and M. A. Straus, eds., *The* Johns Hopkins Symposium on Feminism and the Critique of Capitalism, Baltimore, MD.

Zatz, Marjorie S., and Alan Lizotte. 1985. "Pleas, Priors and Prison: Racial/Ethnic Differences in Sentencing." *Social Science Research* 14: 169–93.

———. 1987. "The Changing Forms of Racial/Ethnic Biases in Sentencing." *Journal of Research in Crime and Delinquency* 24: 69–92.

Zedner, Lucia. 1991. *Women, Crime, and Custody in Victorian England*. Oxford: Clarendon Press.

Index

In this index an "f" after a number indicates a separate reference on the next page, and an "ff" indicates separate references on the next two pages. A continuous discussion over two or more pages is indicated by a span of page numbers, e.g., "57–59." *Passim* is used for a cluster of references in close but not consecutive sequence.

Library of Congress Cataloging-in-Publication data

Crime and inequality / edited by John Hagan and Ruth D. Peterson.
p. cm.
Includes bibliographical references and index.
ISBN 0-8047-2404-0 (cloth) — ISBN
0-8047-2477-6 (pbk.)
1. Crime—United States. 2. Equality—United States.
3. Discrimination in criminal justice administration—United States.
I. Hagan, John. II. Peterson, Ruth D.
HV6791.C735 1995
364.973—dc20 94-17742 CIP Rev.

∞ This book is printed on acid-free, recycled paper. It was typeset in 10/12½ Galliard by Tseng Information Systems, Inc.